I0282199

1990 Dallas Meeting
at the
Doubletree Hotel in Dallas, Texas

Edited and Arranged by

Wayne Seaton

Truth
Publications

Taking His hand,
Helping each other home. ™

© **Truth Publications, Inc. 2018. Second Printing.** All rights reserved. No part of this book may be reproduced in any form without written permission from the publisher. Printed in the United States of America.

ISBN 10: 1-58427-279-1

ISBN 13: 978-158427-279-3

First Printing: 2010

Truth Publications, Inc.
CEI Bookstore
220 S. Marion St., Athens, AL 35611
855-492-6657
sales@truthpublications.com
www.truthbooks.com

Table of Contents

Introduction
Wayne Seaton

(Editor's Disclaimer: I readily admit this work is not error free. It is difficult to produce such a volume free from all errors, no matter how many times the work is edited. However, every effort has been made to minimize any errors.)

The Dallas Meeting was held at the Convention Center of the Doubletree Hotel in Dallas, Texas from July 12th through the 14th, 1990. There were seven themes or subjects of study over the three-day meeting. Participants traveled and spoke at their own expense. They participated, not as a part of some party or division in the brotherhood, but simply represented only themselves. There were fifty-one active participants who were all working together to make the Dallas Meeting possible, but all were working individually representing only themselves in the discussion.

There is another potential division growing in the Lord's body over whether these kinds of collective actions (e.g., brethren working together but as individuals) are scriptural. The argument has always been "the church is the only collectivity authorized to do the work of the church." Over the years, some have morphed this argument into "the church is the only collectivity authorized to teach the scriptures." They teach that all efforts to teach the truth through any other collectivity is sinful. If this thinking continues to fester in the brotherhood, studies of this type (i.e., the 1990 Dallas Meeting, the Arlington Meeting, etc.) will soon cease to exist. It is my prayer that we use the principles in this and other such discussions to unite on how individuals can work together to preach and teach the gospel without violating any principle of scripture. A study of these same principles can help us see the truth on this emerging divisive issue.

There have been multiple divisions that have occurred over some of these same issues within the last two hundred years. Separate connections and separate associations currently exist in the Lord's body, resulting in distinct and separate bodies. The fact that these issues are being discussed again should teach us that, until we learn the lessons of history, we will be forced to repeat it, resulting in even further departures from God's word. The importance of this meeting and others like it is that we are discussing the scriptures and we are studying again the issues that have divided us. The issues that divide us are not one or two minor schisms, but are major differences in how to establish authority and how we view the scriptures. For more than sixty years, these issues have not diminished but have proliferated dramatically. The aim and the purpose of the 1990 Dallas Meeting was to develop a basis for a reconciliation of long estranged groups of brethren. But reconciliation can only take place on the basis of truth; else we are simply uniting in error like the denominations have attempted. Truth is objective and definitive and discernible. Truth must be the basis upon which any and every reconciliation is attempted.

Objective of Publishing This Meeting

Imagine these divisions no longer exist and brethren once again uniting as God demands. How encouraging this would be to every child of God. Many people in the church have the attitude that these issues happened long ago and should be laid to rest so we can move on. Some are tired of hearing about these differences, and have not even taught the next generation that these issues exist. However, God never intended for us to give up on unity, and as long as people are willing to study the issues that divide us, unity is possible. There is much to learn about why this division occurred in the first place. Was it a sinful attitude toward the word of God or toward each other in the brotherhood? If so, we need to learn from this and unite in love, forgiving one another, and once again, share the same faith. The ultimate goal of every Christian is to be with our Father in heaven. Every faithful child of God should want to discuss any and every Bible topic, but especially when division exists, and when souls are in danger of being lost. Whether or not we agree over these issues, we can all benefit from these discussions. To please God, we must have a love for God, but more than that, we must have a love for the souls of each other. It is my hope and prayer that all who read this book will see the changes in work and attitudes that have taken place in the Lord's church over the years that have led us to where we were at the time of the 1990 Dallas Meeting. Fast forward to today, we see many new departures. Had attitudes been different and greater attention been given to some of the differences discussed in this book, we might not be a divided brotherhood. And without stepping back to analyze these issues in light of the divisions in the Lord's church, who knows how the body of Christ will look in another twenty or so years?

About The Dallas Meeting

A moderator from each side led and directed the Dallas Meeting. Roy Lanier was the moderator for the institutional brethren and Jamie Sloan was the moderator for the non-institutional brethren. The moderators worked very effectively to keep the meeting running in an orderly and proper manner. Moderating duties were switched between speeches in order to show no preference to one side or the other of the discussion.

The format of the Dallas Meeting is presented in the order in which the speeches were made. There are seven sections or cycles of speeches that make up the Dallas Meeting. Each section began with a twenty-eight minute major speech followed by a twenty-eight minute rebuttal speech. Four panel speakers then gave four-minute speeches each. Next, there was a freewheeling and less structured panel discussion lasting about forty-five minutes, followed by a question and answer period where the audience was allowed to ask questions of any speaker. Finally, there was a summation session which allowed each main speaker a two-minute summation speech to wrap up each section. Each of the seven sections or topics followed this same format.

The Dallas Meeting was less like a debate and more like the Arlington Meeting. Each side was supplied a full transcript of the opposing speech of the main speaker in advance of his speech. The panel discussion was a freewheeling and unscripted session where the panel speakers were allowed to ask and answer questions of each other as they freely discussed their topic. The moderators were to ensure that equal time was given to each side of the discussion and to make sure the discussion was fair. A question and answer period followed the panel discussion. The audience members were allowed to submit written questions for any of the speakers they desired. These questions were handed to the moderators who read and directed the questions to the proper participant. The two-minute summa-

tion speeches from the main and rebuttal speakers served as concluding remarks about that topic. Breaks were taken throughout as needed.

The sale of a certain number of luncheon and dinner tickets was a part of the rental agreement of the hotel convention center. These tickets were sold to individuals for the dining facility at the hotel and were in no way connected with the work of the church. There were several brethren selected from both sides of the division as after dinner speakers. Both lunch and dinner speakers were given flexibility in their topics but were instructed beforehand to avoid the topics the speakers were discussing. Some of the dinner speeches were funny and entertaining while others were very serious. However all were designed to challenge the thinking of the dinner audience in light of the current division, and to help us see the need to heal the schism that has taken place in the Lord's church.

How This Book Evolved To Its Current Form

This work is the product of many years and many different versions. I attended the discussion and purchased video tapes offered at the meeting. These tapes served as the basis of the different versions of this work. The first version was an outline made of the speeches designed as a springboard for high school classes to study the issues.

I shared with Tom Roberts some of these outlines and he thought it would be useful to make a word-for-word transcription of the entire oral discussion. The second version of this work was a transcription of all speeches except the after dinner speeches. The third and final version is this present form complete with the after dinner speeches and charts. In order to give the reader the feel of being at the discussion, all the charts used in the discussion were recreated as PowerPoint presentations. Every effort was made to preserve the look and feel of the original slides used in the meeting. All conversations caught on tape were preserved to give the reader the feel of being at the discussion. In some cases, explanatory notes were placed inside parenthesis for clarification.

How to Read This Book

It is difficult to discuss division in the Lord's body without identifying in some way the parties that make up the two different parts of the division. Care has been exercised not to use pejorative terms such as "digressives" or "liberals" and "antis" or "anti-cooperation brethren." In order to help identify two groups of brethren without the use of pejoratives, I have used the terms institutional and non-institutional. Other publications including Directories of churches of Christ make these distinctions without any misgivings from either side of this issue. These terms were also used in the discussion and are an accurate portrayal of each other's positions and actions.

The ways the terms have been defined are given here briefly for informational purposes only. The following explanation will primarily be of benefit to those not familiar with the division in the Lord's body over the last sixty plus years. Institutional brethren generally believe or accept the establishment, support, and use of para-church institutions (e.g., colleges, orphan's homes, homes for the aged, etc.) from the church treasury to do the work God commanded the church to do, hence the term "institutional brethren." It should be noted that not all institutional brethren accept all institutions built and maintained by churches of Christ to be supported from the church treasury. But since these brethren are aligned, accept, and maintain fellowship with those who do, they accept and are identified with institutional brethren. Institutional brethren see the institutions as a method or means of the church doing its work. They also believe non-institutional brethren are right in the way they understand and support the work of the truth, but they do not believe it is the only way to do the work of the church.

Non-institutional brethren generally believe the establishment, support, and use of these institutions from the church treasury to do the work of the church is without divine authority and, therefore, sinful. Non-institutional brethren see human institutions not merely means as a means or method of the church doing its work, but are separate institutions doing the work God gave the church to do. Non-institutional brethren oppose any form of centralized control or any work that includes the combining of resources from other churches to do its work. Non-institutional brethren believe the first-day-of-the-week contribution is a fellowship or sharing of all the members in that offering to the Lord as He has commanded. Therefore, the use of those funds puts every member of the church in fellowship with that action. If a church decides to support human institutions from that treasury to do the work God designed the church to do, then every member of that congregation is in fellowship with that work he believes to be sinful. Each member is forced into a strained relationship, no matter what he decides to do. One is in fellowship with sin if he gives his contribution to a work he knows to be sinful. One is in sin if he refuses to give

as he has been prospered. He must then decide if he can worship in good conscience with a group that he knows he cannot share in what God commands the church to do. They will then work and study with the offending church to bring it into conformity with the New Testament pattern of work and worship, or having failed to do this generally believe that a separation must be made from that church participating in some sinful work and worship. They do no see this as causing division. They believe that a division has already taken place between the brethren in sin and the Lord. They see this action as necessary to restore erring brethren to a right relationship with the Lord. If they fail in this effort, they see no alternative but to start a group whose work and worship are scriptural, and where every member can work and worship together with a clear conscience.

The spoken word is vastly different from the written word. It is much more free flowing and less structured than the written word. Transcribing the spoken word presented multiple problems, some of which identified to make the reading of this work more understandable. For example, punctuation, partial sentences, changing thoughts in mid sentence, run on sentences, proper spelling, and paragraph divisions were only a few of the challenges. Misspellings and mispronunciations appear as they were presented. The only things not included in the speeches were the occasional "uhs" and stammering that often are a normal part of speaking. These are distracting from the written text and were omitted to keep the message as clear as possible. Exclusion of these distracters did not change in any way a single word of any speaker. Changes of thought in mid sentence have been preserved by the insertion of an ellipsis (e.g., "I…let's take the hospital for a moment").

There are very few times where I have inserted my own words or comments, but have done so only on an as-needed basis. These comments were added either for clarity or to give the feel of being at the lectures. For example, when there was laughter from the audience, I inserted (Laughter, whs). However when charts were introduced, I simply added the chart number in parenthesis. Since they were not my own thoughts there was no need to put my initials in the parenthesis. Some charts were only partially legible and were, therefore, reproduced as clearly as possible. The age and condition of the VHS tapes made seeing charts with a lot of small text all but impossible. Copies from old newspaper clippings were especially difficult to read, and some charts with these were not legible.

Books and published references are italicized, such as the *Christian Standard*, *Gospel Advocate*, or *Gospel Guardian*, and the Arlington Lectures—under the published title *Arlington Meeting*. References to radio programs, such as the *Herald of Truth*, are also italicized.

Introductions of all speakers appear at the beginning of their speeches and were taken from the Program printed by Gospel Teachers Publications. They were reproduced in this work exactly as they were written in the Program, including all abbreviations and misspelled words. Without including the misspelled words as printed, confusion could have resulted. Some comments of the participants would make no sense because they referenced the errors in the Program during their speeches.

During times when the speakers would speak emphatically, CAPS were used to note the emphasis. The speaking styles of some made emphatic speech difficult to determine. Some speakers spoke emphatically most of the time, so selections were placed in all caps as deemed appropriate by the editor.

All quotations of scripture were given as quoted by the speakers. At times, the speakers gave their own version of the verse being quoted, which was reproduced as spoken. Sometimes speakers would quote scripture without giving the scripture reference. This was reproduced as quoted and the scripture quoted was added in parenthesis, e.g. (Quoting Matthew 5:23-24, whs).

Sentence structure and paragraph placements are particularly difficult and time consuming when transcribing from the spoken word. Speakers sometimes make intricate arguments, making exceptionally long sentences and paragraphs. Sentences and paragraphs were arranged in order to make the speeches as clear and understandable as possible. Side bars and tangents are common practices in the spoken word and also make sentence structure and paragraph placement difficult to determine.

Conclusion

It is my hope and prayer that this work will be helpful to those studying these issues that have divided brethren over the years. Let us work together that the prayer of Jesus might be realized by us. "I do not ask in behalf of these alone, but for those also who believe in Me though their word; that they may all be one; even as Thou, Father, art in Me, and I in Thee, that they also may be in Us; that the world may believe that Thou didst send Me. And the glory which Thou hast given Me I have given to them; that they may be one, just as We are one; I in them, and Thou in Me, that they may be perfected in unity, that the world may know that Thou didst send Me, and didst love them, even as Thou didst love Me. Father, I desire that they also, whom Thou hast given Me, be with Me where I am, in order that they may behold My glory, which Thou hast given Me; for Thou didst love Me before the foundation of the world" (John 17:20-24, NASV).

Special Thanks

Without the help and suggestions of several people this work would not be what it is. I would like to thank Tom Roberts for his suggestions which have been incorporated into the final form of this work, and for his constant encouragement over the years. He has been a friend and mentor for my wife and me when times were tough. Without his prompting, I would never have published this work.

My mother, Viola L. Garner, and father, James B. Seaton, deserve special credit for teaching me at an early age to love the Lord and to make a serious commitment to serve Him. Ron Halbrook and Tom O'Neal made valuable suggestions and took the time to read the manuscripts. I owe a debt of gratitude to Mike Willis for his work in publishing the Dallas Meeting. There were 97 files of various formats which he had to arrange into one consistent volume. I am truly indebted to all these faithful brethren for their work and the encouragement they provided, not only in this work specifically, but also to me in my preaching generally. I must take special note of my son, Tim Seaton, for his extraordinary artwork, cover design, and separator page formatting. His technical design and illustrations have made this work a more professional looking product. I am indebted to all the brethren on both sides of these issues that faced the firing line of a public examination of divisive topics. The Lord is truly glorified whenever disciples of the Lord study and discuss the truth of the gospel. May such discussions continue until division is healed and unity is obtained within a divided brotherhood.

Above all these, I am mostly indebted to my wife, Rita Seaton, who has offered many good suggestions and done a lot of proof reading. It is with great pride that I dedicate this work to Rita for her loving support that enables me to do what I love best, preach the gospel of Christ. She has been, and continues to be, the love of my life. Her suggestions and ideas make me a better preacher and a better person. I love you Rita!!

Historical Perspectives

Day 1 Speech Cycle 1
Thursday, July 12, 1990

Participants

Non-Institutional Brethren
Steve Wolfgang—Rebuttal
Ed Harrell—Panelist 1
Colly Caldwell—Panelist 2

Institutional Brethren
Hulen Jackson—Main
Hardeman Nichols—Panelist 3
Adron Dorn—Panelist 4

Historical Perspectives
Day 1 Speech 1 Main
Hulen Jackson

Introduction: *Jackson, Hulen. Minister for sixty years at Commerce, San Daba, and Dallas, Texas churches, also in Shawnee, Oklahoma. Known for radio and TV work, director at ACU for many years, trustee of Bell Trust, associated with many outstanding events and crises through the years. Long time work with Trinity Heights and Preston Road congregations in Dallas, presently working with Duncanville, Texas congregation.*

Thank you Roy (Lanier), very much. I want to say first that I'm glad he put the map on that folder, how to get to the hotel, because I know a lot of Dallas preachers that stay in a state of confusion, and they're not always sure where they are going, and when they arrive. I'm glad to be here.

What I'm going to say is, more or less, personal, and it to some extent, may sound like I'm bragging about the experience that I've had. But I moved to Dallas in 1942, born about sixty-five miles from here, and preached my first sermon when I was sixteen there in Denison. So Dallas has been our home.

And sincerely I feel that all the troubles that we've had of any magnitude, those troubles have arisen in the years that we've been in Dallas. So I'm going to present the history of the movement, the troubles of the movement, from the standpoint of how it developed in the Dallas area, and the things that I know as the background.

I'm glad the brother, in praying, mentioned the sweet fellowship that we have in Christ. I'm sincerely stating to you that all of you, as far as I'm concerned, are in my fellowship. My wife's oldest brother, Cled Wallace, was one of the most level-handed, level-headed men I've ever known. If you didn't know Cled Wallace, you missed a gem, a rare person, good judgment. But he often said that I'm slow in drawing lines on brethren, lest I get my lines tangled up. And I've thought about that, I know, a thousand times. I've never drawn the line on anybody because of what he believed, or did not believe, relative to the matters that will be discussed this weekend. To me, you're brethren;

you're my brother my sister in Christ. I've tried to show that in every way.

Now that doesn't work both ways, at least in many instances. Several times in meetings in various places over the nation, some brother who was on your side, and I mean that kindly, would be in the service. And I'd purposely request urgently that the preacher there use him in leading a prayer, having a part in the worship. I think it was right, and until I die I'll continue doing that. I'm not going to fall out with somebody because he does not believe exactly what I believe in these matters. We're all brethren as far as I'm concerned.

I disagree with you sincerely and wholeheartedly about a lot of those matters. But I'm not going to say that you are not in my fellowship. But on the other hand, I've attended many times to hear some of my friends of the past who happen to be nearby in meetings. And sometimes I might be the first person present, and you understand the motive in saying this, not one time have I ever been asked to even lead a dismissal prayer. Not one time, as far as I know, has it been mentioned by the local preacher that I happen to be, or some other brother, present. Now to me, that's un-Christian. So if anybody's drawn the line, I haven't drawn the line. And that's the way I feel about it. We're still brethren. And we have fellowship in Christ.

I'm glad to make this speech, but I truly am sad that it's necessary to make it, and I'll hasten to tell you why. Because some of the active men, some of them are here today, who are on the other side, leaders in this movement a long time ago, were some bosom friends of ours. They've been in our home, we've been in their home, we've held meetings together. And so I've lost some of the best friends I ever had in life. It's been a great personal sacrifice to me for these situations to arise and for the condition to get to the point where it is today.

I've never been accused of being liberal. I don't think I am. But I've tried to be consistent. Brother Coleman

Overby used to say so many times that we have to be consistent, and that truth is never inconsistent.

I'll tell you when I think, maybe, the beginning of our troubles of any size began. I moved in '42 to Trinity Heights, moved to Preston Road in '47, and moved back to Trinity Heights in '52, and then to Duncanville where we still are. And when we were at Preston Road in about 1951, our full time, fully supported, one of our missionaries was James Walter Nichol at Cedar Rapids, Iowa. He and James Derwood Williford conceived an idea, who lived in that area, to have a radio program and to have several stations broadcast it, and they called it the *Herald of Truth*. Likely, not a soul here knows this. It ought to be a part of the record. So James came down at the invitation of the elders, and he talked with the elders at Preston Road. And I was present when he asked them, would they accept the responsibility, and back what they called the *Herald of Truth*. We were in the throws of a building program there, and meeting on Wednesday night in a neighboring church building and on Sunday at the Highland Park High School. So we were not in a condition at all to accept the responsibility of that sort, and the elders turned it down. So they went back to Abilene and talked to the elders of the University church, and they, for some reason, decided not to, and then Highland took it on.

I'd never heard of anything, except occasionally somebody saying … and I've been in the church all my life, my family goes back seven generations in the church, and six of those generations had elders in my immediate family. But I never heard these things discussed, that it would be sinful and wrong and do this, that and the other, that those things that have divided us. So I really think sincerely, that when the *Herald of Truth* was announced, that that marks the beginning, and that was in 1951 or '52 when it really got started.

I grew up here, not far from Boles Home. I remember the 20's when that home started. I was just a youngster but we used to go every Thanksgiving, most of us did, and take a basket dinner and join brethren from all over north Texas. The ladies met and canned vegetables and fruit all during the summer and fall season, and truck loaded that to Boles Home. I never heard anybody say anything about it was wrong to send money from the church to help Boles Home. So that's been my expression, my experience, and I don't think we had anything of any consequence to divide the brethren as it has until you might say about in the early '50's.

I learned while I was at Preston Road preaching that a banker friend of mine, who was a banker then, wanted to go to Hawaii to preach. And the Preston Road elders said they'd help him, through the Ferris church. This is a matter of record of the Preston Road church in their minutes. So they accepted it and they sent whatever it was a month to the Ferris elders, who in turn, put that with theirs and other moneys they had collected in supporting a preacher, and he may be present. And I respect him, and he's my brother, and we had him lead in a …the prayer in a meeting not too many years ago, where I was then. But he's violently opposed to it now. That was in about 19... before 1950. And the Preston Road church contributed out of their treasury month after month, and sent it to the Ferris church.

It's been a great personal loss, as you know, for these things to happen. So frankly, if anybody has driven anybody out, and this is a serious charge, but I feel like you brethren have. I'd still gladly ask any of you to pray.

In 1967, five of us and five of the other brethren, I don't know how to say it other than to say it that way, that's terrible, met down at Buchanan Dam. Stayed together, slept together, ate together, had fine, fine, fine fellowship. We studied these matters for three days and nights. They decided then, AND TOLD US SO, that they made mistakes in accusing us of endorsing everything that any church of Christ anywhere in the world, they read in their bulletins, what they were practicing.

I've never been a brotherhood-wide preacher, and I don't feel amenable to anybody for what a church is doing a thousand miles from here. I can't do anything about it anyway. And a lot of things that are going on today, I think they're terrible. But I don't believe I'm the savior of the church and I'm not going to try to be. And I'm not going to go to see the elders where they're doing something that I feel like is unscriptural and wrong, unless they invite me. You may think that's the awfullest, but that's the way I feel about it.

So we had that great period of fellowship. We didn't change anybody's mind but they were convinced they said, that we still preached the Bible, and we believed the Bible and we were trying to follow thus saith the Lord.

Then in 1970, I think it was, fifteen of us and fifteen of them met at Arlington, and those lectures are in print, maybe the book *Arlington Lectures* is still on sale.

And then a year or two later, several met down in the San Antonio area, and since I'd been a part of these other two, they asked me to come down and be a part of that.

So I've been in close contact, in a sense, in these meetings up till some years ago. I don't think we've driven anybody out. But I'm going to tell you candidly, I feel like you have driven us out. There's not a preacher here that preaches for a church that opposes what we practice who would invite me for a meeting. And I'm not asking for a meeting, I'm about through holding meetings. So I'm going to lay at your feet the blame for any break of fellowship. Now if a man divides a church, and I know about it, I think that might be a different matter, likely would.

I want to raise some other questions. And that's in answer to a charge that some of you make. And that is that we're the ones that have changed. Now if you're talking about a lot of things that are being done by churches of Christ today that weren't twenty years ago practiced, I think I'd endorse everything you said. It's not because I'm an older preacher, and I think he thought I was the oldest one around that still remembered some of these things, and that's why he asked me.

But ... who's changed? Not long after the turn of the century there was a children's home at Bowling Green, Kentucky. And I've been there, and I've been through it. It was established and congregations contributed to it; a home in Nashville long before that; Boles Home up here in the early '20's and churches. . . .I never heard of a church that opposed it.

I've never asked a church before I went for a meeting whether they did or didn't. I've never asked them whether or not they gave any money to Boles Home, or to *Herald of Truth*. I don't think it's any of my business. They can do what they want to do. It's not affecting anyone else but those people and it's not affecting the worship and the work of the church, as I see it.

But the changes have been made, eliminating the modern stuff that's going on today, hoopla, maybe I could call it. I think those changes have been made by you brethren. Churches almost universally contributed. Sometimes the statement is made that brother John Akin who established the Akin Fund, and you brethren had charge of that for some time, that brother Akin was opposed to children's homes. He was not.

He was just like a second daddy to my wife; she was the baby of the Wallace's. Sister Akin was the first Bible class teacher my wife ever had. And she remembers asking, as a little tot, asking Sister Akin, what that was on her cheeks. Her stepmother that reared her, she never did use rouge, and Sister Akin had a little on (Laughter, whs). And she couldn't understand what that was on her cheeks that Sunday morning. I guess we knew Brother Akin better than anybody. She grew up under him. He used to say that Foy Junior was a great preacher, but he couldn't hold a light to his daddy, Foy Wallace Senior, my wife's daddy. When he moved to... came to Longview, Texas in 1902 and baptized Sister Akin and got him out of the digressive church, "Man," he said, "he was a preaching machine." They were really like brothers. And Brother Akin reminded me several times when I was preaching, especially at Preston Road. Went and visited with him every day, that Gaylord came to see him some years before that, while superintendent at Boles Home. And they were in a financial jam and they had to have five or ten thousand dollars in a hurry. And Brother Akin gladly let him have it. Brother Akin never was opposed to that, and I'm sure I knew Brother Akin far better than anybody here.

You know, in the '20's I guess it was, the Hardeman Tabernacle Meetings were held. Maybe that's the first big cooperative effort of that magnitude that the churches had, and congregations supported it. I've never read anywhere where anybody opposed it on a scriptural basis.

I moved to Dallas at the beginning of the war and thousands of people were moving in and many of them were Christians, and they didn't know that we had about fifty churches scattered all over the city, the Metroplex. And I told the elders one time, "Let's put a big ad in the Saturday evening paper. Have a map showing the locations of all the church buildings, and down at the bottom a list so they can find one near them." Well, I think that cost $150 a week, and I suspect our contribution didn't run over $500 a week. We couldn't have supported that by ourselves. So we contacted every church in the county, and not a single church turned us down. They all, 100% of them, cooperated and sent it to us so we could sign the contract for the ad.

Not long after, that a brother over at Peak and Eastside, and he thought it would be great to have a little sermonette. Now Foy Wallace always said a sermonette is preached by preacherettes, you know ((Laughter, whs). And they started that, and Peak and Eastside supported it, and they ran that for some time and churches contributed to that.

Brother Coleman Overby, a pioneer in educational work in the church, came over in about '44, and spoke to our teachers at Trinity Heights. He and I talked about thousands of people in the church would like to teach, but they didn't know how. The church has never had any kind of training to teach people how to teach youngsters, young people, and so forth. We need some kind of training school. Brother Overby said, "I've thought about that. Let's have one."

So in 1945 we had the first teacher training school in the history of the church in America. And every church in Dallas County contributed to the expense of that, so Ferlan Bryan could furnish the building and pay these speakers that came, some far and near, their expenses in traveling. Now that was in 1945. We cooperated. We hadn't changed, you have. I don't mean to be blunt, but that's the only way I can preach. Just tell people the way it was, and that's just, not my guess. That's exactly what happened in the Dallas area, and I think that's the pattern of brotherhood-wide experiences.

And then we kept on having those teacher training schools, until they grew so large that we got around 2000 people a night, and had to split it and have one on either side of the Trinity River, and we continued to cooperate.

These situations never did cause much trouble in the Dallas churches as they did in some metroplexes. We've never had much of a difficulty. Very few groups were inclined to go in that direction. Maybe it's because Dallas, when I came there, was considered one of the centers of conservative thinking religiously. And I still believe that that's the way it was. It may not be now. But we continued those schools for years and all the churches helped pay the expenses.

We had the two great downtown revivals. Had about 12,000 people a night at the big coliseum. Fifteen days and during that, I did the baptizing, and Loyd Smith here, the church in Sunset where he was preaching, they sponsored that. But the budget that year was $40,000. Why they couldn't pay $40,000, so they asked churches would they help. And churches helped and nobody lost their autonomy. Baptized 300 people that first week meeting; same time next year we had another one and baptized over 200. Their budget had to be then $50,000, and the churches helped.

I could go on and on in talking about example after example after example of cooperation. And it's sad to think that that's become almost a dirty word today among us. But they cooperated in having teacher training schools.

Then, later I told the elders at Trinity Heights where I still was, that we've never had what we called an elder's workshop. Let's have a gathering here in our auditorium and have, not preachers, but have elders talk to elders about how to conduct a business meeting, and what attitudes they ought to take, and how to shepherd the flock, and things of that sort. Let elders tell elders, elders of long standing. First night we had 900 elders. Next year we had another one. Had an average of around 800. And the churches all cooperated and contributed voluntarily. They decided to or not to, and nobody blackballed anybody. Nobody ever knew except maybe our elders, which churches helped.

Those are things in which I've had a part. That's why I say you might think I'm bragging on my experiences. But from that background, having all of these meetings, three of them at least, with brethren on the other side. And then knowing about all of these activities that we've been carrying on in the Dallas area for years and years.

I speak it from a sincere heart. It breaks my heart, truly it does, that these things have happened. In the Arlington Meeting, I presented some things to some of the brethren, and that speech is in the book. I said, "If we could get an auditorium," and I was talking about ours. Twelve thousand people every night to hear the gospel preached, baptized three hundred. Now if Sunset sinned in having that meeting, tell us brethren, how in the world can we do it? If what we do and the way we do it is wrong, then tell us how we can do that. Preach to 12,000 people for fifteen nights, turn people away because they couldn't get inside, baptized several hundred. Now if our method of doing it…please tell how we can do it and be scriptural.

And I'm going to call his name, because he's one of the dear friends whose friendship I lost. He's been in our home so many times, nearly a lifelong friend. When that session was over and I begged them to tell us how to do it, Roy Cogdill told me that my answer is, they didn't reply publicly at all, but my answer is that no church of the Lord ought to ever get involved in a project of that magnitude. Now I think scare tactics, scare tactics, drives us away from some things. We're afraid of something big. It doesn't have to be sinful because it's big. And I told Roy, "I don't believe that God designed the church so that we cannot take advantage, in some scriptural way, of preaching to millions of people." And we can do that today.

I'd like to say one more thing. Brother Akin set up the Akin Fund when I was there. I was the first man to read the charter. Brother Bell and Sister Bell set up the Bell Trust and I've been a director of that now for thirty some odd years and we give millions of dollars away. And you still have a portion of the Akin Fund; Preston Road has the rest. And I talked to Brian Vinson, Foy's here now, the son. I said, "Brian how can you be a director of the Akin Fund" and he was then, "and send money when brother Akin was not ever a member of the…" whichever church it was. They were sending money to that church for them to support a man some where else. Brian was a good man, honest in heart, and he said, "That worries me." I don't see one bit of difference between what you do in the Akin Fund and the thing you preach against.

God bless you, and I still call you brothers.

Historical Perspectives
Day 1 Speech 1 Rebuttal
Steve Wolfgang

Introduction: *Wolfgang, Steve. Presently works with Danville, KY. (11years) had done other local work in Trenton, Fl, Atlanta, GA, Marion, IN, Franklin, TN, and Louisville, KY. He has taught in a preacher training school at Danville for the last ten years with over seventy-five men graduated. Does extensive meeting work in the States and overseas, and is an adamant student on restoration history.*

I suppose the place to begin is where Brother Lanier left off. He described me as knowledgeable in Restoration History. I call you attention to the program that's been printed. I want to thank Brother Eugene Smith for the time and money that his company has put into printing not only these programs, but the flyers. When they faxed me my copy last week of this program to proof, and to make corrections on the biographical sketches, I noticed that under my name they had put that I was an expert in Restoration History. I think Foy Vincent must have written that because I know Roy Lanier didn't write that about me. And I wasn't real comfortable with it, so I called the *Gospel Teachers Press* and I said, "Why don't you just put that I'm an avid student of Restoration History." And I wandered if I should spell that word, but I figured, no these people they know what they're doing. So I read in the program now that I'm an *adamant* student of Restoration History, and my wife would probably concur with that judgment (laughter, whs).

But I do not intend for this speech to be adamant or aggressive, which is a word that some brethren have used about what I said in Nashville, or at least the printed copy. And I hope all of you have a copy of the address that has been printed. We distributed about 400 copies as I recall in Nashville just type written. And these have been printed up now in a little booklet. If you don't have one there's some others in the seats and some at the back and you can take one with you, and feel free to read it. It's 44 pages and a lot of that is footnotes and small print and some of you may not be interested in reading it. But I just begin there because what I'm going to do for 28 minutes is to do…

I've got several points I want to make like all the speakers, and I'm going to quit in 28 minutes whether I said all of them or not.

I've been accused of rewriting history in this booklet. I tried to go back and as somebody with some formal training in history, and as an avid student of, not only Restoration History, but other forms of it as well, to bring whatever measure of objectivity and fairness that I've been trained to do so as a writer and a student of history to this.

I enjoyed listening to Brother Jackson's speech. I have appreciated his fine spirit. From a historical standpoint what he said is, if I may be so blunt, historically short sighted, because it's anecdotal. That is it deals with one person's experience over a limited period of time and of course that may be interesting as biography but that's just a very small slice of what happened. And many people's experience would be quite different from what we have heard related here today.

Now let me go back to this idea of rewriting history. I've been in print with regard to these kinds of things stating basically what's in this 44 page booklet for fifteen years; it's been accessible to anybody who has access to even a mediocre library. Brother Harrell, whose lead I have followed basically in this and who'll be on the panel, has been in print for thirty years, I suppose on it. I have most recently, I've done this half dozen times, I suppose over the last fifteen years, presented papers like this before professional historical societies, most recently in March, at the American Academy of Religion. It has been well received. They have judged it again, as a fair and objective attempt. People from various institutions including, David Lipscomb University, Abilene, Pepperdine, a number of other institutions that would hold views, I suppose somewhat similar to these brethren who are sitting at the table here have read it. And have… if not commending everything about it, have accepted it as a fair … as an attempt to be fair and objective.

And I guess what I would say to those who think this is a slanted view of history, or a revision of history is, if this isn't right, then one of you fellows needs to write something and tell us what's wrong with it, and where it's wrong, and where it's slanted, and what isn't fair and objective about it. I would make that request of you.

Now what I'm going to do for the remainder of the time that I have is just to walk through this. And read a few paragraphs at a time, and just deal with some things that I think are interesting, that we might pay profitably some attention with.

I'm going to start very near to the front. I won't read the very first quotation that's there because the Brother who I'm quoting, and I don't see any need to call his name, has since he said that, he has recanted somewhat his view and I appreciate the spirit that motivated that. But I quote it not so much as a single person's view, but as what I take to be a representative statement of how members of main stream churches of Christ, if I may use that term, how leaders in what we have come to call institutional churches, viewed those who came to be called "antis" at the end of the 1960's or there about.

Or, if we were to go back to, for example, the … If I can get this focused correctly. Joe I'll scoot out of your picture for just a minute … the head of one of these institutions wrote the kind of rhetoric that reads, for example the bottom of the page (Chart #1). "Infidelity, agnosticism and anti-ism have much in common." That is to be an 'anti' is like being an atheist. "None ever brought a helping hand or healing ministry to the unfortunate of earth living in want and misery," assuming that that ought to be the work of the church to do that, "nor have they ever built a home for homeless children or a hospital," again assuming that we ought to do that as collective groups of Christians, "in which to minister to the sick." And what I do in this particular booklet is just to pose the question. How did it come to this? How did we get to the point that even brethren of fine spirit, perhaps like Brother Jackson, and again I appreciate his spirit, and others who will speak with whom I have had association in the past? I've come to know and appreciate, for example, Brother Doran, who lives in my area and with whom I've had a number of interesting and lively conversations about Restoration History.

What I basically tried to do in this booklet is to go back about fifty years and talk a little bit about some changes that occurred around the time of World War II, not just

> ## Anti-ism and Atheism
> Infidelity, agnosticism, and 'ant-ism' have much in common. None ever brought a helping hand or healing ministry to the unfortunate of earth living in want and misery. Nor have they ever built a home for homeless children or a hospital in which to minister to the sick.
> Tom Holland, Challenge of the Commission: Sermon Outlines From Acts (Brentword, TN: Penman Press, 1980), P.20. See also Gaylor Oler, "No Soup," Boles Home News, March 25, 1954, p.1

in the thinking of one group of brethren but in society as a whole and how that affected churches (Chart #2). What developed in the post war years and what were the issues and some of the arguments that are used to support that? What caused some brethren to hang a yellow tag of quar-

> 1. The Last Fifty Years
> 2. World War II
> 3. The Post-War Era
> 4. What Were "The Issues"
> 5. The Arguments
> 6. The Yellow Tag of Quarantine
> 7. Separation, Growth, and Development
> 8. Current Perceptions
> 9. What of the Future

antine on other brethren? If we're looking for historical causation, if we're trying to explain why things changed from the way they were fifty years ago, we might need to look at facts like, the growth, "the explosion" if you will "after World War II, in the number of institutions supported by churches. From 5 or less to 30 or 40, all of them with their hands out begging for money from churches." We might need to look at what would cause brethren to say, "Let's just quarantine those." A charge probably not fully appreciated by those of us who grew up after a period in which wonder drugs, and those kind of things, became daily facts of life.

And I talk a little in the book about the separation, the growth and the development of the two different, I hesitate to use the phrase, groups of churches, because that approaches speaking the language of Ashdod, but I think you understand what I mean. And then something I hope I'll have time to return to at the end of this address, and that is, what of the future and what can we do?

What I basically tried to describe in the booklet, in the period, for example 1920 – 1940, is a period that might be described as a period of steady growth, of geographic expansion outside what we would roughly call the south or now maybe the sun belt, institutional development (Chart #3) where fledgling, small colleges, some of whom took church money before, and orphanages as well, virtually exploded after 1945, to a much more numerically stronger group of institutions. I see it as a period of relative

---

Between The Wars
1920-1940

A. Steady Growth
B. Geographic Expansion
C. Institutional Development
   1. Colleges
   2. Orphanages
D. Relative Doctrinal Harmony
   1. Denominational Debates
   2. Heretics "scorched"

---

doctrinal harmony." Represented not only by the denominational debates; the fact that heretics, rather than being warned that they would loose their place in the brotherhood, as came to be, I suppose, the main threat after the war, heretics were basically scorched.

I've been handed a note to try to frame this better and I have to tell you that that's the best we can do with this particular projector. We've been having trouble all day with regard to it. I'll apologize for that but it's the best we can do.

Actually, I'm going to edit a lot of stuff out. Let me talk for just a few minutes about an attempt that I make in the booklet to be fair. If you're looking at the booklet, pages 18 and 19 (Chart #4). That's all right, just leaving those; I throw transparencies all over the place generally. I make the statement that, "It is no doubt true that there have been instances of non-institutional brethren who

have used mirror logic. That is, who vacated the premises before they were invited to leave, who displayed rancorous attitudes in the process, who may have heaped derision and vilification upon their 'liberal' opponent." I am not arguing that non-institutional brethren always behaved themselves as they should. Surely there is enough sin and

---

It is no doubt true that there may have been instances of non-institutional brethren who used "mirror logic," vacating the premises before they were invited to leave, displaying rancorous attitudes in the process, heaping derision and vilification upon their "liberal" opponents. I am not arguing that non-institutional brethren always behaved themselves as they should; surely there is enough sin to go around in this or any other division. Whatever the case, the division over institutionalism was clearly induced by much more fundamental causes than that some brethren on either side behaved themselves in a manner unbecoming to Christians - which is at least part of the reason why it will take more than simply "talking" or forming new friendships with each other to heal this breach. Division did not come simply because brethren mistreated each other (though no doubt some did), but was due to much more basic causes. It will not be reversed unless and until those more fundamental problems are remedied.

And whatever may be said of the conduct of individuals of either persuasion, it is certainly true that the levers of brotherhood "power" were clearly with the institutional majority, and the message they sent, as perceived by their non-institutional brethren, was a rough equivalent of "Go play in the traffic."

---

fault to go around in this or any division. I'm not trying to paint all the conservative brethren as guys in white hats and all of the institutional brethren as children of the devil. I don't try to do that. But whatever the case may be, I want us to see that there were more fundamental causes to this division than just the failure to call on somebody to lead in prayer, for example, or that some brethren on either side behaved themselves in a manner unbecoming to Christians.

And at the bottom of this particular transparency, I think probably on the next page, I make the point that whatever maybe said of the conduct of individuals, whether specific individuals behaved themselves or not …just in the nature of the case. (Chart #5) It's true that the levers of power, if you were, in the brotherhood were clearly in the hands of the institutional majority. They controlled the colleges, and the widely circulated papers, and the television programs, and the radio programs and that sort of thing. And the message they sent, as it was clearly perceived by their non-institutional brethren, if you'll pardon the phrase was a rough equivalent of, "Go play in the traffic."

> In short, by the early 1960's a clear message had been delivered to the minority tagged "anti" by the majority. Delivered with all the smug superiority and condescension of an older sibling, it said, "Go away, kid -- you bother me." As Filbeck has demonstrated in his chronicle of the missionary society controversies, a similar mentality had evolved which was no longer willing to consider optional what had been first defended as mere expediencies. The colleges, orphanages and other institutions appended to the churches now seemed to many to be indispensable -- absolutely necessary -- to the work of the church. Seen in this light, it was an easy step to elevate their value well above whatever questionable virtue the maintenance of fellowship with the cantankerous "antis" might possess. Non-institutional brethren could be deemed expendable if they could not agree to go along and get along. Many seemed to believe their fellowship less valuable to the cause than the emerging network of colleges and other institutions erected and funded by the churches, ostensibly to the great glory of God.

Brother Roy Lanier told me . . . in the and I hope he won't mind my referring to him, in the course of preparing for this, that that came as a surprise to him and to some others that we felt that way, many of us. My sense is, that if you polled brethren in non-institutional churches, is that you would find that almost as a man, almost to a man, they would tell you exactly what I have just said. That from the perspective of where many of us, or many of you sat, and I have childhood memories for example of my father, a Deacon in the largest church north of the Ohio River and the treasurer for that church, being told either to write a check to a given orphanage, which I will not name, or get out. I don't think, if we're going to trade anecdotes, I don't think that's an isolated instance. That could be multiplied hundreds, maybe even thousands of times over.

And to go back to what I have written in the booklet. (Chart #6) "In short by the early 1960's a clear message had been delivered to the minority tagged 'antis' by the majority. Delivered with all the smug superiority and condescension of an older sibling." It said, again to use a vernacular, "Go away kid you bother me."

I try to parallel what I see happening in this instance to things that David Filbeck, who's a historian of the Independent Christian Church movement, to what he wrote about the development of those kind of institutions. "A similar mentality it seems to me had evolved…" (I'm reading now from page 18 of the pamphlet if you want to read along), "a similar mentality had evolved which was no longer willing to consider optional what had at first been defended as mere expediencies. The colleges, orphanages, and other institutions appended to the churches, now seemed to many to be indispensable—absolutely necessary—to the work of the church." How can we do the work of the church without big meetings and colleges and training schools, it's just how can we do the work of the church without these kinds of things? That's the mentality that I'm talking about. "Seen in this light it was an easy step to elevate their value well above whatever questionable virtue the maintenance of fellowship with the cantankerous 'antis' might possess. Non-institutional brethren could be deemed expendable if they could not agree to go along and get along. Many seemed to believe their fellowship less valuable to the cause than the emerging network of colleges and other institutions erected and funded by the churches, ostensibly to the greater glory of God."

I had an experience some time ago in Kentucky. I attend the Cain Ridge Lectureship, which Dr. Doran's been involved with for many years. And I posed a question at the last one that was conducted that he and I attended, and many other people as well. And I posed a question to a well known brother, who's … again I see no purpose in calling his name, but you'd recognize it if I did. And among the comments that he made was this one. (Chart #6) He said, "I honestly believe that a lot of the younger men among this movement don't know the history. I really think that they feel like what happened was, we were all opposed to orphan homes at one time, and all opposed to cooperative evangelism, and those of us who support such things have just apostatized and gone the way of all the world; when the fact of the matter is" this brother said this these are the facts, in his version, "the fact of the matter is,

> I honestly believe that a lot of the younger men among this movement don't know the history. I really think that they feel like what happened was, we were all opposed to orphan homes at one time, and all opposed to cooperative evangelism, and those of us who support such things have just apostatized and gone the way of all the world; when the fact of the matter is, back in history when we were united, we were united in the support of such matters and not in opposition.

back in history when we were united, we were united in the support of such matters and not in opposition."

Well, I address that also in this particular booklet and I'd like to just say a few words about that. If you want to, turn to pages 10 and 11 of the booklet and read along, in case this looks fuzzy to you, as I'm sure it does, it may be fuzzy headed as well to some of you, but we'll do the best we can. Again, I'm trying to be objective and honest here. (Chart #7) There is no question about the fact that cooperative works although probably smaller and more… seemingly more innocent in nature than some that we're seeing today, that's been present a long time before even

> That there had been some "historical precedent" for centralized support of city-wide evangelistic endeavors cannot be successfully disputed. The cooperative efforts of the "Tabernacle Meetings" of the Twenties and Thirties were reflected in other such post - World War II endeavors as the Houston Music Hall meetings, in which the Norhill church undertook to oversee funds from Houston-area churches so that Foy E. Wallace, Jr., could preach lessons which, transcribed and later published as *God's Prophetic Word* and *Bulwarks of The Faith*, would provide sermon material on which an entire generation of preachers would "cut their teeth." The local preachers at Norhill at that time were Luther Blackmon and Wallace's close friend, Roy E. Cogdill, who before long would launch his own printing company largely to be able to publish Wallace's books as well as his paper, *The Bible Banner* (later, *The Gospel Guardian* - in which Cogdill would later renounce the centralized arrangement of the music hall meeting).

the 20th century, in the 19th century even. "That there had been some 'historical precedent' for centralized support of city-wide evangelistic endeavors cannot be successfully disputed."

I've talked to some of…brethren who agree with the basic views that I hold. Who have tried to, I guess sort of pick my brain, and say "Can't you establish historically maybe that the…" But the fact is that they have existed for a long time, there's no question about that. "The cooperative efforts of the 'Hardeman Tabernacle Meetings' of the twenties and thirties were reflected in other such post-World War II endeavors as the Houston Music Hall Meetings in which the Norhill church undertook to oversee funds from Houston-area churches so that Foy Wallace, Jr. could preach lessons which, transcribed and later published as *God's Prophetic Word* and *Bulwarks of the Faith*, would provide sermon material on which an entire generation of preachers would 'cut their teeth'. The local preachers at Norhill, at that time, were Luther Blackmon and Wallace's close friend, Roy E. Cogdill, who before long, would launch his own printing company, largely to be able to publish Wallace's books as well as his paper, the *Bible Banner* later the *Gospel Guardian*…" and "in which Cogdill would later renounce the centralized arrangement of the Music Hall Meetings."

And I want to pause for just a moment and refer to that. I talk about the question of who changed. This is from one of the footnotes and I've documented that there. If somebody would like to look at it or challenge it, you're free to do that. (Chart #8) "Cogdill, Blackmon, *Guardian* Editor Yater Tant, and others who initially supported such efforts…" in the 1950's primarily became convicted, or "were forced by conviction of conscience, and, as they saw it, consistency, to withdraw their support for such collective endeavors…" And since this is a history section, I go on to add "…in much the same way as men like Tolbert Fanning and Benjamin Franklin, who were initial supporters and defenders of nineteenth century missionary society endeavors, eventually withdrew their support for such efforts and indeed became vocal opponents of such works."

I meant to go back and check this but I recently spent five weeks in eastern Europe and just had about eight days at home before I came here and I didn't get a chance to do it. Fanning, if I'm not badly mistaken, was the Recording Secretary for the Tennessee Society, and I believe Frank-

> Cogdill, Blackmon, Guardian editor Yater Tant, and others who initially supported such efforts were forced by conviction of conscience, and, as they saw it, consistency, to withdraw their support for such collective endeavors - in much the same way as men like Tolbert Fanning and Benjamin Franklin, initial supporters and defenders of nineteenth - century missionary society endeavors, eventually withdrew their support for such efforts and indeed became vocal opponents of such works.

> The discussion of "historical precedent" is an interesting one which one or both sides often adduce to bolster claims, but which is ultimately meaningless since, even if uniform, what the "pioneers" did provides no validity for doctrine or practice unless one accepts an "authority of tradition" view-point akin to that of Roman Catholicism. In this context, it simply demonstrates that sincere, intelligent, and honorable persons can and do change their minds and actions for a variety of reasons; or, that people sometimes do contradictory things and are not always self-consistent.
> See James R. Wilgburn, *The Hazard of the Die: Tolbert Fanning and the Restoration Movement* (Austin, TX: Sweet Publishing Company, 1959), chapters 10-12, *especially pp,176-181, 187-188, 193-195;* Earl West, *Elder Ben Franklin: Eye of the Storm* (Indianapolis: Religious Book Service, 1983), pp.158-160, 211, 222 ff,: Joseph Franklin and J.A. Headington, *The Life and Times of Benjamin Franklin* (St. Louis: John Burns, Publisher, 1879), 304-305

lin served for a while at least as President of the Indiana Christian Missionary Society.

Now to those who are interested in questions about who changed, I would say several things. One of which is, who cares who changed. I'm happy to go on record as saying, "I don't care what happened in Houston in the '40's or Birmingham in the '50's or Nashville in the '20's or a '30's." (Chart #9) I go on to say in one of the footnotes; "The discussion of 'historical precedent' is an interesting one." I'm interested in studying about that. It's an intriguing way to spend a few hours, reading these sorts of things which, "both sides often adduce to bolster claims, but which is ultimately meaningless since, even if uniform, what the" so called 'pioneers' "did provides no validity for doctrine or practice" unless you're willing to accept a point of view akin to the Roman Catholic idea of the 'authority of tradition,' and I don't think anybody here is. "In this context, it simply demonstrates that sincere, intelligent, and honorable persons can and do change their minds."

Should we say that Franklin and Fanning should not have changed because initially they supported societies? Should they have been locked into that position for the rest of their lives? Or is it better for someone upon studying the scriptures, and seeing that something that began relatively innocently and now threatens, perhaps to take on ... because of the growth and development of a whole tangled web of these things. Maybe we need to go back and take a second look at that and change our minds to conform to what the Bible teaches, rather than the other way around. That's the point I'm trying to make. It may

also indicate "... that people sometimes do contradictory things" or that we're "... not always entirely self-consistent."

Brother Jackson told me that I'd be his lifelong friend if I'd tell him how young he looks. And so I'm going to quote something from David Lipscomb here, and just say Lipscomb died, if I remember correctly, in 1917. Brother Jackson I know you must have been born after that time.

Brother Jackson – Main Speaker: "Yeah I was." (Laughter, whs)

Steve Wolfgang – Rebuttal Speaker: And so I want to talk about something, again just as an illustration, and there's a booklet printed which again you can get in the back. If you don't have a copy of the grey one, there's a yellow one back there on *Congregational Cooperation*. And among other things it quotes, in this case David Lipscomb's comments about the famous Henderson Meetings, where a church in west Tennessee sought to take the oversight for a number of different churches and to oversee their use of funds.

Now if we're going to talk about history, and when opposition to these things developed. And if we're going to discuss the question, have we always been united on these things, and has it been uniform brotherhood opinion that these were OK and we should just go ahead and do that. Well, let me just share with you a few comments from the pen of David Lipscomb (Chart #10). Now I not trying to say that whatever Lipscomb wrote was OK. But read with me what he wrote and see whether this sounds like what's always been done is that we've just supported cooperative

> Now what was that but the organization of a society in the elders of the church? The church elders at Henderson constitute a board to collect and pay out the money and control the evangelist for the brethren of West Tennessee, and all the preachers are solicitors for this work. This very same course was pursued in Texas a number of years ago. The elders of the church at Dallas were made the supervisors of the work, received the money, employed the preacher, directed and counseled him. For a number of years they employed C.M. Wilmeth. He then dropped out of the work and the Texas Missionary Society took the place. Other experiments along the same course have been made. All of them went into the society work.
>
> All meetings of churches or officers of churches to combine more power than a single church possesses is wrong. God's power is in God's churches. He is with them to bless and strengthen their work when they are faithful to Him. A Christian, one or more, may visit a church with or without an invitation and week to stir them up to a faithful discharge of other duties. But for one or more to direct what and how all the churches shall work, or to take charge of their men and money and use it, is to assume the authority God has given to each church. Each one needs the work of distributing and using its funds, as well as in giving them (Gospel Advocate, March 24, 1910, p. 364).

works without anybody questioning them.

This is from the *Gospel Advocate*, March 24, 1910. "Now what was that…" speaking of these Henderson Meetings, where this church became in effect a sponsoring church. "…what was that but the organization of a society in the elders of the church? The church elders at Henderson constitute a board to collect and pay out the money and control the evangelist for the brethren of west Tennessee, and all the preachers are solicitors for this work…" And if you're saying, well so what about west Tennessee. Let's bring it a little closer to where we are. Lipscomb said, "…This very same course was pursued in Texas a number of years ago. The elders of the church at Dallas were made the supervisors of the work, received the money, employed

the preacher, directed and counseled him. For a number of years they employed C.M. Wilmette. He then dropped out of the work and the Texas Missionary Society took the place. Other experiments along the same course have been made" and "all of them" Lipscomb said, "went into society work."

Now here is the point that I want to make as with Lipscomb. "All meetings of churches or officers of churches to combine more power than a single church possesses is wrong. God's power is in God's churches." In local congregations, in individuals doing His work, not in mass meetings, not necessarily in television. I don't have any objection to it, preached on television a time or two myself. You sometimes wonder though, hearing some of the rhetoric, how the first century church survived the first century without those kind of things. Lipscomb goes on to say, "A Christian, one or more, may visit a church, with or without an invitation, and seek to stir them up to faithful discharge of their duties." I suppose he would say maybe even to make a contribution to them even though they technically are not even a member there. "But for one or more to direct what and how all the churches shall work, or to take charge of their men and money and use it to assume the authority God has given to the church. Each one needs the work of distributing and using its funds, as well as in giving them." Now I offer that simply as an exhibit, that this is not something that happened in 1951. And if we're going to talk about historical precedent, perhaps we need to be a little better historically informed when we speak.

How much time do I have brother? OK! I've got 5 minutes then basically.

Roy Lanier – Moderator: Surprise me and end early. (Laughter. whs)

Steve Wolfgang – Rebuttal Speaker: I'll try.

One other thing that I quote in the booklet, and I'll just cover this very briefly. I think it's on page 30 if you want to look at it, is… and I'm trying to give an illustration, in reaction to the kind of session that we're going to hear tonight about the development of this problem of hermeneutics. Some of you may have heard that word before. And I quote an 1893 article from the *Christian Standard*, in which a brother talks about the fact that we just toss off Apostolic examples if we like and we follow them if we like and if we don't like it we just ignore it. Now many of you from both sides of this question, I would ask, when you heard some things like that from some brethren in Nashville were horrified, rightfully so in my opinion. And that sort of thing has been adduced, or introduced, to try to prove and to advance actually a number of things.

I've got a quotation here, I'm not sure you can see it. (Chart #11 illegible) I'll explain what it is. This is an excerpt from a Master of Divinity Thesis at Harvard University several years ago, written by a woman who identifies herself as a co-minister for the Brookline Church of Christ in suburban Boston. And this thesis is written as an open letter to Churches of Christ. And it is an argument advanced on the basis of the fact that since Jesus allowed women to accompany Him when He was on the earth, and since women were important in the life of Jesus, and since He used them in His parables as illustrations, and so forth, therefore women ought to be able to preach. I won't read a lot of this but she identifies the basic argument in this particular way. "Women were important in the life of Jesus from beginning to end. Women are ever present in the birth narratives. Jesus used them in His parables. He talks to women,"etc. And therefore the argument is "if Jesus did it then we ought to be able to do it today. Jesus takes a radical view of women and His response to women was radical. He did give both men and women the commission to evangelize," she says, "and to tell the gospel story."

Now I would guess that even among those if you brethren who would support some of the institutions that I mention in this booklet, that in theory at least that what you would say is we don't buy that argument. We disagree with that kind of hermeneutic, if you will. And yet what is amazing to some of us who you style conservatives, or other kind of language, and I don't mind if you call me an 'anti', by the way. I've been called worse, and by professionals too. We're all 'anti' something or other, I hope.

Here's a Dallas area publication from 1990, (chart #12 illegible) in which a good brother, I'm sure, out of sincere motives, I have no question. But he begins by asking the question "Is medical mission work scriptural?" And he expresses amazement that anybody would even ask that question. "It has always been a source of bewilderment to me, that this is even a tenable question." Can't quite understand why anybody would even ask such a question, "Is medical mission work scriptural?" But will condescend he says, he doesn't say that exactly, but maybe it's a valid ques-

tion and so we'll talk about it. "What is the argument here? We are instructed to be Christ-like. If we believe in lives of action instead of lip service we must follow in the paths the man of Galilee trod. We find in the gospels that he taught, fed people, healed the sick, cast out demons," and so forth. The argument is the same, "if Jesus did it we can do it." Now what I would like somebody to help me understand is, what is the difference in those two arguments? What would some brother who buys into this argument in support of medical missions ... what would he have to say, consistently, to this woman who wants to preach? Again, I suppose out of sincere motives. What kind of argument can be adduced and made in that particular sense?

Well, there are a lot of other things that I'd like to say. I'll just close by reading the last paragraph of my speech.

How much time do I have? One minute! That ought to get it just about right.

I don't mean to be pessimistic, but I pose the question. What can meetings like the Dallas Meeting produce? I think several things. Number one, it might result in some people changing their minds or their lives, perhaps their convictions, about some of these issues. More likely however, in the second place, it may simply reinforce convictions already long held. Third, it will produce an insight, I hope, for learning about each other, which might prove useful, even if nothing else results.

And finally, from my perspective, it may help all of us who are younger, resolve that it will not happen again in our lifetime, if we can help it. Perhaps such divisions are inevitable every two or three generations as new levels of sophistication are obtained, people that I respect have told me so. But I would like to think that by learning from the past, by teaching with great patience and instruction, by recognizing the factors and circumstances that bred division, perhaps our children and their children can avoid the quick rush into another division, which can never be healed. Maybe that task is futile, some whose judgment I respect have said as much, but I must try.

I thank you for your attention.

Historical Perspectives Panel Speaker Ground Rules

Roy H. Lanier - Moderator: (Very beginning not captured on tape whs) …for this session, and they're supposed to get my permission to speak. So they've got to raise their hand like a little schoolboy, and all of that. But we're going to experiment with this. We think it will be interesting to listen to these four men just simply talk to each other across these tables, and we're going to listen in on it for a little while. And that's what this panel discussion is designed to be.

(Roy Lanier refers to instructions to the audience for the Question and Answer Session that followed the Panel Discussion. WHS) Now if you have questions write them down and turn them in, either to me or Jamie Sloan. We are not looking for statements, nor are we looking for arguments. We're looking for questions. And if you turn in a big, long, detailed question that implies everything under the sun that you want it to imply, we probably will toss it, because we just simply want to make brief questions to our four panelists, and also to our two speakers in the next hour, not this one but the next hour; but be remembering that.

Now our four men that are involved in this particular session are: Brother Adrian Doran of Lexington, Kentucky, there's a good . . . a little bit of biographical information in your program; then Brother Hardeman Nichols who lives here in Dallas, both of these men well known and traveled and experienced in the Lord's work though the years; Brother Colly Caldwell who is connected with Florida College in Temple Terrace, Florida and Brother Ed Harrell who is a teacher with the University of Alabama at Birmingham. Ed Harrell will speak first and then Colly Caldwell and then Hardeman Nichols and then Brother Doran. Each one of them will have four minutes.

I just simply want to say that Ed Harrell, whom I have known since high school days, is a basketball playing fool. (Laughter, whs)

Now see, I was kind.

Historical Perspectives
Day 1 Speech 1 Panelist 1
Ed Harrell

Introduction: *Harrell, Ed. He is presently Breeden Eminent Scholar in the Humanities at Auburn University, has formerly taught history at E. Tennessee State, University of Oklahoma, University of Georgia, University of Arkansas, and University of Alabama at Birmingham. Widely recognized as a scholar on evangelism and religion in the American South, Harrell, native of Jacksonville, FL, has authored six books, two of which are biographies of Pat Robertson and Oral Roberts, and is often interviewed on national radio and TV networks.*

You were (referring to brother Lanier's closing "see I was kind"). I'm not going to be as kind. Well it is good to participate in this conference, which it strikes me, is a little piece of historical trivia in its own right. And lest we get too large a notion about what we're doing, I think that is probably what it will be. There is a historical inevitability, I think, about the separation that we're involved in. And in many ways the interesting thing about this conference is that we are here. That's partly personal, because those of us with some age on us once worked in a church that was more united … in churches that were more united.

It's true that I knew R.H. Lanier in high school. We played basketball together and I was the center who took all of the licks and collected all of the rough stuff under the basket and R.H. stood out in the corner and waived his hands to throw the ball to him (Laughter, whs).

But the fact of the matter is that what exists today are: separate communities, separate connections. And the next generation is entirely unlikely to have the same kinds of views and associations that those of us had who predate the 1950's. Furthermore, the issues that have divided us are not going to disappear. And in fact they're not a few issues, but the issues have proliferated as time has gone on. And so the fact is that we're not here to heal some sort of marginal schism, but we're here to discuss what it is that's led us to the point that we're now at.

It seems to me that the nature the historical division in the 20th century and the 19th century are strikingly similar. We obviously don't have time to talk about them right now. But in both centuries what happened is, the time came when critical issues rose to critical heights and people were called on to make decisions about them. The issues were not new in either the 19th or the 20th century. It is true that none of the things that divided institutional and conservative churches began in the 1950's.

What changed in the 1950's, was the size and the nature of the debate that took place. Different people changed sides. Brother Jackson said that he'd never heard anybody oppose these things prior to the 1950's. He didn't read Brother W.W. Ottey then, or Brother John D. Lewis, or Brother James Allen who was for a time editor of the *Gospel Advocate*; men who always opposed institutionalism. Some people changed in one direction, some people changed in another direction. The question is what did you do?

And I believe that the venue for division in the restoration movement has always revolved around how one reacted when elevated issues were raised. I think people react in three ways. Some say we're going to stop doing what's being done because it violates the hermeneutic.

There are others who say the hermeneutic is wrong, and if you want to know about that all you have to do is go to Abilene next weekend. And some people it seems to me, including many in this room, and we perhaps will have time to explain this more fully, essentially have a stronger loyalty to the church of Christ than to the hermeneutic. And I believe in both the 19th and the 20th century what we've ended up with is three groups: one that tried to consistently stay with the hermeneutic; one that abandoned the hermeneutic; and one that essentially showed a primary loyalty to the church.

Historical Perspectives
Day 1 Speech 1 Panelist 2
Colly Caldwell

Introduction: *Caldwell, Colly. He serves as Vice President of Florida College, teacher and administrator since 1971. He was born in Clarksville, TN, has preached in Indiana, Tennessee and Florida, and presently preaches for the Citrus Park church in Tampa.*

I join with all these others in expressing appreciation for the opportunity to be here and I'm glad that all of you are here too. In education sometimes we say, "If you want to touch the past you touch a rock; if you want to touch the present, you feel a rose; and if you want to touch the future, you touch a person." And that's why I think we're here, not so much for the past, but to touch a rose, maybe, in the present and to touch some persons for the future.

When we think about where we are, and I agree with Brother Harrell completely that we are in separate connections, if we want to put it that way. My personal conviction is that the only way that's going to change is by one person deciding that he's doing right, or doing wrong and changing, and becoming right. And I think this whole matter is going to be a one on one kind of a thing, that all of us have to take a look at as we go along.

I appreciated Brother Jackson's comments at least the spirit of them in saying "All of you are in my fellowship. I've never made this a test of fellowship." I have to get down to business though, when we talk about that. And business says to me that this is not just a matter of who leads prayer. It's a matter of what we share in. And I think we're going to have to ask ourselves, "What are we going to share in?" Not so much who we like or who we will even allow to lead a prayer, but what we'll do, and what we will participate in doing in the churches. And I have to ask these

brethren myself to please help us to know what you will share in and who we are talking with this week.

We went to Nashville and we had a little bit of a time with a great variety of dispositions. And I think what one fellowships, what he will share in, and what he will go along with, has a lot to say with how far we've come, historically. And I guess I really want to ask some of these brethren, "Are we going to share with those who question the verbal inspiration of the scriptures, or who call for the new hermeneutic? Should we build gymnasiums? Is recreation and entertainment the work of the church? Is the worldly church just a concept to talk about or is that a reality in action and are we going to do anything about that? And are we going to share in the things that are involved in that?"

Obviously we're going to talk about whether churches can oversee other churches. "But is that important if they do?" is a serious question to me. I think we need to know if we're willing to say to all the brethren who are now willing to accept instrumental music, "I won't draw a line" or "I won't do anything about that," or "I will consider that something that I will share in."

Historical Perspectives
Day 1 Speech 1 Panelist 3
Hardeman Nichols

Introduction: *Nichols, Hardeman. Well known preacher for 43 years in congregations in Cordova, AL, Lubbock, Midland, and Dallas, TX, along with Jackson, MS. Now in full time meeting work, participant in many forums and lectureships and debates, resides in Dallas, TX.*

I'm happy to be a part of such an occasion as this, because I think that good can come of it, because of our spirit of love and devotion to the Lord Jesus Christ, and to the word of God as our only rule of faith and practice.

This is the historical section of our meeting. And I think Brother Hulen Jackson was on line in dealing with these things that are a matter of history; and it doesn't invalidate history when one is a personal observer. I think Brother Wolfgang's comments were missing the point of both the type of discussion that this is at this time, as well as dealing with the fact that this is the historical section. And if the apostles could give a valid historical document, though it by inspiration, of the work of Christ and that would not invalidate their work because it was personal. It certainly doesn't invalidate the work of uninspired men whenever they make their personal comments. It's good that we have people like that who were a part of the immediate things that were going on. And while most of that first generation of those who were involved in these questions are no longer with us, some are.

I was just a young preacher and was invited and was a part of the Arlington Meeting. And I recall very much there the fact that there were divisions among the fifteen of the opposite view, as well as divisions among us. And we'll be talking more about what we are discussing with each other.

I want to deal with what was a part of the two speeches originally, Brother Hulen Jackson's speech and Brother Steve Wolfgang's speech. The idea of the yellow tag that was mentioned was simply one man's statement, and certainly was not the attitude of the brotherhood, over the practice of refusing to support *Herald of Truth*, or of orphan's homes. Most of the division came because people pressed the issues that were a matter of opinion, and they made personalities more important and they divided brethren. And that's a sin to divide brethren over things that are not scriptural.

There are many things that I'd like to discuss about that. And I think that this was very clear in the fact that our late Brother Franklin Puckett, who had the recorder shut off at the Arlington Meeting one afternoon, when it was brought up some had even had public debates that it was a sin to support an orphan not a member of the church out of the treasury. And those that did so would go to Hell. And he said, "Turn off the recorders." And he said, "Brethren I want to make an appeal. I do not believe that things like that ought to divide us, and I will not go to the Judgment over matters that have to do with the support of little children like that. And I'm not going to be driven to an extreme like that."

There were other divisions there and still there are among us, on both sides. Some of them are very serious, and others we need to go back and look at in the very view of history. And I believe that some of these things can be aided if we'll look at them properly in the setting not only of history as to what has happened, that's important, but also from the view of what the Bible principles that are involved in it have to do with these matters.

Historical Perspectives
Day 1 Speech 1 Panelist 4
Adron Doran

Introduction: *Doran, Adron. Noted educator, for many years President of Morehead State University, Lexington, KY, noted preacher and lecturer for over 50 years.*

If this timekeeper decides to shoot, I want a commitment from him before he does that he'll pay my hotel bill and take care of my wife and get her back to Kentucky. (Laughter, whs)

I thought this session was going to be holy, devoted to the historical aspects of the problems that arose, and not the problems themselves. You have outlined in other sessions of this series the issues themselves that you're going to discuss.

Will Rodgers said that he did not know anything except what he read in the paper. Well I don't know much more than Will Rodgers said he knew, but what I do know I know right well.

I know what happened in Kentucky, and it happened long before Steve Wolfgang was born, and I was there. I was baptized in 1927 by Alonzo Williams at the old 100 year old church in Cuba. I did not know anything about division within the church of Christ then. Oh I knew there were some people that opposed bobbed hair, and wearing rouge, and required everybody to wear a hat and some things like that. But it was a long time before I heard of the Bollites, or the Sommerites, or the anti's, or the conservatives or the liberals within the church of Christ.

Back in 1928 I went to Freed Hardeman College. Following that summer, I sang in meetings for preachers. And the only deviant among those preachers during that period of time was a fellow who taught that the kingdom of God had not yet been established. Later Bollism and Premillennialism arose.

Foy E. Wallace held a debate with Charles E. Neal in Winchester, Kentucky in 1933. All of the congregations of central Kentucky supported that debate. Wallace came to Lexington following the debate and held a meeting that was sponsored and financed by all of the congregations of that area. Nobody was opposed to that kind of operation at that time, and no issue was raised about orphan's homes. And in this little old congregation where we lived, we used the fifth Sunday to take up contributions to send to the orphan's home. We sent clothing and food and medicine and anything else we could collect to them. So it was a long time after that, historically, before we began to divide over the question.

So I want to talk about the ancient history, if you want to talk about my day, which I suppose pre-dates most of you except maybe Yater Tant, who's in the audience today, and we're about the same age. And I hope that in our discussion this afternoon we can talk about the time frame in which the division took place. And then let the other folks talk about whether the issues that are between us today aught to be promulgated by us or we aught to all oppose them.

I was just as opposed to the new hermeneutics, if I know what it is, as you are. I'm opposed to all of the liberalism that is represented by a lot of them today as are you. I believe today just what I did when Alonzo Williams put me under the water and I came up a member of the church and I've tried to stay in the church and out of everything else since that time.

Historical Perspectives
Panel Discussion Ground Rules

Roy Lanier - Moderator: I can not believe it. All four of them stopped on time (Laughter, whs). We are delighted with this experiment. (Laughter, whs) You elders, if you go back to your churches and say preachers can do this we're not going to say you're telling the truth. Now then, we will continue this in a panel discussion. Who wants to speak first? Just raise your hand and let me recognize you. And you fellows are just discussing this in front of us.

Adron Doran - Panelist: Well you say who speaks first.

Roy Lanier - Moderator: Ed.

Panel Discussion

Ed Harrell - Panelist: OK. Tell me when to stop. (Laughter, whs) I'm with Brother Doran, I think that I tend to keep my remarks pretty much to history.

I confess I have some problem with the personal anecdotal approach to history as well. I've been teaching history for thirty years, and I've discovered, when you're teaching about a war, the one thing you don't want to do is listen to a guy who was there (Laughter, whs). Because he knows absolutely nothing except what was happening right in his area (Laughter, whs). So clearly we have to look at it in a somewhat broader canvas than that.

I think Brother Doran raised a very important question, that perhaps we should direct some attention to, and that is, "When did this happen?" I have a different date from Brother Jackson. I think his was not bad. I think it happened beginning in about 1942, 1943 when G.C. Brewer wrote a series of articles and made a series of speeches in which he said, "When World War II is over the whole world is going to be open to our evangelization. And we need to pick some good churches that can sponsor the work in Europe and in Asia…," which he did, Broadway and the Memphis church. "And we need to do that work and we need to train some men to do it, and we need to quite arguing about it, and if anybody doesn't like it, they can lump it."

Now actually the debate over sponsoring church arrangements and orphan homes had been going on heatedly in the *Firm Foundation*. Old Brother Showalter sometimes would take an opposing view, but what that did, is it raised the level of the debate. And it raised the size of what was being done so, that people were forced to take a new and much more serious look at it. And essentially what some brethren said is, "We're going to do it, whether anybody likes it or not."

Roy Lanier – Moderator: Hardeman.

Hardeman Nichols – Panelist: Brother Harrell mentioned Brother John T. Lewis and others that have opposed institutionalism as he called it. Brother Lewis did come out very strongly in opposition to orphan's homes. I was a very personal friend of his, knew him well. And what is not told by Brother Harrell is that Brother Lewis started the Homewood church in Birmingham, and collected the money, from whatever source he could, to provide for that congregations beginning, and had it paid for and the property that they had at the beginning. And Brother Lewis was not opposed to cooperation in that view.

Now he did oppose orphan's homes, and when Child Haven began, he very vehemently spoke against it. And made some statements that I think he came to regret in some meetings with regard to some of the things. And brethren on both sides made statements that they came to regret. He mentioned how Brother Brewer had wanted the Union Avenue church and Broadway and others to take over the work. One of the elders at Broadway wrote an article in which he pleaded with brethren, "If they didn't want to spend their own money, didn't know how to spend, send it to them and they'd spend it." And he regretted that. Brother Paul Sharon was his name and he came out against that later and said, "I'm sorry. I didn't mean to leave the impression that I think congregations are not able to carry on their own work."

But we can cooperate in preaching the gospel, and brethren that's been done by the leading proponents of the 'anti' movement as well as by those who believed in cooperation. And if you don't believe it, I can furnish the cancelled checks where some of the brethren who were leaders in the movement right here in this room, have received funds much like the Herald of Truth, sent funds for radio programs. Now that's just the part of the historical aspect of it.

Roy Lanier - Moderator: Colly, do you have a comment?

Colly Caldwell – Panelist: I think I was just going to add to what Brother Ed said a little while ago. He was talking about Brewer's comment. And I think then, some things proceeded from that in the late '40's, particularly around '47, when the thing blew up in the papers between Hardeman and Foy Wallace. And that accented the intensity of the feelings on either side, and made this thing blow up among the brethren like it did.

Roy Lanier - Moderator: Brother Doran?

Adron Doran – Panelist: Back to Brother Harrell's war illustration, the historical aspects of it. You can't discuss a shooting war, if you don't know something about the conditions that led up to the assassination of the Prince of Austria. And that's what I think we ought to give some attention to, the ancient history of the situation as it was. You take Danville, Kentucky where Brother Wolfgang has preached for twelve years. The church was started there in the early 1940's. I preached in Danville when they met at a little residence, and congregations helped support that work, as the Nicholasville church did where I was preaching. And I have a picture of twelve men who attended one of those meetings at Danville. But sometime after 1940, four of those twelve men opposed orphan's homes, and the rest of us preached for places that went along and supported them like they always have. Now what happened at Danville? Well, I'll tell you what happened at Danville. Roy Cogdill came....

Roy Lanier – Moderator: Half a minute. Go ahead.

Adron Doran – Panelist: Oh I'll wait (Laughter, whs).

Roy Lanier – Moderator: Response?

Adron Doran – Panelist: I'll say this when I get back. I just wanted to tell all of it before he responded to it. Roy Cogdill came to Danville to hold a meeting, and he held an afternoon session over at Stanford. And he announced to the congregations, composed of elders and preachers and all of us, that there was inevitable division coming over the question of the orphan's home and cooperation. Well, a lot of people were disturbed about that. And soon after that, the church where Brother Wolfgang preaches went non-institutional. Well, the rest of us in that area stayed like we were. Now I don't know what we could have done to have kept Cogdill from saying that. And I don't know what good he did by coming up and saying that to us, because some of us didn't divide over it. I haven't divided yet. And thank you for the half-minute. (Laughter, whs)

Roy Lanier – Moderator: A minute and a half (Laughter, whs). Ed you look like you're...the back of your head looks like...

Ed Harrell – Panelist: Well, yes. I don't want to denigrate the personal experiences at all, because they are important and they are instructive and I certainly have plenty myself. Nor did I want to imply that anyone's particular historic position was defensible. I simply wanted to point out, that all of those arguments are not brand new in the 1950's. They've been going on for a long time.

A lot of people changed. I changed. I was a protégé of B.C. Goodpasture. My best friend was Clyde. Earl West changed. Bill Humbel changed. All kinds of people changed. I think that's what the division was all about. What issues were elevated? I don't think we divided about the issues, mainly. I think we divided about how you are going to approach the issues. And that, in fact, everybody was forced into decision under the circumstances of history, into making up their mind, what they were going to do about it. And I don't care how far you were off the beaten track; sooner or later you had to decide.

Hardeman Nichols – Panelist: But Ed, do you think that really it should have been a point of division like that? Should it have been? Even where there were divisions over whether or not we should support Herald of Truth, or send money to Germany. Every congregation had its own autonomy. They could do what they wanted to do about it. Couldn't we be brethren?

You brethren certainly don't agree on everything.

Ed Harrell – Panelist: Right!

Hardeman Nichols – Panelist: You've got those who believe God's divine cooperative is the individual, no cooperation of any kind above that level. You have those who oppose Christian colleges, those who believe that Christian colleges are all right, and Christian name is all right connected with them. You have divisions; they haven't divided you, why should these issues divide us? That's the point.

Ed Harrell – Panelist: Ok. I don't want…I could speak to that at great length. (Laughter, whs) But uh…

Roy Lanier – Moderator: You may have two minutes. (Laughter, whs)

Ed Harrell – Panelist: Colly?

Colly Caldwell – Panelist: We're going to have a whole session on that as we… a little later on, on why we divide at certain times. And I think from a doctrinal point of view that is…. I think my response to that simply is, when I can't share in doing something, with brethren that are doing that, then that raises… that forces me into a position of making that decision.

Hardeman Nichols – Panelist: In other words, with Paul and Barnabas you would have said, "Since I can't share with Barnabas' idea we ought to divide." Certainly not! Surely not!

Ed Harrell – Panelist: Well let me give a response. I think the time comes when we have to decide about, number one, what area am I going to spend my life working in if divisions become inevitable. And after all, we don't control history that thoroughly.

But I believe there's two different kinds of divisions that take place in the restoration movement. Some that are divisions between people who are essentially reading the Bible in the same way and reacting to the Bible in the same way. There are other divisions that come when the churches come to include people who are no longer reading the Bible the same way.

Hardeman Nichols – Panelist: Yeah!

Ed Harrell – Panelist: Now what I would say is that, I think you fellows went with an awful lot of people that were reading the Bible that way, and you're still with them. And that what many people did is end up determined that they were going to defend the Church of Christ. And I believe that's what happened in the 19th century as well.

Now individually I wouldn't want to charge any body with that, because I think many of you didn't do that.

Hardeman Nichols – Panelist: Right!

Ed Harrell – Panelist: But I believe that that's the ba-

sis upon which the division comes, when the time comes when we seriously question the way in which we're approaching the scriptures.

Adron Doran – Panelist: But Ed, I was taught early when I was baptized, and I know a little more than you would imply that I have to deal with Kentucky. I've been this side of the Mississippi River before I came to Dallas. (Laughter, whs)

But David Lipscomb wrote in the *Gospel Advocate* on July 23, 1901. And he gave a list of individuals and congregations that contributed to the Fanning's Orphan School, and to the Nashville Bible School. I couldn't find anything that anybody took issue with David Lipscomb on that.

Now the issues that arose between west Tennessee and David Lipscomb… David Lipscomb was accusing the people in west Tennessee of doing the thing which he himself was doing in Nashville. And if you read all of the history in the *Gospel Advocate*, and wherever it was about it, Lipscomb was having similar meetings, so they said, in west Tennessee in Nashville at the time.

Now my point of it all has been … I was baptized and the Lord added me to the church of Christ. Now what else should I defend except the Church of Christ? I'm not going to defend some person who goes off in a tangent with the Church of Christ, and I don't believe I have. I believe I'm preaching it just like I did the first one I preached in 1929 at old Webb's Chapel in Carlyle County. But the issues arose.

Well, why didn't we just let each congregation decide what it was going to do about that as an autonomous body controlled by the elders, or overseen by the elders, and then every body else leave them alone. I think that's where you all flubbed the dub by saying, "Well now you're doing the wrong thing, your supporting orphan's homes." Well what if they did?

Roy Lanier – Moderator: Colly, do you have a response?

Colly Caldwell – Panelist: My response to that simply is that, my responsibility is to teach the truth in all situations. If we teach the truth when we preach to these folks on whether it's right or wrong to change the organization of the church or to contribute to an institution out here, then that's going to make an effect on their practice.

Adron Doran – Panelist: But we didn't change.

Roy Lanier – Moderator: A lot of people can't hear you (rest inaudible, whs).

Adron Doran – Panelist: We didn't change Charlie. WE didn't CHANGE to doing it that way. YOU ALL changed to NOT doing it that way.

Roy Lanier – Moderator: Why don't you repeat what you said? A lot of people didn't hear you.

Colly Caldwell – Panelist: Alright! What I said was, that when we come down to decide what the scripture teaches on these things, on what the church aught to do, what the organization of the church aught to be, we're under obligation to teach the truth on that to these churches. Then each church makes its own mind up. I don't know anybody that set itself up as the divider of all the churches. But I know some preachers who went about preaching the truth on what the organization of the church is. And when they did that, then there had to be some decisions made about what brethren would do, and what they'd share in. That's the point I'm making.

Roy Lanier – Moderator: What Hardeman?

Hardeman Nichols – Panelist: I think that one point of history aught to be brought out, and that is that Brother Cogdill did not begin the *Bible Banner*. In fact, that was begun by the family that owned the *Gospel Advocate*. And they funded the *Bible Banner* for Brother Foy Wallace. I believe that's correct. And I see Brother Furman Kearley nodding his head yes. And he's editor of the *Gospel Advocate*.

Another thing is that Brother Wallace himself said that he would always do what he did in that Houston Music Hall Meeting. He never would change that, and never did. And he said there's a difference between Premillennialism and … Brother Harrell brought up a good point. There are some things that will divide, they're doctrinal. But functional things should not divide us where God hasn't specified the detail. And Brother Foy Wallace stated very clearly, wherever he went in meetings that the questions about orphan's homes and cooperation are not doctrinal like premillennialism, but they're functional. And he said we need to make a distinction between it.

Roy Lanier – Moderator: You're starting to preach Hardeman. (Laughter, whs)

Hardeman Nichols – Panelist: Well, I'll tell you what history says. (Laughter, whs)

Ed Harrell – Panelist: I think the question that is not terribly relevant again is "Who kicked who out?" Every place I ever was, for a little personal history, I got kicked out. But that may have been different in other places, and we can say oh well it doesn't really make any difference; we'd still call on you to lead prayer. The question is "Would you have me on the Abilene Lectures?" And so that's the kind of real division that takes place, and that's real. We can't argue about that.

Now what we divided about, I insist, is not simply that we disagreed about issues. We did disagree about them. Now whether they're functional or doctrinal is a question that is going to have to be discussed here at some other meetings.

I think that we all agree that we ought not to divide about anything that doesn't matter. But the question is whether these things matter or not. And…but I believe that we divided when the time came when many of us, and certainly in my personal case, when I became convinced that the people I was talking to concretely about these issues, were no longer reasoning from the same hermeneutic. Now I believe you've got an awful lot of fellows that travel the road with you who are now saying exactly that, so that you're kind of surrounded.

And on our side I'm saying that you violated the hermeneutic; and on your other side there are people who are saying the hermeneutic doesn't work, if you do the things that you do. So it appears to me, that that's the point that needs to be addressed, and it will be addressed here.

Hardeman Nichols – Panelist: Ed, do you think all of us, though, have been aligned with what you'd call "US" and not some of those that have left the hermeneutic been aligned with "YOU" brethren. Shall I give names?

Ed Harrell – Panelist: Oh no! That's just fine with me. I was sure glad to see them go. (Laughter, whs)

Hardeman Nichols – Panelist: Now that's my point. I don't think that most of the brethren have changed their views toward the scriptures and their authority. There have been mavericks and always will be, and they'll be exposed. But they don't represent, generally, the brotherhood.

I can't tell what the brotherhood is. I hold about forty meetings a year but you know, what is that to all the congregations there are? But I know that some of those at Nashville do not represent most of the congregations in the Dallas, Fort Worth area, in what they said. And I certainly wouldn't agree with them. I feel much closer to you than I do to some of them.

Adron Doran – Panelist: Oh, indeed so! Let me risk saying this to Charlie. When L.R. Wilson left Tampa, in what was then the Florida Christian College, he wrote me a letter and said, "I have recommended to the board, and the board wants you to come to take my place at Florida Christian College when I leave here." Well I wrote and said that I didn't want to leave Kentucky. And I don't want to leave Kentucky, don't want to now leave Kentucky. But I wonder if I had accepted that appointment, where would I be? Where would you be? Where would the college be today? If I remained as I was when they asked me to take the job, and they are not where I was when they asked me to take the job, where would we be in that situation, and who would have caused the difference, you reckon?

Roy Lanier – Moderator: Either one!

Ed Harrell – Panelist: We get Brother Doran down there, we'd probably convert him. (Laughter, whs)

Hardeman Nichols – Panelist: Well, I think that the brethren that I know believe in the autonomy of the local congregation. In fact, we sort of like as my dad used to say, "We're like the Indian's tree. We're so straight up we lean backward on that." We might even treat other congregations as if they were denominations in the area rather than as brethren, and that's sad. We ought to promote fellowship, and that's what I hope can come out of meetings like this.

As we go back in history, we can sort of see some things there that were wrong on both sides. And if we had been big enough to say like Brother Paul Sharon, "Brethren, I'm sorry for what I said. I didn't mean all the implications; I was just so zealous for mission work in Germany that, I want to say to you if you're not doing anything please help us. And let's go preach the gospel to the world." And there's a whole lost world still out there, bigger than it was then. And we need to come together on the basis of the word of God as our only rule of faith and practice, and let's stand there.

Colly Caldwell – Panelist: Are we assuming in that, that the issues that are involved in our discussion here don't have a strong, definitive, scriptural basis?

Hardeman Nichols – Panelist: Colly, I think all of you,

all three of you speakers in opposition to what you call the institutional view, all three of you have used words that it wasn't as big back then as it is now. Is it the size of it that's wrong or the principle back of it? You said that, Brother Ed Harrell said it, and Brother Steve Wolfgang talked about before World War II it wasn't as large as it is now, but the same principle.

Ed Harrell – Panelist: I think it's the basis upon which you try to defend it. And the question of whether after decades of debate, one can any longer consider it defensible or not.

Let me just make a historical comment that gets us back. I am absolutely persuaded and have written much about this, that out of the 19th century what you get is three clear religious communities coming. The Disciple of Christ, the ultra liberal restoration group, the Churches of Christ the ultra conservative and the un-denominational fellowship of Christian Churches and Churches of Christ which essentially was a basically conservative minded group, that defended instrumental music and the Missionary Society, or a group of congregational cooperation.

I believe you've got exactly the same thing happening in the 20th century, have written if it's wrong, it's going to be in every encyclopedia in the country, that what you have is coming at the same kind of three way division, brethren who are conservative, but who defended essentially, the practices that came to be challenged in the middle of the 20th century. And so I think the substance of this discussion clearly has to go on to the sessions that follow, about whether these are scriptural practices or not. I do believe that's what's happened.

Roy Lanier – Moderator: That's a good note on which to pause. And hadn't it been interesting to hear four old men talk about history. (Laughter, whs) I am just delighted that these four old men are able to be so instructive to us younger folks. (Laughter, whs) This has been a good experiment. We're going to take a short break in just a moment and come back. Now you do understand we do have another little session at which your questions can be directed to any of these four, plus the two major speakers for a few moments. Write your question down. Do not make argument or statements simply ask questions and we'll try to give them to the panel, and to the speakers for the next session. We will take a… let me be sure I've got over twenty seven announcements here… yes. We will take a five-minute break right now.

Historical Perspectives
Question and Answer

Roy Lanier – Moderator: (Beginning not caught on tape, whs) section now that will be questions and some answers. We are again, experimenting a little bit. We're hopeful that these men will be able to answer these questions in two minutes or less. (Laughter, whs) This is probably going to give a heart attach to these preachers to have to do this. But we are again hoping or we're experimenting and we're hoping that this will be an informative type session where you can ask the questions that you feel ought to be dealt with in regard to the historical perspectives.

I have been asked to caution each of the speakers to be sure and speak well and clearly and loudly into the microphones. Some of our younger people are having difficulty hearing it. (Laughter, whs) And when our speakers, our two major speakers come, they will come to this microphone, and of course the panelists have each their own microphone.

Question 1:
Roy Lanier - Moderator: The first question, "Does the fact that Lewis, Lipscomb or others were inconsistent"… this is to Hardeman Nichols incidently, excuse me for not telling you Hardeman … "Does the fact that Lewis, Lipscomb or others were inconsistent or that they practiced what they now oppose, justify the thing practiced? That is the sponsoring church."

Hardeman Nichols – Panelist: Well, I don't think they were inconsistent. I don't think they practiced what they opposed. But sometimes we try to assign to their words things that they didn't mean. They believed in the orphan's home. They believed in cooperation. They did not believe in one congregation taking over another congregation, nor do we. We believe in the autonomy of the local congregation.

Question 2:
Roy Lanier - Moderator: Brother Harrell, "Which do you regard as a more important loyalty, to the church or to the hermeneutic, and why?"

Ed Harrell - Panelist: Boy, I want to answer that other one, too! (Laughter, whs) I think that that answer is absolutely correct. That what those men were loyal to, I believe was the hermeneutic, was the principle. And when I read their writings, I would frequently see where, it seems to me, they were clearly violating that. But you know we don't see everything at the same time. So I think they were loyal to the principle.

And my answer to that is that I am loyal only to the hermeneutic. I am loyal to the church of Christ in the divine since, but not in the earthly since at all. I have absolutely no since of denominational pride or loyalty.

Question 3:
Roy Lanier - Moderator: Question to Steve Wolfgang. Oh my! This is sort of a strong implication.

Steve Wolfgang – Rebuttal Speaker: Bring it on. Lay it on me. (Laughter, whs)

Roy Lanier - Moderator: Have you ever…no "Have you read the *Gospel Advocate* of November 15, 1954, December 9, 1954, note thirty-three in your booklet. (Laughter, whs) Note thirty-three in your booklet."

Steve Wolfgang – Rebuttal Speaker: Yeah! (The rest inaudible, whs).

Roy Lanier - Moderator: Ok, here's the question. "Isn't it the case that the expression the yellow tag of quarantine is not used in the *Gospel Advocate* but was Cecil Douthitt's coinage?" Somebody signed this but I can't read the question nor the signature. It must be some doctor that signed it (Laughter, whs). But am I reading the question right? Actually the question is, the yellow tag of quarantine is not used in the *Gospel Advocate* but was used in Brother's Douthitt's coinage alone, or something to that effect?

Steve Wolfgang – Rebuttal Speaker: The short answer to the question is yes. I have read them. Hardeman Nichols asked me that question at the break as a matter of fact and I presume….

Hardeman Nichols - Panelist: I didn't hand in the question. (Laughter, whs)

Steve Wolfgang – Rebuttal Speaker: OK. Well that's all right.

Hardeman Nichols – Panelist: I can write legibly. (Laughter, whs)

Steve Wolfgang – Rebuttal Speaker: Brother Douthitt did use that coinage in the title of his article in the *Guardian* of the next year. But the phrase "yellow tag of quarantine" or "tag of quarantine" is in fact used first in the *Gospel Advocate*. It's not used in the title but the idea is certainly there. And again this is based on my memory of things that I haven't read it for the last two or two and a half years, but when I wrote this material, yes I did go back and read that.

And I will make this observation that arises from this other discussion we've had. That actually what's interesting historically about that, that that call for isolation of people who would not go along with the program if you will, is before any of the published debates ever took place. Now there had been some skirmishes in the papers, but this is before the Indianapolis Debate in '54; it's before either of Brother Tant's debates with Brother Harper; it's before Cogdill's debate in '57; before this question was ever explored in a really public sense as to what the issues were.

We get guys, editors of papers, writing without anybody answering this, by the way. I mean it's interesting to me that now there's some people who maybe want to distance themselves with that. My question is where were they in January of '55? If this is such an offensive thing, why didn't somebody write and say "Brother Goodpasture, you're over the line"? "Brother Goodpasture, this is going too far," or whoever else may have been in charge of it. That's my question.

Question 4:

Roy Lanier - Moderator: This is to Brother Jackson. "The people you think are, quote doing some awful things end of quote, parenthesis your words close parenthesis comma (Laughter, whs). Do you believe you are to fellowship with them? Specifically those who are asking for a new hermeneutic: women preachers, the discipling movement, spelled as if it were the 'disciplining movement,' do you consider them in your fellowship?" Brother Jackson, do you understand that question?

Hulen Jackson – Main Speaker: Now don't count this as part of my two minutes. I want to explain why I have been such a popular preacher and preached in Dallas over forty years, 48 years. It's explained by what a good friend said to me. She thought that I was the only good preacher in the world. But she said after a sermon, "You know what I like about your preaching the best?" Now I thought she meant my oratory, my perfect grammar, enunciation. I said, "What's that?" She said, "Well, there's not much to it." (Laughter, whs) Now I've always been a preacher of short sermons.

Now I'm not going to go into that question of who is to be in fellowship. We met with some of the same ones . . . met with these Independent Christian Church preachers twenty years ago. Had a small group of 5 or 6 of us, they had 15 or 20 of them and 15 or 20 of us. And we considered them baptized believers and brethren in the Lord. But in no sense … now they've changed or our brethren have changed…. the ones that were having those meetings. Did anybody ever compromise? They knew exactly what we believed and that we could not endorse them because of their instrumental music, missionary societies. We talked about and thrashed out those differences. And we can't fellowship them in that sense, but I'd call him a brother. And most of us would. But he's a brother in error.

But I don't know what to say about fellowship or you know where you're going to draw the line. I don't think anybody does frankly. We'd better keep that an open question. But where it affects the worship of the church and affects other people there, the whole congregation, and the practice of the church relative to the plan of salvation and so forth and so on. Those things that are in a sense doctrinal and we can't do it. But I don't know really for sure when to say I would fellowship and would not fellowship. Now I've got two minutes for that?

Roy Lanier - Moderator: NO! Time! (Laughter, whs) That perhaps will come up a little bit later, at least it should in the session on fellowship on Saturday.

Question 5:

To Ed Harrell. "Explicate the differences" (Laughter, whs) Can you do it Ed? (More laughter, whs)

Ed Harrell - Panelist: I'm all right so far. (Laughter, whs)

Roy Lanier - Moderator: This really isn't a question but I guess it can go as a question, it's an instruction. "In three areas of division, explicate the differences in three areas of division: especially, the two areas of hermeneutics, and the church of Christ."

Ed Harrell - Panelist: Well, the difficulty in doing that obviously is to explicate it in a brief period of time. But it strikes me that when you look at the three way divisions that take place in the restoration movement in the 19th century and the 20th century, that the basic frames of references remain the same. And that is, there is a group that remains with the relatively straight forward hermeneutic of arguing that there is biblical authority for restoring the New Testament church. Then there… what emerges is people who really no longer have much confidence in that hermeneutic. Now it takes them twenty or twenty-five years to say that. Actually, in Churches of Christ today, we're just getting to the point where people are forth rightly saying the hermeneutic doesn't work. And that's a part of you brethren's burden, and maybe it's somewhat for us.

Adron Doran - Panelist: What part of it have we said doesn't work?

Ed Harrell – Panelist: I… No you haven't said any… I said, there is a group that you have long been associated with in institutions like Abilene Christian and David Lipscomb who would take that position today. But when that question first arises and the debate takes place, I think what happens is many people say, "Well, we're no longer arguing from the same basic premises." And there is a group that sooner or later will acknowledge that. There's another group I think that says, "We are working from the same set of premises." And what we're doing is entirely scriptural, which I think is exactly where these brethren are. Now I believe without passing individual judgment on anybody, that to a large degree a part of the motivation behind that is a kind of a denominational pride. And that is, that we are doing this, Churches of Christ do this, and consequently I'm going to do defend it. I don't think uniformly that's what the position that people who take your view go from. Nor do I think everybody who takes my position does it from the basis of a conservative hermeneutic. I think when one looks historically at the movement that those three categories are clear.

Question 6:

Roy Lanier - Moderator: OK. A double question for Brother Doran. "If a practice is without Bible authority, does it matter how long it is practiced historically?" And number two. "How can you say churches always supported orphan homes when there were none before 1910?"

Adron Doran - Panelist: Well of course the answer to the first one is that you do not support a principle on the basis of antiquity any more than you disapprove one on the same basis, you know. Tradition is all right so long as tradition conforms to the scriptures. That's what Jesus said. You follow your tradition and that's led you to teach the doctrine of men. It isn't anything wrong with tradition today, except that it conflicts with the doctrine of men. And my point was not that we advocated orphan's homes just on the basis of antiquity. We supported orphan's homes because there was just no reason to oppose them. And being old isn't the thing that we contend for, because we're not the last to lay the old aside, nor yet the first to take the new. Now what was the second one? I can't remember when I'm talking. (Laughter, whs)

Roy Lanier - Moderator: I about lost it. I think it was the one, "How can you say we've always supported orphan homes because there were none before 1910?"

Adron Doran - Panelist: Well, we've … Yes they were before 1910. There was one in Midway, Kentucky in 1845 and Alexander Campbell wrote in his *Millennial Harbinger* great glowing compliments of it, and John William McGarvey served as Chairman of the Board for 35 years. So we date them at least back that far. I don't know whether we had one before 1844 or not, I wasn't here. (Laughter, whs)

Question 7:

Roy Lanier - Moderator: All right, Hardeman Nichols. "If a practice is doctrinally wrong, is the question of who changed important?"

Hardeman Nichols - Panelist: Historically it would be, but changing away from the doctrine of Christ would always be wrong. That'd be sinful, to leave the doctrine of Christ. "Whosoever transgresses and abides not in the doctrine" FROM Christ not about Him but FROM Him "hath not God." 2 John 9. "He that abideth in the doctrine he hath both the Father and the Son," but when you're looking at the history of it then changing might be of order. And our whole discussion is in the historical setting and that's why we need to discuss it from that view.

Question 8:

Roy Lanier - Moderator: All right, here is a question. Good gracious. Is that your wrap up for two minutes?

Here is a question that is not addressed to a specific person and so any on the panel, or the two speakers may deal with it. "Does anything from Historical Perspective of past divisions tell us anything about where the present division will go or how it will develop in the next 25 years?

Will we be closer or further apart?" I think they mean "farther apart," but that's all right. Colly did you have…?

Colly Caldwell - Panelist: I'll just say from my study of history, I would say we'll be farther apart as time goes on as shown though the division of the 19th century.

Adron Doran - Panelist: Can I say something?

Roy Lanier - Moderator: You sure can.

Hulen Jackson – Main Speaker: I think they missed the point. We were talking about who changed, the fact that YOU charged that WE'VE changed. And what we we're doing was showing that most of us stand where all of us stood until YOU changed. Your opposition to these things was known in isolated cases but not necessarily in the mainstream of the church until the dates that we gave you. So we were simply showing that your charge is false. You say, "We haven't changed." Well you have from what the church mainly believed and practiced all of those years. But giving isolated cases that don't prove anything, 'cause we didn't claim 100% of the people believed that and that nobody objected to a children's home and things of that sort.

And while I'm up here I might say I was reading the *Gospel Advocate* before he was born (motioning to Steve Wolfgang, whs). And I read the *Gospel Advocate* when James Allen was the editor and I know all of that but that isn't what I was talking about. I was talking about the movement of trouble in the Dallas Metroplex area. I wasn't trying to cover all over the United States. Showing what happened here. Thank you.

Roy Lanier - Moderator: All right, Ed. That seems to have generated a little bit of interest.

Ed Harrell - Panelist: Well yeah, let me say about the change thing. In my mind, the only thing you need to be careful not to change is your commitment to doing exactly what the scriptures say. The practice may change and may ought to change, but THAT shouldn't change.

On the question whether we're going to be farther or does the past teach us anything about that. I think that, as I said in my opening remarks, our communities of connection increasingly separate. And that can not help but go and even farther. Now actually there'll be people who ideologically will probably still be pretty close together. When I used to teach up in east Tennessee, I knew some of those conservative Christian Church preachers and we were actually very close together. In fact I was a lot closer

to them than I was to the institutional church of Christ preacher. And so that kind of relationship will remain but the truth of the matter is our relationship, associational relationship, will become more distant.

Adron Doran - Panelist: Brother Roy, I think we…I think we are making a false assumption, that because we support the orphan's home that we're going to go farther and farther away from the people who do not support it. That's just not a valid assumption. Because there are people within the church of Christ fellowship today, as we know it, that I'm closer to Ed Harrell than I am to them. And I could worship where he preaches a lot easier and with a greater spirituality than I could worship in where those ultra liberals are preaching today. So I think there may be an element within the church of Christ that's going to go as far away from the Restoration Movement as the Disciples Of Christ have gone, but I don't think it's going to be among the people who are here today.

Question 9:

Roy Lanier - Moderator: All right, right in line with this is the next question where a quote is given concerning Wolfgang, and I suppose the question is to you. "Brother Wolfgang in his speech mentions something about the question of who changed is meaningless. If it is meaningless why is it being discussed?" (Laughter, whs) "Why not discuss what will contribute to unity now?"

Steve Wolfgang – Rebuttal Speaker: Well actually, that is the question I was trying to raise (Laughter, whs) to tell you the truth. And I think numbers of us have been grappling with that kind of thing.

The point is that it doesn't make any difference what the ancient practices used to be or how old they are or who was alive when they started as far as that is concerned.

I think the point that Brother Harrell was trying to make a while ago is that you can have a practice … somebody said earlier, said something about is it the size or the practice that's concerned? You can have a practice that seems to be quite innocent. I'm sure that's what attracted Tolbert Fanning and Benjamin Franklin to the missionary societies in their respective states. It seemed like a good idea to preach the gospel. I have no doubt that many people who initially supported an orphanage or some kind of a sponsoring church thought it was a good idea.

I'll give you an example from here in Dallas. My good friend Jamie Sloan and I several years ago crawled up in an attic at the Skillman Avenue church looking for traces of

Roy Cogdill's career. And some of you know I'm writing a biography of Brother Cogdill. We discovered there that in the 1930's when Skillman was Sears and Summit, Brother Cogdill preached there while he was going to law school, they had a Boy Scout troop, which met in the building. Now would some of you brethren today approve? I mean because that was practiced in Dallas then, does that mean that we ought to continue that practice today? Now Brother Cogdill, I'm sure by the 1950's, would not have approved of a Boy Scout meeting in the church building, so he changed on that issue. He was right to change. He changed because he was bringing his practice in line with his commitment to what we call the hermeneutic, to what in more common language, to what the Biblical principle teaches.

And we all need to change to bring our practice in line with what our commitment to the scripture is rather than saying, "look we've done this since 1845 so let's just continue to do it" and sort of proudly wear this badge that "I've never changed." I have to tell you frankly that I'm nervous about people that have not changed their opinions any at all in 45 years.

Roy Lanier - Moderator: Oh, you're nervous about me. (Laughter, whs)

Adron Doran, - Panelist: You're nervous about me too.

Question 10:

Roy Lanier - Moderator: We have one more question that is addressed to two men on the panel. And then Brother Wolfgang will have two minutes to say his final statement and then Brother Jackson, his two minutes. And then it will be time for us to take a break, after which I will conclude with the other 27 announcements. To Ed Harrell and/or Hardeman Nichols, both of you please be brief about this. "Historically was there a distinction in the definition of cooperation and fellowship?" Is there any…what there're asking is and cooperation and fellowship are in quotes, "Is there any distinction historically between those two? Can you supply any documentation?" The reason I guess this question is asked, it's written on the bottom. "Was a cooperative effort, quote end quote, the pooling of resources prior to the 1900's?" Was a cooperative effort the pooling of resources prior to the 1900's? Do you understand the question? I don't but ….

Hardeman Nichols – Panelist: Do you want me to answer it?

Adron Doran - Panelist: Why yes there was.

Hardeman Nichols - Panelist: Acts 11:28-30, there was a pooling of the resources. It became a CERTAIN contribution that was made for the poor saints. Romans 15:25-26 calls it, not separate contributions but a CERTAIN contribution. Yes there were the pooling of resources but it didn't violate the autonomy of the local congregations. Now if brethren in Acts 11:28-30 could give to those down there in Jerusalem without loosing their autonomy, why can' brethren do it now? That's my point. I haven't changed from my commitment to the word of God and I never intend to change from it.

Ed Harrell - Panelist: I'll let the panel answer that scriptural question and speak to that. But in terms of the historical use of those terms, I don't think the two terms would have been used synonymously. Actually the term "cooperation" has existed all through Restoration History and, in the early Restoration History, was taken over from sectarianism. And that is the question, was whether they should have formal cooperative meetings in the same way that the Baptist's did? And there probably have been forms of pooling of congregational resources almost all through Restoration history. But the question of calling those things into question has always been present as well, and became the focus of the 19th century division in the missionary society debate and became a focus in the 20th century because that sort of activity particularly lends itself to dividing groups.

Roy Lanier - Moderator: Alrighty.

Hardeman Nichols - Panelist: Roy, could I just say one brief word? I think, and I respect these brethren, I don't believe we're getting farther apart. I believe we're coming closer together because of the fact that circumstances change methods that would be used. Even *Herald of Truth*, though I've never been asked by a congregation, "do you support *Herald of Truth* or do you not? Have you given to it or does the congregation where you preach give?" That's never been a question that's asked. I've preached for congregations that would not allow a contribution to be given to *Herald of Truth*, that's their business. The same thing on the orphan's home, I think that methods are changing. There aren't the needs in the same way that there were. But taking care of the poor and evangelizing still remain to be done. And brethren let's find good methods that are scriptural and let's do it. Let's not let this lost world go lost because of our fighting among ourselves.

Historical Perspectives
Summation Speeches

Roy Lanier - Moderator: OK. We have two, two-minute speeches at this point, first by Brother Wolfgang and then by Brother Jackson.

Historical Perspectives
Day 1 Speech 1
Summation Speeches

Steve Wolfgang – Rebuttal Summation Speaker: I don't know that I want to make a speech so much as just to try to wrap up two or three loose ends that I've been taking notes on for the last couple of hours.

Going back to the idea of what history is. First of all, history is certainly more than biography. It includes biography, it is enlightened by, and some of its main sources come from, those who are eyewitnesses, but it's more than biography. It's more than collective biography. If that's not true, that it's much more than personal experience, then none of us could write about anything than 20th century, or about anything that's other than what our own personal experience is. Brother Doran couldn't speak reliably about what happened in the 19th century if history is more valuable ... or you could only write it if you lived through it.

And with regard to that, and I don't mean to be picking on Brother Doran, because I think ... I've enjoyed the times that I've spent with him, but...

Adron Doran – Panelist: Better men than you have picked on me, so... (Laughter whs)

Steve Wolfgang – Rebuttal Speaker: All right, well…

Ed Harrell - Panelist: Me!

Steve Wolfgang – Rebuttal Speaker: Well hold on then.

Adron Doran – Panelist: All right.

Steve Wolfgang – Rebuttal Speaker: Just for example I'm going to challenge...I'll be glad to say that with regard to that yellow tag of quarantine, I could be wrong about that. I'd be glad to go back and read that, and if I'm wrong I'll be glad to retract it.

But for example, when the assertion is made that what Lipscomb was doing in Nashville in 1910 was the same as what was going on in Henderson, that was a charge some individuals made against Lipscomb. You can get the little yellow booklet at the back and read for yourself what Lipscomb said and his response to that. And you make the judgment for yourselves as an audience as to whether, in this case, Dr. Doran's memory of the facts accords with what was written at the time.

And I can't let this pass without answer. The situation in Danville was brought up. What was not told about the situation in Danville is this—that the congregation split was divided by people who left the church in Danville where I preach before I came there, and went off and started another congregation over matters that were admitted to be matters of opinion—over matters that those people who were DEFENDING these things ADMITTED were matters of opinion. Now that's my personal anecdote and story. That doesn't mean that it was either right or wrong, and it doesn't mean for instance that that's the basis on which we ought to run. But the whole story ought to be told in that particular regard.

Hulen Jackson – Main Summation Speaker: I mentioned something a moment ago about the Akin Fund and the Bell Trust. And since maybe, and I'm not bragging on that but I guess maybe I actually know more of the background of both since I am still one of the Directors of the Bell Trust, that's been in existence for more than 30 years. We give away about a million dollars a year. We've never checked when a church writes us and says we need $500 a month to supplement what we're going to pay a preacher to send him to Podunk. We've never in any way tried to find out whether or not they believe what you believe or what we believe. I guess we've sent hundreds of thousands of dollars to churches that maybe disagreed with us, the ones of us on the Board, so that hadn't made any difference to us.

But the point I'm making is, in our meetings with the

brethren three different times they made it crystal clear, and time and again they said it, that no church ought to plan a work bigger than they can pay for themselves. Now to me that's the basic principal or tenet of your position. Now then if that's so, you cannot accept money from the Akin Fund, and you could not accept money from the Bell Trust.

Brother Akin was a member at Preston Road all those years while I was preaching there and he never was a member of Lufkin or some of these other churches, and they'd send money to that church, and they'd support a preacher in another place. Now you claim churches can't do that but what about a trust, a fund of that sort? I'm asking this because I'm seeking an answer. As I say, we give a million dollars away every year to help churches support the gospel. That's all it's for. We don't send money to orphan's homes. We don't send it to colleges. We need to know because I believe that you're inconsistent and through the Akin Fund, any other fund that you may have among you is contrary to the basis of your contention as Bryan Vincent Jr...Sr. told me years ago.

Roy Lanier - Moderator: Well it's been rather rich to have these six men. We appreciate their efforts and their sacrifices of time and expense and I believe our experiments have gone well today in the format of the panel discussions.

Now soon after our dismissal by 5:15 we will start in the evening dinner program where Brother Robert Bolter and Brother John Banister will both give some speeches. And then coming back here for the session where Brother Almond Williams and Wendell Winkler will be discussion the Hermeneutics. And we trust that you will try to be on time and enjoy all of these various things.

Please remember our thanks to Joe MacDonald. If you have need for a video, or audio tapes, he's down front. He does this at his cost. We also thank Jesse Deason and Larry Fain and their crew for the registration and work around that. Please register if you have not done so. We thank Eugene Smith for furnishing the brochures and the programs at his cost. We certainly appreciate him in doing this. We trust you will be with us for dinner and then back at... (The tape cut off at this point. whs)

END OF SPEECH ONE, DAY ONE

Evening Meal

Day 1 Meal Speeches
Thursday, July 12, 1990

Participants

Non-Institutional Brethren	Institutional Brethren
Robert A. Bolton — Meal 1	John Banister — Meal 2

Day 1 Meal Speech 1
Robert A. Bolton

Introduction: *Bolton, Robert A. He is a native of Wichita Falls, TX and has preached for 42 years. His local works include Lefors, Lometa, Ft. Worth, Greenville, Mt. Pleasant, Lancaster, and Richardson, TX, as well as Chowchilla and Ontario, CA. He has been in Richardson, TX for 16 years and has served as pastor for 10 years. He is widely published with many articles in many brotherhood papers. (Polite Applause, whs)*

Thank you Steve (responding to Steve Wolfgang's introductory comments not caught on tape, whs). I might say in passing before we get into what we had prepared to say, that this is the first time I've ever been asked to make an after dinner speech where I had to pay for the meal. (Laughter, Steve Wolfgang says, "We'll give you a refund if the speech is good." Laughter again, whs) I'm going to read this manuscript so that I won't be misquoted.

A few years ago I was invited to conduct a wedding ceremony for a black man and a black woman. The wedding took place at the bride's apartment where about 50 guests were in attendance. All of them were dressed in their best Sunday-go-to-meeting clothes, and each of them was a few shades darker in color than yours truly. I was the only white person there. When I arrived at the apartment, I found everyone in a pleasant and jovial mood. But immediately as I stepped into the room silence reigned supreme. You could have heard a shadow fall. I sat down on a couch between a rather plump black woman and a slightly built black man. The whites of 100 eyes stared at me from curious black faces, saying nothing, just staring. Finally after a couple of minutes of thunderous silence, I spoke up and said to no one in particular but all of them in general, "Do you know how I feel?" Still no answer just continued silence. So I said, "I feel just like a marshmallow in a coal bin." (Some light laughter, whs) When they finally stopped laughing, they realized that I was a friend with whom they could be at ease.

Although I can't say the same thing this evening, I hope you would accept me as a friend with whom you can be at ease, for in this position this evening I feel somewhat uneasy. I appreciate the presence of each and every one of you, as well as this opportunity to speak of some matters that are of eternal consequence and import.

After all of these years, I am especially happy to be able to have an association with many of you whom I have known in years gone by and for whom I have had a kind regard. It is a personal pleasure for me to be with such men as John Banister, and Abe Lincoln, and even Curtis Camp who is not here this evening, and others of whom I have not seen in years. I have fond memories of many of you, memories of days long ago when we worked together as brethren. I even remember giving Curtis Camp one of the books out of my own library, and I think the name of it was *Sermons of Ben Franklin Vol. 2*. If anybody sees him before I do, ask him if he's ready to give it back, after 40 years. (Laughter, whs)

Having been left to decide for myself what subject I might discuss, I have given prayerful thought and consideration to what I should say. I don't want to hinder whatever good might be accomplished during these 3 days of intensive study. Neither do I desire to deal directly with matters that have been assigned to others as subjects for presentation during these sessions. On the other hand, my desire is to speak with related matters that will not only be of concern to all, but to present them in such a manner as will be interesting in CONTENT, constructive in INTENT, and conducive to whatever good might come of these studies between us.

Therefore I have elected to speak on what I consider a most important and very practical matter, *Attitudes and Obstacles to Unity Among Brethren*. Now by unity among brethren, I do NOT mean a BROTHERHOOD unity of congregations, but in view of congregational autonomy and a recognition of the fact that the body of Christ is made up of individual saints not a collectivity of congregations. I have reference to unity among Christians, not churches, even as I believe the scriptures teach that FEL-

LOWSHIP among brethren is between individuals and not between congregations per se, for fellowship or unity between churches is beyond the purview of divine revelation.

But before I get into the subject, I would like for you to permit me a few personal remarks and observations in order that those of you who do not know me will have some insight into my background and interest in the things that are being discussed here this week. Having been raised in denominationalism, as a faithful Baptist for some 12 years during my youth and early manhood, I began to question much of Baptist doctrine and became disillusioned with it.

Shortly after World War II, I met and married Billy Jean Grant, who has been my constant companion and faithful wife for over 44 years. It was SHE who was instrumental in teaching me the pure gospel of Christ, which I believed and obeyed in Lubbock, Texas in 1947, being baptized by M. Norvell Young during a gospel meeting with Batsell Barrett Baxter. And for years I thought, and surely must be correct in my thinking, that both of them thought Norvell should have held me under longer. (Laughter, whs) But at any rate I became a Christian, nothing more and nothing less. As a result, I severed my relationship with the Baptist Church, even though my family remain staunch Baptists to this day, my brother being Chairman of the Board of Deacons at the 1st Baptist Church here in Dallas.

Almost immediately after my conversion, I had an ardent desire to preach the gospel, went to Abilene Christian College where I was granted a degree, the first graduate from ACC with a major in religious education and began full-time preaching in Lafarge, Texas in June of 1949. In fact, the first gospel meeting in which I worked as a local preacher was with Curtis Camp as guest speaker some 40 years ago.

It was during those early years of my preaching that the issues which divided us became prominent, with the sponsoring church concept preeminently manifest in the Broadway church in Lubbock and the Highland church in Abilene. I remember being thrilled when the *Herald of Truth* came into being, thinking that now we have a national broadcast to compete with the sectarians. But upon sober reflection I began to have doubts about such concepts, spent several years in serious study of the issues, attended several debates conducted on those issues, and finally concluded there is no Bible authority for such, and here I took my stand.

As a result, although I was never as militant as were some, and never drew lines of fellowship in those formative years, those lines were drawn FOR me. And I soon found that some of the brethren with whom I had previously labored would no longer come to hear me preach, even though I was still preaching the same principles, having changed only my practice to fit my preaching. This – hurt – tremendously - and - still does, but so it has been ever since. After having worked with churches in Texas and California, I am presently, as Steve indicated, in my 17th year with the College Park church in Richardson, Texas.

Although tearfully and sadly separated from beloved brethren these many years, my heart's desire is that we may once again be united upon truth and march triumphantly together under the blood stained banner of Prince Emmanuel. And to this end I offer the following thoughts for your consideration, realizing that the principles with which I deal will be agreeable to most, while their application to specifics may be more difficult to grasp. And may I say at this point that my name is not Solomon, and I don't have all the answers.

The purpose of this Dallas Meeting between brethren of opposing views, with a desire for peace and unity based upon a "thus saith the Lord," is certainly praiseworthy and commendable. If I know my own heart, I am willing to do anything short of compromising truth in any area, sacrificing my convictions based upon that truth, or violating my own conscience, in order to clasp hands of fellowship and unity with those of you with whom I may differ at this point. I sincerely believe that most of you feel the same way. It is high time that these matters be rethought, and prayerfully studied. And thus I am happy that these meetings are being conducted. And my hope and prayer is that nothing but good may result from these studies.

However, none of us should be so naive as to believe there will be no obstacles encountered in obtaining the desired end. For we may as well admit that any investigation and study of these matters will encounter several serious and perhaps seemingly insurmountable problems, obstacles which MUST be overcome if the desired results are achieved.

The first obstacle that may be encountered by some might be described as HUMAN WEAKNESS, including such things as pride, selfishness, egotism, and prejudice. I fear there have many among us on BOTH sides that have not been interested in truth for truth's sake, but whose loyalties have been to certain preachers, and papers, and colleges, and whose convictions have been shaped by such loyalties. Such personal bias often permits the investigation of only one side of an issue, refuses to see both sides, and prevents the honest consideration of anything not considered as "our position." And may I hasten to point out that this is not to question any one's personal integrity, but simply to call attention to this as a problem of human weakness that SOME of us may have to face and overcome in our quest for truth on these matters, for THIS attitude contributes to a DIVISIVE spirit rather than unity among brethren.

The second obstacle, which must be recognized and overcome, is the apparent inconsistency of some on either side of these issues. Some of these matters that were discussed this afternoon and some of the questions indicated this was on the mind of some. Now when I talk about inconsistency, I do not refer to inconsistency in argument or logic. I'm going to let others deal with that matter. But I have reference to the charge often made that SOME among us are inconsistent because we are now PRACTICING the very OPPOSITE of what we once believed and taught.

Let me illustrate. May I be rightly accused of inconsistency when I no longer practice Baptist doctrine as I did 50 years ago? Certainly not! May I be RIGHTLY accused of inconsistency when I change my practice to conform to my preaching, if that preaching is the truth? Certainly not! Question please! Is there ANYONE here who is willing to honestly admit that he has never changed his convictions on ANY matter, but that he has always been correct on EVERY point in his preaching and practice? If SO, there has never been any growth in knowledge or going on unto perfection. If NOT, because he has learned the truth in some area and changed his position to conform to the truth learned, is he inconsistent? Not - if - he - is - honest.

And I submit to you brethren, that this has frequently happened to each of us, and understandably so. The only way that such things will ever cease, is for us to close our minds, refuse to think for ourselves, and dishonestly affirm that we have never changed, and boastfully declare that we will never change. This attitude is an obstacle that must be overcome, for it is obvious that some of us will have to change, if unity among us is ever attained. And such change based upon truth, does not deserve the prejudicial charge of inconsistency. As Max Dupree says in

Leadership Is an Art, "We cannot become what we need to, by remaining what we are."

From a practical standpoint, it is self evident that a third obstacle which must be overcome is that of "Project Commitment." That is a commitment on the part of an eldership or a church to some major program which they may have undertaken. It stands to reason that an eldership, preacher, or congregation, committed to raising millions of dollars for some project, be it benevolent or evangelistic, will hardly be in a position to be objective in the search for truth on that subject. How many of us have castigated our denominational friends for many years for reading the Bible to defend their practice rather than objectively seeking the truth of God's word on some matter? My brethren WE are not immune to such an attitude.

Again, I am not impugning anyone's motives or honesty. But it is foolish to assume that everyone in the religious world is basically dishonest except us. The fact is that we, as a people, can study the Bible in all sincerity and honesty with just as much prejudice as any people. In order to unite upon truth, this attitude must be dispensed with at all costs. For knowing our tendency to defend what we practice rather than be totally objective, presents us with an obstacle most difficult to overcome. As I have stated, I am assuming that each of us present is honestly and sincerely desirous of seeing unity if at all possible between us, but it is one thing to desire such and quite another to attain it. Therefore again from a practical standpoint, I feel I must point out some obvious facts concerning conditions that always exist, which facts must always be considered if unity is to be attained.

Number one, all men have personal characteristics which may or may not be weaknesses of character. The fact is, we are all different. Some of us are cold logicians who often seem to lack emotional or personal warmth; others are highly emotional and may have great charisma. But whatever be the case, each of us must be able to recognize and understand that not everybody is made alike. And simply because I may not be of the same disposition of you, or you me, is no indication that either of us is dishonest or wrong and therefore unworthy of teaching or fellowship.

Number two, some men are slower to see the light than others, while others are quicker to grasp the point than some. Now this is not intended as a reflection upon the slower, for I am one of them, but simply points out that perhaps much more patience is needed to be exercised by each of us toward one another.

Then number three, all men will not think alike on every point. Yet if a man is honest, he will think for himself and arrive at his own convictions, if he is courageous he will stand up for those convictions. So we must recognize that it is the nth degree of folly to demand of another total conformity to our ideas in every case. How many times have you thought that if you could just sit down with the honest person of strong conviction with whom you disagree, you BOTH might come to realize that your differences were not as much or as many as either of you may have imagined? In each of these situations, we must follow the admonition of the Apostle Paul who wrote, "Let your forbearance be known to all men, the Lord is at hand," Philippians 4 verse 5. Let us, toward one another, practice forbearance. Let us stand for truth with ALL our might, but deal kindly with those who have not yet learned that truth and with those who do not see things OUR way. And let us be aware of the fact that it is not OUR way but the LORD'S way that is important.

As Abraham Lincoln said, "I care not if God is on MY side, MY constant hope and prayer is that I may be found upon GOD'S side." Brethren, to follow such a course is not a sign of weakness or compromise, for no man will ever compromise the truth if he honestly loves the Lord and His word.

In conclusion, may I call your attention to Colossians 3:15, where the Apostle admonishes, "Let the peace of Christ rule in our hearts, to the which also you were called in one body and be ye thankful." My understanding of this passage, according to the footnote as well as Greek scholarship, is that the word 'rule' here means "arbitrate or umpire." Kittel says, and I quote, "this term describes the work of an umpire at the games, then comes to mean to order or control. Paul uses it of the peace which settles strife in the church and maintains unity." As we all well recognize at a ballgame or any athletic contest, notwithstanding instant replay, the umpire has the final word in all discussions. We may not like his ruling, and even 'Boo' his call. But we must accept it as the final word, for there is no changing his decision. True, human umpires are subject to mistake, but not the Divine. And so Paul says that a love for peace among brethren as well as with God must rule as the umpire in our hearts to make such decisions and effect such actions as are acceptable to God.

And thus I make this appeal. As we study these things together, striving to ascertain truth, with no disposition to ask anyone to compromise any truth learned, "let us follow after things which make for peace and things whereby we may edify one another" (Rom. 14:19).

My brethren, none of us may have all the answers to all the questions or problems between us. But our attitudes can go a long way toward helping us understand one another better and assist us in dealing kindly with those with whom we may disagree, while yet standing for the word of truth. Let NONE consider these words as a call for compromise of truth on ANY point by ANYBODY, but rather from one who has seen the body of Christ torn asunder lo these many years, as an humble plea for brethren to strive to dwell together in unity once again. Let us hope and pray that such may soon be realized, even perhaps to some degree at least by what we say and do at these meetings.

To that end, "I commend you to God and to the word of His grace which is able to build you up and to give you the inheritance among all them that are sanctified" (Acts 20:32). For nothing short of the word of His grace can bring about the unity we seek, the unity we need, and the unity we must give diligence to keep. And in the words of Brother Hulen Jackson let us all remember, and I quote, "opinions of men have always caused troubles when pushed," and another, "it is sadly so that one's opinion can easily become a thus saith the Lord."

Thank you for being here and listening to what this babbler had to say. (Applause, whs)

Day 1 Meal Speech 2
John Banister

Introductin: *Banister, John. Semi-retired, preacher for Nocona, Memphis, and Dallas, TX churches, also Elk City and Oklahoma City, OK congregations. Has been preaching 62 years, nationally known for pulpit, radio and TV work, presently resides in Dallas. (Polite applause, whs)*

Thank you Brother Lanier. (Responding to introduction by Roy Lanier not caught on tape whs) Roy invited me several months ago to make this speech and I declined because I'm not a speech maker, I'm a preacher, and there's a lot of difference. And I said I can't make a speech, "Well you can," and he insisted. Roy, he is pretty persistent. He's a little bit like my wife, whom we've been married 57 years. And my wife will not let me wear a red necktie. And she was going down to a ranch recently and I wore it Sunday morning teaching my class. And I said, "Brethren, you observe my red tie." I said, "My wife will not allow me to wear such a tie so she's gone and I'm doing it to prove that I'm the head of the house." (Laughter, whs)

And so Roy, he just kept after me and after me, and I was a like Moses when he received the call of the Lord, I didn't want to go and didn't want to speak. But Roy insisted and I agreed. But after last Friday at our Minister's Luncheon I almost backed out. We were kicking around a lot of funny things and we got to talking about the Bible and the book of Revelation. One preacher said, "Well I don't ever read it and study it and we should never preach from it." And Roy had something to say about it and people have a lot of funny views. I said, "Well I know what Revelation says." And I said, "You want to know anything about Revelation you ask me. And I can say as Paul did (when he was) 'caught up to the third heaven' (Referring evidently to 2 Cor. 12:2, and 1 Cor. 3:20, whs) I don't know, the Lord knows, and that answers everybody." And you know what he said? He said, "You're a nut." I almost resigned this speech right there, Roy.

Well, he said now, he specifically gave me two instructions, "Don't talk very long." And of course everybody that knows me knows that I'm a short-winded preacher. And he said, "Don't talk about what's being discussed this week, because, if you do, why you'll answer all the questions and nobody will have any more room to answer a speech … give a speech." Anyway, he said, "Well just talk over your head." And then he said, "But you don't have much up there so you won't be able to say much." And anyway he said "Well just tell about some of your experiences."

Well, I had an unusual experience yesterday afternoon. I went out to Love Field to meet a plane and my good friend and brother in the Lord, whom I used to know and whom I used to associate, Yater Tant came in from Birmingham. And he was a guest at our home last night, we went to Skillman Avenue church and I introduced him. And Brother John Thompson who is the preacher out at White Rock, I didn't know till last night, in fact I never met him, he is the grandson of the famed Brother Will M. Thompson of Oklahoma fame. So he has a rich heritage there. Anyway, Brother Tant, he got to meet a lot of people and people have known of him and knew of his father, old Brother J.D. Tant.

And incidentally Yater gave me a copy this morning, of a new book he has written, a biography of his mother. Many of you have read *J.D. Tant Texas Preacher*, which he wrote several years ago, and so this is a sequel. And he, I presume has a… I don't see Yater here. Is Yater here? Well, he told me he didn't think I was worth a twenty dollar ticket and I'd …(laughter, whs) I wouldn't call Yater a cheapskate, but I think he went out to get him a hotdog somewhere (laughter, whs). Anyway, he told me this morning we had a good time. We stayed up late and talked and talked, and I got in a few words here and there. And then we got up and I fixed his breakfast and so on and we talked until about 10:30 and I just enjoyed it a great deal. I've known and loved Yater a long long time but he's sort of like some of us, he's a little hard headed, and hard to convince. But I straightened him out on most everything.

Anyway I want to tell you two or three things about Yater Tant. I used to live in Oklahoma City and he did, and we were often together. He preached in Francis and I at Culberson Heights back then. This is before all of these problems arose. And he liked to play Forty-two. Now you fellows east of the Mississippi, if you don't know what Forty-two is, why you need to come live in Texas. I remember 1935 I went out to eastern Texas to hold a meeting and they had a brand new preacher from Ohio. And I knew those people, and he got off and he said, "Brother Banister we've got a problem here. We've got worldliness in this church like you've never heard. They don't do anything but play Forty-two." (laughter, whs) I said, "Well brother didn't you ever…" He said, "I never heard of it. I'm going to have to get on it." I came back the next year for a meeting. And he learned how to play and he enjoyed it more than anybody else (Laughter, whs).

Well anyway, Yater liked to play Forty-two. And I was reared in a home where we played a lot of games. And I considered myself . . . I was the acknowledged Forty-two champion of Oklahoma City for a number of years; everybody admitted that who played against me. Anyway, this really happened, this is not a preacher story now (Laughter, whs). We'd often get together, about once a week, for a Forty-two game and a dinner. And Helen, his wife, and I would be partners and Mary Bell, my wife here, would be partners. And so one night they were over at our house, and by 11:00, time for any respectable Republican to be in bed, and we were ahead about eight or nine games to one. Oh, we just snowed them under. And I said, "Momma it's time to go to bed so the company can go home." But Yater didn't take the hint. You have to hit some people over the head with a 2 X 4. And he says, "I'm not going home till I win." I said, "Oh my goodness alive." And this is the truth if I ever told it, he stayed there and we played until 2:45 that morning. (Laughter, whs) And finally I said, "Helen let's let him win, so he'll go home. (Laughter, whs) Now that really happened (Laughter, whs). And I was going to ask Yater, if he was here tonight, if he remembered it. And if he denies it, he's just a big old you know what. So anyway we had a lot of fun.

About twenty-five years ago, after I moved to Dallas, one Sunday afternoon, (I, whs) telephoned (Yater Tant whs) (and said, whs) "Yater Tant I'm going to spend the night with you." He replied, "Well OK. But I'm going tonight over Florida Christian College's Lectureship," which was on then, and "I'm to be the speaker over there." He said, "I'll go with you." I said, "OK." I went over there and introduced him around; he hadn't seen some of those brethren in a good while. And so my subject was on "Au-

thority." And I preached a good lesson on "Authority," it's in the book. (Light laughter, whs) And after it was over we got in my car to come home, he said, he said "John," he said, "that was a real good sermon." And in his ever so kind and subtle way he said, "If you'd just practice what you preach, you'll be a good preacher." (Laughter, whs) Anyway, we've had a lot of association together and Brother Tant's a great man and it's a joy to be with him. I'm sorry he's not here to hear the speech but anyway joy to be with him. And anyway, well he said …is Brother Tom Roberts here? I'm not sure that I know him. Alright, he's going … said, "To spend the night with you" and said, "If you were crowded he was coming back." But now since he didn't come to hear my speech I'm not going to let him come back. (Laughter, whs) No anyway, we told him he could come back. And if I had known … we fed him last night after church, and fed him breakfast, and I fed him dinner and all that. If I had known how much he eats I don't know whether I would have invited him or not. (Laughter, whs) Anyway so much for that.

Glad to see Brother and Sister Adron Doran here. I'd read after Brother Doran for many years before I first met him in October of '88 at … we were on the lectureship down at Faulkner University together and enjoyed his speeches so much and have read after him. And he told me while ago, he said, "Now we spent forty dollars, two twenty dollar tickets to hear you speak." I said, "Well I didn't know I was worth that much." And Brother Bolton, they put us up here pretty high. And I got a free ticket and you had to pay for yours? (Uproarious laughter, whs) Well you need to… (Robert Bolton speaks out something not understandable, whs) (John Banaster asks, whs) What is it? (Robert Bolton repeats, whs) "That's the difference in liberal and conservative." (Uproarious laughter, whs). Well I'll tell you if that's the case I am an ultra liberal, because I'll take a free meal anytime I can get it.

My wife and I got a sort of a thing, she has a sister, there're sort of funny. "You come eat dinner with us." "No it's my time to have you." And so they're arguing over it. And I said, "Momma, if your asked, say yes before they change their mind." And so, by the way, I was reading in the Thessalonian letter I think it was, the other day where Paul said where he supported himself by his own work and he didn't sponge and eat off of the brethren. And I thought, well I don't know whether any of us can qualify or not.

Well anyway, Brother Doran, getting back to Brother Doran. He had a lot of nice things to say. And this February I was on the Lectureship over at Freed Hardeman as he was, and I heard him give some very nice resumes or actually lectures on biography of some of our men of the restoration. And then he was at Abilene at a lectureship in February of this year, and I heard him again. I really appreciate him. And I have been after him to do a lot more on some of the lesser known men of the restoration movement, and we appreciate him.

But anyway, over at Montgomery he said, "I've got a question to ask for you. My brother Basil" said "when he went to Texas he changed it to Doran (pronouncing it like Dooraan, whs), but I says its Doran." And I said, "Well you know Brother Doran when these guys leave Tennessee and Kentucky and come out here, like old Sam Houston and some of others, they were sort of scalawags back there, and they had to change their name to be respectable in Texas." Anyway, we had a big laugh about that. Well, I'm just talking off my head and that's why you're not getting much. (Laughter, whs) Of course I was instructed not to discuss… I've enjoyed the discussion. I appreciate the fellows here. I've seen some of you brethren … haven't seen you in a long time, and I love all of you and appreciate you and you're my brethren and so on.

Brother Foy Wallace, we all know who he is. He was a great man. He came to my hometown when I was a little boy about eight years old. He had a little s… little boy about six months old, it's back 1919 as I recall. And he came several summers to hold a meetings. He stayed in our home. He stayed in my granddad's home. He stayed in uncle Luke Johnson's home. And we had a Tabernacle and big meetings three Sundays, imported singer, usually Brother Tillit S. Teddlie, and Brother Wallace just preached and he did a tremendous job. And I remember one year, I think it was 1922 was when he was on a bobbed hair kick, and he really got on that. And one of my aunts, my mother's sister, she had already planned it, but during that meeting she had her hair bobbed. And I tell you Brother Wallace felt that as a personal challenge and he really went after it. And I remember one Sunday afternoon sitting in grandpa's yard under the old Mulberry tree and my old granddad, Uncle John Thompson, he was an old pioneer out there. He'd argue with you, and "Brother Wallace why are you against bobbed hair?" Well so on, so on and so on. "Look at your wife and all this jewelry she's got on" and so on. She had a good bit

of jewelry, and Uncle John just couldn't see that that was quite consistent.

But I remember another thing, and this really happened. Brother Wallace was holding a meeting in our Tabernacle, big crowds. The Baptists, Methodists, and church of Christ owned the Tabernacle jointly, and we would each have a two week summer meeting. And about the middle of July we'd start and have preaching every night until the first of September. And there wasn't anything else going on in the community and everybody came to everybody's meetings. Well anyway, Brother Wallace was up preaching and Uncle John sat right over here, my granddad, and he was a slightly hard of hearing. And during Brother Wallace's rather lengthy, would that describe it? (Laughter, whs) I'd say lengthy lengthy sermon. Why this fellow sitting next to Uncle John went to sleep. And Brother Wallace said, "Uncle John wake that fellow up, he's asleep." And my granddad, he thought he was saying it low so nobody could hear. But he was hard of hearing so he said, "By golly you put him to sleep wake him up yourself." (Laughter, whs) I asked Brother Wallace, "Do you remember that?" He said "I sure do, embarrassingly I do remember that." (Laughter, whs) Anyway I loved him very much, he was a great man.

We've had a lot of great preachers. I told Yater last night that I never heard his father preach, but I used to read after him. I read the *Firm Foundation*, the *Gospel Advocate*, and old Brother Joe Warlick's *Gospel Guide*. I was reared on those from a childhood. And I used to read all the notes, preacher… Reuel Lemons called it preacher brag. He didn't think you ought to put in Field Reports. And I used to read those, and I knew a lot of the brethren that were preachers long before I ever met any of them. And many of them I met later. But I met Brother J.D. Tant only one time. He was at an A.C.C. Lectureship, I think it was in maybe February of '33. And it was the same lectureship when old Brother Daniel Sommer was there. He had made a trip down here to Freed Hardeman and, I think, to Harding. And I remember Brother Daniel Sommer said this, you know he was strongly opposed to colleges of any kind in any way. And he didn't make a speech but the brethren asked him to say a few words. And he said, and I remember it quite well, "Brethren if the way these colleges that I have visited recently, if this is the way they've been operated," he says, "I never would have opposed them." Did you know that Brother Doran? Well anyway, I don't know whether he ever changed or not. But he was a man and he had a lot of good convictions. And so, through these lectureships we've seen a lot of good brethren.

Brother G.C. Brewer held his last Gospel Meeting here in Dallas over at the Sunset church, March of 1956. He died in June of that year. And I went over several times to hear him. And he told me the last week morning service; he says, "I'm really sick. I'm going to Memphis and check my doctor." And found that just a lot of malignancy and they didn't do anything. And he quickly wrote his autobiography, which was not very well written because it was done so hurriedly, if you've read it. It's good but it's not up to Brother Brewer's regular writing. But anyway, he died and he was a great man.

And I remember when I was a student at Harding College over at Morrilton, before it ever moved to Searcy. Old Brother Armstrong was the President, had Brother G.C. Brewer come hold a meeting. And he would preach each morning there at the college auditorium and downtown church at night. And his last night's sermon was on Heaven. It's in his book, *The Brewer Sermons*, but the sermon in the book is nothing compared to that one he preached that night. You talk about eloquence in rhetoric; I believe that's the finest and most impressive sermon I've ever heard in my life. And it made me want to live in such a way as to go to heaven, regardless. And he was a great preacher, and we've had a lot of great preachers.

A lot of the men that lived east of the Mississippi, the… Tennessee, Alabama, and Kentucky. And you brethren know a lot of them more than I. I knew them by reputation. We have a great brotherhood. Peter says, "Love the brotherhood." And I do and you do and we all should, and we need to bear with one another. And we need the brotherly love that covers a multitude of sin. That doesn't mean that we sweep it under the rug, or endorse it. But it means that we deal with each other in a charitable, kind way recognizing that we too make many mistakes and have many faults. And so I'm not as pessimistic as one of the brethren who said this afternoon. He didn't think it would ever improve. I think it will. And Brother Bolton's sermon, if we work on this and study and so on.

And as I get older, and I had my 80th birthday in April. I don't know how much longer I'll live. By the way, you said that you and Yater were the same age Brother Doran. Now Yater is two years older than I am, and you and I are the same age. So Yater Tant's older, he… (Brother Doran says whs) "I said Yater's the only one there that was older than I am." Is that what you said? Well, anyway, he is, you're telling the truth (Laughter, whs). I tell you, I enjoy being around Brother Yater Tant a lot. Now I don't know whether he's going to go back home and tell them that he spent the night with me. It might ruin his reputation. But anyway, we've always been close. And it's been a real joy.

And I'm sorry I've got a funeral in the morning and I've got a wedding Saturday morning. I'm going to have to miss these next morning sessions but I hope to be here the rest of the time. And I hope I haven't bored you too much.

But we've got a great brotherhood. And we're not three brotherhoods, in my judgment. I agree with Brother Jackson we're all brethren, and you're my brethren, and I hope that I'm your brother. And if and when we all get to heaven, there'll be a lot about heaven perhaps that we're not all able now to apprehend. But when we get up there, we may kick a lot of these things around. I've got several questions I want to ask Abraham and Paul and so on. But it just may be that when we're all sitting around the throne, the Lord may just say to us, "Well, brethren you did a lot of fussing and fuming and feuding over some things that weren't nearly as important as you thought they were." I don't know whether that'll be true or not, but I wonder if it is.

Well thank you very much. (Applause, whs)

Scriptural Hermeneutics

Day 1 Cycle 2
Thursday, July 12, 1990

Participants

Non-Institutional Brethren
Almon Williams — Main
Melvin Curry — Panelist 3
Maurice Barnett — Panelist 4

Institutional Brethren
Wendell Winkler — Rebuttal
Gary Workman — Panelist 1
Don Tarber — Panelist 2

Scriptural Hermeneutics
Day 1 Speech 2 Main
Almon Williams

Introduction: *Williams, Almon. He is a native of Marmaduke, AR, presently resides in Temple Terrace, FL, and has been on the faculty of Florida College since 1965, teaching Social Science, English, Bible and Bible Languages. He has worked with Castle Heights and Sulphur Springs congregations in the Tampa area.*

As I understand it, my contribution to this series of discussions is to lead off with a discussion of Biblical Hermeneutics and Biblical Authority. However, I should like to say at the outset, that I do not wish for God or any of my brethren to be held responsible for the things which I say. I do wish to be here as a servant of Christ and do the best that I can in talking about what I have learned about Biblical Hermeneutics and Biblical Authority. I'm not so sure, as so many have said, how glad I am to be here. In Ecclesiastes 7:8 the wise man said, "The end of a thing is better than the beginning" (Laughter, whs). I'm just hopeful that that will be the case. However as requested I should like to discuss the following items throughout my discussion this evening: Pattern, Silence, Law of Exclusion, Authority, and Examples.

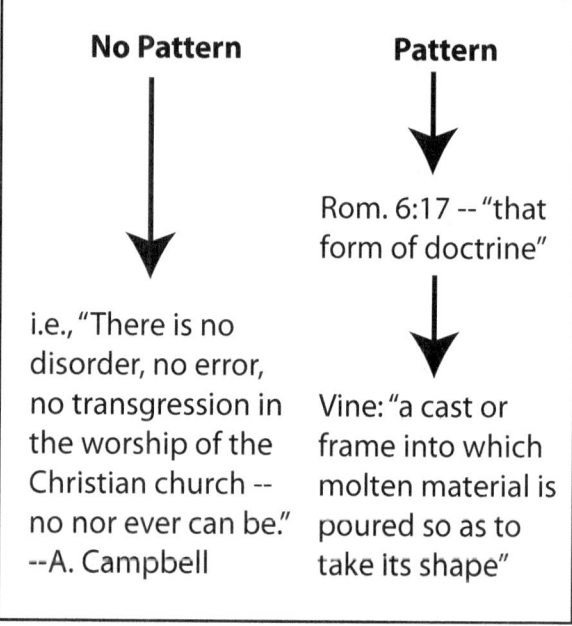

In the first place, I should like to talk about the pattern of the scriptures and the part, if any, which silence plays in the pattern in the scriptures. And so we must ask the question, "Is there a pattern in the scriptures for our practice or not?" As I see it, the issue is between scriptural patternism and scriptural deformation. Some brother I read many years ago, who in commenting on Paul's language, "that form of doctrine" in Romans 6:17-18 once observed thus: "the problem with so many folks was that they wanted to deform Christianity of its divinely established forms." Exactly so, nevertheless the scriptures (Chart #1) still teach that the scriptures contain forms, even substantial forms. For *Vine's* says of the Greek word used in Romans chapter 6, "The metaphor here is that of a cast or frame into which molten material is poured so as to take its shape" (Volume 2, page 124). We ourselves then must be molded to or by

the mold of the gospel.

But in regard to the above quote from this unnamed brother and forgotten brother, I assume that the above mentioned brother was making a pun on the word deform. That is, "Whenever men deform the New Testament by taking away its forms, men have also in effect deformed it by leaving it in a shapeless grotesque mass." And of course here I have this quote from Vine's, how that the word used here is a cast or frame into which molten material is formed. True restorers have always believed that the New Testament contains a pattern for the church and that this pattern must be respected, that is, restored.

Woodrow wrote an article a few years ago in *Restoration Quarterly* entitled *The Silence of the Scripture and the Restoration Movement* and he makes it very clear how Alexander Campbell thought about this matter of there being a pattern in the scriptures. And from a July 1825 *Christian Baptist* essay, Alexander Campbell said that if, "there is no order in our Christian assemblies of worship" etc. "there can be no disorder, no error, no innovation no transgression in the worship of the Christian church no nor ever can be."

And about 35 years ago, Bill Humble a Restorationist Historian and a Restorationist in his own right, wrote two articles in *The Preceptor* 1955 entitled *God's Work In God's*

> "God's work must be done, but God's work must be done in God's way."
> --Bill Humble

Way (Chart #2). And he concluded the second article or the two articles with a ringing exhortation to do God's work in God's way and closed with this final statement, "God's work must be done in God's way. God's work must be done, but God's work must be done in God's way" (page 463). And to the wonderfully balanced idea and attitude of his essays I should like to give a hearty amen. Brethren I confess without any apology that I am a patternist; I am an unrepentant patternist. And I suspect that almost all of us here are the same regardless of how we might understand the pattern. I'm also supposing that we do not have any new hermeneuticists among us, and if so I hope they feel as though they are in a very small minority.

I agree completely with what Roy Cogdill said in the

> ## PATTERN:
> "The sum total of what God said about anything is the pattern of God's will for that thing and it is the exclusive pattern."

Arlington Meeting on page 62, (Chart #3) that "the sum total of what God said about anything is the pattern of God's will on that thing, and it is the exclusive pattern." But what part does silence play in making the pattern or in being any part of the pattern? So far as I am concerned silence is the very essence of non-patternism. And so far as I'm concerned that's what silence is, it's nothing (Chart

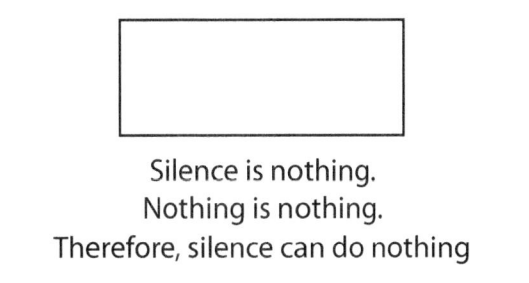

> Silence is nothing.
> Nothing is nothing.
> Therefore, silence can do nothing

#4). And since nothing does nothing, therefore silence can not do anything. Silence was not a creative force in the original creation of God; neither does silence have any creative force in the new creation.

Does Genesis 1 teach fiat creationism or not, or some combination of fiat creationism with something else? To ask the question is to answer it. I believe that fiat creationism and fiat creationism alone is taught in Genesis 1 as the creative power of God. And that, if we are fiat creationists in the Old Testament and in the old creation, we, to be consistent, must be fiat creationists when it comes to the New Testament. These transparencies were made for me by a couple of former students from the data I gave them, the rough data. And now they are former friends, because they were supposed to write there, "Nothing does nothing." And of course students make mistakes and I understand that, even ex-students.

I wish I had time this evening to talk about how that in the Old Testament in regard to God's silence, men sometimes asked, "why can't we" do thus and so? And God in the Old Testament has answered that question. What should be our proper response to its silence and whenever we think about asking the "why can't we" question?

But now some people, the Restoration historians, for example Woody Woodrow, have tried to show that the restorers were ambivalent about this matter of silence. That sometimes they spoke of silence as though it excluded a thing or a thing was excluded because the scriptures were silent about it. At other times a thing was permitted before…because the scriptures were silent about it. I don't know for sure what Woodrow's idea was in this article, because he explains quite clearly how that this ambivalence of Campbell and others in regard to this matter of silence is only an apparent ambivalence and not an actual ambivalence. And that's the question as I see it (Chart #5). Whenever the restorers, and we ourselves, show an am-

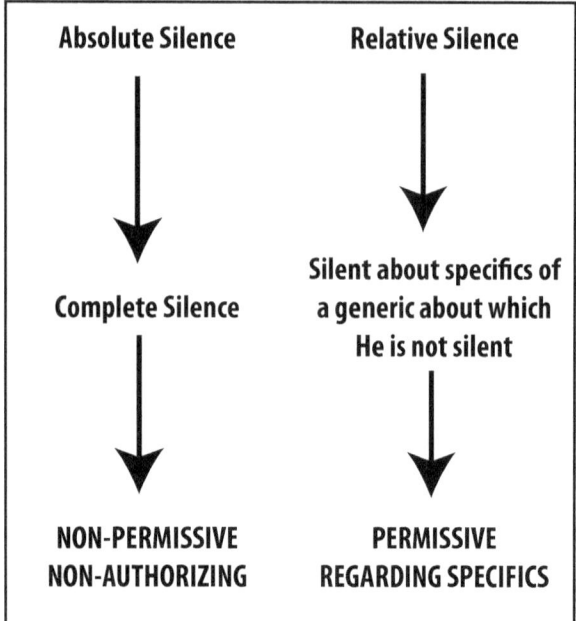

bivalence on this matter of silence it better be this kind of ambivalence or else something is wrong. It must be only an apparent ambivalence and not an actual one.

Now when the scriptures were absolutely silent about something, then the silence was non-permissive, non-authorizing. And we were not to do the thing because the scriptures were absolutely silent on that matter. However once the scriptures specified, say generically something, and did not give the how of doing it, this was only a relative silence. The generic thing was established by God's speech and is so because God said it's so. He was not silent on that. But in regard to various matters where He does not express the how and He's silent about the how or the specifics of a generic, then of course that silence is permissive because the general category, or whatever, has been authorized by God's speech.

Now we come to the second part of my speech. How do things get into the pattern then? Well, this deals with the law of inclusion or authorization by God's speech. But is there a law of … I hope I said that right, inclusion?

Is there a law of exclusion? There are two ways of looking at the law of exclusion. One way is generally to ignore it and seemingly to question even whether it really exists. My FC colleague, Melvin Curry, expressed this view very effectively in *The Arlington Meeting* on page 91 when he said, "I have discovered in discussion with individuals that

it is much better to speak about what is included than what is excluded. I do not know if there is such a thing as the law of exclusion. The emphasis in the New Testament is always on what God says."

Another way to look at the law of exclusion is to see two laws of exclusion. I take this way to be supplementary to the way I've just mentioned rather than contradictory to it. First, there is the strict law of exclusion, which I take to be nothing more than the law of self-contradiction (Chart

> ## Strict Law of Exclusion:
> the law of self-contradiction
>
> (balance of chart was covered and could not be seen)

#6). That is, we can not logically in the very nature of reality have the object A and the object non-A at the same time, for such would be a self-contradiction. When we apply this rule, the law of self-contradiction to the Bible, we know that logically we can not possibly, in the nature of things, have singing, an authorized matter, and non-singing, its opposite, at the same time by the same persons. For the former necessarily excludes the latter but nothing more. However singing does not necessarily exclude playing, or for that matter a thousand and one other things, for the simple reason that it is possible for one to sing and to play at the same time. But it is not possible to sing and not to sing at the same time, and by the same people. The most that we can say is that singing just does not include playing; playing must stand by itself and for itself.

Well, I've got to hurry along here, because if I only have 15 minutes, I've got to get to the second part of my

> ## The Relationship of Examples To Commands:
> 1. They provide structure or substance.
> 2. They provide essentials the commands may lack.
> 3. They substitute for specific commands.
> 4. They provide the setting for the commands.

third major point. (Chart #7) My third major point is concerned with the part that examples play in commands.

And here it is as I see it. The following relationship examples sustain to commands. In regard to general commands or principles they provide us some structure or substance we can get our teeth in, and not just go swimming around in the Atlantic Ocean thinking that some generic thing or principle authorizes something.

Two, in regard to some specific commands, which lack certain essential elements they must have, examples can provide us some of the essentials of the specific commands which the commands themselves lack.

In the third place, sometimes I believe, since examples represent specific binding authority, they even can substitute for certain commands or virtually be equal to commands.

And in the forth place, examples provide the setting for commands. Commands do not exist by themselves. Now then, my thesis is that commands cannot stand by themselves but that they need examples at least in four particular ways.

One, examples serve in their relationship to general principles or commands to give them some substance or structure. General principles or commands by themselves are often so vague that one person can take them one way and another person can take them another way.

But examples can give them some needed skeleton or parameters. Consider the following examples. Love is often used as the normative general principle and thereby the love advocate can overlook the specific teaching and examples of the scriptures, which just don't seem to jive with his view of love. But the problem of such a generalized love is also obvious in that, when we get down to the New Testament specifics of love, we soon have a parting of the ways, because one group takes love one way, and another group takes it another way.

I wish I had time to quote Brother Ketcherside on this to show how, in my estimation, he was so out of step with the New Testament teaching on love. But I do want to emphasize this. There is no way generally to obey the general commandment of love. The only way to love is to do specific loving things. And the New Testament in the examples of the New Testament give us the structure or the specifics, the nitty gritty of what it means to live, "loving the Lord your God with all your heart and your neighbor as yourself," etc..

In the second place, the golden rule, in the 1850's, was used by abolitionist brethren to prove that slave holding was sinful. Therefore any church which fellowshipped slaveholders or which had not taken a stand against slave holding was in fellowship with sin. And therefore ought to be disfellowshipped by all churches which took Matthew 7:12 seriously (see Ed Harrell: *A Quest For A Christian America*, pages 107 – 21 and 133 – 38). Harrell's pointed observation, "The injunction to do unto all men as they would do unto you, became to them the all consuming design of Christianity" (page 114). And this portrays clearly the attitude of some who are determined to go by some general principle, and to ignore examples. Their argument that slave holding based on the golden rule was sinful, sounds very good doesn't it? I've often made an argument like that myself, but it's so easy to draw a conclusion from that general principle that just won't line up with the specific facts in the New Testament.

Well, various other examples could be given where people want to go by some general scriptural principle, and ignore the examples as irrelevant or merely permissive. How is the argument, which is based on the generic commands of the great commission to preach the gospel… we're not told how and we ignore examples; or the good of Galatians 6:10, and we ignore examples, how is an augment based on the great commission this way, or the good of Galatians 6:10 essentially different from those which I have given? I insist it's not and it won't hold up.

In conclusion on this point, I assert and this made me, as much as anything, change from the institutional position to the non-institutional position…no that's…yes… "I assert that without examples to give us some parameters to limit general principles and commands, there are hardly any outer limits to how far we can go in the work, worship and organization of the church, when we try to pursue such generalities to their seemingly logically ultimate end." And when we hear brethren saying, "The Roman Catholic Church is the ultimate end of such." I say "yes," and I'm willing to defend that.

Now then, the second function of examples in relationship to the commands is to fill in on specifics of specific commands, which don't contain their specifics. Take for example just one example to save time, the element of baptism in the command to baptize. For example, the great commission says that the Apostles should baptize the taught, but it does not say in what they should baptize them, Mark 16:16 and Matthew 28:19. Unless the examples of baptism in water are more than just permissive, there is no one and only element for baptism. Even if one tried to get the element of baptism from John 3:5 "born of water," or Ephesians 5:26 "the washing of water by the Word," he would still need the examples so as to know that the water of those two passages was not figurative but literal water, and to know that these passages are indeed talking about baptism. And the same thing could be said about the Lord's Supper.

But let's go on to our third. Well, what would you say, one, to the following argument. The great commission says to baptize, in general, but not in what. And examples cannot give specific binding authority; therefore we are at liberty to baptize in whatever expedient element we wish to. The New Testament does not say to have both the cup and the loaf in the Lord's Supper. Now what would you say if a person said then, that you can have either one you want and you can have them in whatever order you want to.

In the third place, examples serve in relationship to some matters without specific commands recorded in the New Testament, to be in effect the equivalent or substitutes for such commands. And after all, there are commands in the scriptures to follow examples. Any viewpoint which argues that examples are only permissive is going to collapse or stumble over the statement in the scriptures to follow examples. Now I've read numerous things whereby people try to cut down the force of these passages, but all of their efforts fail. And I'll be glad to talk about that more if necessary later on.

But in regard to something for which we have no specific command, take the time of the day for the Lord's Supper. There is no specific command to have the Lord's Supper on any day of the week, the month, or the year. However there is the example in Acts 20:7, of the disciples coming together "upon the first day of the week to break bread." Does not this example preserve the essence of the apostolic teaching or command on what the disciples should….on when the disciple should have the Lord's Supper?

Roy Lanier – Moderator: 5 Minutes

Almon Williams – Main Speaker: OK.

Now a second specific command, or two specific commands, we don't have. And if the examples don't give us the gist of these specific commands, then one of our most prized positions of all goes down the drain, or two of them. The scriptures never teach us, give us a command to organize autonomous local churches. There's no command to do such. In fact, what is even more interesting is that there is not a command even to form local churches. But if I understand the New Testament properly, local churches not only existed but also were independent of one another. Further, do not these examples of local churches and independent local churches, preserve the essence of the apostolic teaching or command on the nature of the local churches as well as the need for local churches to exist?

And finally, examples in relationship to commands, they are the setting. We don't have any isolated commands floating around. They all come to us from other times and from other people. Examples are the setting in which examples come to us, so that commands are reducible to examples. And to think about the value of a setting, just think about the value of a ring to a diamond. None of you fellows better ask…if you ask a woman to marry you, better bring her a bare diamond. She may love diamonds but she doesn't want a diamond in her hand. She wants a diamond in a ring and she wants the ring with a diamond on her hand. And apparently God's the same way, when it comes to examples and commands. We don't have any bare commands. We have commands always in the setting of examples.

Some talk about direct commands. Well, direct to whom? You know I've read the Bible and I never found anything specifically directed to Almon Williams. I recall one time, I was reading in Joshua some of the cities that were given to the Israelites, one in the King James Version was spelled Almon. And I was glad to see that, I finally found my name in the Bible. Then I looked at the margin of the King James, it says the Hebrew is Alemeth, and there my name was gone. There are no scriptures directed to me or to anybody in this group. They come to us via examples or they don't come to us at all. And if examples are not binding neither are…I mean if … yes … neither are commands.

In conclusion brethren, as Christians whenever we get anyone of our practices called in question, we must give it up for a "thus saith the Lord" and not a "thus saith not the Lord." If we cannot do so, that is give scripture for what we practice when it's questioned, we must give up the practice. Nowhere else has the truly spiritual devotion of Thomas Campbell, in my judgement, come to us any more forcefully than the following pledge to all the like minded people of his day. "But this we do sincerely declare. That there is nothing we have hitherto received, as matter of faith or practice, which is not expressly taught and enjoined in the Word of God either in expressed terms or proof precedent, that we would not heartily relinquish," if it didn't have that, "that so we might return to the original, constitutional unity of the Christian church. And in this happy unity enjoy full communion with all our brethren in peace and charity." Ah! What noble heart beckoning words and how I should like to go and do likewise.

And I'll tell you just one thing. Back in 1951, an elder said to me in Flint, Michigan, "I want you to go to Harding College. And I want you to become a great defender of cooperative work among the brethren." I thought cooperative work was right. James D. Bales was in favor of it. Of course you might not like that, but I thought, James D. Bales was in favor of it, and if it was good enough for James D. Bales it must be good enough for anybody else. But as Brother Harrell said, my hermeneutic made me give up such co-operational practices, because I can't prove them beyond a reasonable shadow of doubt.

Scriptural Hermeneutics
Day 1 Speech 2 Rebuttal
Wendell Winkler

Introduction: *Winkler, Wendell. Presently heads College of Bible at Faulkner Univ., former director of Brown Trail School of Preaching, noted author, lecturer, known for local works for 46 years in Rayville and Bossier City, LA, Neosho MO, Huston and Fr. Worth, TX.*

When the preacher went to the store to buy a dozen eggs, and he got ready to pay for them, he lacked ten cents. And so he said to the owner of the store, he said, "I'll just put them back on the shelf." And the owner of the store said, "Oh no"! He said "that's not necessary preacher." He said, "Just go ahead and take the eggs." He said, "It's not but a dime." And the preacher said, "Oh no," he said, "I don't do business like that." He said, "I'll just put them back on the shelf." And again the owner of the store, he said, "Preacher, "It's not but a dime. Go ahead and take the eggs." And again the preacher was going to protest and then the owner of the store having been one who attended where he preached said, "Now preacher, go ahead and take those eggs. It's not but a dime." He said "I'll just take it out in preaching." And the preacher said, "Well, I don't have any ten-cent sermons." The fellow said, "In that case I'll come and hear you twice." (Laughter, whs)

So anyway, we got two of us on tonight and I appreciate so much the privilege of listening to Brother Williams and appreciate, as others have said, the spirit in which his presentation was given. I'm very grateful to Brother Lanier and to Brother Wolfgang for the work that they have done and for the invitation that they have extended and for the confidence that has been expressed. And I stand before you tonight understanding the seriousness of the position wherein I stand and the seriousness of the topic that has been assigned.

I want to spend a few moments tonight by way of some introductory material. And as we thus begin I would like to say from a personal perspective, that I believe that most of us, if not all of us tonight can say that we are not here tonight to castigate or to malign. Nor are we here to con-

tribute to polarization and divisiveness. Nor are we here to assume a polemical stature or position, though there have been such discussions in the past and no doubt there will be profitably others in the future. We're not here to speak for a school, nor a segment of the brotherhood. Nor are we here to sweep a divisive problem under the rug, or to put a Band-Aid on a wound of many years' deep concern. But, from the positive standpoint, I believe that we can say we are here tonight to accentuate our similarities; again, to emphasize the need, yea, the mandate for unity upon God's platform.

Thirdly, we're here representing ourselves as 20th century Bereans who had open hearts. "They received the word of God with all readiness of mind." They had open Bibles, "They searched the scriptures daily." And that's the happy combination that must be present, open hearts and open Bibles. Further we're here to foster and improve understanding between the persuasions that are present, and to begin and or to continue a healing of a too long forgotten open wound in the body of our Lord, and thus to contribute to world evangelism (John 17:20-21).

But now a transition but still by way of introductory material, I believe tonight that there are some presuppositions that we can all take to heart. And among them are these: that the Bible is divine in origin, 2 Timothy 3:16-17; secondly that it is God's full complete and final revelation of His will to man (Jude 3; Gal. 1:6-9); thirdly that it is to be held in profound reverence, as the Psalmist said, "My heart standeth in awe of thy word." That's why we take off our shoes when we open the Bible, because we're standing on holy ground (Psa. 119:161).

We are presupposing that all of us believe that the Bible must be believed (2 Thess. 2:13), that the Bible must be obeyed (Rom. 6:16-18), and the Bible must be taught (2 Tim. 2:2). Additionally we are presupposing that we love the brotherhood (1 Pet. 2:17-18), but that we recognize that a segmentation exists among us (1 Cor. 1:11), but that "my brethren these things ought not so to be" (James 2:10); and that we recognize that God instructs us to be united (1 Cor. 1:10).

And we are presupposing additionally, that we all recognize per this gathering, that there is a deep-seated desire in the hearts of all present to restore and to cultivate "the unity of the spirit in the bond of peace." But we all recognize that the present state of affairs largely exists because of a lack of unanimity when it comes to the field of hermeneutics. First why are we here, secondly presuppositions, thirdly what about hermeneutics?

Duncan said, "Hermeneutics is simply the science of interpretation." We would like to expand on that very briefly by saying that Hermeneutics consist of the approach and the application; approach – application that we make of the word of God. Therefore we're dealing in the field of Hermeneutics where how does the Bible guide us, direct us, lead us, authorize us, instruct us and restrain us?

But still by way of introductory material, the field of hermeneutics is not a field that somehow or another in the 20th century produced now some real problems and all of a sudden this is just peculiar to our given day and time. When the Jerusalem council was conducted in the book of Acts chapter 15 about AD 50, such resulted in a letter being penned. Now upon receiving that epistle, the recipients were faced with a hermeneutical challenge. They had first of all to make a decision concerning the origin of that epistle. And then secondly they had to determine something about the nature of the content of that epistle. When the epistle said to refrain from fornication, was that to be taken figuratively as it was often used in the Old Testament for idolatry, or to be taken figuratively. And so tonight we're not faced with any really new challenge.

Now the field of Biblical Hermeneutics is a very broad field. And for the brevity of the time allotted to this section tonight, that's certainly so. Now with these background thoughts in mind: Why are we here? Presuppositions? What is Hermeneutics? And it's not a really new challenge to us. I want to enter into the body of the study tonight, in which we will pursue the following approach. First we will make some general observations concerning the matter of authority. Secondly, we will deal with the ways that the Bible authorizes. And thirdly, speak to what should our response be to the silence of the scriptures, and close with some observations.

First, some general observations concerning Biblical authority. Ladies and Gentlemen we must have authority in our lives, otherwise the condition of the judges exists, Judges 21:25, wherein men "do that, that is right in their own eyes." But what do we mean when we speak of authority? Webster sometimes misses it, but many times hits it on the target, and thus he does relative to authority. He says authority is, "superiority derived from status that carries with it the right to demand and give final decisions." Thus authority has to do with that to which we can make our final appeal. Relative to this matter of Bible authority, this audience needs not have developed in its hearing the chain of Biblical authority. Thus I will not so do except to state it's God, Christ, the Holy Spirit, the Apostles and the Bible.

Now relative to the last point, the Bible is our exclusive authority in religion, in matters of faith and practice. Such is taught implicitly in 2 John 9-11, Galatians 1:6-9 and in a multitude of other places. And because that is the case, the list almost becomes endless as to what then does NOT constitute authority in religion. For example: subjective experience, human reasoning, the religion of parents, the human conscience, the will and practice of either the majority or the minority, the church, the school, the paper, a preacher, human tradition, democratic vote, what are sister churches doing, what are growing denominational bodies doing, what's the motive of action? None of these constitute really Biblical authority for our action. But rather, "What sayeth the Bible?"

Now we must have Biblical authority for all that we preach and practice. Colossians 3:17 says, "Whatsoever ye do in word or deed do all," "whatsoever" and "all" are corollaries in that given passage, that's the generalization. But then Paul becomes specific and breaks down the "whatsoever" and the "all" and says, "in word or deed," word – preaching, deed – practice. And so this then must be what's done in the name of the Lord or as our Lord authorizes. Yes, Biblical authority we must have for what we practice. Does not the Bible say, "We walk by faith" (2 Cor. 5:7) and that "faith comes by hearing" God's word (Rom. 10:17). Indeed then Biblical authority must be present.

But brethren sadly we must observe that the condition has already arrived it seems, in some places, where Biblical authority is no longer believed to be absolutely necessary, a further indication incidentally of repudiation of pattern authority. And such has grown out of, and resulted from the view of the Bible as primarily being a compilation of love letters and not being constitutional, with the message of the Bible being primarily relational and not coital. I believe, THAT in a nutshell, is the new hermeneutic, and I repudiate it.

Now having established the fact of some just general points on the subject of Bible authority, I want to make the transition to the second emphasis of the evening. And that is how does the Bible authorize? The Bible authorizes by commands and or directives, by examples, by implicate or inference and by expedience, with the silence of the scriptures avidly being respected.

But now, let's break that down for our study. First of all, Bible authority being established by commands. In our study of that particular matter, I would like first of all to observe that commands or directives in the New Testament differ in the form in which they come to us. Sometimes these commands come to us in the form of a direct mandate, "believe on the Lord Jesus Christ" (Acts 16:31).

Secondly, sometimes they come to us in the form of an expressed desire. Paul said to the Thessalonians (2 Thess. 3:5), "may the Lord direct your heart," that's my desire, "into the love of God."

Thirdly, sometimes these commands come to us in the form of a conditional statement, "if ye then be risen with Christ." Doesn't that come to us indeed stating that we are to have been risen with Christ? But it's in the form of a conditional statement.

Again sometimes they come in the form of an exhortation. For example 1 John 4:7, "beloved let us love one another."

Then sometimes they come to us in the form of a question. "Shall we continue in sin that grace may abound?" That rhetorical question, equal to simply, we're not to continue, brethren don't continue in sin that you might be a recipient of a greater measure of the grace of God. But it comes to us in the form of a question.

Then sometimes it comes to us in the form of a declaration, "He that believeth and is baptized shall be saved" (Mark 16:16); and so, varying forms.

Now these commands or directives of God can either be generic or specific, to which Brother Williams made reference a moment ago. Now if the command is generic, such authorizes the action without the details. If the command is specific, such authorizes the action and specifies and authorizes the details. And such can be illustrated by, naturally, the building of the ark. Noah was told, for example, to put a door in that ark, but he was not told specifically where to locate the door. And so he was specifically told to put a door in the ark, and that's specific authority, but there was a generic…there was a generic part to that as well. Why? Well, what side of the ark? God did not legislate, so that was left to his discretion.

Then relative to these commands or directives, what is man's relationship to these? When the commands are generic, we are at liberty to choose, not binding one to the exclusion of the other, while we are judicious and expediential. But when the commands are specific we do not have the right to change or to loose. Binding and loosing were prerogatives of the Apostles. And brethren we have apostolic authority, Galatians 1:6 and following, but we do not have Apostolic succession. When God commands, then we are not to change by addition, subtraction, or modification, neither are we to question. But when God commands we have the privilege to obey regardless of the cost, regardless of how foolish the command may seem, regardless of whether we can see connection between the command given and the necessary results to be followed.

But again, Biblical authority established or cooperated by example. There are abuses in this field of Biblical Hermeneutics. Some doubt, if not out rightly deny, the authority of Biblical examples. Such ones advocate Biblical authority is primarily limited to commands or directives; others make examples an exclusive way of establishing what can be done. That's why these ask "Where is the example for individual communion cups? Where is the example for a meeting house or for visual aids?" Such illustrates why this phase of hermeneutical study is vital.

Now what do we mean by example? An example is that which is to be followed or to be imitated. Now let it be understood that examples are authorized in two senses. An example authorizes in the sense that the matter must be done, that is, it's a matter that is obligatory. Examples also authorize in the sense that they *may* be done, that is, the matter is permitted but optional. And thus in the field of Biblical examples there is a must and a may authorization in them.

Now to expound on that a little further. Biblical examples or events fall into certain classifications. And I will be very brief here. There are examples in the Bible of things done that are sinful (Acts 5:1-11, Ananias and Sapphira).

Next there are examples or events that were right when they took place, but would be improper now, delaying preaching to the gentiles for ten years.

Thirdly, there are actions in the New Testament that were temporary but obligatory. 1 Corinthians 14:1, desire spiritual gifts, was what the Corinthians were to do. Well that's temporary as we read back in chapter 13:8-10, but it was certainly obligatory then. Then there are actions which were temporary and optional. What about the circumcision of Timothy?

Then there are actions, which are permanent, and optional. What about the Macedonians? That example of giving to the standpoint of they were reduced to abject penury. Now that's permanent in that we can still do it, but it's not required, optional.

And then there are events that are permanent and obligatory, such as 1 Corinthians 16:1-2, giving of our means, and the Lord's Supper and so on. It can be readily seen then from this study, that for an example to be binding today, it must be right, it must be permanent, and either must be either optional or obligatory.

Now out of this list of classifications, how do we determine into which category an event or an action falls? And perhaps we'll have time to deal with that a little later, so I'll just mention it very briefly. I believe that it can be told in the following ways.

First by the employment of hermeneutical principles, primarily these that are applied to commands, apply in examples and such matters. Therefore in the exercise of the application of hermeneutical principles, we will do what? Study the action per se, then the immediate context, and then the remote context.

Add to that secondly, for us to understand into which category a given event falls, we then must exercise rational thinking, common sense. God made man and the mind of man and God gave us the Bible adapted to man. That being the case then, God adapted the Bible to man's rational concept and behavior. Thus we can exercise rational thought in these matters.

And then add to that thirdly and somewhat redundant, but I'll mention it because I believe it's so important. We must come to understand the totality of the Bible's instruction on a given matter at hand before we can determine whether or not that given example falls into the area of being obligatory for today.

Friends, a repudiation of the authority of Biblical example will result in serious consequences. It will result in the repudiation of the Restoration principle. Secondly it will constitute a capitulation to the modernist of our day who denies pattern authority, and that the Bible is our blueprint. And thirdly, it will result in the loss of the distinctive nature of the New Testament church, per the Lord's Supper.

But again, Bible authority by implication and necessary inference. All the Bible says, it says either explicitly or implicitly. And what it says implicitly is as binding as what it says explicitly. And when God's word says something implicitly, I may be just now in 1990 inferring that it is thus implied, but not just because I inferred it does it become authoritative, but simply because it's been in the Bible all the time, and because God said it, because God said it, not because we're just now inferring it. We must see that God implies and man infers. And that it is authoritative because God implied it.

Now what do we mean by implication and necessary inference? An implication or a necessary inference is a deduction reached by sound rational reasoning based upon facts. When any action or fact is absolutely demanded by the Biblical information at hand, though not specifically stated, that fact, that action or information is implication or inference.

Now to illustrate, it is implied that Jesus went down into the water. The Bible never said He did. The Bible says he came up out of the water. But the implication is that he went down into it. Our Lord used implication when dealing with the Sadducees in Matthew 22 relative to the resurrection from the dead.

But then authority established implemented by expediency. What do we mean by expediency? Expediency friends, is that that expedites naturally or assists in the implementation of an obligation.

An obligation has an expediency. So where there is no obligation, then naturally we would have no expediency. And furthermore if there is no advantage we would have no expediency. So there must be, one, there must be an obligation; two, there must be an advantage for an expediency to result.

Now relative to this matter of expediency, let's examine some illustrations. The Lord, for example, says that we are to assemble (Heb. 10:25). This constitutes the obligation. But in the area of expediency, we can assemble in a tent, under a tree or in a meetinghouse.

And let it be understood that there is a vast difference between as expedient and an addition. For example, it would have been an addition in the use of an unauthorized kind of wood if Noah had a used Pine. Or it would have been indeed an addition if he had of built it out of Aluminum. But that no way at all prohibited him from using a hammer and a crowbar. One is in the area of an expedient whereas the other is not the case.

And of course such can be reasoned relative to songbooks and the use of an organ. One is not authorized, not in the field of expediency, whereas the other is.

Ladies and Gentlemen, let me say that we must come to understand that we have to have Biblical authority for what we do. And when somebody says where is the authority for a songbook, and if I...the implication being that well we don't have that therefore we still do it, therefore we can do anything else that's not authorized, is false reasoning. I believe songbooks are authorized in the Bible in the field of expediency.

Now as we draw toward the close, I wanted to have considerable time to deal with this matter of respecting the silence of the scriptures. But let me just say that Colossians 3:17, as well as other texts we have previously mentioned tonight, establish the fact that the silence of the word of God must be avidly respected. And that such can be illustrated throughout the New Testament and the Old Testament.

But since my time has transpired let me bring to a close the observations of this hour by simply saying that tonight, by way of introductory material, we observed some presuppositions. We observed some reasons for our having assembled. We observed the definition of hermeneutics, and we observed that that's the challenge of the hour. In the transition we then observed how the Bible authorizes, by command, by example, by necessary inference, implication, and by expediency. We then observed that Bible authority is necessary for all that we do and say in the field of religion, and with the silence of the scriptures being avidly, avidly respected.

Let us call to memory that 1 Peter 2:17-18 says, "Love

the Brotherhood," and that Psalms 133:1 says, "Behold how good and how pleasant it is for brethren to dwell together in unity," and that "God hates the sin of division" (Prov. 6:16-19). And that when my Lord died on Calvary and when his body was bathed in his own blood and in human spittle, one of the reasons for which he was dying is stated in Ephesians 2:13-16, wherein we read, "That he might reconcile both unto God in one body by the cross having slain the enmity thereby." Unjustified division among the people of God is a reproach upon the death of our Lord on Calvary's hill.

Scriptural Hermeneutics
Day 1 Speech 2 Panelist 1
Gary Workman

Introduction: *Workman, Gary. Presently in meeting and publishing work, former overseas evangelist in Lebanon, noted author and lecturer, frequent participant in lectures and unity forums. He is a native of California with 31 years of preaching in Big Bear, San Pedro, and Simi, CA, Las Vegas, NV, and Dallas, TX. Resides in Mesquite, TX.*

It certainly is a pleasure, I want to express along with these other brethren that have spoken today, to have a part in the program this evening. The time constraint is always against us and there's so much that we would like to say that we will not have time to say. So let me get right in to it lest I loose any of this four minutes.

I believe that much of the problems that have arisen, have come about because of different hermeneutical perspectives. Now to put that down in everyday language, we simply haven't approached the Bible with the same principles of interpretation, and we therefore have these problems. I believe that if this one session tonight could be the only session, and we didn't even have all the rest of them to follow, we could solve the problem in this area alone, because I believe this is where we must solve it. Never mind the new hermeneutic on this occasion, we have enough problems with the old one. (Subdued laughter, whs). And we need to look at the old one. If we could solve these things about the hermeneutics of the thing, the principles of interpretation, then I believe the issues would disappear. They would take care of themselves.

We've heard and continue to hear and see in print over the years and up to the present day, that some are conservative and some are liberal. And I want to address that for just a moment. Brethren I don't believe that I'm a liberal. And I believe that I'm just as conservative as anybody in this room. Now I think that we have some liberals in the church, but I don't identify with them. And so we need to, I think, look at these terms that we sometimes use about ourselves and maybe make some corrections.

I want to state for the record also that I don't believe in church support of human institutions. And therefore I'm not an institutionalist, and I don't claim any allegiance with that mode of thinking. I think that all three of us, who on this occasion are on our side of the table, all three of us want to conserve everything that is laid out in the Bible for us to believe and practice. And that's why we say we are conservative. We don't want to violate a single principle of authority that God has put in that book. There are some who say, "It doesn't matter, you can just love God and do as you please." We don't take that position. We never have and we never will.

These two speeches though, reveal that we do have some differences in principles of interpretation. And there is virtual agreement. I think you've noticed by the hearing of these tonight, there is virtual agreement on much of what was covered tonight. In other words, when it comes to direct statements, sometimes called commands, we have agreement. When it comes to the matter of implication or necessary inference we have virtual agreement. Where we differ has to do with examples. Brethren I believe in patternism. I am a patternist. I believe the Bible is a blueprint. But I do not believe that an example taken by itself, an example alone, where there is no statement, whether explicit or implicit, that no example can be binding. If you have it by itself and there's no implicit or explicit statement to bind that thing, it cannot be bound. And this is where I think the crux of the matter lies. We must not think that if one says that an example alone cannot bind, that this is equivalent to saying that all examples therefore are in the realm of permissiveness. This doesn't follow because some examples may simply reflect what is bound in some other place.

Scriptural Hermeneutics
Day 1 Speech 2 Panelist 2
Don Tarbet

Introduction: *Tarbet, Don. Speaker on many lectureships, debater, respected author, businessman, and preacher for 39 years at Farwell, Paducah, and Sherman, TX, as well as Albuquerque, NM. Presently preaching at Calvin, OK and living in Denison, TX.*

I express my appreciation for the opportunity to be here this evening, though with fear and trembling. Seldom do I stand in an audience of this many preachers.

I appreciate the things that Brother Winkler had to say with which I agree regarding the emphasis upon examples. And also what Gary has just expressed, that examples alone are not binding.

I'd like to touch on the three major points of Brother Williams' speech. I have the advantage of having it in written form here. I'd like to make some quotes from it, "That the New Testament is a pattern of the gospel and the pattern of the law of inclusion and the pattern and nature of the authority of examples." And he spent approximately one half of his material on that subject. I can appreciate the fact that he believes in the same principles or hermeneutics that most of us would accept. The problem of course is in the application.

I liked many things that he had to say. On page three of his message he talked about being a patternist, and I say that I too believe in following the pattern of the New Testament. And I'm impressed with the statement that "the sum total of all of God's will is all of its parts." And on page seven there's a statement though that I'd like for you to pay special attention to and by way of commendation regarding his statement. "God's silence regarding the specifics of the generic allows us to use our judgment and to use any expedient specifics in carrying out the generic matter." Of course any time we fail to recognize that, we do have some problems. Then on page nine, he said, "In other words we should do in religion only those things authorized in God's word."

Now I would question some statements that he has made regarding examples. And we had a fine presentation, highly technical matter, being presented to us tonight. But I am somewhat confused about some of the statements regarding examples. Under generic authority, he stated, "In relationship to the command go, he has not made the choice of any specific way to go, to leave the choice up to our judgment." Then he said, "in the matter of specifics, or carrying out the generic, we have the choice of using our best judgment in the matter." I agree with that, but then we have other statements that lead me to consider the difficulty of some of the other statements. For instance on page 16, rather page 17, he said, "The residual problem of examples. Whenever we find no helpful pertinent data at all to help us to decide this matter, or only enough presumably to confuse us, what should we do? I answer that we should take the deed in question to be specific binding authority until we learn otherwise for the following reasons."

Then on page 18 he referred to the fact that "commands cannot stand by themselves," and on page 21 he emphasized the fact, "without examples to give us parameters to limit general principles and commands there are hardly any outer limits as to how far we can go."

I wanted to mention these things because these no doubt will be areas that we'll be discussing, along with the example of the Lord's Supper, and the example of establishing local congregations.

Scriptural Hermeneutics
Day 1 Speech 2 Panelist 3
Melvin Curry

Introduction: *Curry, Melvin. He is a native of Orlando, FL and has been on the faculty of Florida College since 1963 and head of the Bible Dept. since 1975. Presently preaches in Dover, FL.*

I too appreciate the opportunity of being here this evening and sharing with you just a couple of minutes of introductory thoughts.

Long ago I was impressed with two principles that seem to be imbedded in the New Testament, that speak to the kind of attitude that I must have, and that all of us should share with respect to the scriptures.

The first is that we respect the individual conscience of one another. And the older I become and the more involved I get in various issues, no matter what they are, the more I respect what Paul had to say in passages like 1 Corinthians chapter 8, or Romans 14 or other passages that have a bearing on the question of conscience. We should not under any circumstance cause a brother to offend by a liberty that we possess. And I suppose that the whole question of authority comes down to the matter, "Are we really and sincerely willing to give up our liberty for unity?" I have many many head on discussions with individuals with whom I differ, and sooner or latter it just comes down to that.

The other principle that seams to me to be imbedded in the scripture is that of congregational independence. It is something that the New Testament guarded jealously. All one has to do is study carefully the matter of the contribution for the poor saints in Jerusalem, and all that Paul had to write about it to understand how important it was that each congregation through their own messengers, guard their deposits and fulfill and accomplish the will of God.

I hope that each of us who is present, is willing to recognize these principles as we study commands and examples and inferences. And when we see clearly what the New Testament teaches, that we are willing to defer to the conscience of others.

I also would like to suggest that when it comes to the matter of examples, there is no better instructor than God's Old Testament book of examples. As Brother Williams had said, there are a number of examples that he would like to have cited. I would like to share simply one of them with you. Look with me, if you will, at Numbers the 15th chapter for just a moment. There was a case that came up in which an individual was caught violating the Sabbath, picking up sticks on the Sabbath day. In the light of the Old Testament it was quite obvious, in the light of the Ten Commandments, that Sabbath violation was to result in the penalty of death. But the question is "What kind of death?" And I would like for you, carefully, on your own, to read Numbers the 15th chapter and notice that when they found this man picking up sticks they knew he was worthy of death, but they knew not what kind of death. And they simply put him in ward until God revealed to them what to be done. Had God not spoken, I suppose the man would have rotted in jail. But the fact is God did speak. And it is the sum total of what He says, as He comments on His own statements, that gives us our basis of authority.

Scriptural Hermeneutics
Day 1 Speech 2 Panelist 4
Maurice Barnett

Introduction: *Barnett, Maurice. He has preached for 38 years, the past 25 in Phoenix, AZ. Also serves as a pastor, and is author of 7 books, most of which examine various cult movements.*

I suppose that at some time or another all of us had wished that we had the Apostle Paul here, or if we just had spiritual gifts why things would be so much easier, that'd settle so many of these problems. But I remind you that in the first century when they had inspired men and they had spiritual gifts, they didn't have any fewer problems nor any less division than we have today. The churches divided over any number of things: there were doctrinal matters, there were moral issues, there were false teachers on every hand. And groups that pulled away from the disciples did not necessarily become atheists. They still believed in God, they still believed in Jesus Christ, and yet they had formed their own particular group. Churches had to be reprimanded because of the course that they were taking. So here was a situation, In a day when there were inspired men and spiritual gifts and we still find a lot of mess in the New Testament.

The question is, of course, "How was it handled?" I don't find in any place where any of the Apostles or even when Jesus was handling the divisions in His day among the Jews, where there was any appeal to "Well let's just try to get along and have unity because that's more important than anything else. We'll love one another to death." The constant appeal that Jesus made and the Apostles made was to truth. They revealed truth at that moment, but it was still an appeal to truth and it was truth that was presented in any number of ways. It was presented in the very ways that we read now, and ways in which we determine what they had to say and what they want us to know. That truth is for us now as much as it was in the first century. God designed it that way.

I believe that there are three principles engraved in stone that we have to keep in mind. Number one, we have an absolute standard of truth revealed in the scriptures. Secondly, we are capable of understanding it. And when two people disagree, someone is wrong and perhaps both are, but at least one of the persons is wrong. And the only way that they can become right is to come back to the scriptures. When two people disagree, somebody's left the truth. And thirdly, after reasonable time and effort to try to correct the error of someone, God demands division. He requires a break be made. And those things are clearly clearly taught in the word of God.

The studies that we have tonight have to do with getting back to "What does the Bible teach? How does it teach us?" I think there's a good deal of fuzzy thinking on the subject and I think we've heard some of it tonight. For the most part, I appreciate the presentations that have been made. But I think we need to define some things more clearly. I don't think that we really clearly have defined what we mean by specific directives, or specific commands and what we mean by generic authority, or what we mean by expediencies, or examples. And I think there's some definitions that need to be clarified in regard to those. We can be wrong because we are wrong about the principles and we don't have the correct approach to the word of God. But we can also be wrong when we do not apply those principles consistently throughout the word of God and that's important. Thank you.

Scriptural Hermeneutics
Panel Discussion

Jamie Sloan – Moderator: Reminding you that the specific areas of application regarding the cooperation question are to be discussed in subsequent sessions. Yet it may be that in the next 20 minutes or so we can accomplish some things by allowing these brethren to take turns for about 2 minutes apiece; trying to give some further definition to the differences between the two views that have been expressed this evening; trying to clarify these different areas of discussion. Brother Reeves is going to help us with that, if you need some help about the two minutes you can…I think he's going to give a one minute warning and then time's up. If you can handle that yourself all right, that's fine too.

Melvin Curry – Panelist: Are we going to do this with each speaker?

Jamie Sloan – Moderator: Yes.

Melvin Curry – Panelist: I wonder if he could move over here so we can see him.

Jamie Sloan – Moderator: All right, is that good?

Melvin Curry – Panelist: The speaker is blocking it.

Maurice Barnett – Panelist: Move that microphone up close to you.

Panel Discussion

Jamie Sloan – Moderator: We need to get you as close to the microphone as you can. All right who would like to go first then? Any volunteers? Gary?

Gary Workman – Panelist: One thing that Brother Williams brought out in his position, that if we didn't go by examples alone we would not know the element in which to baptize, and I think he also mentioned the day of the Lord's Supper. And I'd like to respond to that to start with.

Because I made the statement that I don't believe that any example is binding, if that's all you have. And Brother Barnett asked for definitions, we really do need some. I don't know if we have time for them. By example I don't mean something that's obligatory, I simply mean the record of some action. And so that's the way I'll be using it this evening.

But here's the way that I would establish the day of the week for the Lord's Supper. If I never had Acts 20 verse 7, I would know that it's to be taken on the first day of the week, and I think that it can be proved. Here's the way I would do it. I would say an assembly of Christians was commanded to take place on the first day of the week, 1 Corinthians 16 verses 1-2. An essential part of an assembly is the observance of the Lord's Supper, 1 Corinthians 11 verses 20 and following. Therefore the Lord's Supper was commanded to take place on the first day of the week. I don't need Acts 20 verse 7. It illustrates, it corroborates, it substantiates, but if that's the only passage we had, we couldn't bind the day of the Lord's Supper any more than we could bind the time of day of the Lord's Supper, and insist that it be in the evening as some brethren have done. Or bind the place, and say that it must be in an upper room, as some other brethren have also done.

And then further more regarding the baptism in water, if we never had Acts 8, Phillip and the Eunuch, we wouldn't need to wonder about what the element is. Because in Acts 10 Peter said, "Can any one forbid the water" and he commanded them to be baptized.

Jamie Sloan – Moderator: All right, response on the other side over here?

Maurice Barnett – Panelist: I really don't agree with the use of 1 Corinthians 16 and that particular interpretation, because there is not inherent, in the instructions of 1 Corinthinas 16, an assembly.

Now the way that we would establish an assembly in 1 Corinthians 16 is to take it in conjunction with other passages that have to do with the first day of the week assembly. You look at the instructions of 1 Corinthians 16, and it simply says "on the first day of every week you lay by him in store as he may prosper that no collections be made when I come." And there's nothing said about an assembly, we have to assume and assert an assembly in the passage. So this is why some brethren will mail their check in. I have no objections to that, or they'll leave it with the preacher and say, "put this in the plate for me Sunday," or any number of other ways. I know of one congregation that has a box in the vestibule, where members just drop it in the box as they go in the door, and then they assemble in the auditorium. This doesn't state assembly.

I agree that this is a collection made by a congregation that's placed in a common place, a common treasury. But to say that this requires alone, standing by itself, an assembly every first day of the week, is to say something that this passage do not say. I would take Acts 20:7 only in relationship and reference to another way of proving it. I don't think that Acts 20:7 alone, by itself, will establish an every first day of the week assembly, but we can get into that in just a few moments. I think my time is up.

Jamie Sloan – Moderator: Don, or...?

Don Tarbet – Panelist: I'll just make comment that the fact that the Lord's Supper, when instituted in Matthew Mark and Luke, all refer to the fact that the Lord's Supper was to be in the kingdom. And then we have Paul saying, "I'm giving instructions that I received from the Lord," and the fact that he said to do it, and the often-ness of it is suggested. Then when we have the assembly mentioned, or the assembling in Hebrews 10:25, along with the reinforcement of 1 Corinthians 16:2; I see Acts 20 verse 7 as the demonstration, the example of what we are to do. But I believe we have all this, the text and the context, all that have some bearing on it.

Jamie Sloan – Moderator: Melvin?

Melvin Curry – Panelist: I want to address what Brother Workman said just a minute ago. I may have misunderstood Brother Williams' point, but I don't think so. When he talked about examples alone, he was simply saying that there is no commandment in the New Testament that is directed to us in the 20th century. It is directed to first century Christians, Paul to the Corinthians, or to the Ephesians, or whatever. And therefore that whatever authority we have is by way of New Testament examples, and it was the commands themselves in the New Testament that become examples for us. And our only basis of authority is by way of examples. That's what I understood him to be saying.

Maurice Barnett – Panelist: Gary, can I make another point? I think before we get into some of these applications, as you pointed out Gary, we need to define some terms. We've got several areas where we need to understand what the principles are before we can really start applying them. And I think that that starts with this matter of generics and specifics. I've heard a good deal about generic commands and specific commands, as though there were two different categories. There's no such thing as that. All commands are specific. Generic simply refers to the options or choices found in specific statements and commands that are left up to us to carry out. Those are the unspecified options.

Here's where I would disagree with the point at the beginning of Brother Winkler's presentation. I don't find much to disagree with his presentation. But here's a point in which he stated the Bible authorizes by directives, by inferences, by examples, and expediencies. The Bible does not authorize by expediency. An expediency is an option of generic authority. It is what is authorized by authority, but it does not authorize something. Now he got around at the close of it and straightened that out and talked about obligations bringing about expediencies. But we've got to keep our language proper and correct that we're talking about in generics and specifics.

We're talking about the specific command or statement, and we're talking about those unspecified choices that we can make, that are found in specific authority. And that's where we have to start. And that has a bearing on 1 Corinthians 16 and all these others.

Jamie Sloan – Moderator: This side went twice in a row. You guys want to go twice in a row?

Gary Workman – Panelist: I think that we again, we may have some semantic differences among us, where we don't really differ in our viewpoint, but we might be expressing it in different ways. I know Brother Winkler, and I know what he believes in this, and I know that he understands that for anything to be an expedient it must first be authorized. And while it may not have sounded that way at the initial presentation of it, it was contained in his material.

But again, I agree that when we say generic and specific, every command...this is the way I typically say it. Every command has both a specific and generic aspect. So if you take the great commission we can't say that's generic, but sing is specific. The great commission is specific when it says "go." It means "go," not "stay." That's specific, we have to go. But it's generic or optional as to how we go.

If we take the other thing, we have the generic aspect of making music, making melody to the Lord. That would be the generic part of that and the sing is the specific. Or you could even say that after you mention the sing, there are still some options because it still doesn't say whether you have to have 4-part harmony or unison. It doesn't say what the style of the music might be, whether classical, or bluegrass like in the red songbook that's used so much, or whatever. (Laughter, whs) So we recognize all of these things.

And I think that Brother Williams said, "Well this one is generic, this one's specific." But I think that even he would agree with what we're saying on this point. I don't think we disagree on this. We expressed it a little bit differently but that's not where the disagreement lies.

Back to 1 Corinthians 16, I don't agree with the observation made regarding that. Because if this were simply a private matter of laying by in store, stuffing it under your mattress, or in your drawer, or putting it out of one bag into another, the first day of the week would not be specified. And "by him" doesn't mean at home as some people have insisted. I think an assembly has to be implied in the understanding of that passage.

Jamie Sloan – Moderator: Don. Don.

Maurice Barnett – Panelist: Let me just say that I didn't say that. So…

Jamie Sloan – Moderator: OK.

Don Tarbet – Panelist: Brother Barnett, is not expediency authorized by the Lord? In other words, I believe Brother Winkler was not trying to say that expediency was not doing something unauthorized, but rather it is a way of carrying out that which God does authorize, such as songbooks and so on.

Maurice Barnett – Panelist: Can I respond to that now?

Jamie Sloan – Moderator: Yeah, it's you're turn.

Maurice Barnett – Panelist: OK. No. What he did at the beginning of his presentation, he put it on the level with directives, inferences, examples, expediencies. All of those things authorize expediencies, but expediencies do not authorize anything. It's the way that he had it worded.

Now as I say he corrected that on over in his presentation. But what I'm wanting to get across is we're going to have to get our concept of the principles correct before we can make a correct application of them. We've got to understand that. And I think that there are a lot of people here tonight that are confused by some of these things. Unless we get those straight, then we're not going to be able to properly apply them consistently whenever we need to.

Jamie Sloan – Moderator: Brother Curry?

Melvin Curry – Panelist: Why don't you go back across the table and then we'll get caught up again.

Jamie Sloan – Moderator: All right.

Melvin Curry – Panelist: Yeah.

Gary Workman – Panelist: I believe that we do have the principle of the obligation to love our brother, as was brought out in Brother Williams' speech, and as Maurice said in his brief comments at the microphone there. And we should forebear in various matters, but none of us are willing to forebear in every single objection that some brother might raise. The very things that was said by these two brethren about how that for the sake of unity we ought to be willing to sacrifice our liberty, have been said to me by those who hold to the one cup quote, unquote, and no class position. And they've said, "If these are matters of indifference, then what difference does it make? Why don't you give it up for the sake of unity?" These brethren won't give it up. And so why make the application to us to give up the liberty on these things that we have divided over, when they won't do the same with these other brethren?

Jamie Sloan – Moderator: Melvin?

Melvin Curry – Panelist: I think maybe we need to talk to the one-cup brethren, and we need to talk to other individuals, the no class brethren or whatever the situation is. Frankly I will give it up. I'll use the one-cup if it will bring harmony to the body of Christ. And I will give up the class situation, because it's not authorized by God directly anyway. I mean I think its expedient, but I don't think it's necessary. That's my only answer to it. I'll be glad to give it up if it will bring unity to the body of Christ.

Jamie Sloan – Moderator: Don?

Don Tarbet – Panelist: What about the use of songbooks, someone objected to that, should we give it up remembering Paul's attitude toward having Titus circumcised in Galatians 2?

Melvin Curry – Panelist: I don't really suppose I have to have a songbook. If that becomes a critical issue to stand in the way of the unity of brethren, yes sir. I'll give up meeting houses, I'll give up songbooks; I'll give up any expediency that's necessary to bring brethren together. Yes sir, I don't see any problem with that.

Gary Workman – Panelist: Well…

Melvin Curry – Panelist: I don't think it's necessary mind you, but I'd give it up gladly.

Gary Workman – Panelist: In that case, we could all be united tonight. Let's all of those of us sitting on this side of the table give up the various things that divide us, and let's all you brethren give up the individual communion cups along with us, and the Bible classes.

Maurice Barnett – Panelist: Wait a minute. You haven't heard from me yet. (Laughter, whs)

Gary Workman – Panelist: Are you really willing to do it? See I don't really think that this is going to happen. I think that when matters like this are perceived by one side to be making laws where God didn't make them, that brethren are going to feel like it is not within the bounds of what the scriptures demand of us, regarding loving the brotherhood, to concede to a point that is presented as doctrine rather than opinion. And you brethren deal with that the same way that we do to those that are on our right in some matter.

Maurice Barnett – Panelist: Let's get back on track and get with our definitions. All authority answers to the questions: who, what, where, why, when, how, how many, how often, how far. And God will specify some of those at times and that's what we mean by specific authority. All of those, that He does not specify, are the matter of generic options.

Let me illustrate it this way; this is a favorite illustration of mine. I step into a room of teenagers and I say, "Go get some bread." They assume that I mean the kind that you eat. But I've given a specific directive, "Go get some bread." Now as far as I'm concerned it doesn't matter to me, who gets it, where they go, what kind of bread, where they get it, how they paid for it, how they get there, or anything else, as long as they do what I've specified, "Go get some bread." So they might … the whole room go, or it might be one or two or what have you.

But if I want to be a little more specific, and there are other things that are more important to me, I'll specify a little bit more. And I'll say, "Charles, here's the money. You go down to the corner drug store, you get one loaf of thin sliced wholesome sandwich bread, white, and you bring it right back here immediately." And that means that those items are important to me. Now he's still got a lot of choices, and those unspecified choices still I've left up to him, because they're not important to me.

This is what God's done in His word. He may tell us "the who" and "the what" and leave "the how" and "the when" unspecified. When He does that, then we can decide on "the how" and "the when," as long as we get "the who" and "the what" correct. That's the difference between specific authority and the options that are our choices.

Now when it comes to examples, examples may reflect either the specific or the options, either specific or generic authority. And we have to determine that in dealing with examples. OK.

Jamie Sloan – Moderator: Gary?

Gary Workman – Panelist: Ah well, let me continue that line of thinking on. We…our two-minute limit restricts us. I know that Maurice wanted to say more there. But I think regarding the example thing, this is where the rubber meets the road. This is the point on which we divide. We won't divide on necessary inference, now that's the new hermeneuticists. They say, "We have to throw that out, there's no such thing as necessary inference, no such thing as binding implications." We all, who are battling this out on this occasion, disagree with those brethren.

What we disagree on among ourselves is the matter regarding an example, or the record of an action to be more precise. Some brethren have said, well here's the record of an action about a church sending to another church, and what it was for, and whether it could be done or whether it couldn't be done. But there's no statement contained anywhere in the Bible that says that it must be done one way verses the other way.

If we're going to take simply the narrative record of some action as binding in the absence of some explicit or implicit information that is contained in the Bible on that subject, then there's no way in the world that we can avoid being forced to the position that every time you pray you must kneel, since that's the only position mentioned for Christians in the New Testament. And there's no way in the world that you can avoid taking the position that you must fast.

There's no way in the world that you can avoid taking the position that you must use only one container in the Lord's Supper. You may think there were other containers involved but you can't prove it, and you know there was one. There's no way that you can avoid taking the position that we must have an undivided assembly every time the church gets together on some occasion of study. And there's no way you can avoid saying that when we go overseas to do missionary work, evangelistic work overseas, we must go by ship. All of those things are recorded in the Bible. And if we're going to take narrative action as binding, we have to bind those things.

Melvin Curry – Panelist: Maurice did you want to add something else to what you…?

Maurice Barnett – Panelist: No, I'll get to it. Go ahead.

Melvin Curry – Panelist: I suppose that sooner or later we have to clothe examples in flesh and blood. And I certainly believe that we do have to look at each example, as Brother Workman was suggesting, and determine whether it is in reality today binding upon us. And if it is, then we'd better do it. All I can say is, if it really comes down to the licking log and such things as you mentioned are absolutely, unequivocally the bottom line on it, I certainly better yield to it. I may question your conclusions with respect to that. But I don't think that I can question the fact that when finally we have reasoned ourselves down to the fact that this is it and this is the example that if it is authorization we need to do it, no matter what it is. No matter how it might grate our own liberties. That I think is something that maybe the speakers themselves need to get back to in their own lessons.

Jamie Sloan – Moderator: Don?

Don Tarbet – Panelist: Would you believe, Brother Curry, that the idea the Lord's Supper being in an upper room in Acts 20 and verse 7 would always be binding upon us, that we ought to yield to that command on the part of someone? Or where there would be many lights instead of one light where they were gathered together?

Melvin Curry – Panelist: Well, I would say that if what Brother Workman said is true, and apparently you agree with him, that you have to have a command clothed in an example. The fact is…I mean an example backed up by a commandment. There are various commands for assembly and I gather that the brethren assembled in various places. I don't think to the upper room is the only place brethren assembled and therefore I don't think we're limited to the upper room.

Don Tarbet – Panelist: But that's the only record we have of the communion, being in an upper room, is it not?

Melvin Curry – Panelist: Were they in an upper room in 1 Corinthians the 11th chapter?

Don Tarbet – Panelist: We have instructions there, rather than an example. It doesn't tell us what place they did use. But Acts 20:7 mentions the upper room. It was instituted in the upper room in Matthew 26.

Maurice Barnett – Panelist: Can I go now?

Jamie Sloan – Moderator: We're about out of time. We need to decide here maybe one more if we're going to come out equal. One more response from each side. Go ahead.

Maurice Barnett – Panelist: OK. What we find in Acts 20:7 is both reflective of generic options and specific authority. I believe the first day of the week in Acts 20:7 is a reflection of specific authority, not generic. The upper room, the undivided assembly, the one assembly on Sunday, the nighttime, whatever that is, all reflect their choice of options. I believe that the first day of the week Lord's Supper was a result of specific instruction, and there's the difference.

As was pointed out a moment ago, that examples will show choices by first century disciples. Let me word it this way, that choices by first century disciples of options do not limit us to their choices. We're not limited to the choices that they made. In other words, the examples do not limit nor alter generic authority, is what it amounts to.

So that what we have to determine is, first of all, where the specifics are. And in my study I always start, and I think you're correct in that Gary, that I always start with the specific statements of scripture on whatever subject. Get all the passages together that deal with that particular subject, even related passages and related subjects. Find out what the specific instructions are, determine what the options are, and fit the examples into the picture. Now I think that's the correct way to approach the study and then we get all of these different parts correct.

Now I'm not going to have time to develop Acts 20:7 at this particular point. But that states what I think about it.

Gary Workman – Panelist: Well, here's some observations I want to make. If we take the position that some examples that stand alone, that is apart from any explicit or implicit information related to them elsewhere in the Bible. If we take the position that some so called examples are binding and some of them are not binding, we're doomed to disunity. We'll never see it alike. Men simply won't come to the same conclusion.

I noticed in Brother Williams's paper over on page 18, he spoke of MY intuitive responses, MY understanding, MY initial reaction. And Brother Barnett just said I BE-LIEVE, I BELIEVE. Well we all have our assumptions, our approaches, our beliefs, our opinions, what ever it is. But you see if that's what we're going to depend on to decide that this narrative action is binding, and this one over here is not, in the absence of some other information somewhere, we'll never see it alike. And that's why we need to get back to a more consistent position.

The only consistent position, I believe, that we can possibly take is to see all examples as either permissive but not binding, that is an optional way of doing something; or as illustrative of an obligation that is binding that is stated either right there in connection with that narrative or somewhere else on that same subject. I believe this is the only consistent position that we're going to be able to take, and the only way that we'll ever see the Bible alike. So it's in the matter of examples where we really part ways. And we must solve this problem or we're never going to solve these other issues, because it's going to come down to the fact that narrative action is where we differ in the conclusions that we've come to on those points.

Jamie Sloan – Moderator: I know that you're impressed and encouraged, as I am, by the abilities and the spirits of these men. We're thankful to them for this final discussion. Now we're going to spend some time in a question and answer period. And so if you'll please, get those to Brother Lanier or myself. I'll tell you, judging by the nature of this topic, I just have a suspicion that some of these questions are going to be doozies, as we used to say in the country. But we'll take about a 5 or 10-minute break and then look to some question and answers.

Scriptural Hermeneutics
Question and Answer Ground Rules

Jamie Sloan – Moderator: All right, let's get ready to begin again. I've been asked to push meal tickets. (Subdued Laughter, whs) Tomorrow noon still a number left to sell. I know you have enough concern for Brother Wolfgang and his being able to send his children to college, (Laughter, whs) that you are not going to allow him to have to eat or dispose of 57 meals tomorrow at noon. So please….

Steve Wolfgang – Coordinator: 65.

Jamie Sloan – Moderator: 65? 65. So we need you to purchase meal tickets. Will this help? Who's, if we announce who's speaking at that dinner is that going to help? (Subdued Laughter, whs) Brother R. J. Stevens and who? Brother Curtis Camp. That ought to do it right there. So let's please help in regard to that. Brother Barnett said that he was concerned that some of this might confuse. We certainly do have a lot of questions up here, so we're either awfully interested in this or maybe a little confused. And we've got one more.

Maurice Barnett - Panelist: Are we going to continue this speech until midnight? (Laughter, whs)

Jamie Sloan – Moderator: We may have to. There's no way that we can answer all these questions but we'll do the best with them that we can.

Maurice Barnett - Panelist: You'll let Terry Green fall out of a window. (Laughter, whs)

Jamie Sloan – Moderator: That's one thing he could probably do. Again we appreciate very much the sincere efforts of these brethren to be honest. Their convictions honest with the word of God, and addressing these questions in the fine way that they are, encourage us a great deal. And I know that this will be profitable.

Question and Answer Session

Question 1: The first question is to Brother Williams. It says, "What example is followed when women teach classes of children, what command is obeyed?"

Almon Williams – Main Speaker: Well I would say the generic command to teach and that's all I have to say about that. But I would like to say here also at the outset in the two-minutes I have, that in writing 25 pages I probably expressed a lot of stupidity and fuzziness too for that matter. And that's why I'm so willing to listen to people criticize what I have to say, because I'm just the beneficiary thereby. And we should always be that way in regard to our practice as well as in regard, you know, to our preaching.

I believe that generic authority can authorize some things. But that authorizes the generic thing, and it authorizes whatever is essential or reasonable in good judgment to do what God tells us to do. But I think we can push generic authority just as we can take an addition and say it's just an aid when in fact it has become an addition. For example, I would not argue that in some cases instrumental music might aid the singing. I don't know that that's always the case but I would be willing to admit that it might do so. But instrumental music is another kind of music and one can't just justify instrumental music on the basis of an aid. And I don't think we can justify all the things we want to on the basis of generic authority.

Well my mind slipped there, you know on what I wanted to say about that so I'll probably . . . my time is about up now anyway and I'll probably get a chance to talk about this matter of generic authority even more. Do I have any seconds at all?

OK now, I said that I gave up the cooperational approach because I couldn't prove it beyond a reasonable shadow of doubt. Oh yes I could prove, in generic authority of one kind or another, that it might be so. But as Moses E. Lard said many years ago in regard to infant baptism in the households, "What might be so might not be so. And are we going to base a Christian practice on what might not be so?"

Question 2:

Jamie Sloan – Moderator: This question is to Brother Winkler. Brother Winkler, "Where did Paul receive the authority to go to the temple during the days of purification, and purify himself and offer sacrifices as a Christian? Acts 21:26 please give Biblical references. If this is an example that comes from apostolic authority, why isn't it binding today?" Do you want to look at that?

Wendell Winkler – Rebuttal Speaker: I believe an answer to that question is found in 1 Corinthians chapter 9, where Paul said that he became all things to all men to win some to Christ. And of the area, some things that were in the area of custom, and engraven into those given practices, I believe in that day and time, that they could so do by way of accommodation without the compromise of truth in an effort to become all things to all men to win men to Christ. That would be my response to this particular question.

And I practice that same thing today. If I moved into a given community where there was a given practice that was in the area of no sacrifice of principle or faith involved, that I would practice that in order to win people to Jesus Christ. If I thought my influence would be curtailed and or that my influence would be greater in winning Adventists to the Lord, if I moved into a total saturated Adventist community and feeling as they do about pork, I would just not eat pork. But I wouldn't bind that on anybody by any means. But that would be my answer to that particular question.

And I don't want to take a polemic posture here, but I am…Have you given me a time signal that my time is up? I want to explore this matter about an example, and commands are examples, and that commands do not stand alone. If I understood it correctly, correct me if I'm saying that incorrectly. But the commands are examples and that they're binding because they're examples. What about Acts 2:38? There was no example to which these people could relate when they were told to repent and to be baptized. Suppose the New Testament just stopped right there? There was no example in anyway at all pertaining to that. It was a directive, it was a command, and I believe it will stand alone.

Question 3:
Jamie Sloan – Moderator: All right. Brother Barnett, I've got two here relative to Acts 20 and 7. I wonder if you could take both of them and thoroughly discuss them in two minutes or less? (Laughter, whs) The first one says, "Brother Barnett would you please explain further why examples do not limit generic authority using Acts 20 and

7 as point of discussion?" And the other one says, "Why is the first day of the week observance of the Lord's Supper binding but the upper room is not? What is the specific instruction related to Acts 20:7?" Do you want to just look at while you…?

Maurice Barnett – Panelist: No, I've got it, thank you. In Matthew 26:29, Jesus said that he would not drink that fruit of the vine with them again until that day in the kingdom. The verbs in the passage are all present tense verbs that require repetition, require something that continues. It is a phrase that says it is that day in the kingdom, not that day of the kingdom. The phrase "that day" is from the Greek phrase *tes hemaras ekeines,* "that the day." Which in every place in the New Testament always refers to a 24-hour period, without exception. Jesus had a particular day in mind for the continued performance of the elements that he had prescribed.

And then you can go to Acts 20 and 7 that when the disciples came together on the first day of the week to break bread, it is a specific. It is a specific of what Jesus was talking about in Matthew 26:29, so it is a reflection of specific authority. Acts 20 and 7 identified the day that Jesus was talking about in Matthew 26.

The other elements in Acts 20 refer to elements of option. The number of meetings on the first day of the week are in the realm of option. The place, geography and topography are in the realm of option. The time of day is a matter of option. That makes it a matter of generic authority. But the first day of the week as the day for eating the Lord's Supper is a reflection of specific authority.

Question 4:
Jamie Sloan – Moderator: All right, thank you. All right. Let's see, we'll go to the other side and come back over here. Brother Workman I have two questions that seem to be the same question regarding "What about the plurality of elders?." One question says, "Where is the related instruction regarding the plurality of elders except in simple examples? Must there be a plurality of elders in each local congregation, if so why?"

Gary Workman – Panelist: Well, Acts 14:23 is not the only verse you have on that subject in the Bible. Titus 1:5 says "elders in every city," and I think by implication we have to understand that they had one church in each city. When you go, for example, to the letter to the Philippians. You have right at the outset in verse 1, it's mentioned the

Bishops and the Deacons and all the saints. And you go over to chapter 4 and Paul refers to them as no church but you, singular. And we understand that was one church in that city. And therefore it's by the process of implication that we gather, by necessary inference, that we can determine that Titus 1:5 specifies a plurality of elders. You don't need Acts 14:23 to prove that.

Jamie Sloan – Moderator: All right.

Gary Workman – Panelist: I wonder if I might add just a little bit to what was said just here, real quick.

Jamie Sloan – Moderator: Does he have time left?

Gary Workman – Panelist: I believe what you said about that day, I think that specifies it. That shows though, that the Acts 20:7 passage does not stand alone. And that's the very point that I was making. I would go however, from Matthew 26:29 on that day and jump over to Revelation 1:10 and say that is the Lord's Day. And what day is that? 1 Corinthians 16:1-2, it was the first day of the week. I don't need Acts 20 verse 7 on that.

Maurice Barnett – Panelist: Yeah, and that's the point. Take your Matthew 26 and Acts 20:7 then fit 1 Corinthians 16 into the picture and you've got first day of the week service.

Gary Workman – Panelist: And of course, we agree that an example can corroborate or substantiate something that is specified, but what we're saying is if all you had was that and you didn't have Matthew 26:29 then you couldn't bind it. See?

Question 5:

Jamie Sloan – Moderator: Thank you. Brother Curry "Please deal with Paul's refusal to circumcise Titus as it bears on your willingness to give up classes, cups, etc."

Melvin Curry – Panelist: Well, I don't know what the problem is. I said that in the first place about the giving up, you . . . that you do it in the light of what Paul said in 1 Corinthians chapter 8, 1 Corthinans chapter 10, and Romans 14th chapter. Paul is not saying that simply because an individual has an opinion and wants to bind that on everyone that I'm going to have to yield to it. What I said is, if a person unequivocally establishes that this is our authority, and our only authority, then we need to yield to what God says. And we need to defer to the individuals judgment in the matter. That doesn't mean that I have to simply do whatever everybody wants me to do, or give

up what everybody wants me to give up. There are limitations, in other words, scriptural limitations.

Question 6:

Jamie Sloan – Moderator: Brother Tarbet this fellow writes just like me, but it's not my question, so I'll try to read this. "If examples are only authoritative when there is a commandment or necessary implication behind them, would not the commandment or necessary implication be the binding force rather than the examples themselves?"

Don Tarbet – Panelist: I believe in taking all of the scriptures on a topic and the example would be a demonstration of the binding force. But you have to have more than just the example alone in order to know what God wants us to do.

Question 7:

Jamie Sloan – Moderator: All right we're back to Brother Williams. "You stated that absolute silence is non permissive and non authorizing. In view of this, how do you explain the origin and use of synagogues in the Old Testament which are sanctioned by Jesus and by the Apostles? The Old Testament is absolutely silent concerning the synagogue, that is in origin, use, design, etc."

Almon Williams – Main Speaker: I believe that this argument is often used by Christian Church brethren; of course I'm not saying that someone asked that question. And I've thought about it quite a bit because it's often brought up in discussions about the New Testament silence on instrumental music. And I know especially Lewis Foster, R.C. Foster's son, tried to make this argument about the synagogue.

In the first place, I would observe that I don't know for sure that just because Jesus attended a synagogue that he necessarily approved of synagogue worship, although I'm . . . that'd have to be proven. You just can't assume it. But I think you know, if you look at the scriptures you'll see, I forget the passage, I think it's in Leviticus chapter 23 or so, where God calls for a holy convocation on the Sabbath day, as well as holy convocations or assemblies on certain other holy days.

And it gets right down to what we've talked about here, that the New Testament teaches the church to come together in one place. And that requires a common place to come together. And the nature of a place is for our judgment.

The Old Testament authorized throughout their cities

a local convocation on the Sabbath day and they just built buildings, synagogues, to gather in for that purpose. Now if one means the organization of the synagogue let him say so and I might be able to speak to that point, and maybe not.

Do I have any more time? OK now, I certainly agree with a lot that's being said here, how that we must always look at everything God has to say about something. And we'll find clues here and there about whether an action is meant to be for general practice. But I still go by the four things I said about the relationship between examples and commands. Now … (Time expired and Almon quits in mid sentence, whs)

Jamie Sloan – Moderator: Don't you marvel at the self-control of these regarding these time limits? It is beyond my wildest imagination. I'm trying to find ones that pursues a little different area.

Question 8:

Brother Winkler this says "Both speakers tonight took a strong stand against the new hermeneutic. It was suggested earlier today that we can't know for sure whether such a question interferes with fellowship. Can we successfully avoid the new hermeneutic while continuing in fellowship with those who teach it? Can we successfully avoid the new hermeneutic while continuing to fellowship with those who teach it?"

Wendell Winkler – Rebuttal Speaker: This gets into a discussion of really what is the new hermeneutic. I'll just simply say this, that if the new hermeneutic is followed to its ultimate conclusion, if I understand it correctly, it will automatically result in a failure to fellowship those who espouse the ultimate consequences of it.

And this may be an oversimplification of it but the new hermeneutic is that to which I made reference a moment ago in the speech. In which, these brethren have made the statement, that the New Testament is to be looked upon as a collection of love letters and not as being constitutional. And that it is largely relational and not coital.

Now the bottom-line of all of that, is that we can treat divine legislation that has to do with the work and the worship and the organization of the church rather loosely. And that's just the bottom line of it. And so if the bottom line of that is pursued, then the purity of New Testament worship will have been destroyed. And that being the case, I would have no qualms about the fellowship being drawn

right there as it's drawn with the digressives today over the use of the mechanical instrument of music.

Question 9:

Jamie Sloan – Moderator: Brother Barnett it's your turn I guess. "Do you believe that elders of one church assuming the oversight of a work that all are equally related to violates any rule of hermeneutics, if so what or how? Must options be lawful?"

Maurice Barnett – Panelist: Gary brought up a little bit ago that we base our opposition to some of these plans and establish our picture of the New Testament church from examples. I took it that that meant examples alone. That is not so. We have never done that.

We always start and have always started with the organization: autonomy of the local church, the oversight of elders, and the limitation of the oversight of elders. And we're talking there about specific commandments; we're talking about specific statements. And then we go from there in talking about the work of the local church and fit the examples into the picture to show them as illustrations. I agree that what we mean by examples is simply a description of the way disciples acted in the first century in carrying out commands. And what we have attempted to show is that the specific statements in regard to the work of the church and the oversight of elders is in complete harmony with the image of the examples presented, the examples are in keeping with that. That's where we've always started.

As far as expediencies are concerned and options are concerned, they are acceptable only if they are lawful, but expediencies and options must first be lawful, which means that there has to be some authority for it to start with, and we're talking about specific authority. You do not have expediencies and options without specific instruction of some kind.

Gary Workman – Panelist: When James . . . I wonder if I might comment on that just a second. This really isn't our field, I don't think, this question, not directly at least. But here's the thing where you talk about autonomy, the position seems to be taken that one church sends to another church for the purpose of benevolence there's no autonomy violated. But if one church sends to another church for the purpose of evangelism somehow that robs the sending church of their autonomy.

This is something that somebody has concluded on

their own. You don't find a statement on this in the Bible. There's no hermeneutical principle to lead you to that conclusion. The only way you come to that conclusion is by saying, "Well look, we find an example here where they sent this for this purpose and we find no example where they sent it for this other purpose therefore we're going to say that that's binding on us and we've got to do it that very same way." If that's the way we establish Bible authority, then we must also bind sending that money for, to the evangelist out in the field by the method of personal messenger, rather than putting it in the United States Mail.

Maurice Barnett – Panelist: No. The problem involved in that, as far as the oversight of elders are concerned, is that an eldership, in regard to the practice that we see generally, is that they assume the oversight or take the oversight of work of other congregations and they oversee their money. And the work is done out here away from the supervising church. So here the church is that sent the money to the supervising church, who does the work out here, it's not something that's done here, something that's done out here. And in that they violate autonomy, in that one eldership is overseeing the work of other churches.

When the benevolent…when the money was sent to the churches that were in need, it went to the place that was in need, just exactly as the money that was sent to evangelists was sent to where the need was. So it isn't a matter of an inconsistency on the subject of autonomy.

Gary Workman – Panelist: But I think the same position has been taken if the sending….from the one church to the other church was for their own needs, right there in that locality, the same objection has been raised, and saying that's a violation of the autonomy of that sending church.

Maurice Barnett – Panelist: But not in the area of benevolence.

Gary Workman – Panelist: No, in the area of evangelism.

Maurice Barnett – Panelist: I see. No.

Gary Workman – Panelist: See. So there's an inconsistency. If it was for their benevolent needs it didn't violate the sending church's autonomy, if it was for their evangelistic needs, it did somehow violate the sending churches autonomy. That doesn't make sense.

Maurice Barnett – Panelist: It has to with the realm of

what you're talking about as need. Now you've used the word "need" in two different ways. You have to define your word "need." Everybody needs the gospel, not every body needs a loaf of bread. Now what do we mean by need?

Gary Workman – Panelist: Well, in other words, here's a church that cannot afford to pay a preacher. If another congregation sends the money to that church and they take the money and then they pay the preacher the position that I've read from many of you brethren is that that would violate the autonomy of the sending church.

Maurice Barnett – Panelist: Now let's put the preacher in Germany. Now let's let this eldership take care of 100 preachers in Germany and let's send this money by these churches over there, what do you have?

Gary Workman – Panelist: Well, see…

Maurice Barnett – Panelist: That's the…whether he's preaching right there on the spot or whether he's in Germany is beside the point.

Gary Workman – Panelist: OK. If it is beside the point, then we need to get back to the first illustration and say that would…do you agree that would violate the sending churches too, in that case?

Maurice Barnett – Panelist: Oh yeah. There's autonomy that's violated.

Gary Workman – Panelist: Yeah.

Maurice Barnett – Panelist: But his turning of work to which they're both equally related over to one eldership, and this is the point. They're both equally related to evangelism…

Gary Workman – Panelist: No, I mean…I mean…

Maurice Barnett – Panelist: …it's not so in regard to benevolence. You have too different circumstances, again you have two different definitions of "need."

Gary Workman – Panelist: Maybe you misunderstood my question. What I mean is, a needy church up in Idaho that can't afford to pay the preacher. Could a church in Dallas send money up to that church and let that church take that money and then pay the preacher?

Maurice Barnett – Panelist: Again you're using…

Gary Workman – Panelist: They're not equally related.

Maurice Barnett – Panelist: You've got the word "need"

again in the picture and you're using the word "need" in two different ways. Who says they NEED a preacher? That's the question.

Gary Workman – Panelist: Ooooh, I thought we all needed a preacher. (Laughter, whs)

Jamie Sloan – Moderator: I think I just lost oversight of the question.

Maurice Barnett – Panelist: Do you want control back? (Laughter, whs)

Jamie Sloan – Moderator: I only marginally possessed it, but I certainly lost it. (Laughter, whs) But I actually believe that it was for the benefit for the question and answer discussion that I did. So I don't lament the passing of it. (Laughter, whs)

Question 10:

Brother Tarbet, "What would you say to the question, "What role does human reasoning play in hermeneutics?"

Don Talbert – Panelist: I think good common sense needs to be applied all the time. But human reasoning apart from divine directive of course would be out of the question. I believe that the scripture is logical and human reasoning will help us to determine what God's will is.

Question 11:

Jamie Sloan – Moderator: Brother Curry, "Is there an example for paying an evangelist from the first day of the week contribution? Should there be for us to practice that?"

Melvin Curry – Panelist: That's a case in which I personally would go to more than one passage to establish the principle. There certainly is the statement that is made by Paul, "I robbed other churches taking wages of them to do you service." The case of the Philippians as they supported Paul. And as far as the contribution on the Lord's Day is concerned, I think that really there is more than one issue involved in 1 Corinthians 16. And we might make a mistake on that of saying that it is all related to simply the authorization of the... I mean of the contribution. There is, I think a day of assembly, and I don't know Maurice and I might argue with each other on this, that there is a day of assembly that is authorized in 1 Corinthians, if you take the context of the 11th chapter and the 16th chapter together. But I couldn't do it by one simple passage, I would do it on the basis of putting together what is said in several passages to draw that conclusion.

Question 12:

Jamie Sloan – Moderator: All right, we're back to Brother Williams and what may lamentably be our final round. Brother Almon "Please explain why the two specific examples of the Lord's Supper being served in an upper room, Luke 22:12, Acts 27:8, do not bind meeting in the upper room, whereas we partake of the Lord's Supper in the absence of any example of the Lord's Supper being eaten anywhere else?"

Almon Williams – Main Speaker: Well, of course we realize that there has to be... for a thing to be something we ought to practice or must practice, we must have uniformity in the thing. I'm not sure we have as much uniformity in regard to this upper room as we seem to think. For example, in the Gospels the Lord gave a preview in the Lord's Supper in an upper room. As a guest he asked for the guestroom. That seems to be the circumstances of the case and that seems to explain perfectly why he instituted or gave a preview of it in the upper room. Now in Acts 20 we don't just have an upper room, we have an upper room upper room. The fellow who fell down, Eutychus, I think that was his name wasn't it, who had had...he was in the third story. So there's a upper room of an upper room. And I'm not sure it's just as cut and dried an upper room thing as we think.

A moment ago I think Brother Curry was trying to think of a passage that might show that this was not so uniform as we sometimes get the impression. Now do we agree that in Acts chapter 2 and the following chapters when the church met in the Temple that they were having the Lord's Supper steadfastly? Now I don't think the Temple was an upper room there but they were having it in the Temple on the ground floor so to speak. So I think if you study the facts in the case you will see that we don't have uniformity in regard to the Lord's Supper having to be in an upper room. Now, if I could remember what I wanted to say. How much time do I have?

I want to say something about this matter of giving up something for a brother's conscience. It seems to me sometimes brethren we say, "Well you won't give up anything for a brother's conscience and I won't either." How does that show the spirit of Christ? Are we trying to win some argument? Are we trying to say that you're as wrong as we are, and there...? (Time ends and quits in mid sentence. Laughter, whs)

Jamie Sloan – Moderator: A lot of your questions that

we're not going to be able to get to tonight are excellent questions and the reason it parallels in regard to a lot of the issues that we're going to be discussing tomorrow and Saturday. And so for that reason I'm…

Maurice Barnett – Panelist: Would you mind if we took one more? Do we have the time?

Jamie Sloan – Moderator: What say you other brethren?

Maurice Barnett – Panelist: David Tant came to me. He especially wanted me to deal with one particular subject that on…

Jamie Sloan – Moderator: You…you have got a… each one of you is going to have another …

Maurice Barnett – Panelist: Oh, you're going to get back to….

Jamie Sloan – Moderator: Yeah.

Maurice Barnett – Panelist: Gooood. (Laughter, whs)

Jamie Sloan – Moderator: Yeah. So Brother Winkler …

Maurice Barnett – Panelist: I thought you were cutting this off. That's why. (Laughter, whs)

Jamie Sloan – Moderator: No, no, no. We reserve the right to go overtime a little bit. It's still only ten minutes till ten. We're going to take another round of questions among the panel and then our two speakers get a final closing two minutes.

Question 13:

Brother Winkler, "What scriptures teach that expediency is a means of expressing or establishing authority?"

Wendell Winkler – Rebuttal Speaker: Brethren, I'm concerned when people ask the question, "By what authority do you have a local preacher? By what authority do you have songbooks? By what authority do you have a visual aid?," as if there is no authority for it. And the reason why that's asked is, now since you can't give any Bible authority for it and yet you practice it, then we can engage in other activities for which there is no Bible authority, namely for example the use of a mechanical instrument of music.

I think the Primus of all of that is false. I believe there is Biblical authority for a songbook, for this reason. Obligations of necessity involve an expedient, that is, that that expedites the carrying through with the command that assists in the implementation of the command. And the

command is to sing. The book is an expedient that assists us, that aids us, that expedites in the carrying through with that, and because of that, is authorized thus in the field of expediency.

And I think also that gets back to the question a moment ago asked. And that is, "How does the human reasoning enter into this matter of establishing Biblical authority?" God made man a rational being. And he adapted the Bible to man's mind, and therefore He intended for him to use some rational reasoning in working out these matters, 1 Thessalonians chapter 5 verse 21.

But brethren, in the few minutes that I have left here, I think we're getting down to some crux of the matter. I wish we could go till midnight, we do have that example in Acts 20 (Laughter, whs), but it's probably one of those optionals and not obligatory. (Laughter, whs) I would not want to follow the example of Eutychus (subdued Laughter, whs).

But I want to ask these good brethren, and I do count them as good brethren, good in heart and good in attitude. If they get their paycheck out of the contribution of 1 Corinthians 16:2? Now, I believe with all my heart that you good brethren have preached that. Now if I'm wrong I want to stand corrected. But I believe that you've been teaching that your paycheck comes from 1 Corinthians 16:2. Now if our paychecks come from 1 Corinthians 16 and verse 2, let's suppose that the church in Corinth sent that contribution to the Jerusalem saints. And let's suppose that Paul was preaching in Jerusalem. My question is, could his salary come from the contribution that had been sent? And so if his salary could be taken from the contribution that had been sent, then we have an example of one church sending to another church in the field of preaching the gospel.

Maurice Barnett – Panelist: No we don't. (Laughter, whs)

Wendell Winkler – Rebuttal Speaker: Never have? Not one among you?

Maurice Barnett – Panelist: You were talking to the Panelist. You weren't talking to … You were talking to us. No, we don't.

Question 14:

Jamie Sloan – Moderator: So many of these questions are dealing with the Lord's Supper in Acts 20:7; that's…

we've focused on so much. This is the same song but a little different verse. Gary, "If narratives or examples do not express binding authority, then are the parables of Jesus binding or what's binding in the example Jesus used, remember Lots' wife?"

Gary Workman – Panelist: Well, here's where I think, that we're mixing up example with implication. And by the way I don't know that any of the three of us on this side of the table really expressed this as clearly as we needed to about Brother Williams remarks right at the end of his presentation. We don't believe that all commands come down to examples. When you say you can't find your name written in the Bible and therefore it was written to somebody else and that's simply an example. No we don't call that an example. It's by implication that we get this. We understand that by the process of necessary inference. It's not example, there is an implied command to us, via those first readers or hearers of what was said. But I'm kind of like brother whatever his name was earlier, who said he can't remember the question. What, what, what, read that again for me. What… (Laughter, whs)

Jamie Sloan – Moderator: Remember Lot's wife, I think it was.

Gary Workman – Panelist: Yeah. Thank you, thank you, thank you, thank you… (Laughter, whs) There. You see when you're dealing with something like that, or a parable, you're dealing with matters that are stated either explicitly or implicitly. This is not an example; this is something Jesus is saying. He's giving teaching.

When we read about patternism in the New Testament, we don't read a thing about the patternism of examples. We read about the pattern of sound words. We read about that form, that pattern of doctrine, which was delivered you. That's patternism in the New Testament. None of this relates to examples, and so I think we need to get our focus back sharper on what's example, what's direct statement, what is implication, and many of these problems will be solved.

And furthermore, if I can get this in quickly. I don't believe that when Paul said, "The things which you saw and heard" and so forth "in me these things do," or "be ye imitators of me as I also am of Christ," that this means every deed that Paul did we have to do it that way. If he rode on a donkey, then we have to do it to. Certainly it doesn't mean that. It's simply talking about his manner of life. He-

brew 13:7, "Remember those that have the rule over you and considering the issue of their life imitate their faith." That is the imitation of Paul. And any other individual or church mentioned in the New Testament, and we can be just as good examples on that as any of those first century Christians were.

Jamie Sloan – Moderator: Brother Barnett you're allowed to ask and answer your own question sir.

Maurice Barnett – Panelist: You don't have one there for me?

Jamie Sloan – Moderator: Well, I thought you said Brother Tant …

Maurice Barnett – Panelist: I think one is in there. I thought you were going to cut them off there but I think it's there.

Jamie Sloan – Moderator: Well, I didn't see it. Do you remember what it was?

Maurice Barnett – Panelist: OK, it has to do with the examples limiting generic authority. And the point was that Acts 14:23 is the only passage that we've got in regard to elders being appointed in every church, which is an example and therefore examples do limit generic authority. I want to point out that in 1 Peter chapter 5, and it's a point I think Gary made, 1 Peter chapter 5 is a statement in regard to elders, plural, with flocks. And tend the flock of God which is among you. The epistle was written to the dispersion in Asia Minor and wherever those flocks were, there were plurality of elders.

The book of James was written to the dispersion, in chapter 5 he talks…says that if any among you were sick let him call for the elders of the church, which meant the elders of the church where they were. By necessary conclusion, there are elders in churches where men are qualified to be elders and those are statements, statements not examples, then Acts 14:23 will fit into the picture. If we say that examples limit generic authority then we will be limited to an upper room, we will be limited to one assembly on Sunday, we will be limited to the choices, the options of disciples in the first century. And we have to take care of that.

Now, one other thing in regard to Brother Winkler. I take it that he was saying that 1 Corinthians 16 was a contribution for the poor. And if we are supported out of the contribution like 1 Corinthians 16 then we're in violation of it because that's support of preachers. No we do not use that exclusively. We have passages that talk about church support of preachers. Paul says that, "The laborer is worthy of his hire," you'll "not muzzle the ox that treadeth out the corn." He told the Corinthians he had a right to receive from them, that was church support of the preacher. What 1 Corinthians 16 does, is it shows God's way of getting the money together. It was done for all of the churches, the churches of Galatia, the churches of Achaia, the churches of Macedonia; they were all instructed to do it that way. That's God's way of getting money together for whatever work that he has. But our authority for support of preachers comes from other passages. Thank you.

Question 15:

Jamie Sloan – Moderator: Thank you Brother Barnett. Brother Tarbet, "I assume that you believe that brethren forming congregations and that congregational autonomy are binding. How do we learn of these except through examples of such being the case in the first century?"

Don Tarbet – Panelist: I gather the question has to do with learning of local congregations? Well, I think that can be established in three ways: through example, through implication, and through command. We have examples of congregations and their autonomy being established, without question. We also have in 1 Timothy 3:15 how that we're to behave properly in the church. So that implies the church must exist before this command can be carried out. Then in Acts 11 we find where the disciples sent to the needy in Judea. We sometimes say that that means the church. And if that be the case then we have in the Great Commission, Christ saying, "Go and make disciple of all the nations." Therefore He's commanding that local congregation be established with their autonomy.

Question 16:

Jamie Sloan – Moderator: All right. And Brother Curry, your final question. "What would you say is the main difference between Almon and Wendell's approach to hermeneutics establishing Bible authority?" Kind of a summing up conflict here.

Melvin Curry – Panelist: My own impression is that, based on what Brother Winkler said, I don't think there is much he said that Brother Williams would not agree with. I think there's some things that Brother Williams said that Brother Winkler wouldn't agree with. That's just a general impression that I have. It seemed to me that Brother Winkler talked more in generalities.

But I want to take the opportunity to say something in maybe the minute or so that I have left, because I'm not going to be able to stay here the entire time. I want to express my own personal gratitude to the attitude that everybody's manifested this evening. We're all here as individuals. Nobody's representing anybody but himself.

Brothers and sisters, I wish we would talk more. I wish we would sit down and open our Bibles more. I wish we'd pray together more. And I wish we would, as we grow older, have more and more of a disposition to give up, rather than to lay down and put up barriers. I'm not a Universalist, I'm not looking for peace at the price of no truth, but the wholesome, open investigation of truth will always be productive. You know what happened to us? We quit talking, we quit studying the Bible together, and we drifted apart. And we began to raise barriers that in many instances should never have been raised.

I don't know the solutions to all of our problems. But please, on a one on one basis, and however way we can be open about it, let's take this as very serious for the God of Heaven, for our Lord Jesus Christ. And let's really pursue the reality of what it means to be a Christian.

Scriptural Hermeneutics
Day 1 Speech 2
Summation Speeches

Jamie Sloan – Moderator: All right! We want to ask the two main speakers if they would like to take two minutes each for a final summary Statement.

Almon Williams – Main Summation Speaker: I should like to express my appreciation to Brother Winkler for his fine attitude. And as Brother Curry said, I virtually agree with every thing he said with maybe just a few exceptions. And as Brother Curry also said, I've just come here to speak for myself, not even for Brother Barnett or Brother Curry, or the non-institutional brethren per say. Whatever value that I've been able to express, that may have been of help to you, I'm glad to be able to do so. And I think I can learn as much from the criticisms of Brother Barnett and Curry as I can from the other brethren who have spoken up here.

But I want to explain this one thing. I still insist that when you get right down to the whole . . . you know… brass tacks, that there is not a command in the Bible or any other fact that is not incased in an example. Take for example Brother Winkler's example, Acts 2:38. To whom was it spoken? It wasn't spoken to people in the 20th Century. It wasn't spoken to me. It was spoken to people on the day of Pentecost who lived 2000 years ago. Now, if by necessary inference, I conclude that I'm in the same boat with them dispensationally and otherwise; then I'll say that example is an imitable action for me to follow, if I wish to have remission of sins.

And I still insist; now maybe this is just a matter of definition of terms. And it's just my way of dealing with the matter, especially when people say, "Well commands are binding but examples are not." Really, everything is reducible to an example of some kind. But some actions are really put forth as imitable actions, or samples of what we should do.

Brother Bill Humble explained in the Arlington Meeting why he changed from being a non-institutionalist to an institutionalist. I've just gone the other way. And

I would say you can just prove it. You can just prove the local church from his arguments. You can't prove the pastor system, and you can't prove the type of congregational cooperation from his data which he was trying to prove. It might be true but it might not be true.

Wendell Winkler – Rebuttal Summation Speaker: The question that I want to ask about the Acts passage is to those in Acts 2, to the Pentecostians, "Where is the example? What example did they have?" I can use an example to me, but what about them? Did not the command stand on its own two feet, when given to them in 2:38? Where is the example related to that particular passage, and to that particular conversion?

In my closing comments, I would like to echo the statements that have been sincerely expressed by all of the Panelists, concerning the attitudes that have been manifested by the participants, and how grateful I am to have seen that and to have been a part of it. I want to express also appreciation to Brother Lanier and to Brother Wolfgang again, for their contributions to the efforts that are now being expended.

I do want to conclude by saying this by way of a summational statement on examples. Again there are examples in the Bible that are obligatory, that must be followed. Acts chapter 20 and all the corroborating passages that we've been given this evening substantiate that. There're examples that are optional, and may be followed. I think we need to keep that in mind, about the authority wrapped up in examples.

I think also that we need to do more study in the area of the generic and the specific areas of authority. Not binding in areas that are generic and not loosing in areas that are specific. I believe that the study today indicates that if there is such a meeting such as this conducted again that we need to deal with that by way of a concentration, being more concentrated in that given study.

In Acts chapters 13 and 14 a wonderful, wonderful thing occurred, the evangelization of the then known world. Then all of a sudden a problem arose in Acts 15, and incidentally hermeneutical studies of Acts chapter 15 become extremely interesting. There was a command there; there were examples there; there were implications there in Acts 15. But there was a problem that arose, and so they took time out to deal with the problem or with the issue. And then right back into chapter 16 and 17 they went back to the job of evangelizing.

And brethren, before we had these segmenting that has occurred among us, we were evangelizing. We have some challenges that have presented themselves among us. Surely we will not stay here forever in our generation and give as a heritage to our children a divided brotherhood over these matters. Let us leave Acts 15 and get over to Acts 16 and start evangelizing a lost world. For remember according to John 17:20-21, a lost world is the price we're paying for a divided brotherhood.

Jamie Sloan – Moderator: Do we have any more in closing? Steve do you have any announcements?

Steve Wolfgang: Registration cards.

Jamie Sloan – Moderator: We've had excellent attendance today but a number of you have not found the time or thought about registering. We plead . . . we need for you to do that. Please stop by and fill out a registration card, also remember the luncheon tomorrow. We will look to have a good rest tonight and be back in the morning to start. Yes Steve? (The tape ends here whs)

END OF SPEECH TWO, DAY ONE.

END OF DAY ONE

Congregational
vs. Individual Activities

Day 2 Cycle 1
Friday, July 13, 1990

Participants

Non-Institutional Brethren
Ferrel Jenkins — Rebuttal
Martin C. Pickup — Panelist 1
Robert Harkrider — Panelist 2

Institutional Brethren
Cecil May — Main
Joe Blakeney — Panelist 3
Avon Malone — Panelist 4

Congregational Versus Individual Activities
Day 2 Speech 1 Main
Cecil May

Introduction: *May, Cecil. Presently heads the Magnolia Bible College, noted lecturer, author and educational man for 39 years in Holly Sprints, Ripley, Ashland, and Fulton, MS, and Portland, OR. Former Teacher at Columbia Christian.*

Thank you. Thanks to each of you for being here. And to those who are responsible for it, thank you for inviting me. I edit a little publication called *Preacher Talk*, and one thing about it that preachers like particularly, it's free. And if you would like to receive it and do not, if you will give me something with your name and address on it before you leave here, I'll be delighted to, or even send it to me later, I'll be glad to add you to the mailing list to that publication.

To give you a little bit of an orientation as to where, at least I perceive that I'm coming from, I'd like to begin by saying that I am a Christian. And I'm saved by the grace of God through faith in our Lord Jesus Christ, and that's all I am. And by deliberate determination, that's all I ever intend to be, in terms of labels that can be applied to one religiously. I don't like camping, a lot of camping going on, this camp and that camp. And I realize that the heart is deceitful and difficult to know. But in so far as I know MY heart, the only camp that I'm interested in being a part of is the one that Jesus Christ makes me a part of when He redeems me by His blood.

I cherish the fact that I have a letter in my files from Brother Yater Tant, who was reacting to an article in *Preacher Talk*, and who referred to me as a closet anti. He meant that as a compliment and I took it as such, and as I said I cherish it. I have another letter from one of you whom I won't name, who says that, and this is a quote I think, "Some of you conservative liberals and some of us liberal conservatives, are probably closer to either other, than each of us is to the radicals in our own camp." And having already said that I try my best to stay out of camps, I still understood what he was saying, and appreciated the remark.

Brother Ed Harrell preached a sermon at the Helton Street church in Florence, Alabama a number of years ago that I was privileged to hear. He dealt with some of the same matters he dealt with up here last night in regard to what he refers to as the hermeneutic, the commitment to believing the Bible and doing what the Bible says and the way by which one determines what the Bible says. And he outlined a great lesson on that beginning with what it takes to become a Christian and continuing on with what that hermeneutic suggests some Christians ought to do. And toward the end of that lessen he outlined some things that, though he didn't give great emphasis to it, I understood where he was coming from and understood that he was suggesting some thing that I would not agree with. But at the same time, at the conclusion of that lesson, I remember very distinctly that he said, "Now some of the details of this may be arguable. And it might be possible" he said, "that there are some honest and good hearted people trying to work through this hermeneutic. And still committed to the basic principle in the word of God, might come out in a different place." And he said, "If you're in that category," he was not talking to me he was talking to the whole audience, but he said, "if you're in that category then," he said, "there's a basis for us to talk." He said, "Only if you're not interested in the process have we no basis for conversation." And I think the reason that we are here today is because we have a basis for conversation.

The writer of the 119th Psalm, verse 63 said, "I am a companion of all them that fear thee, and of all them that keep thy precepts." I heard Brother Johnny Ramsey say one time, "That's one of the finest texts on the subject of fellowship that there is in the Bible." And that is my aim.

What we're talking about this night...this morning, individual verses congregational activity, is kind of an inside topic. I don't know if ever you've been around when an inside joke was told. That's a joke that's funny to all of those people who know about something else that has gone before, but means nothing to anybody else. And if you're ever around when an inside joke is told, and you're not inside, it leave you sort of feeling left out. You really just don't know what, you know, what's going on and why are they laughing and what's so funny.

This is an inside topic. The majority of the religious world would have not the slightest inkling of what we'd be talking about, looking at the announced topic for this morning. And even if they could figure out what it was that we were talking about, the majority of them would not have the slightest inclination to be interested in it. And yet it's a topic that is interesting enough to have brought some of us from Florida, from Mississippi, and from Canada, out here at 9:00 in the morning on a hot Friday the 13th, because we are concerned about it.

At the Nashville Meeting I sat next to a young man who in the course of a discussion, like some of the ones that we're having this week said, "I don't understand this mentality." He said, "I don't think like this, and I don't understand those who do." He said that to me as an aside, as we were sitting on a platform just about like that (pointing to a Panelist table, whs). And as he has developed further in, if not in his thinking, at least in the enunciation of his thinking, it's become very obvious to me at least that his expression, "I don't think like this," meant explicitly that, "I don't think in terms of coming to the Bible with deciding what the Bible teaches us, that as a church we can do and cannot do." It's becoming increasingly evident that he doesn't think like that.

A great portion of the religious world doesn't think like that. But you and I both think like that. And that's why we are here and why we are having this discussion. So even though it's an inside topic, and a lot of people might even think it's the inside joke, it's serious to us. And that's, in a sense a compliment I believe to us, because of the particular concern that we have.

To define the issue of individual and congregational activity and the difference between them, let me read a conversation. The conversation never occurred, but it's a typical composite of conversations that do occur, and that sort of set the reason why this issue is discussed. (Person 1 whs) "The church cannot scripturally give material aid to a non-Christian. As individuals we should be good Samaritans to anybody in need, but the Bible only authorizes the church from its treasury to support saints. 1 Corinthians

16:1 speaks of the contribution for the saints, and all the examples in the New Testament are the same." (Person 2, whs) "Yeah, but doesn't the Bible tell us to do good to all men and especially to them that are of the household of faith? Doesn't it tell us, to visit the fatherless and the widows in their affliction? Don't those passages say that every one in need is the object of our benevolence that we're just to give special attention to members of the church?" (Person 1, whs) "Yes. But those passages are to individuals. Individual duties must not be confused with cooperate duties. There's a difference between what individuals can do and what the church can do. Individuals are told to go into business or do gainful work so as to have to give to him that needeth, the church is not authorized to do that. Individuals are specifically told to take care of their own parents in order that the church not be burdened. There's no way to say that the church is authorized to do everything that individuals are commanded to do."

That, as I perceive it, is the issue that this question of individual verses congregational activity has grown out of, and the reason that it is discussed. And we raise the question then, "Is it sinful to use funds from congregational treasuries to feed the poor, at the same time sinful for me, as an individual, not to feed them?" Are only individuals permitted to practice what the Bible calls pure and undefiled religion, and are churches specifically forbidden to… or are churches forbidden to do so, not specifically but at lease implicitly, as the discussion would go. This is the issue under discussion.

I'd like to deal with it this morning in the limited time that is available, in three ways. I want to talk about a definition of the church. I want to talk about some difficulties with consistence. And then I want to talk about what we mean by, or what I mean at least, by a matter of judgement.

First of all a matter of definition, because to me this whole issue is basically definitional. The church is the people who are redeemed. That's the Bible definition of the church. "The Lord added to the church daily such as should be saved" (Acts 2:47). Even if you don't use the King James Version, and even if you acknowledge that the word "church" is not in the Greek text, you take the composite of the scriptures in the first part of the book of Acts, and it is evident that's what the church is. It is the saved; the people are the church. I could quote those scriptures but so can you. And you've used them and I'm not telling you something that you don't know, but I'm going to make a point from it that perhaps some of you will not see.

But in Acts 8:1-3 the Bible says, concerning the Apostle Paul before he was the Apostle Paul, when he was Saul the persecutor, that he made havoc of the church. And then it tells how he did that, that he did that by going into every house and hailing men and women and carrying them to prison. The church is the church wherever it may be, whether or not it is assembled. And the church can do something, or the church can have something done to it, as that is done in a scattered manner to individuals, as surely as if it is done collectively through a treasury or through a group of people who are gathered together.

And the essence of what has failed to penetrate at least my mind ... I read a sentence in Brother Wolfgang's history that somebody said that they just couldn't understand, couldn't perceive the distinction between individual and collective activity. He rightly acknowledged that's one of the primary pillars of the thing that creates this difference between us. And I, I don't understand it. I have, I've read what you said about it. I've looked at it; it's not a matter of not having tried to understand it. But definitionally, it simply continues to come out, to me, that the church is the people and the people are the church. And if one can go from house to house and persecute Christians, and when he does that, biblically he persecutes the church. That if one goes from house to house to people because they are Christians collecting money from some cause for them, when he gets through and takes that money, that's still the church that has given that money and that again, to me, is definitional.

Revelation 2:3, Jesus at the end of every sermon that he ... every letter that he wrote to the seven churches of Asia said, "He that hath an ear let him that hear what the Spirit sayeth to the churches." And again, the way that that is communicated to the church is to individuals. What the church does, in the FINAL ANALYSIS, is in EVERY INSTANCE a compilation of what the collection of the individuals who make up the church have done.

I was in college when this issue arose. The early '50's are my college years, and I went to school with some of you with whom we don't have much association any more. But I was in school in the time when the people who ended up on different sides of this issue, at that time were all still attending the same schools and all still speak-

ing in the same lectureships and all still writing for the same papers.

And I remember vividly some years after that, that there was a proposal made on the pages of the *Gospel Guardian* that we've tried to come to a kind of understanding, accommodation on this matter. Maybe while we continue to discuss them and try to convince one another, let's put a "box in the vestibule," it was proposed. "And let the institutions, the orphans homes," there weren't any Bible colleges around at that time that I know of, but if that were the case, the Bible colleges, "be supported by means of people who put money in that box specifically designed for them. They can be encouraged to do that, but keep it out of the church treasury."

I felt then, and I said then, that I wish that people would have listened to that. I wish there had been an honest reaction on the part of some of US, to receive that in the spirit in which I hope that it was given and try to work through that. I doubt very seriously if that would have been necessary to do, even for the sake of unity, in every place. But I KNOW that there are some places where if that had been done, then unity could have been maintained. And I think that would have been worth doing. That was ridiculed on BOTH sides of the aisle. And I've always wished that those, who seemed to be somewhat at that time, had received that with greater appreciation and respect, and at least given it a try in some places where it might would have helped. I honestly believed that, and said that at the time, although my voice is still not very heavy and it certainly wasn't in those days.

But having said that, I must also say that the response that was made to it, even though it was almost ... was sometimes... was made in ridicule. And I don't want to say it in a way that smacks of ridicule. But it is a fact, and on reflection I think we need to be recognized even if we were going to try it... It is a fact that all that does is substitute passing the people by the plate, for passing the plate by the people. And you've still got the same people doing the giving out of the same basic motivation and purpose and end and aim. And again, I suggest to you that definitionally, it is simply a distinction without a difference.

In 1 Timothy 5:4-16, there is a passage there about caring for widows, and is one that is most frequently used to suggest that this distinction is a valid one that needs to be maintained. We have a person told that as a Christian, every Christian is obligated to care for his own. And we are not allowed to foist that off on the church, so we're not to allow the church to be burdened. We are to carry that obligation ourselves because it is our own. But that's not properly a distinction between the work of an individual as opposed to the work of a congregation when it's something that everybody is obligated to do. On the contrary, what that is, is a recognition of the fact that that's an obligation of an individual which he doesn't have a right to foist out off upon every Christian. And to make the point that I'm making, definitionally, I would simply say that it would be just as wrong, if I was able to take care of my own aged parents, for me to go from house to house among the Christians where I worship and other Christians nearby, and solicit money from them to help me to take care of my aged parents, that I'm able to take care of, and have an obligation to take care of. It would be just as wrong to do it that way, as it would to go to the treasury of the church and ask for it. There is not that distinction, again I suggest, definitionally.

The viewpoint that I'm looking at, it seems to me, in effect, and I emphasize that word "in effect." I'm not saying that this is the definition that anybody would give, but in effect it seems to me, that the definition of the church becomes the treasury. And what is done through the treasury is what the church does and nothing else is. And the definition of the church is not the treasury but it is the people. The church is people and when the people act the church acts. Definitionally, that's my point. Whatever scripture obligated all Christians to do, it obligates the church to do. And whether the church does it through one bank account, or another bank account, or through no bank account at all, is simply not a matter over which Christians ought to divide. Definition is a point here that I would stress.

Secondly, I would emphasize some… Who is the timekeeper? Are you the timekeeper?

Jamie Sloan – Moderator: You have five minutes.

Cecil May – Main Speaker: OK, thank you. Difficulties with consistency, is another point that I want to make regarding this. There are two saying going around that are contradictory. You've heard both of them. "Ah consistency, thou art such a jewel." I've looked up every quotation book that I've got in our library and I've never been able to find who said that verse. But it's been said a lot, enough times that everybody's aware that consistency is indeed a jewel, and is indeed a rare one. It's something

to be desired, something to be sought for. We need to be consistent, because if we find ourselves saying something here, and then saying something or doing something over here that contradicts what we said over here, then there's something wrong with what we've said in one of those two places. That's why we need to recognize the virtue and the value of consistency.

But the other saying that goes around is … I did find the source of it; it's from Emerson in his *Essay on Self-Reliance*. And he said, "A foolish consistency is the hobgoblin of little minds." You've probably heard that one quoted too. And the point that he was making there is not one we probably, to its ultimate conclusion, we would agree with at all. But beginning with simply what is said on the surface, "Consistency is the hobgoblin of little minds," in the since in which we have talked about consistency before already. And that is in the since in which we decide that I can't say this today, even though I now think it's right, because I've already said or done this yesterday and I don't want to contradict that. The kind of consistency that makes us hold to something that is foolish and wrong because we have to, to be consistent with something we have said before, is the kind of consistency that needs to be turned away from. We need to be willing to change. And we don't need to take foolish positions in order to be consistent with something we said before. What we need to do is go back and analyze what we said before and see what's wrong with it that causes an outcome of it to be so foolish.

I have here some illustrations that I think would illustrate that. But I'm going to skip over those in the interest of time, and come to one that's directly related to the point. In Galatians 6:6 there's an admonition to Christians, "Let him that is taught in the word communicate unto him that teacheth in all good things." Now the Elizabethan Language of the King James Version obscures the point a little bit. But most of us, I think nevertheless, in reading that can come out to understand that what that's saying is, that those who are taught by teachers of the word, need to be willing to share their material thinks with those who taught them. It's one of the texts that teach that preachers are to be supported for the work of preaching. But notice that this text is couched very very clearly in individual terms. "Let Him that is taught in the word communicate," share "with Him that teacheth in all good things."

The Galatians 6:10 passage, very much under consideration in this, "Let … as we have opportunity let us do good unto all men, especially to those who are of the household of faith," just four verses away from this one. And both of them are couched very clearly in individual language. And yet while we argue that one cannot be fulfilled by the church collectively through its treasury and it becomes sin if it is done that way, the other we ordinarily and regularly do by the church through its treasury. I suggest that there is at least a problem of inconsistency there that needs to be looked at.

I realize there are other factors involved. I am aware of the fact that the Apostle Paul said that he received funds from churches, "I robbed other churches," he said, "that you might be helped and not be burdened" (2 Cor. 11:8). But I would prefer for us to suggest, first of all, that if you say that that came out of the treasury, that's an assumption that is not stated. The only thing that is explicitly stated that the funds out of the treasury, if the treasury is the lay by in store on the first day of the week, and we all believe that it is and I do too, the only thing that it's ever explicitly stated that that treasury was used for was benevolence for saints. Well, let me be more specific than that, it was benevolence for the poor saints in Jerusalem. It was for a, one specific instance for, benevolence for a particular people.

And we've already seen that if individuals do something together, even though, however it might be done, whatever form might be used to do it, it's still the church doing it. So it would be an assumption unproved that would say that it necessarily came through the treasury, as Acts 8:3 the church in the house is still the church, would clearly indicate. But still if this distinction were maintained, then this still is an individual obligation. And if we say that individual obligations can be met collectively, then what you have done is stated my point. Because that's what I am saying, individual obligations can be met collectively. Collective obligations can be met individually. They presuppose one another.

1 Corinthians 16:1-2 is not, if you take a limited view of what that authorizes, what the pattern is. I believe in the pattern as much as you do. The thing is, we have to decide what the pattern is. And if we decide that the pattern is saints only, then I raise the question, "Why not saints at Jerusalem only?" or "Why not benevolence only and no preacher support from that particular treasury?" I suggest that if you reason on to show how you include

saints anywhere other than Jerusalem number one, and two, preacher support, and then extend the same reason, then you've got caring for the fatherless by the process of that same reason.

There has been kind of an embarrassing thing going around, I know, that it's all right to take church funds out of the treasury to fertilize the preacher's yard but not all right to take funds out of the treasury to care for a starving child. I understand the rational that is used for that, the preacher's yard is … providing a house is part of his support. If you can do preacher support, then you can do the details of that, I understand that. But again I suggest that when you hear that, and you look at it in terms of the totality of the teaching and emphases and priorities of Christ and what He's given the church to do. That again that could surely become an inconsistency that maybe ought to make us look back to see what's wrong with our reasoning back here, that would cause us to come out with that kind of thing.

The last thing I want to say, and I've only got a minute to do so, has to do with matters of judgement. When we say that a thing is a matter of judgment that does not necessarily mean that therefore anything's OK, and anybody can do anything they want to, and everything is a matter of judgment. There is such a thing as poor judgment. There is such a thing of judgment that is so poor and based upon such wrong priorities that it even becomes sinful. And just saying that a thing is a matter of judgment does not say that therefore anything that anybody does in that area is all right. That's not the thing that proceeds from that, and it doesn't mean that therefore that opens up an area where it's not even possible for us to help one another and correct one another in that area.

We say that the church cannot enter into business. And I realize that there are all kinds of ramifications of that, and a lot of different people conclude different things about that kind of thing. But I would suppose, at least, that all of us would recognize that it would not be an appropriate use of church funds, and emphasis and purpose, to go buy a piece of real-estate with the idea that it's going to appreciate, and 15 years down the road, we can have 15 times more money to preach the gospel with. That would not be something that would be appropriate for the church to do.

On the other hand, I do suppose that we would all recognize that if the church bought a piece of ground for a parking lot, and later it appreciated 15 times, and the needs of the church for parking or for other things came to be able to be fulfilled in some other way, that it would be all right for the church to sell that property, and they wouldn't necessarily have to sell it for they had given for it to begin with.

What I'm saying is that if there is an absolute principle that the church cannot go into business, then the church can't sell property. But if there is a matter of judgment involved in which purposes and basic intent and of that sort of thing gets involved, then there comes room for discussion. But it does not mean that there is an absolute principle that completely takes everything out.

Let me conclude with this word. We may need to learn some things, including not to assume wrong motives so quickly when others differ from us in judgment. Not to be so quick to bind our judgements on others, and to talk and to listen to each other more, to learn what we don't know than to defend what we've already decided. And if we learn some of those things this week, then it will have been a week worth while.

Congregational Versus Individual Activities
Day 2 Speech 1 Rebuttal
Ferrell Jenkins

Introduction: *Jenkins, Ferrell. He is a native of Huntsville, AL and has done local works in Florida, Kentucky, Missouri, Tennessee, Indiana, and Ohio. He presently works with the Carrollwood church in Tampa, FL, and formerly taught at Florida College for 15 years. He is a participant in archaeological expeditions, widely used author and specializes in Bible land tours for Christians.*

It certainly is a pleasure to be here with you this morning and to see so many who got here this early on Friday the 13th to be able to come and hear us. Brother Banister said yesterday that while his wife was away he wore the tie she would never let him wear and that he proved that he was head of the house. (Laughter whs) Well, I'm just the opposite. I called at 7:20 this morning to ask my wife if I had on the right thing. (Laughter whs) So if I don't it's her fault.

It's good to be with you again, and of course it's good to listen to Brother May. I only met him a few years ago at some professional meetings that we were attending. And have come to know him a little bit better and to appreciate him and to enjoy his *Preacher Talk* and some of the very nice things that he has said in that paper, even since the Nashville Meeting.

And I think that meetings like this do help us to see one another and learn one another as people and as brethren in Christ. And to perhaps more seriously consider one another and what one another has to say than perhaps has been done for a number of years. It's hoped that this effort will result in a better understanding of the scriptures and also that it will help in a better attitude toward one another. And of course I believe that it has the possibility of paving the way toward a possible reconciliation. Not by large numbers of people, but at least by some of us in our interest of the truth. I'd like to thank Roy Lanier and Steve Wolfgang and all of the others, all of the participants and the audience and everyone who has made this meeting possible.

Now my assignment is to speak on the collective or church activity and individual activity. And as you know we write our speeches independent of one another, and this is not a debate in which I'm going to take up each of the points that Brother May has suggested. But if we didn't deal with some of the same topics, it would indicate that at least one of us didn't even understand what the controversy was over. And so indeed we will be dealing with some of the same things, but I'll not be trying to make a reply specifically to things that he has said.

I think that every one of us recognizes that there are peculiar individual responsibilities. For example, the matter of the husband's relationship to the wife, the wife to the husband, parents to children, and that sort of thing. Many have maintained that there is no distinction to be made between the individual and church responsibilities in certain areas, especially in the care of the needy. And others have pointed out that this is also true in the areas of recreation, and the support of the colleges, and so on. We've been told by many that whatever the individual does, that is the same as the church doing that. And when an individual acts then the church is acting.

But some of us have maintained that there are some responsibilities that belong exclusively to the individual and that the church should not be burdened. And we recognize also that there are parallel duties which are to be fulfilled by both the individual and the congregation or the church, like the study of scriptures and prayer and benevolence and evangelism and so on.

I want to start by using one or two quotations from some people who have stated this in the past, because I think we must keep this in perspective of the controversy that has raged or did rage in the '50's and early '60's. (Chart #1) And of course all of us remember Brother G.C. Brewer in 1947 said, "They say it is all right for Christians to support colleges, but that it is wrong for a church to do so. And thus they make a difference between Christian

---

Some Have Maintained That No Distinction Should Be Made Between The Individual Christian And The Church

G.C. Brewer - 1947
The Harding College Lectures, p.113
"They say it is all right for Christians to support colleges but that it is wrong for a church to do so. Thus, they make a difference between Christian duties and church duties, Christian responsibilities and church responsibilities, Christian work and church work, all of which is absurd on its face."

---

duties and church duties, Christian responsibilities and church responsibilities, Christian work and church work, all of which is absurd on its face." You will notice of course that he was saying, in effect, that if individuals can support the college, then of course the church can support the college as well.

So the issue was much more, and it is much more than just the care of the needy. But it also involves the matter of the colleges, and other institutions, para-church institutions, that might want the funds of the church. I have quotations in my notes and there are copies of them on the front pews here or seats and along here and at the table at the back. And you can get these quotations and things of that sort. (Chart #2) Have one from Brother Guy

---

Some Have Maintained That No Distinction Should Be Made Between The Individual Christian And The Church

Batsell Barrett Baxter - 1963
Questions and Issues of the Day
"In view of all that has been said above, it is now possible to state what I believe to be a broad general principle. Any 'good work' which the Individual, as a Christian, is obligated to support financially, the church is equally obligated to support financially. There has been a great deal of talk about what the individual can do in supporting good works and what the church cannot do in supporting the same good works, which the Lord wanted all the obligation falls equally upon individuals and when the (the rest obscured by the overhead device).

Woods, but here's one from Brother Batsell Barrett Baxter

in 1963 when he wrote his *Questions and Issues of the Day*. He pointed out in the part that is highlighted there, he emphasized that, "Any good work which the individual, as a Christian is obligated to support financially, the church is equally obligated to support financially." And of course he was advocating the church support of the college at that time. He also went on to say that, "Individuals are the church." The same thing that Brother May has said for us, and we don't disagree with that. But we believe there is such a thing as a distinction to be made between the church, meaning all of God's saved, all of the people in the universal sense, and the church meaning a local church, with overseers and deacons and its own work and its own treasury and so on.

Now the New Testament teaches that God's people, both individually and collectively, have a responsibility in the care of those that are needy. I believe that "Whatever we do in word or in dead we should do all to the glory of God through our Lord Jesus Christ" (Col. 3:17). (Chart #3) And I believe that whether we act as an individual or

New Testament Teaching On The Christian's Concern And Care For Others

Individual	Church to its own	Church to Church(es)	Church to Benevolent institutions
Mt. 5:43-48	Acts 2:44-45	Acts 11:27-30	?
Mt. 25:35-40	Acts 4:32-34	Rom. 15:25-26	
Lk. 10:30-36	Acts 6:1-5	(not visible)	
Acts 4:36-37	1 Tim. 5:16	1 Cor. 16:1-2	
Acts 9:36-39		2 Cor. 8:6-9	
Acts 20:34-35			
I Cor. 16:15			
Gal. 6:10			
Eph. 4:23			
I Tim. 5:15			
I Tim. 5:16			
Heb. 13:15-16			
Jas. 1:26-27			
Jas. 2:15-16			
I Jn. 3:17-18			

whether we act in some collective form, that we are giving God the glory in the church and in Christ Jesus, as Ephesians 3:21 suggests.

I have here a list of passages that, I think, basically we all would agree on, passages that emphasize the responsibility that individuals have with regard to benevolent care and concern for those that are needy. Everything from Jesus' statement that we should love all men, to Galatians 6 that we should do good unto all men. And it seems that perhaps this is an individual passage, though there would be some who would…who might differ on that particular point. But basically, we would all agree that these passages do place a responsibility upon us to be benevolent toward those that are in need. And so I'm not going to read them all due to the lack of time that we have, because I think we understand that.

I have also listed what I understand to be passages that talk about the responsibility of the church, a congregation of God's people, providing for its own. And in the book of Acts, and I think these examples are very instructive for us, we have Acts 2:44-45 where these brethren sold their property. "And they brought the funds and laid them at the Apostles' feet and there was the distribution as any had need." And the needs of the people were met. According to Acts 4:34, there was not a needy person among them. In other words, they were able to, in some way, pool their funds and collectively meet the need of that particular group at that time. The widows in Acts 6 were being neglected. And there you see as the Apostles began to set in effect what would be a way for a group to act, when they no longer can do this they said, "Look out among yourself and select seven men of good report." And these men then were appointed over this work, this business, this responsibility of the congregation, and of course it corrected the situation at that time. And in 1Timothy 5:16 there is a reference to the fact that the church should relieve those who are widows indeed.

Ok, it says try to get microphone closer. There's about the best I can do. I can stand closer to it that would be better, try to get closer to the microphone. OK.

Now let's talk also about the responsibility of church to churches, or churches to a church. In the New Testament we also have examples of churches, congregations of God's people, as they were doing this very thing. In the reign of Claudius, there was a famine that adversely affected the brethren in Judea. And the disciples at Antioch determined to send a contribution for their relief (Acts 11:27-30). And the Bible says that "they sent it by the hands of Barnabas and Saul."

I believe it's very important to observe in this case, that Acts 11 is not the same incident of Romans 15 and 2 Corinthinas 8:9, 1 Corinthians16:1-2. Those latter passages refer to something that happened about a decade later. And so we need to realize the difference in the two cases. In the first instance, you have disciples at Antioch who pooled their funds and by the hands of Barnabas and Saul they sent it to the brethren, to the elders of the brethren that dwelt in Judea. And it's sometimes confused and we use that as a case of Jerusalem receiving those funds. But it says that the brethren in Judea were the ones who were needy, and it says that the funds were sent to the elders in that particular place. And then over in Romans 15 and 2 Corinthians 8:9 and 1 Corinthians 16:1-2, the Apostle Paul talks about several churches throughout Macedonia and Achaia, as these churches were sending funds to the poor among the saints that were at Jerusalem. And so there are two distinct cases, but what it shows is that a congregation may have a responsibility toward helping other congregations in benevolent needs of that sort.

Now there is no example in the New Testament of churches ever sending contributions to human benevolent organizations through which to do their work or a separately set up cooperation. I'm not sure when some are talking about they don't support human institutions, if they're making a play on the fact that they think that home is a divine institution. I'm not sure I'm clear on everything that's being said on those points and perhaps it will come out in some of the latter sessions.

I believe the Bible makes a distinction between the individual action and church action. I think our Lord made that kind of distinction in Matthew 18:15-17. (Chart #4) There, Jesus said, "And if your brother sins, go and reprove

---

Jesus Taught A Distinction Between Individual Action and church Action
Mt. 16:15-17 (NASB)

15 "And if your brother sins, go and reprove him in private; if he listens to you, you have won your brother."
16 "But if he does not listen to you, take one or two more with you, so that by the mouth of two or three witnesses every fact may be confirmed."
17 "And if he refuses to listen to them, tell it to the church; and if he refuses to listen even to the church, let him be to you as a Gentile and a Tax-gatherer."

him in private, if he listens to you," it says that "you have won your brother. But if he does not listen to you, take one or two more with you so that by the mouth of two or three witnesses every fact may be confirmed. And if he refuses to listen to them, tell it to the church. And if he refuses to listen even to the church, let him be to you as a Gentile and a tax-gather." Now you will notice the term church is used. It implies a group. It implies an assembly. It implies a called-out group of people, and one person does not constitute that called-out group or that assembly. One individual and even the two or three witnesses in this case, did not constitute what Jesus referred to as a church.

Paul Taught A Distinction Between the Individual and the Church.

1 Corinthians 12

20 "But now there are many members, but one body."

21 "Now you are Christ's body, and individually members of it."

I Timothy 5

15 "But if anyone does not provide for his own, and especially for those of his household, he had denied the faith, and is worse than an unbeliever."

16 "If any woman who is a believer has dependent widows, let her assist them and let not the church be burdened, so that it may assist those who are widows indeed."

(Chart #5) The Apostle Paul taught also the distinction between the individual and the church. In 1Corinthians 12:20 Paul says, "But now there are many members but one body." Now he says, "You are Christ's body and all individually members of it." I think we all recognize that the finger is not the body, the ear is not the body, the nose is not the body. Paul used all those illustrations and we would recognize that one body, one individual is not the church, or is not the total of the body of Jesus Christ. If we recognize that there is a church universal, that is that all of the Christians make up the church of the Lord which He purchased with His blood. And we recognize that God

has ordained that there should be local churches, like the church at Philippi and at Corinth and at other places. Paul, for example, wrote to the brethren, "to the church of God at Corinth and all who dwell in Achaia." There were people in Achaia who were not members of the church at Corinth. There may have been some at Cenchrea, there may have been some at Athens, and there may have been some at other localities who were not a part of the church at Corinth. And so it shows the distinction between individual and church activity.

A distinction between the individual and the church is also made in 1 Timothy 5. In this chapter, Paul discusses the responsibility of a Christian to his family. Personal responsibilities toward one's immediate and extended family are set forth in that passage of scripture. A clear distinction between the individual and the church is made in verse 16. It says, "If any woman who is a believer has dependent widows, let her assist them and let not the church be burdened so that it may assist those who are widows indeed."

Back in 1955 Brother Bill Humble had, I think, at that time already debated Leroy Garrett on the located preacher question. And in his…and also the right of Christians to maintain colleges. And in the defense of the right of Christians to build and maintain colleges in which the Bible could be taught, he clearly set forth the distinction between the individual and the church. He said, "When we consider the care of widows, the difference between individual and congregational responsibility stands out clearly. If a Christian has a widowed mother, it is his duty as an individual…" and he emphasized that, "to provide for her needs. Paul taught this clearly when he wrote…" and he sites the same passages I've sited. He goes on to say, "However he does this as an individual and it is not a work of the church. We know that it is not the work of the church because Paul wrote, let not the church" he emphasized that, "let not the church be burdened." And so I think this is not the first time that people have made the distinction between individual and church activity. And it was commonly done in order to show that individuals could build and maintain colleges and other institutions, and the church was not responsible for those. In fact, the church was not doing those things.

Now the distinction between the individual and the church is seen also in the difference between the individual's money and the church's money. (Chart #6) I have here a passage that shows three things about the individual's

Two Treasuries - Acts 5:1

Individual	Local Church

1. Method of Raising

A. By honest labor - Eph.4:28   A. By voluntary Offering -
                                                  I Cor.16:1-2; 2 Cor.5:6-7

2. Oversight

A. The Individual Acts 5:4   A. Local Elders - I Th. 1:7;
                                                  Acts 11:30

3. Use

A. Liberal Contribution I Cor.16:2   A. Preaching Gospel
B. Pay taxes Rom.13:7   Phil. 4:15-16;
                                                          2 Cor.11:8
C. Provide for Family I Tim. 5:8, 16   : Edify Saints
D. Good Words I Tim. 5:16   : Preach to lost

                                              B. Not readable

fund, the two treasuries as I've called this. There is a difference in the method of raising funds for the individual and for the congregation, or church. There is also a difference in the oversight of those funds and there is a difference in the use of those funds. In Acts 5:4, the Bible tells us about Ananias and Sapphira. They, like Barnabas, had a tract of land and they sold it. But, unlike Barnabas, they wanted to keep back a portion of that and yet claim that they had given the whole amount. They lied of course. And as they brought these funds and laid it at the Apostles' feet claiming that they were giving everything, the Bible tells us that Peter said to them, "While this property remained it was your own, and it was under your control." He said, "After it was sold, it was under your control." I thought it was interesting to note there that the word "control" is the word *exousia*. The same term that our Lord used when He said, "All authority has been given unto Me in Heaven and on earth." They had the total authority and control over that piece of property and they had the control of those funds once it was sent, once it was sold. And so you can see then that they had their treasury, which was distinct from the treasury of the church.

My first recollection of this particular issue was in an open forum at Florida College, back in 19... probably 55 or 6 somewhere along there. And I remember a brother who then lived around the Miami area and he reached in his billfold and he took out a dollar bill. And he said, "If I

spend this dollar bill that's the same as the church spending it." Someone asked him, "If he went to the picture show had the church gone to the picture show?" Feelings were much stronger about picture shows then before television and HBO were so common. And so of course he said, "Oh, no, no, I don't mean that."

And all of us who are older remember Brother W. Curtis Porter. And someone told me, a friend of mine, said, "I was seated by Brother Porter and in his style he began to write, and he wrote this. He said, 'One sheep is a flock, one cow is a herd, one hen is a flock, one boxcar is a train.'" You know of course what he would have done with that in discussion. It simply shows the folly. One member is not the body and there is a distinction that is drawn and this thing about the money clearly illustrates that difference.

Now Christians raised their money by honest labor, not by going into business. Brother May and I are on agreement on that. And he didn't get to say everything he had written in his paper there, but I am in agreement with what he said on that particular point. And the church raises its funds by voluntary offering of its members.

The oversight of the fund is different. I oversee my fund, well my wife keeps the check book but I do get a little bit. And the church oversees . . . I thought maybe that's a good deal. It'd be better to be able to pick your own clothes than to be able . . . and not have control over your check book though, you see. So I don't know I'll have to talk to Brother Banister about that and see how to work that out. But the individual controls his funds. And when money is turned into the group, then the group is the one who has that responsibility. And I believe that God who has given elders as stewards, they are men who are responsible. And when I look also at 1 Corinthians (Acts, whs) 11:30, and I see that funds were sent to the ELDERS in Judea, I believe that they have something to do with the oversight of that particular fund.

Think about the use of these funds also. The church may use its money for preaching the gospel. It may use its money to . . . and I usually say that and I include edification and evangelism in that one category, and also relieving needy saints. And as I look at the examples in the book of Acts, these are the examples that I have. But I see the individual as he uses his money to make a liberal contribution, to pay taxes, to provide for his family, and to maintain good works. Again, that whole list of passages that direct him, including support of gospel preachers (Gal. 6:6)and other passages that would show that.

Now congregational activity obligates every member of the congregation. And I believe that this is an important issue as it pertains to what we're discussing in this total meeting. A failure to recognize that congregational activity obligates every member of the church has brought division into the body of Christ several times. There are examples of some things that have brought disruptions into the body of Christ, for example the use of musical instruments, mechanical instruments of music. You see there, you do not have just someone who thinks differently from the way you do, but you have some individual who has done something that is just a tangible sign of his way of thinking. Treasury contributions by one church to another church, or to organizations, involve EVERY MEMBER of that congregation, every member of that group. The Missionary Society to do evangelistic work was like that. The sponsoring church, through which many churches pool their funds in order to accomplish a chosen work, is like that. The college, though which the Bible is to be taught and leaders are to be trained, is like that. And the publishing business, through which the gospel is to be spread by means of the printed word, also falls into that category. Also I believe that the benevolent institutions, the hospitals, the orphan homes, the homes for the aged, through which the church will care for it's needy, fall also into that category. The use of church property for social and recreational purposes OBLIGATES EVERY MEMBER OF THE CONGREGATION in the support of such. I think we must come to bear with all of these issues.

I think if we had a box in the vestibule, OUR approach, MY approach, and I don't really ridicule the box in the vestibule idea at all, but my approach is the box is on the corner of the street. And let each person put his OWN envelope in that and mail it to whom ever he wishes that he thinks is doing a good work. That out of his liberal contribution, or rather out of his abundance, he is able to help in whatever work he sees is right, and not obligate the entire group. When these things are bound upon the GROUP, upon the congregation, the Christian who cannot conscientiously approve of them has no choice but to fight or change, because you see conscience is involved in these matters.

Now there are individual differences that we all have with all of our brethren, whether there's just a handful in the group we are with, or whether we are talking about the church universal, or we are talking about camps, or whatever. I thought about the camp that said the devil will come down and try to attack, and I'd like to be that camp so that the Lord will protect me. And I agree with that attitude of not being in camps and parties, and that whole concept I think is abhorrent and totally contrary to the spirit of Jesus Christ and to the teaching of the New Testament, and I deplore it. But individual differences do not OBLIGATE other members of the church and should not bring division. Oh I've got a whole list of these things like: the covering, and participation in the military, and INDIVIDUAL support of colleges and benevolent societies and so on, television and movies, and trees in your home at Christmas or not, and the use of religious pictures and objects and crosses and so on. There are many of these things that we can keep INDIVIDUALLY, every one of us has our own opinion about them, I have a strong opinion about every one of these. And yet I know that if I talk to as many as two or three and we talked more over, . . . , talked about more than two or three of these issues, we would find that we would have differences. But that doesn't keep us from working together when we agree on CERTAIN things, that as a group we're going to do.

I'm impressed with how few COLLECTIVE responsibilities there are. I'm talking about responsibilities that God has BOUND upon us to do as a group. For example, there's worship. Well, this involves the assembly, it involves the singing together, it involves the Lord's Supper, it involves the contribution. I think also of the use of those funds, the work of the church, the evangelism, the edification, and the benevolence. And if we can limit our COLLECTIVE functions to THESE THINGS, then fewer problems would exist among us. You see we don't have all that many things that we really would have to agree on in order to say we can work TOGETHER, and we can put these others into a realm where the individual is free to do these if he so chooses to do them.

And I tell you, I believe that there is a world lost, and I believe that there are people who are concerned about those, among ALL of us. And I believe that in our responsibilities as a group like I'm talking about, and in our individual realms, that we can see many people won to Jesus Christ. We must each teach and practice what we understand to be the truth. In Philippians 3:15-16, Paul talked about that matter of living by the rule whereunto you have attained. None of us can do less than we understand and know, but we must do everything that we understand and know.

One of the great principles of the Restoration Movement was the principle "In faith unity, in opinions liberty, in all things charity," or love. Since Thomas Campbell's statement of that in 1809, it has been one of the classic statements of Restoration Literature. I believe then that we should limit our collective function then, to those things that are authorized by direct commands, by approved examples, or by necessary inference. And let us do those things that are right and which cannot be wrong. In this way, group activities will not be bound on the individual who conscientiously opposes such. Is that possible for us to agree on these essentials, or matters of faith? Is it possible for us to recognize a list of individual requirements as non-essentials or matters of opinion, and thus leave them in the realm of liberty? Without this I fear that unity will never exist among us.

The individual Christian should feel free to participate in whatever type of good works he believes is in harmony with the scripture and with his commitment to Jesus Christ. This program of course, makes us aware that there are many areas that need to be discussed, some already and more to come today and tomorrow. And I think of course, that it's good for us to do this. In my heart, I want to do the will of God. I want to glorify Him in everything that I do. I feel confident that this is a true sentiment of each one who is participating in this meeting. And I do not now, nor have I ever, knowingly felt any ill will toward my brethren with whom I have differed over these matters.

We need to seek to bring about a situation where the word of God is respected and obeyed and where none is expected to violate HIS conscience in order to enjoy the fellowship of his brethren. Let us strive for "unity in essentials, liberty in non-essentials, and love in all things." And may the Lord bless us as we seek to rectify a situation which we know is not pleasing to Him. Our Lord prayed for us, "I do not ask on behalf of these alone, but for those also who believe in Me through their word. That they may all be one even as Thou Father art in Me and I in Thee. And that they also might be in Us, that the world might believe that Thou didst send Me." Thank you very much.

Congregational Versus Individual Activities
Day 2 Speech 1 Panelist 1
Martin Pickup

Jamie Sloan – Moderator: (Beginning not recorded whs) . . . to introduce the panel to you. On my far right, Brother Avon Malone who teaches at Oklahoma Christian University, Brother Joe Blakeney who is a full time elder in Whitney, Texas, Brother Robert Harkrider a Texas preacher transplanted in Orlando, Florida, Brother Martin C. Pickup who is preaching with the Carrollwood church in Tampa, Florida and teaching at Florida College. And now who wants to go first? Marty?

Congregational Versus Individual Activities

Introduction: *Pickup, Martin. He is the son and grandson of well-known preachers, was born in Ft. Worth, TX, and has preached in Texas, Kansas, and Florida churches. He presently is with the Carrollwood congregation in Tampa, FL and is in his third year as instructor at Florida College.*

The very fact that I have been asked to be on this program and that I am here, is an indication of the fact that there is now a second generation of people involved in this division. And I think that I can speak a little bit from the perspective of those of my peer group, probably on both sides of this issue.

And I think, and I'm quite confident of the fact, that as we've heard yesterday so many times, people speaking about, "Well this is what happened and this group is to blame" or "this was said" or "this was not the proper thing that was done." People from my generation, in the first place by in large, don't have any idea what happened. In the second place, there are many of those, and I'm not saying this is good, I think this is extreme, but there are many of those who perhaps do have some idea of what is happening, an inkling of an idea, whose attitude toward it is that it was silly. And in their minds surely this could have been avoided. And many of those go to the extreme, where they just toss everything out the window and say all of this just must be church of Christ traditionalism, and they just give the whole thing up.

Then there are others on the other extreme, and I'm speaking specifically about my own peers, who I think uncritically accept what they've been taught. And I think that's so on both sides. If they know anything about the issues, it's just that well, the other side's wrong and we are right. And I think both of those extremes are improper.

Now I believe firmly that those of my generation cannot be blamed for the division that has happened. But there is one charge that might be labeled against us, that we go to those extremes that I've talked about and that we today, or though out our lives, just uncritically accept what has happened without studying. I can't do that. I wasn't involved in all of this but I have inherited it. But more than that, as a Christian it's my responsibility to look at these issues and to decide for myself what does the Bible really teach. And that's the responsibility of every one, but especially do I make that appeal to those who are in the younger generation on both persuasions, both sides of this.

Before God I'm going to stand. And I'm going to be judged not on the basis of what I was taught, but I'm going to be judged on the basis of what the truth is. And I have to make a decision for myself about that.

Now having said that, and coming from that perspective, I would like to affirm, that as Brother May has said in his speech, as he spoke about some differences in concept that he had with those at the Nashville Meeting. And the brother, who said, "You know I just don't THINK the way these people think." I am compelled to say to Brother May, "I don't think the way that you THINK about the church, especially about the local church."

And as Brother May defines what he means by the local church as simply being people, Christian people. Well, I agree that the local church is Christian people, but that's not a sufficient definition. Because when Paul, for instance, addresses his first Corinthian letter to the CHURCH at Corinth, and when he speaks about the church in Philippi with elders and deacons, he's not just talking about SAINTS at a local area who HAPPEN to be

Christians, and who function individually. But He's talking about saints at a local area who have agreed to function collectively to do God ordained work. They function not merely as individuals but as a collective group, as a local church. That to me is a fundamental principle. I think that's the issue we're talking about in this portion of the program and that's the real essence of the debate that I have with Brother May and what he said, "What is the local church?" Thank you.

Congregational Versus Individual Activities
Day 2 Speech 1 Panelist 2
Robert Harkrider

Introduction: *Harkrider, Robert. He is a native of Beaumont, TX and reared in Nacodoches, TX. Has preached in Birmingham, Pinson, Hueytown and E. Florence, AL churches, also in Houston and Nacodoches, TX, and is presently in Orlando, FL. He was two years in Sydney, Australia. Author of 14 workbooks and he presently has a weekly TV program.*

Good Morning Ladies and Gentlemen. I thank God that, by his grace, I'm able to participate in such a discussion where brethren are willing to keep an open Bible and an open mind, like the Bereans of Acts 17:11. I'm grateful to every man who had a part in making the arrangements, in making this possible.

And I must say that I am encouraged really, by the fact that many of us who are present at this meeting, not only agree that Bible authority is essential for what we do, but our approach to hermeneutics is not that far apart. My prayer is that we'll keep lines of communication open and that we will sincerely strive to be consistent in the application of the principles that we understand to be the truth.

In response to Brother May's speech, I agree that the church is people who are redeemed. Saved people make up the church as he used Acts 2:47, we would all agree. But if that is the only definition and designation found in the Bible, then a consistent application would mean that Oklahoma Christian University should begin accepting contributions from churches. Because his implication is that it would be individual Christians acting, nothing more than like passing the plate by the people or the people by the plate.

Furthermore, no one should object any longer to churches building and maintaining hospitals, or to churches building gymnasiums and bowling alleys and family life centers. For that matter, if the church is nothing more than individual Christians, then we could open a wing of our buildings to operate a grocery store business, because what is scripturally lawful for individuals to do should be right for the church to do.

But most of you gathered here would disagree with every one of these applications. Why? Because in reality you understand the difference between the term CHURCH as used in the universal sense, and is distinguished from its use in a local sense. In its universal sense, the church is just people, all saved people. But there is no way to activate the church universal. It has no collective function as a unit, because it has no organizational structure except Christ as its head (Col. 1:18). Haven't we all preached that any organization larger than or smaller than a local church is without Bible authority?

But the term church when used in a local sense, has organization that permits a collective of Christians to function as a unit. Elders were ordained in every church (Acts 14:23). Philippi had its bishops and deacons with the saints (Phil. 1:1). In fact, several times in these lectures we've talked about autonomy of local churches. I know you believe in it. Therefore let us keep our thinking clear, that when we're discussing the work the Bible authorizes an individual CHRISTIAN to do, in distinction from the work that it authorizes the CHURCH to do, then we're talking about the church in that local sense. For it is the only way a collective of God's people is authorized to act as a unit.

In fact, this shifting of terms not only confuses the listener, but really, it reminds me of the inconsistency of the Premillennialist when he describes the reason Christ died on the cross. If the Premillennialist is talking about salvation, he'll say that Christ's death was necessary for redemption. But when he's talking about the kingdom, he said that Christ died because the world was not ready to accept him as a king. But you can't have it both ways. And neither can we talk about a local collective of Christians, who are functioning as an autonomous unit under the oversight of elders, as though they are only individual Christians acting. As surely as you do, some of your listeners will be consistent, and WILL send support to OCU, WILL build hospitals, the gymnasiums, and they might even open a grocery store business. God forbid.

Congregational Versus Individual Activities
Day 2 Speech 1 Panelist 3
Joe Blakeney

Introduction: *Blakeney, Joe. Businessman for many years in West Texas, preacher for over 30 years, camp director, elder of a congregation, presently serves the congregation in Whitney, TX as fulltime pastor.*

Now I don't know whenever I felt more inadequate. I used to preach. Then they made me an elder and won't let me preach, and I'm hating preachers already. (Laughter, whs) Naugh, I'm really just kidding.

I really appreciate what's been said here today. And I think our assignment is probably… what we're supposed to do is tell you what the two men said in four minutes. And they said so much, that what most of us do is say what WE THINK they said in about four minutes.

But when we talk about the individual work and the work of the church, and I understand I think, where the issues are. When you get down to the nitty gritty and when it really comes down it most of the time, "What are you going to do with the Lord's money out of the treasury, how do you handle that?" There's not very many individuals doing anything outside of that, now some are. And I think if we pinpoint the problem, that's about where we are.

Off the subject a moment, and I really do appreciate the youngest man up here. I've been working on these baby boomers for quite a while. (Subdued Laughter, whs) Know more about them than almost anybody. But someone mentioned yesterday, "Where are we headed in the next twenty years?" And the worst problem I see with individualism, is that there is going to be a group of individualists that we have in our congregation, now we may be exclusive at Lake Whitney, Texas, that want to do their own thing, separate and apart from the work of the church. At the same time would like to call the shots for the eldership and for everyone else. And one of the great frustrations, now I understand this is not the issue here today, is with individuals and what they're doing in the church today. I think individualism may come to the point to where it's going to be more frustration, the next decade probably, than what the church can and cannot do.

The distinction between the individual and the church, I believe Brother Jenkins addressed that pretty well. But then he concluded part of that with the way the money is raised, the oversight of the money and the use of the money. And I think that's the key to the thing. And down in the latter part, he talked about the collective requirements are few, meaning the church as a whole, not including the individuals, as I understand the way it was put. Worship, the assembly, singing together, Lord's Supper, and the contribution, use of the funds, the work of the church, evangelism, edification, benevolence. And probably that may be where we need to key into. Most elderships are not frustrated with what the individuals are doing per se, but how do we handle the money in the mission field and in the field of benevolence itself. Now that may be where the root of the thing is.

As far as the other side of that is, whether we send it directly to a missionary or whether we send it to a supporting church and they send it to a missionary. We do it both ways. We understand where the missionary is, we understand what he is doing with the money. We understand that he's not receiving money from ten or twelve other congregations directly. And the right hand does not know what the left hand is doing in that situation.

Does that mean enough? Thank you. That thing looks defiant. (Laughter, whs)

Congregational Versus Individual Activities
Day 2 Speech 1 Panelist 4
Avon Malone

Introduction: *Malone, Avon. Teaches at Oklahoma Christian University past teacher at Harding U. and several preaching schools, noted local work for 39 years in Waukegan, IL, Aurora and Denver, CO, Denton and Amarillo, TX.*

I'm finding today that I have a great affinity for one statement Paul made, 1 Corinthians 2:3, "I was with you in weakness and in fear and in much trembling." And I identify, in fact I told some fellows from Oklahoma City, I felt a little bit like the guy that was ridden out of town on a rail. He said, "If it hadn't been for the honor of the thing, I'd just as soon walk." (Laughter, whs)

You know though, I'm very much encouraged by a spirit that I think is discernable. And by some things that have been said that emphasize there's so much common ground. We sometimes forget that. Brother Harkrider I think, made mention of the fact that we do share much in common. And even in the area of interpretation of scripture, hermeneutics, how we would do an exegesis of a passage. We really have more in common than we might realize. And we are respectful of the word, and believe it to be God breathed. We believe it to be inerrant. We believe it to be all sufficient. I think we ought to emphasize that common ground.

We had a fellow speak on a lectureship where I teach, and he seemed to leave us with two options. That either the New Testament, particularly the New Testament letters, are epistolary or they're constitutional. And he made it look like these were mutually exclusive and that it was either/or. Some of the implications of this, "not constitutional," are frightening. And I have an idea that all of us ought to be more and more united and press the battle, not only 'ere the night shall vale the glowing skies, but press it where the real problem exists. You know it's interesting that in the Thessalonian letter, that Paul said, "If any man obey not my word by this epistle, note that man that he may be ashamed" (2 Thess. 3:14). It is an epistle. He follows a letter form. But Paul sees his letters as authoritative, "I adjure you in the name of the Lord Jesus Christ that this epistle be read unto all of the brethren." He will write near the close of 1 Thessalonians 5 "Hold fast the traditions, whether by word of by epistle of ours."

I somehow have an idea that the greater foe and the greater peril may be in another era, another area. But that's somewhat beside the point, and our part is to respond and to comment on two speeches, both of which were excellent. And I found much in both with which I could concur.

Let me say something very quickly. I do not at all believe in the church support of liberal arts schools. I believe there is no Biblical authority for that. I believe the school is the adjunct of the home. I do not believe that the church is to support the school. And if I may just speak from my heart, and obviously you understand I do not represent all the brethren, and all brethren with whom I might be rather close. I…are you already calling time? I'm just warming up. (Laughter, whs) Boy! Am I going to have to hurry! Every time I think about it. Say the book says, "Be swift to hear" so you be swift to hear, and I'm going to try to "be swift to speak."

I'm not enthusiastic about some structures that we've erected. And my lack of enthusiasm is not simply in an area of judgment or expediency. With so many not having heard the gospel, the funds could have been better used. I think we constructed certain structures that betray a mistaken conception of what our real responsibility is, and what this work of the church and the local church really is.

But let me try to comment quickly on the speeches. I appreciated both of them a great deal. I appreciate Brother May, and I had an earlier copy of that prior to this, and I thought it had fine things in it. There is one thing that I would like to register just a bit of a critique on, at least raise a question. Maybe I'm mistaken, you can correct me. I think it's something we've all been inclined to say. We all agree that in Galatians 6:6 that's individual, "Let him who is taught the word communicate unto him that teacheth in all good things." And by the way, there's some things that can be fulfilled individually or collectively. Paul said, "I robbed other churches, taking wages of them" (2 Cor. 11:8). And so, that one who teaches the word might be supported by an individual (Gal. 6:6), or might be supported by churches.

Paul tells the church in Corinth, "when you're come together to deliver such a one unto Satan for the destruction of the flesh that the spirit might be saved" (1 Cor. 5:3-5). And then Paul will write, in 1 Timothy 1:19-20, of "Hymaneus and Alexander whom I have delivered unto Satan that they may be taught not to blaspheme." And we could add to that list, "The woman that's believing has a responsibility to a certain widow and yet the church is to relieve those that are widows indeed." And so there's some works, and I recognize 1 Timothy 5:16 indicates a difference in collective and individual responsibility. But it's rather significant, that really both are doing much the same work. And she relieved a certain widow in order that the church might relieve others. What I'm trying to say is that while there are some responsibilities that may be simply congregational responsibility and other that may be individual responsibility, there are some that will go in both categories.

Now let me get back to that critique. I didn't get through with that. I've got to quit. Hold it gently, can I finish this? (Laughter, whs) Brother May made this statement, that 6:6 and 6:10 are both couched in individual terms. I know I've thought that. I think I've said that. I wish you'd take a look at 6:10 of Galatians in its larger and immediate context. Paul writes in the prescript of the letter to the CHURCHES OF GALATIA. And then as we come here to chapter six, let me read the previous verse, "and let US not be weary in well doing." That sounds somewhat collective to me. "Let US not be weary in well doing for in due season we shall reap if we faint not. So then as WE have opportunity, let us work that which is good toward all men and especially toward them that are of the household of faith." Listen to the next verse, "You see how LARGE LETTERS" Paul has grabbed the pen from the amanuenses; he's going to finish that letter with his own writing. "You see how large letters" (by the way plural "you" twice in the original language), "You see how large letters I write unto with mine OWN HAND" (plural "you" there). I'm wonder if we ought not take another look at some things about that very familiar verse, that's been involved in this discussion.

I appreciate Brother Ferrell Jenkins' presentation. And with a great deal of that I could concur. Thank you very much.

Congregational Verses Individual Activities
Panel Discussion Ground Rules

Jamie Sloan – Moderator: I think Brother Malone's used all of his opportunities up. (Laughter, whs)

Joe Blakeney - Panelist: That was a good exegesis.

Avon Malone – Panelist: Can I leave now since my time is up? (Laughter, whs)

Jamie Sloan – Moderator: I was afraid for a minute these fellows were going to get along so well it was going to ruin the whole session. (Laughter, whs) But, I think Brother Malone has helped us out there, to begin to focus on the difference over these passages. And so let's go from there to discuss this further. All right brethren, who wants to go first?

Panel Discussion

Martin Pickup – Panelist: I suppose my first thought from listening to the good comments that were made, is it seems to me that there's a key difference between you and between Cecil May, on whether or not there is a distinction that should be made between the individual and the church. And I'm not saying that because I'm trying to divide your ranks or anything, but I'm trying to understand where you're coming from. My whole contention with the speech of Brother May is, that he approaches this whole subject from the standpoint of there really, at least in effect his argument would be, there's no such thing really as a local church organization that has distinct work that it should do as opposed to individual action. But yet from the comments you are making, it seams like you recognize that distinction. You would be in agreement with us on that, but not Brother May.

Avon Malone – Panelist: I have an idea he recognizes that distinction. I would be reluctant to speak for him in that regard. But I think we best be careful lest we impute to him something he maybe does not hold or has not said. I have an idea there's a great deal of agreement between us, and I'm reluctant to speak for him.

I do believe there is a distinction between the responsibility of the church and the individual. I do not believe that we go through and mentally color code every single passage in the New Testament and we say individual or collective. I doubt seriously that the Spirit or the inspired writer had that in mind. But I think there are passages where it is very apparent. I think however in some of those passages, that when we'll look very carefully, we find that the congregation and individual are doing the, essentially, same thing.

Matthew 18 is so often used, "If thy brother trespass against thee go and show him his fault between thee and him alone. If he'll hear thee thou hast gained thy brother, if he will not hear thee take with thee one or two more, that at the mouth of two or three witnesses every word may be established. If he will not hear THEM tell it to the CHURCH" and the point's made, there is a distinction. Well, in a sense I see that, "Tell it to the church if he will not hear THEM," "let him be unto thee as an heathen man and a publican." You look at the passage very carefully and the INDIVIDUAL and the CHURCH are doing essentially the same thing, reasoning with the offender with regard to his wrong, with regard to his offense. There is an order, individual FIRST. And then if the method first described herein, (to) bring about a reconciliation of this personal offense, does not resolve it then it becomes a matter for the church to be concerned about. But it seems to me, that in one sense both the individual and church are doing very much the same thing, reasoning with the offender about his offense.

I think there is something like that in 1 Timothy 5:16. Though I readily concede that that passage indicates there is a distinction, this widow has a PARTICULAR responsibility to her own widowed mother or mother-in-law or whatever it might be, if a woman hath widows that believe. And yet she and the CHURCH are in one sense doing very much the same thing, they're taking care of widows. And she takes care of THIS one so that the church might be able to take care of ANOTHER one. I believe there is a distinction. I believe though, it's possible to take that and make it something more than maybe it's intended in the New Testament.

Robert Harkrider – Panelist: The fact that you state there is a difference and a distinction is commendable, yet when you begin to make the applications you begin to dilute that in such a way that you leave us somewhat wondering. It is certainly true the Matthew 18 and 1 Timothy 5 certainly clarify a difference between individual action and that which is church action. And I think, as Brother Jenkins pointed out, there are some things that run concurrently. That is, some things individual action does and some things church do.

Avon Malone – Panelist: Yeah, yeah.

Robert Harkrider – Panelist: But in the matter of discipline, would you take the view that as an individual that we can mark an individual or is this church action? Like 1 Corinthians 5 when he said, "when you are gathered together to deliver such an one unto Satan." There comes a time when there's distinctive collective action, as a unit under the oversight of elders. And so there is a clear distinction. While we both may have a process, have a part of the process of discipline, yet there is some action that is DISTINCTLY exclusively for that congregation as a unit to function. And we need to keep those lines clear.

Jamie Sloan – Moderator: Brother Blakeney.

Joe Blakeney - Panelist: I think a good Panelist ought to be a good listener. (Laughter, whs) When you've got brethren that handle situations like this, I think they ought to handle it. The individual in, for instance ... you represent the church wherever you are as an individual. If I jaywalk across the street in the little town of Whitney, the reflection is upon the church itself not upon me as a personality. And so whatever we do as individuals reflects upon the body of Christ as a whole. It's difficult to separate the two when it comes down to the bare essentials. I still think our main argument is about what do we do with the money, when it comes down to dispensing the money of the church.

Jamie Sloan – Moderator: Brother Pickup.

Martin Pickup – Panelist: Well I think that the argument comes down often times to what do we do with the church money, since the pooled funds is not THE only way but certainly one of the main ways that those saints act collectively as a church.

So I do think it comes down to that, but I think that the real issue is "What is the work of a local church?" How do we know that? If we are admitting, Brother May perhaps didn't clearly, but if we are admitting that there is a distinction that the Bible makes between individual Christians functioning and then functioning in a local church organization collectively. How do we know what is the God ordained work of the local church organization? If we say, "Well it's just whatever God has told the individuals to do". Well that won't work because, as we've seen, 1 Timothy 5 clearly makes a distinction between individual responsibility and then collective church responsibility. So it sees to me the only way that we can ever answer that question, as to what is the work of the local church, is to go to the Bible and read these passages. And make a determination, is this talking about my responsibility as an individual member of the body of Christ, or is this talking about my responsibility COLLECTIVELY with other saints in a local church?

And you know we look at . . . how much time have I got . . . OK. You know, we look at James 1:27 and it just seems to me, and I'll tell you what, I've really tried to be honest with this. Like I said at the beginning, I'm not trying just to inherit my interpretation of a passage. But I cannot for the life of me see how you can get church responsibility, collective responsibility, out of James 1:27, when in the context he so clearly is talking about the individual. And I would also say the same thing about the Galatians 6 passage, but I want to say something else about that later.

Jamie Sloan – Moderator: Avon.

Avon Malone – Panelist: Well, I'd be interested in what he would say about Galatians 6:10, because I think that one deserves a new look. I need to get up closer? (Speaking to the moderators, whs)

With regard to your James 1, "if any MAN among you," one much loved translation has it, "seems to be religious and bridles not his own tongue but deceives his own heart, this MAN's religion is vain." If any MAN among you and we might argue about the translation, but it is rendered that way. "Pure religion and undefiled before God and the father is this is, to visit the widows and fatherless in their affliction and to keep oneself unspotted by the world."

And obviously the matter of purity from the world is going to be involved, one's individual life, no doubt about that. I know from other passages that, you do too, that the church can take care of widows (Acts 6:1-6; 1 Tim. 5:1-16). So, I know at least a part of that, the church can do in the light of other passages.

I also know that that particular letter is addressed to the twelve tribes of the dispersion, the twelve tribes of the *diaspora*, which is probably a term for the church. Maybe…I have an idea he may be writing to Jewish Christians. I know he's writing to Christians from 2:1 and from 5:19-20, but I have an idea he might be writing to Jewish Christians. But it's a collective term and we put it as a general epistle. I have an idea there's the possibility, in the light of other passages, I wouldn't state just with that, but I know from Acts 6 and from 1 Timothy 5 the church can care for some widows, that we may have something here that can be done by both church and individual.

Truth about the matter is though, that we have great areas of agreement. You're talking about how are we're going to determine what we are to do? You had the right idea. You went right to this book. I agree with you on that. And we would agree its evangelism, edification, and benevolence; we don't have any problems there. I think that we need to SEE we have a great deal in common.

When I came in here last night, I happened to run into George Bailey. You know those things happen, you don't have a choice on some of these, it just happens. (Subdued laughter, whs) No I was glad to. And he made a statement with which I can identify. He said, "I have a much greater affinity for these brethren than for some fellows way off there to the left that are saying some things that would" destroy all respect for Biblical authority. I think we need to emphasize something that we do have in common and continue to work in these areas. I'm not trying to minimize the areas but I'm not sure that we have selected the most significant battleground of our day.

Jamie Sloan – Moderator: All right, Robert.

Robert Harkrider – Panelist: As I said in my four-minute speech, sometimes I am reminded of the premillennialist who argues about the death of Christ from different points of view depending on what he's trying to talk about. On one breath you say that the individual and the church are separate, in fact you discuss the fact and said in your four-minute speech Brother Malone, that you would not believe that individuals could support liberal arts education.

 Avon Malone – Panelist: I believe that.

Robert Harkrider – Panelist: And yet in your discussion of James and Galatians, you seem to confuse the difference between DISTRIBUTIVE action and COLLECTIVE action. And you know we're talking about collective action as the difference between that of individuals. And I find it difficult to understand how you could deny the fact of individuals building hospitals or churches doing the same. If our action together is Galatians 6, if we're running together on the same ground, if that is really collective action and not distributive action, then we're going to run into some problems in the application of these, as many of your brethren have done in fact. They've applied the very principle that you set forth.

Avon Malone – Panelist: Well, I don't want to get over that and I won't, but let's go back to James 1:27.

Robert Harkrider – Panelist: But you see, they have followed consistently what terms that you have set forth. And that's really why this is a very vital discussion, and you said you doubted that this was right on the issue of what we needed to be talking about. But I think if you'll face this squarely, this is at the root of many of the problems of brethren within fellowship at least many of you have had, that are doing some things now that embarrass you and you wish they were not doing. And yet they have justified it on the basis of the very thing we're talking about here.

Avon Malone – Panelist: Yeah.

Jamie Sloan – Moderator: Yeah. Just, Avon just to keep the heat off of me, let's formally ask Joe if he'll surrender his two minutes to you.

Avon Malone – Panelist: Naugh I don't want to do that. (Laughter, whs)

Joe Blakeney - Panelist: I will in a minute. (Laughter, whs)

Jamie Sloan – Moderator: Because I'm going to have to take the blame for all this when it's all over. Joe?

Joe Blakeney - Panelist: I still think, and I may not even know what the issue is now (Laughter, whs), I still think there's a problem with what the individual can do and what the church can do. Do I understand you to say that the church can support only those that are members of the church, of the body of Christ? That individuals can go out and help anybody they want to, is that . . . did I just dream that up?

Robert Harkrider – Panelist: We haven't addressed that really.

Joe Blakeney - Panelist: But, is it true? I'm talking about in doing benevolent work, not mission work, benevolent work.

Robert Harkrider – Panelist: If you'd like to get into the hermeneutics, then there is such a thing as the silence of the scriptures. That what the scripture authorizes, is the churches always helped saints. And yet there were individuals who helped those who were even not saints. And I think that there is a distinction there. As we take the scripture there and follow through the scriptural hermeneutics, and as we would deal with others. whether talking about instrumental music, we talk about hermeneutics there. We talk about the law of exclusion and the silence of the scripture, so why not deal with the same type of logic in this.

Joe Blakeney - Panelist: If the Good Samaritan had been a member of the church of Christ and he had run across that fellow on the side of the road he said, "Are you a member of the church of Christ, yet… and what is your hermeneutic?"

Robert Harkrider – Panelist: The Good Samaritan is not the church; he is an individual. You see that's our problem, we don't recognize that difference.

Joe Blakeney - Panelist: But what if he had been? What if it was a group of elders representing the church?

Robert Harkrider – Panelist: Well, I think every one of those elders…Why represent the church as elders? Are you a Christian? Can you as an individual do It?

Joe Blakeney - Panelist: Yea, I think the individual Christian can do a lot of things that represent the church.

Robert Harkrider – Panelist: Absolutely!

Joe Blakeney - Panelist: I think everything we do as Christians should represent the body of Christ.

Robert Harkrider – Panelist: Well, Epaphroditus there represented the church at Philippi as their messenger in Philippians 2, but there's still actions that we do individually. Timothy also, in Philippians 2, was willing even to sacrifice his life, he loved him. He loved the Apostle Paul and gave himself in to the work. He said, "No man likeminded will naturally care for your state, all seek their own but not the things which are Jesus Christ." So there are things we do individually, but there are things we do as a collective unit. And that's what we're talking about, that DIFFERENCE. That's what's our problem, not understanding it.

Joe Blakeney - Panelist: Individually though, you're saying we can help non-Christians, but as the church we must help only those that are Christians.

Robert Harkrider – Panelist: Can you find one passage where the church helped those who were not Christians?

Joe Blakeney - Panelist: Not off the top of my head. (Subdued Laughter, whs)

Robert Harkrider – Panelist: Not off the top of mine either. (Laughter, whs)

Jamie Sloan – Moderator: Avon, I'm not sure whose turn it is, but we need to hear from you again, I think.

Joe Blakeney - Panelist: Yeah. (Laughter, whs)

Avon Malone – Panelist: Well, you want that kind of authority? Can you find one passage for the Bible classes as you have them?

Robert Harkrider – Panelist: Yes.

Avon Malone – Panelist: All right!

Robert Harkrider – Panelist: Yes, in passages that teach the responsibility of teaching. I know in 1 Corinthians…

Avon Malone – Panelist: Under a generic kind of authority?

Robert Harkrider – Panelist: Well, generic authority starts with a command doesn't it?

Avon Malone – Panelist: Yeah, but now don't take up all my time, I just wanted to know…(Laughter, whs). See here's the problem that bothers me. The problem that bothers me, we want a certain kind of proof. But if some of us had to produce for non-class brethren the same kind of proof that we're demanding, some very clear example or Biblical precedent, you know I think I could make, I think you could make a pretty good defense for this as an expedient. But if we require … if others required of us the same kind of proof we ask for, we'd be hard pressed.

But let me make a point here. Whether it's the individual or whether it's the church, whatever we do needs to be authorized. We leave the impression that the church is under very specific and limited authority. I think there may be something to that. I don't differ as much with you brethren as some might think. But on the other hand if an individual does it, why he's completely free to do it however he wants to because this is the individual doing it.

He can buy services. He can transact business with some institution. He can do it in his own home, do it some other way that's the individual, he has complete liberty. Stop and think about that a minute. "Whatever you do in word or in deed do all in the name of the Lord" does that apply to individuals? I believe it does.

I believe then, that we need to have some pattern you need to produce. Tell us somehow, if I'm going to do it in my own home, how am I going to do it? You see if the individual does it, there needs to be some precedent or pattern to establish how he does it. And if he has some liberty, and I think we see he does, if he has some liberty then it seems to me that in SOME areas in expediting divine commands the church also does it.

I think we've never thought about this thing in terms of the fact that, OK the individual's going to take care of these orphans, or this widow. Now how is he going to do it? Well, "whatever he does in word or in deed" he needs to do it "in the name of the Lord."

A number of years ago I was living in Aurora, Colorado. A situation developed where I felt I had a personal responsibility to a widow, and at that same time, and because of that same death, to three fatherless boys. We took them into our home. But the Hoffman Heights church converted a garage into a bedroom, and those three boys lived in there. The individual whatever he does though needs to do it in keeping with Biblical authority. Now I thought then and I think now, that maybe we did the thing we should have done. I didn't know anything else to do. I didn't wrestle with some of the technicalities that we might here. But I'd like to remind you that if the church needs to produce authority for what they're doing, and then we say this is individual responsibility and this is not church responsibility, there needs to be some authority over here. How's the individual to do it? Well, we generally agree he's left pretty free. And I've often wondered, "How is it that he's under such generic authority and the church is under so much specific authority?"

With regard to one of the things you mentioned, you agreed with me that other passages, Brother Harkrider, would indicate the church CAN care for some widows. So what we're saying about James 1 was not limited JUST to James 1. I share much in common with you brethren, but I have an uneasiness when we demand a kind of proof that we would have a hard time providing for things that we generally accept.

And I guess, I have quite frankly, some difficulty with this. I know that among YOU brethren, there are some sharp differences with regard to marriage and divorce, with regard to some vital areas, and yet there is still fellowship. And I'm wondering why can't WE have fellowship? What we're talking about is important, but if you can have fellowship and differ over things like THAT, as vital as THAT is, why can't we somehow work to work together and have fellowship?

Jamie Sloan – Moderator: All right I'm going to give Brother…for this session, Brother Pickup's going to have the last word here.

Martin Pickup – Panelist: I agree that the question that you just asked about fellowship is a vital question, and if that's why we have the last section, I think that needs to be discussed then.

As far as your statement about we need authority for everything whether we're talking about individual action or church action, I certainly believe that we all need to work under the authority of God. But the fact of the matter is that, as you pointed out, the individual passages are much more general, much more generic. But what you see as you look at the New Testament, is that these saints that were called upon under apostolic guidance to form a local congregation, did PARTICULAR, SPECIFIC work.

You don't see them as…you don't see the local church as a general benevolent society. That's not what was established. And the way I KNOW that is simply by looking at the evidence here in the New Testament, from what those churches did as part of their work. They did relieve needy saints in time of famine, but there were a lot of other needy non-Christian people that their money didn't go to. That wasn't the work of that church in its collective work.

And may I say this? I think a large part of our problem here is that when we talk about individual action as opposed to church action, we maybe have in our minds that the local church is really supposed to have the EMPHASIS in the way, in GOD'S mind, the way the church universal is to function and do the will of God. We've over emphasized the importance of the local church and the stature it is to have. I believe that the New Testament clearly puts the emphasis upon the individual and what he is supposed to be doing. That's where the real stress lies and the local church, as an organization, is chiefly for the purpose of edifying and strengthening its own, so that then they as individuals can go out and do the work of individual members of the body of Jesus Christ. And I think we have our emphasis wrong then.

Avon Malone – Panelist: Could I make one response? It was indicated that scripture is much clearer with regard to the churches function than the individuals.

Martin Pickup – Panelist: Specific.

Avon Malone – Panelist: I think there's a bit of a judgment call in that. I want to ask you something. How did the church in Ephesus, where Timothy was when Paul wrote that letter, how did they take care of those enrolled widows? Exactly what did that involve? And in verse 16, "let not the church be burdened that it may relieve them that are widows in deed," exactly how did they do that? Did they put them in one structure? Did they…

Robert Harkrider – Panelist: Your question is really over 'the how' and we don't disagree about that, that there may be methods…

Avon Malone – Panelist: But the point I'm trying to make is…

Robert Harkrider – Panelist: The question is the 'who' that we're talking in this discussion, the difference between the individual and the church, and the 'who' did it? There's a difference between the believer who hath widows providing, that's the 'who,' let not the church be charged, that's a different 'who.'

Avon Malone – Panelist: I understand what you're saying.

Robert Harkrider – Panelist: So our question is not over 'the how' but over 'the who.'

Avon Malone – Panelist: I understand what you're saying, but the impression was left that there is very clear with regard to church activity.

Martin Pickup – Panelist: I said specific.

Avon Malone – Panelist: And among other things that might include how it's done.

Martin Pickup – Panelist: I said specific, the church had specific things that it was doing, and it's…it goes back to the question of generic authority versus specific authority. And when God specifies…

Avon Malone – Panelist: I agree there's some specific things the church needs to be doing.

Martin Pickup – Panelist: And when God specifies, and I think we've all agreed on this, we must abide by what God has specified.

Jamie Sloan – Moderator: All right, we do have some questions that focus on this in the next hour, while there still is a next hour. (Laughter, whs) We need to get these main speakers back up here. We're doing great with the meal tickets; we just need a few more of those sold. Please, let's take care of that. We could maybe use some more questions. I'm really…

Avon Malone – Panelist: This is not going to take any time, but I have a problem, individually with those meal tickets. Could we do something collective (Laughter, whs) to ease . . . I can't handle these twenty dollar . . . can we do something collective (Laughter, whs) to help me with my individual responsibility? (Laughter, whs)

Martin Pickup – Panelist: Just don't use church funds for it. (Laughter, whs)

Congregational Versus Individual Activities
Question and Answer

Jamie Sloan – Moderator: Make sure everybody understands the ground rules before we go to breaking them too much (Laughter, whs). I will ask you a question and you will have two minutes to answer that question. This brother down here will give you a one-minute signal and then, however many frantic no time signals he needs to give (Subdued Laughter, whs). But seriously, I'm very encouraged by the interest in this particular segment. And I do believe that the questions really help us to focus on some of the different aspects of this. So we'll ask Brother May the first question, and that says…

Question 1:

Brother May, "1 Corinthians 12:14 says, 'for the body is not one member but many' do you believe one member is the body?"

Cecil May – Main Speaker: No. One member is not the body, but one…the members of the body make up the body, and the body is not in existence apart from the members. I wrote down here a little bit go, "I don't need to be told that one Christian is not the whole church." I know that, and Ferrell knows I know that. But he's obviously telling me that because he thinks I'm missing some implications of that. Ferrell doesn't need me to tell him that the church is composed of the people. He knows that and I know he knows that. But I'm obviously telling him that because I think he's missing some implications of that fact.

I admitted that I don't understand really where you're coming from in this thing of individual and congregation. It's also very obvious to me you haven't yet, or at least the ones that have talked to me here including Avon, haven't understood where I'm coming from on it. My point is not that there is never a difference between an individual and the church. Obviously one individual is not the church. My point is that when a group of individuals do something together because God has given it them to do, that that is the church doing it. Not a question of MAY the church do it, they HAVE done it. The church has done it, when it's done that way.

The distinction on Matthew 18 again makes THAT POINT. I…take one individual, later tell it to the church. Those are two separate things. But tell it to the church is not just getting up before the local church. That's one way to doing it. But writing it in the papers and printing it all over the brotherhood is another way to do that. And one violates that principle as much as the other, and violates the point that is being made.

We were getting close to the point that needs to be discussed. We have talked last night almost to *ad nauseum* I guess, about the first day of the week and the upper room. And I think everybody agreed last night that there's a difference. And the difference is in the background of why it's essential to follow that example of the first day of the week, and not essential to do it exactly that way when we get to the upper room. And I think if we apply those same principles to some of these examples of the church working, then we'll be getting down to what we need to do. And I understand that's going to happen later, even if it doesn't happen in this session.

Question 2:

Jamie Sloan – Moderator: All right Brother Ferrell Jenkins, "If Brother Jenkins agrees we can fulfill Galatians 6:6 through the church treasury, why can't we fulfill Galatians 6:10 and James 1:27 through the church treasury? If the church can build a preacher's home and pay him why can't the church build medical clinics and pay doctors and nurses?"

Ferrell Jenkins – Rebuttal Speaker: OK, I'm glad to address the matter of Galatians 6:6 and 6:10. I believe that the context of this passage is addressed to individuals that he's writing to, a group of people, not one particular church but a group of churches throughout an area. And that he is dealing with the responsibilities that they have individually in the sixth chapter.

I think that 6:6 is devoted to the individual, and I think that we have other examples in the New Testament of individual Christians who did this very thing. John for example, commends Gaius in 3 John because he had supported the individuals who had come his way, and he had sent them on their way because they took nothing from the gentiles.

I see that there are other passages, as some have already brought out, that there are mutual responsibilities. There are some common responsibilities. And Paul said in 2 Corinthians 11:8-9 that "he robbed other churches taking wages from them," and in Philippians 4:15-16 the church at Philippi sent once and again to Paul. No other church had fellowship with him in the matter of giving and receiving but only the church at Philippi. So there is a difference. There are mutual responsibilities, and are overlapping responsibilities. But the church does not learn its responsibilities from Galatians 6:6 and the individual does not learn his from 2 Corinthians 8:9 except as he is a part of a local church.

Now let me see the last part. "If the church can build the preacher's house to pay him why can't the church build medical clinics to pay doctors and nurses?" Well, the church has a responsibility to preach the gospel and Paul taught that those who preach the gospel should live of the gospel. And New Testament churches did support preachers, same passages I've already used and 2 Corinthians 11:8-9 and Philippians 4:15-16, and so a church has a responsibility to do that.

And this thing, I kind of agree with Brother May on this thing about *ad nauseum*, when you get into the upper room and all of this. I mean all of us recognize the area of expediency. We may not yet be agreed exactly how far it extends, but in our hermeneutic, we all think that there are generic commands that do give us an area of expediency. And how big a house the preacher has and all of that's included. But I don't see any authority at all for the church to build medical clinics or anything of the sort, except as those would be a part of its particular care of the widows that it might be responsible for. Whatever is involved in the incidentals of caring for the needy, the "how," the "who" will supervise, what kind of building they'll be in, what kind of care will be given. All of that falls within the category of caring for those that are the needy, or the needy ones.

And so really in a sense, it's the same. But if you're talking about a separate Preacher House Building Society and a separate Hospital Society, an institution, then I oppose both of those.

Question 3:

Jamie Sloan – Moderator: Avon, This question! "The church and the individual both have responsibility toward some widows. The church should relieve the widows indeed; the woman should relieve her widows. Should the church relieve her widows?"

Avon Malone – Panelist: I'd say only if she did not or could not. That's her responsibility and she needs to fulfill it. If she cannot or will not, then that might be something else. But she has a personal responsibility and needs to fulfill it.

Jamie Sloan – Moderator: And in regard, by the way about these two minutes, if your answer to that doesn't take your two minutes and you want to go ahead and fill that out in…

Avon Malone – Panelist: Well, somebody put a question up here about…and maybe it would better go to someone else, because I may be in agreement with what seems to be implied by the question. But it does mention the passage that I want to introduce. I'd like to hear more about 6:10 of Galatians in its context, "let us not be weary in well doing" and "behold how large letters I write unto YOU," plural you, that's the immediate context. And he's writing to the churches of Galatia. In that connection, this question was put up here, if I've got a minute or two. 2 Corinthians 9:13, if you will look at that with me, you might want to turn to it…

Jamie Sloan – Moderator: I've got…Avon; Brother Pickup's… the question I've got addressed to him I think is this very question.

Avon Malone – Panelist: All right, well it may better go to someone else.

Jamie Sloan – Moderator: All right! Let me see if this does, if it doesn't well bring it up again we'll…

Avon Malone – Panelist: All right!

Jamie Sloan – Moderator: Marty, "If Galatians 6:10 is individual responsibility and 2 Corinthians 9 is church responsibility how do you explain this striking parallel." The parallel he gives is this, "Galatians 6:8-10 says, 'he soweth…do good unto all men,'" 2 Corinthians 9:6-8 and 13 says, 'he sowth…good works unto all men'?"

Martin Pickup – Panelist: I'm not quite sure I understand exactly the point he's making. But it seems to me that what's being said here is the fact that a plural pronoun is used in the context of talking to individual Christians. Does that necessarily then mean that, OK now we've switched to a local church collectively. And I don't think that that follows. Ephesians 5 talks about 'wives be subject to your own husbands,' plural pronoun, but obviously talking about those women in the church individually in that relationship. And the fact the plural pronoun is used doesn't affect that.

As I...this is the point I was going to make on Galatians 6:6, 10. As you look at the context it seems to me that he clearly is talking about individuals. I think you had made the statement a while back that the letter is addressed to the churches of Galatia. And so you were trying to say, that therefore because it's addressed that way that we should understand the plural pronoun is referring to a... these local churches, then doing that as part of their work, unless I misunderstood you. And I would just say that I don't think that follows at all. I mean if you can use that line of reasoning, if addressing the churches of Galatia, he would be talking about some church wide organization or something.

Avon Malone – Panelist: It says local churches.

Martin Pickup – Panelist: Which obviously doesn't follow, and you know that because you look at the passage and you determine, no he can't be talking about that. He's talking about the churches of Galatia distributively, in regard to various responsibilities. And in the same way even among those individual CHURCHES of Galatia, there are distributive responsibilities of the members. And it just seems to me, that's clearly what's going on in Galatians 6:10.

Avon Malone – Panelist: How do you get individual out of all plural terms though? I heard what you said, but I still have a little trouble with that. Let us…

Martin Pickup – Panelist: If you look at the epistles that are addressed to the various CHURCHES in the New Testament, and if you were going to go down the line and look at the information that is given, I think what you'll see is that most of the information in these letters, that is addressed to these CHURCHES, really refers to the members of that church in their individual life. And that there really are very few collective responsibilities that are talked about. Now of course there obviously are collective responsibilities, say in 1 Timothy, talks about the elders

and deacons and the widows indeed and all of that. But, well my time is up.

Jamie Sloan – Moderator: Joe, next question.

Joe Blakeney – Panelist: 2 Corinthians 9:13 does not talk about an individual responsibility; it's talking about the church collectively. The whole 8th and 9th chapter is.

Jamie Sloan – Moderator: Let's…Question for you Joe.

Joe Blakeney – Panelist: Oh I thought you wanted me to answer him.

Jamie Sloan – Moderator: No.

Joe Blakeney – Panelist: Oh, I'm sorry.

Jamie Sloan – Moderator: It's all right, your doing great.

Joe Blakeney – Panelist: I did good didn't I? (Laughter, whs).

Jamie Sloan – Moderator: I know you'd rather talk about that, but somebody wants you to talk about Jay walking again, so let me… (Laughter, whs)

Joe Blakeney – Panelist: I didn't say that did I?

Question 4:

Jamie Sloan – Moderator: "Although your Jay walking may reflect negatively upon the church, would the church be thus responsible for paying the fine for the Jay walking? (Laughter, whs). Would the collective group be charged with the same crime?"

Joe Blakeney – Panelist: Yes sir, in my town it would (Laughter, whs). I represent the church of Christ in Whitney, Texas, probably a little bit more than ordinary members do. Every member should. When you individually are out doing anything you do as a child of God, your representing the Lord's body, I don't care what it is.

Question 5:

Jamie Sloan – Moderator: All right Brother Harkrider, I am in order, it's your turn, right? "Do we need an example for a church to assist a non-saint? Do we need an example for a woman to teach classes of children?"

Robert Harkrider – Panelist: If we believe in Bible, the authority of the Bible, we need to determine the command that can be obeyed in any one of these, either by an expressed statement, or by an approved example, or by a necessary inference. The question says, "Do we need an example?" I'd have to say, well no, if it could be established by some other means.

But yes, I would say that whatever is the work of the church then let it be authorized in the Bible. There may be aids and expediencies about "the how" to carrying out the teaching, and yet we must begin with the command, or with Bible authority. And that's the difference between aids and additions very clearly. We say that there is authority for the use of the projector, or Bible class material. Are we to divide into Bible classes? We know it is not specified, and therefore it is not an essential that we have Bible classes, these are but aids or expediencies. But we start with the command of teaching.

I'm itching to address Galatians 6. Can I address that? (Laughter, whs).

Jamie Sloan – Moderator: You can use two minutes whatever…

Robert Harkrider – Panelist: I've got a minute. I find while much of that language, because it's in the plural, "BRETHREN" verse 1 "if a man be overtaken in a fault YE which are spiritual," is that plural? "Restore such an one in a spirit of meekness considering THYSELF" he uses the plural "brethren" there, that's certain. But we understand that's distributive action because we don't act as a unit. Even in verse 9 "let US not be weary in well doing for in due time WE shall reap" is judgment day…are we going to be saved as a church, or as individuals? We understand the language while it uses plural can be distributive in its meaning, and it is individual in its application. And even though the plural of Galatians 3:27, "as many of YOU as have been baptized into Christ have put on Christ," it's plural. Though the book is addressed to churches, it has many instructions that have individual application and are obeyed by individuals.

Question 6:

Jamie Sloan – Moderator: All right, Brother Cecil. "Would the good to be done in Galatians 6:10 include providing medical needs? Does this authorize the church to build hospitals, or does the Bible pattern exclude medical mission work as sinful?"

Cecil May – Main Speaker: This is the part of this thing that I don't like. I'm not really a debater and I always think of exactly the smart, exactly right thing to say the next morning in the bathtub. (Laughter, whs).

But, yes I believe that Galatians 6:10 does authorize benevolence as needed according upon the judgment and opportunity of the people who have to give it for anyone who is in need. I think it would be obviously foolish, poor judgment, probably to the point of sin to build a hospital in Dallas to try to compete with what's going on in the Baptist Hospital and charge room rates that…you know that gets into a lot of other things. But for a person to go to Africa or to South America where people are dying and there's nobody there to help them, is the kind of benevolent work that I do think that the church is authorized to do.

I've mentioned, and again let me keep trying to get this…what I'm saying about this individual—collective thing put together. I emphasized that the support of preachers in Galatians 6 is individual, "let him that is taught in the word communicate to him that teacheth in all good things," that everybody has agreed that's individual. Somebody has said, "that might be fulfilled either way," because it also says for the church to do it.

But I'm saying that that passage in Galatians 6 is an individual obligation, a responsibility that every individual has to meet. And the only way you can get that into the collective thing, is to say that it's possible for individual duties that all Christians admittedly have, to be done collectively. And indeed when they do them collectively the individuals have still done them. When the individuals all…if every member of the church gave the preacher something and it ended up being enough, then the church would have still supported him. There's just…that's the point that I making, and again, I'm suggesting that a great deal of our problem is still definitional. And I don't think we've yet really come to terms with that.

Question 7:

Jamie Sloan – Moderator: All right, Brother Jenkins. This is a little bit lengthy but I'll leave it up here for you. "Does 1 Timothy 5:16 or Matthew 18:15-18 teach a difference in *action*," action underlined "or a distinction in *responsibility*," responsibility underlined. "In 1 Timothy 5:16 both aided widows, same action. In Matthew 18:15-18 both dealt with a brother at fault, same action, not a question of action but who is to be responsible for the action?"

Ferrell Jenkins – Rebuttal Speaker: Well, the question took two minutes. (Subdued Laughter, whs). I don't see really any question here, it's more of a statement, because indeed the showing the difference in 'the who' did the certain thing. And in the case of the going and talking to the brother, or whether the church talks to the brother, and the matter of the individual providing for the widow or the church providing for the widow. You pointed out that actually the same details or the means or the methods or how this is to be accomplished, would be identically the same. And I make this point very frequently when I'm discussing our options in obeying the Lord, generic and specific and talk about that very thing.

I think we need to distinguish in this whole thing about the giving in Galatians 6:6 and this about the difference between the individual and the church. I had…I closed a meeting Wednesday evening in Indiana. And in fact Tuesday evening, I'm really gaining the acceptance of brethren, they paid me Tuesday evening and I stayed. (Laughter, whs). But there was a check that was signed by the Treasurer of the congregation and it was from them and I understood that that church was supporting me as a gospel preacher. And on Wednesday evening, just before I went to bed, the godly couple that I stayed with knew I was coming here, and they asked me about my expenses and they gave me an envelope with a note on it that said, "We would like to share in your expenses."

Well I consider this part of my work as a gospel preacher being here, I think every preacher here does. And there an… just a perfect illustration of the two different ways that a gospel preacher may be supported in his work. The church supported me, and individual Christians supported me, but it was two distinct treasuries and two distinct acts. I believe the Lord was glorified in each.

Question 8:

Jamie Sloan – Moderator: Avon this may not take you very long. You may want to use your time for something else, but the question says, "Be definitive about those structures where we have wasted the churches funds." Do you know what they mean by that?

Avon Malone – Panelist: Yeah, I think I know what they mean by that. We got some guys at Harding, I mean at… well we had them at Harding too; we got them at Oklahoma Christian. We get together in the school gym, we whoop and holler and we foul each other and we call it basketball. And as antiquated as I am, I do that like three or four days a week. I do not believe that the local church ought to be producing facilities like that. That's the sort of structure, and there's some others, that that would illustrate. I don't have, you know, a lot of fellows may differ, a lot of brethren, I don't want to use the designations or terms we ordinarily use, might not agree with me. I have

no enthusiasm for the church building structures like that. Although I make use of some buildings like that, but not so constructed. That's what I meant by that.

Let me use some time on something real quickly. The…and Brother May brought this out early in the hypothetical conversation, in illustrating what's done with this individual collective distinction. I believe there is such a distinction. But I think we can go to some extremes with it. The practical thing that usually comes out of that is the individual can be a Good Samaritan to all men, saint and sinner alike, but the church cannot. And one reason that we pressed on Galatians 6:10 has to do with that. I don't believe that authorizes the building of some things that have been mentioned. But I'm not all together convinced in my mind that that particular passage in its immediate and larger context, directed to local congregations in the larger context, and with what we have there, is simply talking about something that's done individually, "as we have opportunity."

But let me add to that another passage or two. I think Brother Blakeney mentioned one of these. Read with me in 2 Corinthians at 9:13, "Seeing that through the proving of you by this ministration, they glorify God for the obedience of your confession unto the gospel of Christ, and for the liberality of your contribution unto THEM". Them what? Pardon the grammar. Them saints. There, but that's not all, "unto them" referring to saints "and unto all."

Along with 2 Corinthians 9:13 just read, let's add a passage from a speech of Paul in Acts 24, "And now after some years I come to bring alms to my NATION." I come to bring alms to my nation and offerings, etc.

We have some passages in the Thessalonian correspondence, where "I love" and I believe love to be Biblical love must be expressed is toward all. 1 Thessanonians 3:12, "And the Lord make you to increase and abound in love one to another and toward all men." Love, to be Bible love, needs to express itself.

1 Corinthians, and I'm going to quit with this one. I see these subtle signs and they're pressing in on me. I shouldn't have taken so long on that first question. I could have been briefer. "See that none render unto any evil for evil but always follow after that which is good one toward another and toward all," written to the church of the Thessalonians and in a context which I think opens some possibilities we need to honestly look at.

Let me, can I say one more thing very quickly. And I realize that if every time we see church we think only of the local church then this may not mean much. But we all agree that while the church functions as the church in the local congregation, the church is used in another sense. God has given "Christ to be head over all things to the church which is his body, the fullness," the *pleroma*, meaning amplitude, plentitude, fullness, "of Him that filleth all in all." Somehow I have difficulty. . . . you may not have this problem with believing that the one who said "love your enemies, bless them that curse you, do good to them that hate you, pray for them that spitefully use you and persecute you, if you salute them that salute you what do ye more than others?" I have a little difficulty in believing that that church, which is the fullness of Him, concerns itself only with saints in that area.

I know in evangelism we're obviously, because of the very nature of evangelism, concerned about the whole world. And I think that's our primary work, and I think that's where we need to unite. But I think we need to take a look at the Acts 24, 2 Corinthians 9:13 passage. And I'm not sure I'm completely convinced yet on Galatians 6:10. Thank you.

Jamie Sloan – Moderator:

All right thank you Avon. If Brother Jeff Asher is here you have a message, if you'll go and see Brother Fain back in the back. Where am I, Brother Harkrider? For some reason I think we're at Brother Harkrider.

Question 9:

OK, Brother Pickup, you can have Brother Harkrider's question. (Laughter, whs). Was the non-Christian helped by the church, in 2 Corinthians 9:13?

Martin Pickup – Panelist: Is this for me?

Jamie Sloan – Moderator: Yes sir.

Martin Pickup – Panelist: Ok. I think that when you look at the contribution that is being talked about here, you have to look at all the passages to understand what contribution is being discussed. You have to look at 2 Corinthians 8:9, you have to look at 1 Corinthians 16, you have to look at Romans 15, and I think clearly that the passages indicate that this was a contribution to the saints.

I think that when you look at the contribution that is being talked about here, you have to look at all the pas-

sages to understand what contribution is being discussed. You have to look at 2 Corinthians 8 and 9. You have to look at 1 Corinthians 16. You have to look at Romans 15. And I think clearly that the passage indicates this was a contribution to the saints. If you look at 2 Corinthians 9, he even talks about one of the reasons for this contribution as being a expression of liberality given to these people who had enriched these gentiles spiritually. And so there was the reciprocation, that you assist in their time of material need and there is the sign of that, that you are sharing with them in these things. And if you look at other passages, you look at Romans 15, Paul's point is that in verse 25—"but now I am going to Jerusalem serving the saints, for Macedonia and Achaia have been pleased to make a contribution for the poor among the saints at Jerusalem." I think that that contribution that's being discussed there, is clearly a contribution those gentile churches were making to saints in Jerusalem.

Avon Malone – Panelist: What about the 'all'.

Martin Pickup – Panelist: And the 'all' is a relative term. You have to look at. OK, all what?

Avon Malone – Panelist: "All men," in my translation.

Martin Pickup – Panelist: No. The word 'men' is an interpolation. You have to look at, all right, all what? And in context Paul's whole point is, this is a sign of the spiritual fellowship that you have with those people in Jesus Christ.

Avon Malone – Panelist: But you....

Martin Pickup – Panelist: And you're helping them materially because of the assistance they have given you spiritually.

Avon Malone – Panelist: But being honest... (Spoken softly behind the scenes whs)

Jamie Sloan – Moderator: Here is a question, I think that focuses on something that's been said a couple of times. Joe it's for you.

Joe Blakeney – Panelist: (Talking to Avon in the background whs) Does it not say men in the American Standard?

Avon Malone – Panelist: (Talking to Joe in the background whs) No.

Question 10:

Jamie Sloan – Moderator: Brother Blakeney, "You say whether an individual...you say whatever an individual does reflects on the church. Are you not confusing Christian reputation and influence with collective action? Isn't there a difference?"

Joe Blakeney – Panelist: Is that for me?

Jamie Sloan – Moderator: Yes sir.

Joe Blakeney – Panelist: If I understand the question right, yes it does reflect upon the church win lose or draw, as a Christian. It may not in the large community but it definitely does in a small community. Is that the question or did I miss it?

Jamie Sloan – Moderator: The question says, "You say whatever an individual does reflects on the church are you not confusing Christian reputation and influence with collective action?" Do you want to discuss the difference between action and reputation and influence? That's their question.

Joe Blakeney – Panelist: Well, I'm a little dense; I just don't see any difference.

Jamie Sloan – Moderator: OK. We got… I want to get as many of these in as we can. We're going to be running out of time here. I guess we're back to Brother May.

Question 11:

"Keep himself unspotted from the world includes promotion of and participation in clean recreation. This is a part of pure and undefiled religion. Can a church practice this phrase of pure and undefiled religion by planning, promoting, and providing recreational gatherings, church kitchens, gymnasiums? If the church can't build a gym does this mean that the church can't practice pure and undefiled religion?"

Cecil May – Main Speaker: You may think that I'm not answering the question. But I . . . before I get to it you'll see that I am . . . reference was made to the fact that maybe I had not recognized the existence of the local church as opposed to just the universal church. I do recognize that. I realize that. I did not comment on that in the speech that I made.

I do believe that the church comes into existence at the point when people are baptized into Christ. The church is there when that happens. Then the church being in existence, there are certain things the New Testament says the church is supposed to do. They are to begin to meet, they are to organize, they are to select elders and deacons,

if there are men that are qualified. They are to do certain things, and in certain cases they are to do those certain things in certain ways. And everything they do has to be authorized. I believe all of that, and not only believe that, I preach that. And I believe that I practice in accordance to that.

But having said that, I also say that there are a great number of the things that we talk about that are not so much a matter of absolute principle, the church is not authorized to do that, as it is a matter of judgment. And again I say that saying a thing is a matter of judgment doesn't mean that anything that anybody does it is all right. There can be such poor judgment that it's sin.

I made mention…was made of the college in the budget. I don't think that it's the…that there's anything in what the Lord has given the church to do that suggests that the church's obligation to provide education and how to be a lawyer or a doctor or a school teacher, or anything of that sort, for all of its members. That again is very closely akin to the fact that the church as a whole doesn't have any obligation to provide for my mother, if I'm able to do that. The church might enter in if I couldn't do that, then they would help me, and if I couldn't provide an education for my children then they might help that child. But that's not an obligation.

But it seems to me that you do not have to say that it is sinful for a congregation to allow a brother to put up a… use a basketball goal on the edge of the parking lot because the tennis shoes will ultimately wear away the church's asphalt. You don't have to say that in order for you to say that it's wrong for the church to spend a million dollars to build a gymnasium when a lost world needs to hear the gospel. There's some judgment involved and I think that there's more judgment involved than some kind of absolute principle that says that you can't use the church's pavement that way.

Jamie Sloan – Moderator: Well we're going to be out of time. I've got one more question for Brother Jenkins. And then in accord with our guidelines, then Brother May can have a two minute summary and then Brother Jenkins a two minute summary.

Question 12:

Brother Jenkins this question says, "Do you believe the mainstream view on interpreting this church and individual's responsibility issue, has anything to do with the new hermeneutic? If so how and why, if not don't you agree all of this issue is a judgment call rather than a pattern principle?"

Ferrell Jenkins – Rebuttal Speaker: I'm not sure I know what the mainstream is. "Does it have anything to do with the new hermeneutic and, if so, how or why? If not don't you agree all of this issue is a judgment call rather than a principle?" I don't see what this issue and having something to do with the new hermeneutic has anything to do with whether or not it's a pattern principle. I don't understand the import of that question. I think that the people who are here think that this is an important question. And we believe that indeed we do need to have an answer for it from the scriptures. I think the new hermeneutic people would say that this is all a useless discussion and that we really don't need any of this at all and no authority and just do what Jesus did, however nebulous that is and so on.

I'd like to take just a minute of this time to address 2 Corinthians 9:13. It is in a sense a new issue and not brought up by Brother May or myself. I would agree with what Marty said about the passages. The collection was taken for the saints, 1 Corinthians 16:1-2. In Romans 15 and the other passages Paul said he was going to Jerusalem to minister to the saints. And then 2 Corinthians 9:12-ff he talked about the ministry of this service. He uses the word *koinonao*, a word which carries the idea of sharing. I don't believe that word is EVER used in the relationship between a Christian and a non-Christian. And then he talks about the thanksgiving that would overflow to God. I believe these are Christians as they prayed. And then of course, when as he talks about the liberality of the contribution, the *koinonao*, unto them and unto all. "Unto them," I believe Romans 15:25-26 would suggest are the poor among the saints. The "all" which is simply *pantas*, and the men is italicized, it's not part of the Greek text. And the point is simply it could be all the saints. I mean we have to add a word there in order to supply, to fill out the context, and it could be all the saints, that the poor among the saints received a material benefit, all the saints received the benefit from that.

Jamie Sloan – Moderator: At last report there were approximately a half-dozen tickets left for lunch. Those can be purchased there.

Again may God be praised for the good spirit that has prevailed and certainly we do earnestly pray that the truth has been presented and that it will be perceived in our hearts and bear fruit in our lives. Again we're very glad for the opportunity. Steve do you have. . . . (Tape ends here whs).

Congregational Versus Individual Activities
Day 2 Speech 1
Summation Speeches

Cecil May – Main Summation Speaker

Number one, let me wholeheartedly agree with Avon that at essence of this matter has to do with the thrust of goodness and love going to all who are in need in so far as we have opportunity and ability to provide that. And the idea that the church, the body of Christ collectively, cannot participate in that, it seems to me, is completely inconsistent with the whole thrust of Jesus' whole ministry. And that's the reason why I think this issue of individual collective is essential to discuss because this is the point at which that obviously is made to be so, of the church.

Secondly, I…this is the second time I've participated in a meeting like this. I was at Nashville and now I'm here. And both times I had to deal with a topic that relates to the issues that divide us. And I realize that has to be done. I realize that's…that you can't smooth everything over and say, "Let's all agree and let's all love one another and forget our differences." I said that to Brother Ketcherside thirty years ago when he first began to apply that to instrumental music. You can't just fuzz it over; you've got to deal with the issue if brethren are conscientious about the issue. I realize you've got to do that. But this is just a personal request. I've done this twice now. And if this kind of meeting is held again, and I guess I hope that it is. And if I'm invited again and I hope that I will be and I'll do what I can to help it if I am. Next time put me on one of those speeches where I can talk about what we have in common and how much we love one another (Laughter) and let somebody else do this. Thank you.

Ferrell Jenkins – Rebuttal Summation Speaker

It has been a pleasure to be here and to participate in this meeting and I look forward to the other sessions. I would like to suggest that while we are talking about differences here and while indeed perhaps some undue time has necessarily been spent on dealing with differences, as Brother Winkler said with Acts 15. I do not believe that those brethren with whom I am associated have totally neglected Acts 16. I think that we recognized our responsibilities toward reaching those that are lost and I do not believe there will ever become a time, nor did there in the history of New Testament churches, that they did not face problems. I'm impressed with the fact that churches that had Apostles that visited them and churches that received letters written by Apostles still had questions and still had problems and still had to seek the resolution of those problems, see 1 Corinthians, 1 & 2 Thessalonians, you all know the cases. And so we're going to always have some kind of problems that are going to arise. But that doesn't mean that we should stop the work of preaching the gospel.

I believe also that we need to recognize that the church universal, of which our Lord…for which He died, that that is made up of all Christians, all individuals who have been baptized into Christ. The church indeed is people. Sometimes these people are spoken of distributively, "great fear came upon the whole church," "the church was scattered abroad and went everywhere preaching the word," and so on. Not a local church, not an individual Christian, not spoken of as the church universal, but simply a group of Christians. There are many Christians in Dallas who are not a part of this meeting. We don't constitute a local church, we don't constitute the church universal, but we each acting in our individual realm. And we can do many things that way and glorify the Lord and be pleasing to Him.

The local church has been given certain work, certain oversight, certain responsibilities, and it can fulfill those. And each one of us in our individual realms can do those things that we believe are in harmony with the will of God. I think that we need to be so very careful about our influence and our reputation. But we also need to recognize some distinctions in our responsibilities and works. Thank you so much for your very good attention to this series.

Jamie Sloan – Moderator:

At last report there were approximately a half dozen tickets left for lunch that can be purchased. There. Again, may God be praised for the good spirit that has prevailed and certainly we do earnestly pray that the truth has been presented and that it will be perceived in our hearts and bear fruit in our lives. Again, we're very glad for the opportunity. Steve do you have the… (The tape ends here. whs)

END OF SPEECH ONE, DAY TWO

Afternoon Meal

Day 2 Meal Speeches
Friday, July 13, 1990

Participants

Non-Institutional Brethren	Institutional Brethren
R.J. Stevens — Meal 2	Curtis Camp — Meal 1

Day 2 Meal Speech 1
Curtis Camp

Introduction: *Camp, Curtis. Preached for forty-three years in Oklahoma, California and Texas. Is currently doing full-time meeting and singing school work. Resides in Kemp, Texas.*

Thank you, Brother Roy. (Responding to introduction by Roy Lanier not caught on tape, whs) I don't think I can say that I'm really glad to be here. Because the first speaker this morning said he was against camping (laughter, whs), he didn't like camps, and he said please do not connect me with a camp. So I feel somewhat depreciated, defeated and downhearted.

But really and seriously, this is something that sort of breaks my heart all over again. Because I've had the privilege of seeing those with whom I've served, renewing acquaintances as it were. And I think of the great times we had in serving in places where they lived and their serving in places where I've lived, but seemingly we can't do that anymore. We both are still preaching the gospel just as we did, but we cannot have these experiences anymore.

Where I've lived In recent years, we worship just as we did when these good brethren, and they are my dear brethren, preached in meetings and we enjoyed association from the first service throughout the last. But it's been a while since we've been able to do that. I could wish to have those warm visits which characterized our association in the past. And so personally, my heart breaks even as we try to examine what happened. I think there is reason for hope. So long as we live surely there's reason for hope. The fact that we are here together this week is good and it's thrilling to us. And brethren, I think I see a little light.

Whatever has alienated us is not worthy. I suspect we would all subscribe to that. Our Lord does not want us apart. We need each other and we need to be together for the glory to which we are called. ("Amen" from the audience, whs) I refuse to believe and will not accept any testimony that you and you are insincere, or that you despise those with whom you used to work and to be associated. Why should we who are united in fighting against

immorality, hypocrisy, and all religious error, stand apart from each other whose lives and services are so desperately needed? It seems we've manufactured and fashioned more issues and problems to alienate members of the body today than did the Corinthians in New Testament times or any other group of people who have begun to follow the Lord.

I was deeply impressed by an editorial written by Brother Alan Highers, in which he pleads for a kinder and gentler brotherhood. There's not the slightest intimation of compromise in doctrine or in practice in what he wrote in the January's issue of the *Spiritual Sword*. I loved his appeal to all of us. I think we'd do well to think about it through the day and take it to bed with us. Wouldn't it be great for all of us to get back to what are the real basics of preaching and living the pure gospel of Jesus Christ?

It's no compliment to us that we've been very busy putting brethren into separate and warring camps and cliques. It's so unlike the will and the way of our Lord. Surely we must adhere to the precious word of God. And when we do, we'll come across 1 Peter 2:17, "Love the brotherhood," and Romans 12 and 10, "be kindly affectioned one to another with brotherly love." John asks, "For he that loveth not his brother whom he hath seen, how can he love God whom he hath not seen?" (1 John 4:20). One can do and be all these things without one bit of toleration of false doctrine or unholy living. We can and we must believe in sound doctrine (Tit. 2:1). We must earnestly contend for the faith once delivered (Jude 3). We ought to speak with boldness (Eph. 6: 19, 20; Acts 4:13).

But surely there is no place for slander or of speech that is injurious to another's good name and character in the body of our Lord. Even in New Testament times some brethren disagreed, yet they remained faithful in the one body, and continued to recognize others as being important members of that body. If we would please our Lord, there cannot be anger, hostility, and suspicion. The power we have is for the preaching of the gospel to the lost. Therefore our energy cannot be expended fighting among ourselves. There are many things we are strictly forbidden to love. There are some things we can love, but there are other things we must love more. With loving the church there are no restrictions, there is no limit. Our love for it can grow and grow and God will be pleased and we will continually increase in our love for one another in our Lord's body.

Our question has never been if we're all in the one body. But there is a question, "Are we behaving as God's children in the one body?" It must be something less than love that motivates us to treat each other so strangely and sometime even shabbily. Our faith has not been strengthened nor our love increased by these past experiences. The effectiveness of many has declined and our usefulness has been markedly lessened. We once marched together and the church was growing and the gospel was being spread into every community across the land. Then it became harder to preach upon any occasion without divisive issues being discussed and stressed. The greater part of all of us have been guilty, and now we realize that and regrets are in our hearts. But in a way I guess that's good, for now we can objectively look at ourselves. And we can look at this world of ours. And when we do, we're going to see that there are far more unsaved people today than 35 or 40 years ago. But still I think I see a little light.

Sylvia and I have a hideaway place in the mountains of northern New Mexico. Every preacher ought to have at least two preacher's homes. There's now a meeting place for the church in that area about 4 or 5 miles from our place, and we delight to attend services there. Likely some of you have visited the Marina Valley church, it's called. There we meet with brethren from many sections of the country, sometimes from several states in a single service. We worship together. We visit together. We embrace each other, those of us who've known each other over a considerable length of time.

One Saturday a brother who has a hideaway place down below ours, down the mountainside, walked by our place. I was high on a ladder painting the gable of the house. This brother called up to me and he said, "Curt if you'll preach in the morning, I'll teach the adult class and I'll lead the singing." He does both really well. And I said I'd do it, so he did and I did, and we both were uplifted by that service. The sad part of this story is that we can't do that where he lives back in Texas, nor we can do that where I live. And my question is, "Why can't we?"

On another occasion on Wednesday evening, following the Bible class to which I had been invited to speak, three brethren whom I have known since 1940 visited together. We had not been in a service together for years. In fact we'd not seen each other in a considerable length of time. We had a great time visiting. We embraced each other. What a delight. But back at home we can't do that. It's for… is it for the fear of condemnation of others, preachers perhaps? I didn't say it was, I'm just wondering, maybe with you. Is it necessary for me to question everyone to discover if his stand on certain questionable matters is the same as mine before I can worship or serve with him? If indeed we can fellowship and worship together away from home, why can't we do it at home? In that mountain church, though we may know the feelings of each, we worship together as if we did not know. If there, why not here and everywhere? I still think I see a little light.

Just a few years ago Brother Homer Hailey came to our city to preach in a Gospel Meeting. A number of miles from there I was with the Bell Avenue church and we were engaged in a Gospel Meeting the same week. But I felt fortunate because their services were at 10:00 in the morning and ours at 7:00 in the morning. I went out each morning to hear Brother Hailey. He recognized me publically and spoke of his being in meetings with us when we lived in Oklahoma City and when we lived in Elk City, Oklahoma. Following the service I invited him and the local preacher to our early service. And when I got to the building the next morning they were there. I asked Brother Hailey to lead the first prayer in that service and I asked the local preacher of that congregation to lead the closing prayer. And under their capable leadership we prayed together. Surely we can worship together. We did that morning.

I made my first efforts at preaching on the last Sunday night in February 1933. Three young men in the congregation started that same month. Brother Robert Gullie had the second Wednesday night, Brother Charles Richie had the third Wednesday night, and I had the forth. Brother Garner came out from Quanah to North Groesbeck, a country church, and preached on the first Sunday and the first Sunday night. And this went on for a good while. And then in time Brother Gullie and I decided we should go to college. Weren't doing any good farming cotton anyway. And so we went away to college, and Charlie got married to Robert's sister. Over several years we preached in meetings in the place where we lived. I was with Charles in meetings where he lived and he preached in meetings where I lived, and so it was with Robert as well. And then we could not do that anymore. And that hurt both them and me.

This past April Brother Charlie Richie passed away. After his retirement in a city near Amarillo, he moved in to Amarillo. We had great times together. We had our favorite coffee place. Charlie liked ice cream and we found a place that would give us an ice cream cone with a cup of coffee. And we enjoyed many sessions. When I would leave the house to go pick up Charlie to go to our date, Sylvia would always say, "I'll see you sometime after dark." (Laughter, whs) We had long sessions. I'm thankful for those.

A little more than a year ago Charles said, with his emphysema, "I'm not going to live very long and I know it and I want you to preach my funeral, if you will." I said, "Charles it'll be no special delight, but if that is your wish, I'll do my best I can." Charlie passed. His son called confirming this, that I'd been asked to speak at that service. In that memorial service we worshiped together. We sang together. The assisting brother led a prayer and made some very appropriate comments on the passages he read. We worshiped together. Can we not worship together in other meeting houses and at other times? I still think I see a little light.

I'm heartened, I'm encouraged, and I'm praying that our tie in Christ will be recognized and strengthened. Many of us have no more than just a few years at the most. How we wish we might live to see once again the warm and sincere fellowship which characterized the first half of our years in the Lord's service. There are two things for which I frequently and fervently pray—that our cherished fellowship might be restored, and that I might live to see it. May God bless all of you my brethren. (Several in the audience say "amen" and "God bless you" combined with warm applause, whs).

Day 2 Meal Speech 2
R. J. Stevens

Introduction: *Stevens, R. J. Preached for 43 years in Oklahoma, California and Texas. Is currently doing full-time meeting and singing school work. Resides in Kemp, Texas.*

Thank you John. (Responding to introduction not caught on tape whs) I want to express my appreciation to Steve Wolfgang and Brother Roy Lanier. And I appreciate so much Brother Camp's lesson. I was moved by that. I know he was a friend of a very dear friend of mine, Brother J. M. Gilpatrick, who also to many of us, was a brother Panhandle preacher too.

Many of you knew my dad, M. Roy Stevens and also you knew my brother, Eldred Stevens. Dad passed away in '68, and Eldred was killed in a plane crash in 1979. These two men meant more to me than nearly any men I've ever known. (Weeping as he speaks, whs) Both of them loved the truth about as well as any men I've ever known. But there was a division among us. It broke Eldred's heart. It broke my heart.

I talked with Eldred in 1954 about the sponsoring eldership question. I was only about 27 years of age then. And Eldred said, "Well R.J., it seems to me that every church falls into one of two categories, either a sponsoring eldership church or a supporting eldership church." I thought that was well put, and I began to think about that. I told him later, I said, "Eldred you had a lot to do with me taking a position that I believe that the silence of the scriptures on the supporting eldership is without authority and therefore I cannot accept the sponsoring eldership arrangement."

Later in that year a very dear friend of mine, who held a meeting in Houston, and I was wrestling with the problem of making up my mind. And I asked this man whom I loved, who has passed on and I'll not mention his name, but he is well known by most of you who are here. I said, "Could you explain to me how that we can send money to a board of directors to do benevolence for the churches in Texas, but we cannot send money to a board of directors to do missionary work for the churches in Texas." I said

,"Now I don't really want to believe this. I'm very happy where I am here at Lindale in Houston. But I'm afraid that I'm going to have to take the position that either the board being support to do benevolence is wrong or the board to do missionary work is right." Maybe you don't see the parallel, but I felt that I saw that. And I felt it rather inconsistent on my part to get up and preach against the church supporting a missionary society but at the same time we were supporting a benevolent society.

And I also began to study 1 Peter 5. And I felt that 1 Peter 5 taught us that the elders are to oversee the flock that's among them, and taking the oversight thereof. Most of us of course in teaching our home study lesson, we always taught that it was in the eldership that the apostasy started. In Acts the 20th chapter, Paul told the Ephesian elders to "take heed unto yourselves and to the all flock over the which the Holy Ghost hath made you overseers to feed the church of God which he hath purchased with His blood." He said, "After my departing grievous wolves would enter in among you not sparing the flock, also of your own selves shall men shall arise speaking perverse things to draw away disciples after them."

And toward the end of 1954, I begged the brethren where I was, I said, "Brethren you know I love you. You love me. But I cannot conscientiously accept our sending money out of the treasury to a sponsoring eldership. I cannot conscientiously accept us sending money to a board of directors to do benevolence for the church here. Please understand that I am not leaving with any animosity in my heart." We almost left with tears in our eyes, all of us. At first it hurt, it hurt so much. But then later we started not talking to each other. We didn't communicate. And years have passed and the hurt hasn't been there. I'll be honest with you, I have not really cared. But there's something about this week that's made me want to care. (Weeping as he speaks, whs) Things that I've heard bring to my mind that there are some people out there that I believe that love the Lord and want to go to heaven. And I believe I too see a little light.

We've used a lot of labels. We've used the label, and I guess we've been really satisfied with these labels. When someone asks us about a certain group we say well they're liberal and institutional. What does that imply? That implies that they don't respect Bible authority because they're liberal. It's sort of a political term. And we know that's not so, all the way. It maybe in certain areas, but in most of the areas that we've heard, the men who are here this week are not liberal in all of their views. And so that's really not fair. And I believe if I was in that particular group I would resent that, being called liberal. I would even resent being called institutional, because the majority of them don't do their work through institutions. They do some of it, very little of it, but some of it is done through institutions. So isn't it fair… I mean isn't it unfair and we might even say untrue to make such an implication as that?

But on the other side we're called anti (pronounced with a long "I" whs) or antis and legalists. Someone asks about us and someone might say, "Well, what do you mean by anti?" "Well, that I mean that they are anti cooperation. They don't believe in cooperating in the field of area … in benevolence. They don't believe in cooperating in the field of evangelism." Has that read true? I do believe in cooperation. I believe churches can cooperate together in the support of as many preachers as we can support in the field. We can support, also we can cooperate together in the field of benevolence. So really I'm not anti cooperation, that's just not a true statement. Someone said, "Yeah but your anti benevolence." No, that's not true either.

I just came from New Jersey. And I met a man, I'm not sure that I can call his name, Robener I think, a preacher of the gospel in that area. He just adopted three children, problem children. I had dinner with them and I told my wife, "We've got to help them. They need help. They need financial help. But they need our prayers." But Brother Robener would be considered an anti preacher, with three children that are not related to him at all, problem children that had been abused, and reaching their teen years. He's not an anti. And to say that we're anti benevolent, we don't really care about the poor orphans or the poor widows, that's not so, and I think we all know that's not so.

But through the years we've used those terms and it seems that we've sort of been satisfied with them. The term legalism is sort of an ugly term. But I heard yesterday about patternists, we believe that we should follow a pattern. And to be legal is simply to do what's lawful and what is right.

So what has this done to us? Well, I think this has blinded our eyes or our hearts to the many things on which we are in agreement. (Some from the audience say Amen, whs) My, if I were to stand up here, I could stand up here and talk for an hour or two. Talking about all of us believe that there is one body, one Spirit, one hope of your calling, one Lord, one faith, one baptism, one God and Father of all who is above all and through all and in you all. That the Bible is God's revealed word. That we're to teach God's plan of salvation through grace, and on and on I could go. And we have… I'd have an "amen" on every one of these things. And it looks to me like that we have just sort of taken our differences and have just made those differences all we can see. Now I am not minimizing them. I believe they are important. I believe we ought to try to work them out.

There's nothing wrong with questioning what's been done. I know the Apostle Paul questioned the Judaizing teachers and they had a hot argument about it in Antioch, and then later had another one in Jerusalem. Galatians the 2nd chapter verses 11 through 14, the Apostle Paul talked about Peter and Barnabas. You know Paul loved Peter and he loved Barnabas probably more than anybody. But he rebuked them sharply because they were to be blamed, they were not walking according… they were not walking uprightly according to the gospel. And when Paul wrote in Galatians 3, he said, "O foolish Galatians, who hath bewitched you that you should not obey the truth?" And then later he says, "Am I therefore your enemy because I tell you the truth?"

I'm thankful that men such as W. W. Otey questioned some of the things that were going on. I'm not saying these men were perfect men. I'm thankful for men like Curtis Porter, who defended the truth, who debated, who stood for the truth. I'm thankful for men like Roy Cogdill who also debated and who loved the truth. Men like Luther Blackmon, I knew from a boy. I'm grateful to those men, and I'm indebted to them for much of the conviction that I have in my heart today.

I want to say in closing, in Matthew the 7th chapter verse 21, I find my Lord saying, "Not everyone that saith unto me Lord Lord shall enter the Kingdom of Heaven, but he that doeth the will of my Father which is in heaven. For many will say to me in that day, Lord Lord have we not prophesied in thy name and in thy name cast out devils, and in thy name done many wonderful works. Then will I profess unto them I never knew you, depart from me ye that work iniquity." Brethren we've got to learn what the will of the Lord is. We've got to do it to go to heaven. We've got to understand that we've got to know that law of the Lord, because the Lord said "Depart from me ye that work iniquity," you that are lawless. We've got to know the law of the Lord and we've got to do it.

And then Jesus goes on and says in Matthew 7, "He that hearth these saying of mine and doeth them, I'll liken him unto a wise man who built his house upon a rock" and so on. "But he that hearth these sayings of mine and doeth them not, I will liken him unto a foolish man." Now we've got to hear the sayings of Jesus, we've got to respect his authority. All of us are agreed on that I am sure.

But I'll tell you what, we need to take the words of Jesus in Matthew 23:23 and 24, for Jesus said to those Pharisees "You pay tithe of mint, anise… and anise and cummin, and have omitted the weightier matters of the law, judgment, mercy, faith. These ought you to have done and not to leave the other undone. You strain at a gnat and you swallow a camel." Is Jesus telling us it's wrong to strain out a gnat? Absolutely not! But let's strain out the gnat and let's strain out the camel. We must respect, we must respect his teaching. And I hope that as a result of this meeting this week, that all of us will look at the weightier matters. I know that judgment, discretion, is a weightier matter because Jesus said so. I know that faith is a greater matter. I know, I know that mercy is a greater matter. I didn't say that, Jesus said it. And I also know of that above all that, love is even greater. "Now abideth faith, hope and love, but the greatest of these is love."

There are wonderful things happening in our world today. Who would have ever thought that we'd have Czecho-slovakia like it is today? Doors of opportunity are opening there. In Poland, doors of opportunity are opening there. Who would have ever thought that at the next NATO conference Khruschchev would be invited to speak? And one year ago how many of the world, of our people, would have thought that the wall in Germany would be torn down between the west and the east? I watched that on television, and I saw the joy as those people crossed that wall. What a joy it was to take the wall down, and they were hugging each other and they were happy because the wall between them had been torn down. The wall's being torn down today, but it's going to be on a one on one basis. We don't have a hierarchy to tell us that this is what we've got to do. Each one of us is going to have to do our part in chipping that old wall down, on both sides. ("Amen" from some in the audience, whs)

Let's then respect the consciences of one another, but above all let's love the Lord and respect his truth. Paul said in Ephesians 4:31, "Let all bitterness and wrath and clamor and evil speaking with all malice be put away from you. Be kind one to another, tenderhearted, forgiving one another, even as God for Christ's sake hath forgiven you." Thank you. (Several in the audience say "amen" and warm applause, whs)

Work of the Congregation

Day 2 Cycle 2
Friday, July 13, 1990

Participants

Non-Institutional Brethren
Weldon Warnock — Main
J.T. Smith — Panelist 2
Paul Earnhart — Panelist 4

Institutional Brethren
Owen Cosgrove — Rebuttal
Hershel Dyer — Panelist 1
Charles Horn — Panelist 3

Work of the Congregation
Day 2 Speech 2 Main
Weldon Warnock

Introduction: *Warnock, Weldon. He presently works with Beckley, WV church and has preached for 35 years with works in Ohio, Kentucky, Tennessee, Mississippi and Florida. He is an experienced debater, TV and radio speaker, staff writer for several papers, and author of commentaries and workbooks.*

I want to express my appreciation for the work that Brother Lanier and Brother Wolfgang did to make this a reality and all the others that participated. It's been a long time since I've seen Brother Lanier. The last time I saw him we were face to face in a confrontation. And I was looking him right in the eye, and he swung, that is he let his arm go, and I backed up and the umpire called strike three. (Laughter, whs). He was a great softball pitcher. We played in the city league in Tampa, Florida and I remember him very well.

I feel like the fellow that fell into a barrel of molasses headfirst and became stuck down in the Okefenokee, Oke swamp in southeast Georgia. He thought for a moment, "What am I going to do?" And then he prayed, "Lord give me a mouth for this occasion." (Laughter, whs). I feel that's what I need this afternoon.

The subject assigned is the *Work of the Church*. That's what we'll be discussing. And as in other phases and areas of the church, the work is the same as far as needing to conform to a pattern. We've heard some discussion about the pattern. We hear that we must have authority in all that we do. Well, that's true and that's a nice platitude. I believe that, these brethren believe the same. But we need to learn how to establish authority and then make the application. And it behooves each and every one of us to learn how to establish authority and make the application.

Now God had a pattern for His Old Testament tabernacle and the same is true with His spiritual tabernacle (Heb. 8:5). And I hear brethren today, the loose livers if you might describe them that way, as saying that we want free congregations, we don't want to be circumscribed. You know years ago you women, your not old enough to remember that song *Don't Fence Me In*. You

men are. (Laughter, whs). But we don't want to be fenced in. And yet Jesus said, "Why call ye me Lord, Lord and do not the things that I say." John said, "He that goeth onward, whosoever transgresseth, and abideth not in the doctrine of Christ hath not God. He that abideth in the doctrine of Christ hath both the Father and the Son." And Paul said he taught the same thing in every church (1 Cor.4:17). And in verse 6 that we're not to think of men more, above that which is written. We're not to go beyond that which is written. Indeed we have a model for the church of the Lord, and that's true from the standpoint of its work.

What do we mean by the word "church"? The word "church" is used at least in two senses in the New Testament. And this has been addressed already, especially this morning. The word church is used in a universal or distributive sense. Jesus said, "Upon this rock I will build My church." Here are all the Christians who've been redeemed by the blood of Christ. All men who've been cleansed by the blood of Christ compose this church and it's a relationship. There's not any organizational arrangement for the universal church. If God wanted it to function or act, He'd have given it an organizational arrangement.

Here is the church in the distributive sense. In Eph. 4:4 "There's one body." Chapter 5:23, "Christ is the head of the church" and other passages that could be sited. Now as individual Christians we have a function. The church has a responsibility, distributively speaking. And from that standpoint we have a relationship or obligation to the state (Rom.13:1-7), the family (Eph.5:23-6:4), as well as other scriptures. We have a duty to our neighbors and to our enemies and to our brethren and to our jobs. And we have a responsibility to ourselves. We're to grow in the grace and knowledge of Jesus Christ. Our love is to abound in all knowledge and discernment. We're to learn the scriptures that we might be able to teach others. And so from a distributive standpoint, the universal standpoint, here are individuals acting. I think we all agree on that.

It's also used in the New Testament from a local sense: 1 Corinthians 1:2 "Unto the church of God at Corinth," Acts 14:23, "ordain elders in every church," Romans 16:16, "the churches of Christ salute you," Philippians1:1, "Paul and Timotheus servants of Jesus Christ unto the saints at Philippi with the bishops and deacons." From the local standpoint, or in the local sense, there's organization. It's the biggest and the smallest. And it is to have elders and deacons and members (Phil.1:1, Acts 14:23). The qualifications are in 1 Timothy 3 and Titus 1. And it's to have a plurality of elders and they're to oversee the flock.

And here is the limitation of the authority of elders, "Tend the flock of God among you," or Paul said to the Ephesian elders at Militias, "Take heed to yourselves and the flock over which the Holy Ghost has made you overseers, to feed or tend or shepherd the church of God, or the church of the Lord, which He hath purchased with His own blood."

And the local church is something we join, we're fellowshipped into it. In Acts 9:26, Paul joined the church at Jerusalem, "assayed to join himself to the disciples at Jerusalem." And if there was not a distinction between Christians and the church in the collective sense how would we join it, we're already in it?

In 1 Corinthians 16 the Bible teaches plainly that there's a common treasury. And here's where a lot of our problems have developed, as one brother stated this morning. How do we spend the money? And all I know about it, Ladies and Gentlemen, is that we spend the money on the things that God has prescribed the church to do; what He's authorized it to do, in every function, its worship and its work. Whatever God has designated a function of the church, its money, the church's money may be spent on and nothing else. It's not ours, it belongs to the Lord, we've given it to Him. As Brother Ferrell Jenkins said this morning, we have power over it while it's ours in Acts 5:4. But then when we give it to the Lord it belongs to Him.

Now here are the senses in which the word church is used in the Bible, the universal or distributive and the local sense, which has organizational structure or arrangement. And that's what we want to focus our attention on this afternoon, the work of the local church. And that work brethren, and I'm not telling you something you don't believe most of us here anyway that you don't already know, consists of preaching the gospel, of edifying the saints, and taking care of the needy, at least the needy saints, taking care of its own.

Concerning evangelism, in 1 Thessalonians 1:8 Paul said, "For from you sounded out the word of the Lord not only in Macedonia and Achaia but also in every place." They were missionary minded, and I want to drive home this afternoon brethren, that we need to be the same. We need to cry out the gospel story around the world. When I was in China a couple of years ago and I came home and talking about the need in China and I couldn't speak without shedding tears as I see a BILLION people who've never heard the gospel of Christ for the most part. And doors are beginning to open there in Eastern Europe and we need to use EVERY means at our disposal to be sure to take the gospel of Jesus Christ unto them. We need to sound it out, and there's no issue there among us.

In Philippians 2:16, "Holding forth the word of life" Paul says, or presenting it or offering it. And in 1Timothy 3:15, "the church is the pillar and ground of the truth." It supports the truth, yea it is the very foundation of it. Acts 13:3, "When they had fasted and prayed and laid their hands upon them, they sent them away." And so the church at Antioch sent out Paul and Barnabas on the first missionary journey. And by implication in the Great Commission, "Go ye into all the world and preach the gospel unto every creature." Go teach all nations. And by statements and examples and implication we see that the church comes within the purview of the Great Commission. Though it was given before the church was established and to the apostles of Jesus Christ, the church of our Lord indeed is to carry out the Great Commission.

Then in 2 Corinthians 11:8 and Philippians 4:15-16, churches preached the gospel by supporting preachers. Brethren we need to search out men that we can support. And there are good men around the world today that need financial aid and assistance. First century churches were missionary minded. In a period of thirty years, Paul could say in Colossians 1:23 that the gospel had been "preached to every creature under Heaven." And they had no TV, they had no radio, they didn't have the printing press, they didn't have the facilities that we have, and yet they were able to take the gospel to the world. And we need to use every lawful method at our disposal.

You know, it's just as timely today as when Jesus said in John 4:35, "the field is white unto harvest." And you know friends, the church did this without a missionary society, and we can do the same today. We have all the machinery that's necessary in the CHURCH that was designed in the mind of God before the foundation of the WORLD to carry the gospel to dying men and women. And I believe it's complete, and I believe it's sufficient, I believe it's adequate. And to try to establish something in its place, try to improve on it, is a reflection upon the wisdom of all mighty God. In Ephesians 3:10-11 Paul said, "To the intent that now unto the principalities and powers in heavenly places might be known by the church the manifold wisdom of God, according to the eternal purpose which he purposed in Christ Jesus our Lord." And that's not the mission of the church, in that passage, but the church showed to the angels when it was established God's manifold wisdom. And the same is true with us, as revealed on the pages of Holy Writ. Well we need to be evangelistic, that's one function of the church.

Number two, the church is to edify. Referring to the gifts in Ephesians 4 Paul said that "He gave some to be apostles and some prophets and some evangelists and some pastors and teachers." That's in verse 11. These are the gifts. I don't believe they're miraculous, though some would differ. These are functions, works for the equipping of the saints, for the perfecting of the saints, that the saints might do a service and in turn build up the body of Christ until we all come to the unity of the faith. Here in this text, the saints are brought to the unity of the faith, rather than the unity of the faith brought unto the saints. And that's why I don't believe it's miraculous gifts in the text.

But here the apostles and prophets revealed the truth (Eph. 3:5). The evangelists were to proclaim the truth and the pastors, elders, teaches are to shepherd and superintend the local flock. By a faithful teaching of the truth and training, the saints will be perfected, or equipped to do the work of ministry and so forth.

Now they're to be brought unto maturity, they're to be developed. We need training. We need to develop young men to be preachers. We need to educate our members to be teachers; we need to develop song leaders, and everything else. The members of the church need to be developed, they need to be edified, they need to be educated, they need to be trained. Paul said in 1 Corinthians 14:12, "forasmuch as ye are zealous of spiritual gifts, seek that ye may excel to the edifying of the church." And then he says in verse 26 of that same chapter, "Let all things be done to edify."

Now brethren let me tell you. The church did all of this without subsidizing human institutions. I'm not against the Christian college, so called, but I want to tell you, it's not the business of the church to subsidize it. As Brother H. Leo Boles said, "It's not the function, the business of the church to subsidize any human institution." And that's so; I don't care what it is. If they're human, the church has no business subsidizing, and that's true for a so-called Christian college. Let the college be the college, and let the church be the church and we'd eliminate a lot of our problems, I suppose.

Well not only is it the function to edify, but also to do the work of benevolence, to help, to care, to be kind, to be generous. The church at Jerusalem relieved the needs of its destitute members (Acts 2:44-45; 4:32-35). There wasn't any of them that lacked. Those that owned property thought it wasn't their own but sold it and brought the price that they gained and laid it at the feet of the apostles. And all of them were cared for. And then in Acts 6, here they took care of their widows. In Acts 11:27-30, they sent relief to the disciples, to the churches, brethren in Judea and gave it to the ELDERS IN Judea. Here was the church that raised the money, gave it to the needy saints in Judea and was overseen by the elders. And brethren if it was good enough for them it ought to be good enough for us. And I want to tell you, just let me inject here, there wasn't any benevolent society or institution involved in the benevolent work of the church. They had all of the machinery, all of the equipment that they needed in order to get the job done.

Somebody says, "Well preacher, is a home the church?" No. You see the church provides it. If we had widows we can provide a house, we can rent a house, buy a house, put the widows there, give them whatever they need. If they need doctors, provide a doctor. If they need medicine, medicine, clothes, whatever it is, food, that's the church taking care of its own work. And they took care of those widows in Acts 6 as it selected seven servants, seven men to see about it, and we can do the same.

Well here were the churches in Macedonia and Achaia and Galatia as they relieved the needs of the saints at Jerusalem. In all this brethren the work was limited. Now we all believe in limited benevolence. None of us believes in unlimited benevolence. The only difference is we draw our circles differently. Mine's more narrow than these brethren here perhaps on the podium with me, except … (Laughter, whs) Here you are down here. (Laughter, whs). They haven't deserted me yet. (Subdued Laughter, whs) All right.

Concerning limited benevolence, it's my position or conviction that was to the saints, to the members of the church. And you know brethren, the problem by in large through the years should have been on the institutions. May the church subsidize institutions? I doubt very seriously if churches who believe that they may support aliens out of the treasury do very much of it. At least that's been my observation over in the Ohio valley where I live. Once in a while they may do it, but that'd be an isolated thing. It seems to me like the real issue through the years should be human institutions. May we subsidize it? That doesn't mean I condone it, that I uphold it. My position is saints alone, saints only. But even regardless of what our position may be, if it's more extended than mine, it's still limited by them. We don't believe in helping those who won't work, which would be a violation of Paul's statement in 2 Thessalonians 3:10.

But now, let's for just the few minutes we've got left, let's talk about what's not the church's work. You know the church today, in many ways is, in many places, is not the same as when I was a boy growing up, and the same thing with a lot of you brethren. There's been a change in the church in the last few years. It has changed from adhering to the New Testament order, to emphasizing secular education, day car centers, athletics, recreation, fun and frolic. The modern church of Christ is little more than a social club or a community recreational center. And sadly many of us don't care. We want it that way and we like it that way. But when we get into these areas we're without any Biblical authority whatsoever.

What isn't the work of the church? Well it's not the work to provide secular education. And yet we see kindergartens, we see day care centers these day schools. That's not the business of the church to teach these secular things. It's not the work of the church to subsidize a college as we've already stated. And then they furnish… it's not the work of the church to furnish recreation and entertainment.

Here's a church over in Tennessee, and I won't call its name but you'll probably recognize it, that built a complex called the Family Life and Education Center. Special speakers from some of our so-called Christian colleges were on hand to help commemorate the occasion. It included a gymnasium, exercise room, sunset room, reception room, fellowship room. It planned activities including walking, jogging, bowling, volley ball, ping pong, tennis, golf, ladies slimnastics, some of us men need it too, basketball, officiating clinics for referees of church sporting events, class on first aid, CPR, and arts and crafts. BEFORE GOD BRETHREN WHAT IN THE WORLD HAS THIS TO DO WITH THE WORK OF THE CHURCH? JESUS PAID HIS LIFE'S BLOOD TO REDEEM US AND GAVE IT A HOLY WORK TO DO, TO SAVE THE LOST. And we've made nothing more than a recreational center or a glorified country club out of it.

N.B. Hardeman said, "Again I say to you with caution and thought that it is not the work of the church to furnish entertainment for the members. And yet many members have drifted into such an effort." I don't have time to quote it all. *Gospel Advocate Teachers Annual* said, "Building recreation rooms and providing and supervising recreational activities at the expense of the church is a departure from the simple gospel plan as revealed in the New Testament. The church might as well relieve the parents of feeding and disciplining all the young people at church expense as to take over the job of entertaining and supervising their recreation at church expense." And I'd say "amen" to that.

It's not the business of the church to engage in social activities and yet we see these fellowship halls and kitchens being built. And I'm not opposed to eating in the church house, that's not the issue. The issue, brethren, is building the kitchen and the fellowship halls with the money we've given on Sunday morning or Sunday evening on the Lord's day, to do the work of the church and prostituting that, using that for play and recreation and social activities and fun and frolic. That's what's wrong with it. And these brethren need to address that more adamantly than they have.

There seems to be like it's silent consent. "Oh, I'm against that." Well is it equivalent to instrumental music? Is it equivalent to a missionary society? Are you just going to say, "Well I know they're wrong but I'm not going to say anything about that much, they're my brethren." Yeah, they're my brethren. But I want to tell you friends, if we got conviction about it, if it's equivalent to instrumental music in worship, we need to speak out on it. We need to take a stand on it. I can tell you where I stand on a post card. You ask me and I'll tell you immediately. I won't vacillate, or equivocate. I'll tell you immediately where I stand or every issue. And I learned a long time ago, I do my own thinking. And I take my positions based on my study, I don't care what these other brethren think. I hope I'm in harmony with their position, I hope that's the way it is, but I take my own stand. Sometimes it got me in a little hot water but that's where I stand. I don't determine my position, my conviction, by what brethren are doing. I determine it by the word of God, by a proper hermeneutic.

Well, what about these clinics, these hospitals? Churches are sponsoring and building them all over the world. Is that a work of the church? No sir! You know Brother Foy Wallace; I thought a lot of Brother Wallace. And he was in a meeting where I preached years ago in New Martinsville, West Virginia, sitting on the front pew. And Brother Wallace gave me an outline on the back of the old sermon outline that I had. He gave me a diagram really, on the back of a sermon outline. How do you turn that thing on? Yellow Bar? All right thank you. And here's what he gave me. (Chart #1) Of course I've recopied it for this, but that's what he gave me. Brother Wallace said, "The church, what it may and may not do." He said, "The church may feed the hungry yes, but it may not put in the budget a grocery store. It may cloth the naked, it may help the sick, it may provide for the infirmed, shelter the wayfarer, provide material for the meeting house, pay the preacher,

Bibles and songbooks and so forth and literature, and help the orphan yes. But what it may not do, budget in the grocery store, a mercantile company, hospital, clinic, drug store, sanatorium, hotel, inn, lumber company, college, publishing house." He says, "Those may not be in the budget of the church." And I thought it was so then and I believe it's now. That's what he believed then. But as Brother Williamson said and we all know that Brother Foy changed his position on some of these things. But in spite of that, I'd always respected him, and thought he was the greatest pulpiter that I ever heard in all my life, or among the greatest.

My time has come and gone, hasn't it Brother Neil? One minute, all right. I got time to finish this. Let me just say this. The church of our Lord has a holy and divine mission in this world, and that mission is spiritual and not carnal. And the means for accomplishing that mission is the gospel not gymnastics. Her work has to do with sanctifying the heart not with satisfying the stomach. And food and fun and recreation and entertainment, secular education and so forth have their legitimate place in life. But their place is not a part of the work of the church. I love to play softball, I love golf, I tell you I could play it every day. And I like entertainment and I like to eat better than anybody ever was. You name it and I like it, hot and cold whatever I like it. But that's not the function of the CHURCH. Let the HOME be the home, let the COLLEGE be the college and the CHURCH be the church and get on with its business of saving the souls of lost men and women. Thank you so much.

Church

	May			**May Not**	
1	Hungry Feed	Yes		Grocery Store	No
2	Naked Clothe	Yes		Mercantile Co.	No
3	Sick Help	Yes		Hospital/Clinic Drug Store	No
4	Infirm Provide	Yes		Sanitorium	No
5	Wayfarer Shelter	Yes		Hotel -- Inn	No
6	Meeting House	Yes		Lumber Co.	No
	Material				
7	Preacher Pay	Yes		College	No
8	Literature Books/Song Books	Yes		Publishing House	No
9	Orphan Homes Help	Yes		Institutional Orphanage	No

Work of the Congregation
Day 2 Speech 2 Rebuttal
Owen Cosgrove

Introduction: *Cosgrove, Owen. Native Oklahoman, Bible chair and Christian College teacher, preacher for 39 years, script writer for Herald of Truth, noted author and publisher, presently with College St. church in Waxahachie, TX, a second time there. Has preached in Alpine and Clyde, TX, as well as Moore, OK.*

I was reading through the program of this meeting, and among others I read Brother Maxie Boren. Maxie and I were roommates at *Abilene Christian*, and vanity being that it is, I didn't have my glasses on and I read "Maxie Boren – full time meeting and lecture speaker, Director of *The Brown Trail School Of Preaching*, noted for evangelistic efforts and presently lives out of his pickup and fifth wheel trailer…" and so forth and so very good. A little later I put on my glasses and read that again and it says, "Maxie Boren – full time meeting and lecture speaker, Director of *The Brown Trail Scholl of Preaching*, RIOTED for evangelistic efforts." And somebody told me, if you have Maxie for a meeting now he won't let them go to sleep. This reminds me of Acts 19. There it is, not in black and white, but in brown and ecru, Brother Maxie Boren stirred up a riot.

Unless brethren in our discussion of differences . . . we need to be able to look though each other's eyes. We're never going to have harmony; we're never going to have the proper understanding I think, until we're able at least part of the time, to see these issues through each other's eyes. In other words, if we're going to have insight, we're first going to have to have empathy, and that involves the golden rule, and it involves the love that the Lord has commanded us to have toward one another.

This has been such an enjoyable experience. But yesterday evening someone asked the question "What do you think will be the outcome of this meeting?" Some were very optimistic, and some were not so optimistic. And I thought of this old preacher's story that maybe many of you have heard, about an old sage in the little village that

could answer almost any question. A couple of mean boys said, "We're going to fool that old man." Do you remember the story? One of them said, "I'll tell you what I'm going to do. I'm going to get a little bird, and I'm going to go to him and I'm going to ask him, 'Old man, is this bird dead or is it alive?' And if he says, 'That bird is dead,' I'm going to open my hand and let it fly away. And if he says, 'That bird is alive,' I'm going to squeeze it and kill it, and say, 'Old man you're wrong!'" So they asked the old gentleman the question. And he looked with a gleam in his eye, and he said, "Boys, that's strictly up to you." Whether this meeting does the good that all of us want it to, is strictly up to us.

But I want to tell you before I get into my speech, and by the way, Brother Warnock, your speech is one of the best I ever heard. With just the exception, in my mind, or two or three points, an excellent speech with the Jerusalem ring about it, and I appreciate it. But if we're going to do the good that we need to do to make this meeting accomplish the purposes that we want it to accomplish, we're going to have to have love and respect for each other. We're going to have to continue communication; we're going to have to continue inquiry. When you arrest inquiry, and take a position, you kill it. Inquiry is a living thing, its curative action. If we want to stop it now, so that we can list our creed, we kill that inquiry. Let's leave our minds open; all of us. I'm not scolding anybody; I'm saying all of us. And in the meantime, let us exercise good manners toward one another, especially in the communities where we live. God forbid that we go at each other's throats before the eyes and ears of a doubting lost world.

Now my speech! The Lord often talked about the work of God. He emphasized doing. Many like to talk about the work of the church. Jesus stressed and accentuated "Doing the will of My Father who is in Heaven." Christ's way, involves much more than talking. God wants fruits, not just words. True religion requires sweat, effort, sacrifice, performance, doing the will of God. I do not want to belabor this point, which all of us in fact believe. Neither do I wish to make any accusations or unfair appraisals of brethren as has all too often been done in the past. But we do want to warn all of us against the danger of becoming so obsessed with the "how" of our work that we neglect the "what," the substance, the work itself.

There are, it seems to me, two extremes that threaten the work of the local church. One is what we might call *Promotionalism*, often done with the best of intentions, but with such zeal that it is untempered by scriptural restraints and considerations, and without proper regard for the reservations and the scruples of honest brethren who have honest objections. The other extreme, is a negative and controversial spirit that in obstructing and opposing the ideas and efforts of others, can have a very discouraging and stultifying effect on people who are trying to do the Lord's work. And yet we know that a certain amount of promoting, in the best sense of that word, and a certain amount of restraint or negativism, in the best sense of that word, are necessary to the proper functioning of the church.

I have felt for many years that the strains put on the fellowship of many of us gathered here today have been very harmful to the church of the Lord. The loss of some of our great talent in the old conservative rear guard left us more exposed to a liberal movement that rivals some of the things that happened in the *Restoration Movement* a century ago. Though many of us have grieved at the rancor and bitterness that we have sometimes seen in the discussion of our differences, I have always felt a greater affinity for and a greater closeness to our conservative brethren than for those whose loose ways doctrinally, show a disregard for the book and little concern for the body of Christ as we have known it.

Some have indicated they do not know if I'm a "liberal conservative," or a "conservative liberal." That may be *no man's land* to some, but it's just fine for me. I do not want to be in any person's coterie, and I don't want to be any one's champion. I am glad that this assembly has no official power at all; that we cannot legislate, adjudicate, or execute one jot or tittle that God's law does not already state. I know that we are all equally glad that there is no human President, or Pope, or Pontiff, or Chief who can send out some dogma to be bound upon the churches. That after all of our reason is done, we still will be free

people under God, with both the freedom and responsibility, and understanding of inquiry that will lead us in God's ways as we endeavor to find and "keep the unity of the spirit in the bond of peace."

In discussing the work of the congregation, please note these general implications of John 9:4 "I must do the works of Him that sent Me while it is yet day, for the night cometh when no man can work." *I* – the personal responsibility that each one of us has in God's work. *Must* – The urgency of the gospel and everything about it. Brethren, the Lord has given us His word and it's not a bunch of suggestions, there's an urgency about it. We're talking about the work of the Lord. *I Must Work* – The need for action, performance and individual involvement. *I Must Work The Works Of Him That Sent Me* – The importance of God's authority and the need to be guided by His wishes. *While It Is Yet Day* – The very real limitations of our opportunity and time. We must get on with the work. *For The Night Cometh* – The reminder for us to cease and to use the precious opportunities that we have. *When No Man Can Work* – Again a reminder to work, and to work now! "Whatever thy hand findeth to do, do it with all thy might for there is no work, no device, no knowledge, no wisdom in the grave whither thou goest" (Eccl. 9:10).

Promotionalism and *controversy* are both honorable when done honorably. But both or each can be as blatant a flight from duty as was Jonah's flight from Tarshish. One tends to turn the Lord's work into a circus, and the other tends to turn it into a grave yard. And both of them can be inimical to the actual performance of Christian duty. He will not try to be tedious in referring to the hundreds of New Testament admonitions to work, do, obey, serve, minister, help, and bear fruit to Christians. All of us are aware that the Bible is replete with such admonitions, and the ubiquitous and recurring emphasis is characteristic of the Lord's own life and work. It's when we get into the "how" and "what" that we sometimes run into difficulties, and into honest difference in understanding and conviction.

So let us discuss what we have for years considered the main area of the church's work. We've often said, and well, the church's work is in three main areas: evangelism, edification, benevolence. These areas overlap. They are interrelated and interdependent. In fact, they are almost inseparable. How often, has an act of benevolence edified those who did it, and those who received it, and led to teaching and encouragement and conversion? Our good works can cause others to glorify God, and a wife's good manner of life can win her husband to the Lord. I could quote references on these first things, but you brethren know them and you preach them and we understand them.

Often the Lord's mode of operation began with benevolence, and yet His main emphasis was always spiritual rather than just physical. And I think that this is a part of the problems that face the church today. There is too much carnality in the church, always has been, and there is today. This is the crux of many of our disagreements, the emphasis, whether it's spiritual or carnal. But I want to tell you something. The carnality of a troublesome spirit is just as destructive and sinful as the carnality of the fun seekers and glory seekers. In Galatians 5:19-21 of the seventeen "works of the flesh" that the apostle Paul lists, that he says "are evident which are these," two of them primarily refer to our relationship to God, five of them primarily refer to morality, and nine of them primarily refer to how we get along with our brethren.

In the first order of the church's spiritual work, is the evangelization of the world. In evangelizing, we've resisted and rejected the Missionary Society because it usurped the role of the local church as the sending agency in the New Testament church. There's an important difference in one or more churches helping another church with one or more of its programs, and in several churches sending to a society or a group or some separate institution to do the church's work. And we understand, I think, the difference in using a brotherhood paper, a bookstore, or some enterprise to help the local church to do its work. So can we also see the principle of helping a church to do a work that may extend beyond the neighborhood or the community where it is located.

To be sure, all types of abuses of this principle are possible. And I personally have no quarrel with the brothers who are very cautious in this regard, especially in light of the advent of the Missionary Society.

And we are well advised to respect the autonomy of each congregation and each individual church answering to Christ directly. And by the way, this principle should also be observed by Preachers and editors and coteries and pressure groups and political groups, as well as by someone that's trying to promote some big brotherhood project.

Individuals from the church at Antioch went on the second journey of Paul, no doubt sent forth by the church, as they had been on the first journey (Acts 13:1-3). A member of another congregation, Timothy, joined them at Lystra. Luke joined them at Troas. Aquilla and Pricilla joined them at Corinth. And they all associated in a great evangelistic endeavor and of course there is not a single hint of any evangelistic or missionary organization machinery that existed, much less dominated or superseded the freedom and autonomy of the local church. Yet, Paul often received assistance from other churches (2 Cor. 11:8).

May I emphasize again without trying to be tedious, that many of the church's problems would be alleviated or certainly ameliorated, if individuals in congregations would get to work on this matter of supreme priority. I believe that the church and the Lord would be infinitely better served, as would all of mankind, if many of our sideways motions were put into saving the lost. There is a vast difference in wrestling in the barracks, and fighting the foes of the Lord. "Negativism" and "Promotionalism" both can be flights from the Lord. Many brotherhood peacocks would do well to attend more of their own work at home; to brighten the corner where they are; to try to baptize somebody; and to concentrate on building strong local congregations. And I'm convinced brethren that the more we keep the baptistery waters troubled, the better we will be able to resolve and avoid our other troubles. In other words, one of the first responsibilities of the local congregation is to evangelize, and we must be about our Father's business.

In the matter of edification, historically we've emphasized the responsibility of Christians in the local congregation to encourage one another and to build each other up. "Let all things be done unto edifying." Every loose cannon in the brotherhood, whatever his personal or doctrinal conviction, would do well to pay extensive and conscience and conscientious attention to this admonition from God. Whatever side, on whatever issue may do, the Lord has quite an investment in the church, and our efforts to edify and encourage each other must begin with genuine love and friendship for him and for one another. Concordance searches for such words as: edify, encourage, exhort, teach, comfort, build up, and many other related concepts, add up to an extensive and pervasive New Testament emphasis.

On our helping one another to grow in the grace and

admonition of the Lord, and on considering one another to provoke unto love and good works, some very real dangers face the church in this area of edification. Efforts to entertain, and to play and generally to appeal to the flesh, are defended on the basis of their value in edifying. It seems to me that there are three types of approaching this fun, food, and fellowship business in the local church. And by the way, I think that the word "fellowship" is one of the most desecrated words of the New Testament. In its original uses in God's word, it generally meant the most sensitive and beautiful sharing of faith and work and suffering for Christ. Now it often conveys the idea of chips and dip and soda pop. One fellow announced at the end of a worship service there would be no fellowship after the services that night, when in reality all that the folks had done was to postpone a party.

Anyway, the three general approaches to entertainment as it relates to the church rather than the individual, may be categorized as: incidental, privately sponsored, and church sponsored. Incidental activity may refer to something as innocuous or innocent as children playing in the church yard after services, or during a break from Vacation Bible School; or a neighborhood child playing with a skateboard on the parking lot during the week; or serving refreshments during Vacation Bible School. It seems to me that brethren who say you can serve refreshments in the yard but not in the church building are attaching a spiritual significance to a meeting house that's not found In the New Testament. Indeed, often churches in the first century, as do some now, met in private homes where eating facilities were already in place. Paul's admonition in 1 Corinthians 11:22 refers more to the corruption of an occasion, the worship service and the Lord's Supper, than to a place. If this scripture restricts eating to our own houses, it would forbid eating at a café or at a park, or at someone else's home, you eat in your OWN houses.

A second type of association, meant to encourage friendship and enjoyment of other Christian's company. By the way, we do quite a bit on this word social. I think we'd do well to look up the word "social" in a good dictionary. Most of them have about eleven meanings, all of them good. They talk about friendship. It's all right to be social, that's what the foyers for. There are two meanings however I don't like: one is socialism; and the other is social diseases. But aside from that, the rest of them are all right. We allow people to have social activities in our home, or some public place, or some rented hall, or some similar location or facility. And although I know it could be subject to abuse, I find no problem in the judicious use of church facilities for social activities, as long as they are recognized and support it as individual actions, and they do not impose a financial burden on the church.

I'm aware of the temptation to build an Olympic sized swimming pool baptistery, or a gymnasium auditorium, or a country club type of family service room or something else. But frankly brethren, it can be difficult to draw a line where incidental becomes church sponsored, or even when individually sponsored becomes church sponsored. And these sometimes difficult distinctions pose two challenges to me within my home congregation. I have the challenge to express myself in love and respect for others and to respect their judgment as I expect them to respect mine. Within my relationship to brethren in other congregations, I must respect their autonomy and even their opinions in matters of judgment. Probably, if I were the President of the universal church of Christ, I would send out an edict forbidding brethren to build a church auditorium that even incidentally could be used as a gymnasium. But since I am not such a President or Pope, it behooves me to express myself about it and then go home and try to baptize someone in Waxahachie, Texas.

When it comes to church sponsored efforts at edification, such things as Gospel Meetings, Vacation Bible Schools, Singing Schools, Bible Classes, Cottage Meetings, and many other efforts, are readily seen as legitimate congregational efforts to build up the church. And I have no problem whatever with the church being involved with camps, and Youth Ministries, and Campus Ministries, as long as they are the teaching arms of the church, and clear distinctions are made in edification, and mere entertainment, and in individual and church support. Now brethren, the apprehension of many is that a program or pet project may become more than that; that it may become a project that predominates and even supersedes the local church, the tail wagging the dog so to speak; that uses the Lord's church as a front for the program rather than the programs being a working arm of the local church, is a justifiable concern. A good church can be ruined by becoming the lackey of a pet project, but this does not preclude good programs, or one congregation helping another.

I have five minutes and three pages! I am worried. I'm going to have to summarize some things brethren.

On the matter of benevolence, I have many scriptures

here listed about our doing benevolence. We all believe them. As the apostle wrote, "If there is any other commandment, it is briefly comprehended in the saying, 'thou shalt love thy neighbor as thyself.'" Dare we ask the Lord as did the lawyer of old "Who is my neighbor?" We have long endeavored to differentiate between individual and congregational responsibilities, as well we should. But while others emphasize PERSONAL, I want to emphasis RESPONSIBILITY. Everything that the Lord ever commanded comes down to individuals, whether they work as individuals or in groups, or part of the congregation, or part of the brotherhood. If it were not so, there could not be an individual judgment.

I've mentioned here in Galatians 6:10 that I believe that the obstructions that some brethren put on this to make it purely individual are artificial. I'm sorry I don't have time to go into that except to say, it's almost inconceivable that the Lord would say to an antagonistic and proud lawyer, "Go thou and do likewise" but I will forbid My church from ever showing benevolence whether as a church or as the body politic. We know there are things that a person can do scripturally as individuals, but churches cannot. But to deny the right of the church ever to do good to those that are not saints, is to deny to the body the opportunity to do what her head constantly practiced during His ministry. Sometimes we become so concerned with the "How" that we almost forget the "What." This, ought we to have done and not left the other undone.

Helping orphans. Incidentally, some individuals have taken fatherless or otherwise needy children and raised them, and it's cruel and unfair to say those folks don't believe in helping orphans. They have helped orphans in very noble and unselfish ways. That's one way to do it, it's not the only way, but it's one way. Some folks would have a difficult time doing it this way, but there are various ways to do it, whether it's in a natural or an arranged home. The collection box in the foyer is another way to do it. Many of us don't think it's the only way to do it, but it's one way to do it. BUT BRETHREN, WE'D BETTER BE GITTING SOME RECEIPTS, whichever way we do it. There may be some things I don't like about certain homes and how they do it, but they're still homes.

I want to say in quick summary here, UUUH! One minute! We don't believe in church support of Christian Colleges. Brethren, most of us that I know don't believe in supporting Christian Colleges out of the church treasury.

I wish we had more time to talk about this more in length, but the time just gets away.

But let me have this conclusion. Brethren, let's concentrate on the work of the church and how we "can" do it rather than on how we "cannot" do it. In a world that's on a collision course with eternity, let us get on with the work. Let us have as our consuming desire to pitch the battle against the Devil; to work hard and faithfully. Let us determine in this generation and sooner, out of a pure love for God and His church, we will proclaim the gospel to every creature everywhere, and encourage in every place that we can and in every way the church for which the Savior died. And I believe that everyone here has that motive, at least to some degree. May God grant us the wisdom, the faith, the will, the brotherly love, to do the very best of our ability to do these things.

And thank you brethren for your kind attention, and may God bless us all.

Work of the Congregation
Day 2 Speech 2 Panelist 1
Hershel Dyer

Lewis Hale – Moderator: You don't have to come to the microphone, just speak from your microphone. Sir? Oh, I'm sorry.

Introduction: *Dyer, Hershel. Presently with 10th Rockford congregation in Tulsa, OK where he has worked for over 30 years. Well known lecturer and preacher of note for 40 years in Oklahoma, Texas, and Nebraska, assisted in the beginning of York College, NE.*

Before getting into any kind of a review of what's been said, I want to say just a few personal words. This is a very wonderful place for me to be, not up here where I am, I'd like to be where you are. But it's a joy to see so many good brethren whom I have known in the past. If you didn't hear those two speeches at the noon hour, you missed two of the finest during this whole series. Brother Curtis Camp and Brother R.J. Stevens delivered such moving addresses that I think everybody present was really moved, maybe to tears.

So we're very much In earnest about what we're doing here. And we're talking things over as brethren. These brethren, who are sitting here on the platform with me, are not antagonists to me. We're discussing things over which we may differ, but we differ in love, and we differ in mutual respect.

Brother J.T. Smith, who will be speaking in a few moments, is a fellow preacher along with myself in the city of Tulsa. We love each other very much, and have very great regard for one another's feelings and attitudes. We had a Preacher's Meeting and we've been talking of resent times with people who have all together a different approach to Bible authority than what we do. Some of us here in this room, several of the brethren along with myself, we were engaged in discussion just a few weeks ago with a man who just simply doesn't know where his hermeneutic is. There's scarcely any person in this room today who doesn't know the name of that man if I were to call him.

So we're glad to be talking with brethren that believe

that when something is not authorized, it is forbidden. It must be authorized in some way in the scriptures, or the word of God, or it is forbidden.

I would like this afternoon for us to test a principle that I want to see duly tested. It was brought up two or three times in the discussion this morning but I want to lay it before you again. And I would like for these brethren, along with myself, to test it. If there's something radically wrong with it, or wrong at all with it I want to know, and I think every sincere person here wants to know. Can a congregation be wrong in doing what every member of that congregation is obligated to do? I would like to test that to the fullest. Is it wrong for the congregation, Christians in a collective sense, to do what every individual in that congregation is duty bound to do. We'll probably have a good deal of discussion on that.

We've had a good deal said about edification along with evangelism and benevolence. In the work of edification, there are a lot of things that enter into this. For example, suppose we had some new converts that we're trying very hard to draw closer to the rest of the members of the body, and we decide that we're going to get together for a meeting, and maybe have some refreshments in that meeting. The church provides the preacher, the teacher, or the teachers to help work these new converts into the active work of the congregation. Is it wrong for the church, as such, as it supplies the teachers and the teaching, to supply maybe the facilities with some refreshments or something of that nature? We're not talking about the extremes to which brethren go to, but I'd like to know. We say we don't believe in the church doing anything that's carnal, but a building itself is carnal. The facilities we have are carnal facilities, they're earthly, they're material.

Is my time gone? OK.

Work of the Congregation
Day 2 Speech 2 Panelist 2
J.T. Smith

Introduction: *Smith, J. T. Since 1961 he has done local work in Indiana, Tennessee, Florida, Ohio, Kentucky, Arkansas, California and Oklahoma, also preaching in meetings in 32 states, the Philippine Islands and Panama City, Panama. He is now in his 5th year with the East Central Church of Christ in Tulsa, Oklahoma. He is also the owner and editor of Gospel Truths, a 24 page monthly journal.*

I too would like to express my appreciation to Brother Steve Wolfgang, to Brother Roy Lanier, and Brother Jamie Sloan for giving me this opportunity of being with you today that we might discuss these things that pertain to life and godliness.

I was thrilled and excited last evening so that I could hardly sleep, about the things that were said in the speeches last night.

Regarding our session on History, it makes little difference whom this problem, or when this problem began, or how it started, or with whom it began, for I heard yesterday the solution to the problem. When Brother Hardeman Nichols said yesterday that John said, "Whosoever goeth onward, and abideth not in the teaching of Christ, hath not God. He that abideth in the teaching of Christ, he hath both the Father and the Son." I recognized then, that others were quoting the same passages of Scripture that I quote on these matters. And I said, "Thank God that we have found brethren who do not believe in going beyond God's word."

Then last evening as I reflected on Brother Winkler's excellent lesson on Biblical Hermeneutics, that many of us wish that we had the ability to present and how to establish Bible authority, I was thrilled. Again when I heard my good friend and brother Gary Workman say that he did not believe in the church support of any human institutions, I said thank God we agree on that. We are not divided on whether or not to take the Lord's Supper in an upper room. Besides Jesus settled that when he said in John the fourth chapter to the woman at the well, the place where you worship God does not matter.

But my brethren, I know one thing that I can depend on. That when we look at the passages of Scripture in the Bible, in the New Testament, that talk about the work of the church and the church in evangelism, I know that the local church selected a preacher, defined the territory of labor and sent out a preacher. I can give book, chapter and verse for that; that local churches paid a preacher Philippians 4, and 1 Corinthians 9 and 2 Corinthians 12 and 13; that the local church sent directly to a preacher in Acts 14:26-27; that the local church received the report from the preacher. But I do not know of a single passage where the Bible teaches that the sponsoring church arrangement may be used. (Chart #1) Now if we will stick with what we found yesterday, "that whosoever goeth onward and abideth not in the teaching of Christ hath not God," we can settle this thing. We can settle it. And I was thrilled to understand and to know that it could be settled.

What Has God Assigned to the Church in Evangelism?

Local Church Selected A Preacher

Local Church Defined Territory Of Labor

Local Church Sent Out Preacher (Acts 11:22-24)

Local Church Paid Preacher (Phil. 4:15-16; 2 Cor. 9:12; 12:13)

Local Church(es) Sent Directly To Preacher (2 Cor. 11:8-9)

Local Church Received Report From Preacher (Acts 14:26-27)

The Bible Does Not Teach The "Sponsoring Church" Arrangement

You say well, "What about those who would go out from among you because of these things?" Or "Why would you go out from among brethren?" Brother Dub McLish, I get his bulletin, and he's had a number of articles on this new hermeneutics and other matters of liberalism, called *Come Forth My People*, in which he said, "Good people who are in bad churches need to hear the Lord's warning in Revelation 18:4, 'Come forth my people out of her that ye have no fellowship with her sins and that ye receive not of her plagues'." Faithful brethren who continue in liberal, apostate churches offer excuses for doing so and give many examples. But we need to come back to the word of God. And when I tell brethren that we can do these things in matters of evangelism let me tell you something, I can give you book, chapter and verse and you can too. Let's go to the Bible.

Work of the Congregation
Day 2 Speech 2 Panelist 3
Charles Horn

Introduction: *Horn, Charles. Respected for 32 years of service in congregations at Columbia, MS, Independence, MO, Hot Springs, AR and Whitney, TX. Is active in summer camp work, serves both as preacher and pastor at Whitney, TX.*

It's been a wonderful experience to be with you, and I thank God for the attitude that's been manifested. And it's my understanding that we're to observe and make comments on the speeches that have been made. You know Jesus on one occasion prayed, "Father I thank you that you revealed these things to children, the unwise and not to the wise." And so I thank God for what we've heard today.

The work of the church is evangelism, edification, and benevolence. We're in agreement. Let's go to work. But of course the problem comes beyond that. Hebrews 8:5, I believe as strongly as any brethren here, that the new tabernacle must be built according to God's pattern just like the old tabernacle was. If God gave us a pattern for a church building, we'd all have to build it alike. But he says, "build upon the foundation of the Apostles and Prophets," the inspired Apostles and Prophets and their teaching, Jesus Christ being the chief cornerstone.

What I've heard today, Brother Warnock and Brother Cosgrove, has been very much the same thing. As a student in 1953 in Abilene Christian College, I thought then as I heard brethren discuss these matters, "These brethren have a point. They're warning of where a digression can go to. They're warning about where they're afraid the church might be." Sadly enough some have not heard their warnings. But I thanked God then, and I thank God now, for you brethren who have offered those warnings. And many of us, and I believe most of us, have heard those warnings. I think you heard Brother Owen Cosgrove say, "We've heard the warnings." We hear and see where we go off on a tangent. Either extreme is not good. Let's keep balance in this matter. "Faith comes by hearing and hearing by the word of God."

The sad thing that I see in all this is that the conviction that you brethren may have on the limiting of the church, of how many churches can cooperate together, and where that's been pushed to a point of intensity of division among the Lord's brothers, is sad. And I thank God for the spirit that we've come to a better understanding of one another.

I compare it to this. There's the marrow and there's the bone. "Jesus is head of the body, the church." "By one Spirit we've all been baptized into one body." And whether that finger and this finger and this hand and arm, and… I don't know where the symbolism of the local congregation is in that. But I know that when Christ is the head and that every congregation and every individual are going "into all the world and preaching the gospel to every creature, teaching them to observe all things" that He has commanded. That they will be working in harmony with one another for the lost souls, preaching the gospel, that Jesus died for our sin, was buried and raised again the third day according to the scriptures.

Brethren I don't have the wisdom to discern all those intricacies between the individual and between the congregation, because they're one and the same.

Work of the Congregation
Day 2 Speech 2 Panelist 4
Paul Earnhart

Instruction to Panel Speaker

Neil Abbot – Moderator: OK Brother Earnhart, four minutes please.

Introduction: *Earnhart, Paul. He preaches in Louisville, KY, edits Christianity Magazine, served three congregations in Nigeria for four years. He has done local works in Kenosha, WI, Waukegan and Zion, IL, St. Paul, MN, Joplin, MO, Mt. Sterling and Louisville, KY. He is widely used in evangelistic meetings.*

I would like very much to express appreciation for the opportunity to be a part of this study group, and to those who have planned it, and worked so earnestly to provide it, and to those whose spirit and attitude is making it possible.

I stand before you, as our brother this morning said, as a disciple of the Lord and as one committed to Christ, absolutely. And as a consequence of that, I have reached certain convictions about His will. It is not out of any animosity or ill will that I've had differences with brethren of other persuasions, and I have none now. But there were things I believed that caused me difficulty, and things I refused to practice that caused me difficulty, and things I was compelled to preach that caused me difficulty.

I went to school with Charles. We were there in 1953, also with Owen. Avon Malone was my best friend in college. We were roommates. It was not a marriage made in Heaven. He liked to go to bed at 10:00 with the chickens and I liked to stay up all hours of the night. And he had to cover his head with the bedclothes and everything else. And he stood and performed the wedding ceremony for myself and my wife. That's not the difficulty with me.

The problem is substantial differences. We agree on many, many things. And I thank God for each one. I have rejoiced and reveled in the statement that has been made about sound biblical hermeneutics. I rejoice in it. And as Brother Smith has said "it thrills our heart to hear it." It's good to be here and to hear one another state these things.

If I have a problem, it's a difficulty in those areas that have to do with the activities of the local church that involve every single member in those activities in a personal way, and with which I cannot have part. And as long as those are true local assemblies, I cannot join together with you in doing them, as long as my conscience moves me in the direction that it presently does.

Galatians 6:10 has become the doorway through which so many things have come in to the work of the local church, every good thing to all men. If this is applied to all because the pronouns are in the plural number, then absolutely 2 Thessalonians 3:10-12 "if any will not work neither let him eat" is applied to everybody. And verse 12, it suggests ought to work diligently and not to be busy bodies is applied to everybody and therefore must be a part of the work of the local church. To interpret this individually is, I believe, the basic thrust of the passage. I see no basis for understanding any collective action here. I have no difficulty seeing collective action when people are told and instructed or by example are shown to be acting together, not because of the number of the pronouns.

But the problem that I'm having, and I'll just speak to this briefly, is I'm not sure always what you're opposed to. I've heard, I think, some unequivocal statements that churches ought not to support colleges. But I'm not sure you're opposed to churches building health spas. I'm not sure you're opposed to gymnasiums. I've hear words about "judgement," I hear words about "I am not enthusiastic about these things." But we need to hear from you, I'm pleading with you brethren, we need to hear from you, "These things are sinful, not to be practiced." When we know that, we'll know where you've come down with both feet on the thing and we'll be able to talk further about it.

I thank God for your openness and your directness. I pray that we'll go on being just that candid and open. And we can, as we've been pled with, love one another from a pure heart fervently.

Work of the Congregation
Panel Discussion

Neil Abbot – Moderator: OK, thank you very much. Now our next panel discussion will be a little bit different. And I don't know if you brethren were here during the first panel discussion when Brother Lanier said, "Let's just pretend that you're around the dinner table and discussing these matters. And we'll just pretend like we're looking in on it."

And so this type of panel discussion won't lend itself to transparencies and the use of the overhead. But just talk among yourselves just like you would at the dinner table and we're just kind of overlooking it. Or over, yeah looking at it, (Laughter, whs) and overlooking it. (Laughter, whs)

And you have two minutes for each speech that you have, or each talk. But you can talk as many times as time will allow. And I'll draw the discussion to a close at the proper time. So you can either start your discussion with a question or a statement or whatever. Who wants to start?

Panel Discussion

Hershel Dyer - Panelist: All right, as I stated in my remarks, I'd like to see us test this principle. We realize that in a congregation there are people of all different circumstances and settings. There are some people that are married. There are others unmarried and therefore those instructions for husbands to love their wives, wives to love their husbands, children to obey their parents, parents to train up their children the right way and so forth, those duties belong to people in their given circumstances and do not belong to the membership all together, that is to every solitary member.

But I raise the question, "Can the church support and even support out of its treasury to do some work of evangelism or benevolence, edification? It could fall into one of those realms, the duty that every individual in that congregation has to perform. I mean he has that obligation; she has that obligation to God. Can the church itself support that, if that is the duty that applies to every member?" I'd like for us to explore that a little bit.

Paul Earnhart – Panelist: Brother Dyer, it seems to me that you're operating on the basis of a tautology there, that since every member… All members of the body of Christ are the church. Therefore, whatever all members of the body of Christ are commanded to do, the church can do. And of course that would be true if we were talking about the church universal, not about a local assembly.

And I've heard this before, but I've never heard it demonstrated from the Bible to be true. It's an interesting presupposition, but I don't think there's a biblical basis for it.

But if it were presumed to be true, Ephesians 4:28 is certainly something that every Christian is commanded to do. "Not to steal anymore but to labor with his hands the thing which is good that he may have wherewith to give to those that have need." And therefore the church ought to be right in involving itself in any enterprise of a business sort that was honorable and honest. And I would suppose that 2 Thessalonians 3:10 and going through 12 would also apply because "if any will not work neither let him eat." So all are expected to labor, all are expected to do honorable employment. I don't know on what basis, if you took this principle, you couldn't object to the churches involvement in enterprise. That's my concern there.

I've heard this point before. And it's accurate to say that what every member of the church is commanded to do the church is commanded to do. But that is the universal body. We're not talking there, about the local assembly and what Christ has given it to accomplish. I believe that's a team with a team responsibility. Most of what we're commanded to do we're commanded to do as individuals.

And I come to you with a deep conviction that this collectivist mentality is destroying us. We need the personal commitment to Christ. And then out of that, let us join together in these teams that the Lord has arranged and we'll bring the fervor of our own personal commitment and discipleship to that, and they're going to go like they ought to go, if we do in them what the Lord expects.

Hershel Dyer - Panelist: Let me ask you now. "In the realm of evangelism you would have no objection to the church supporting or aiding any individual or any group of individuals in the work of evangelism, would you?" Because the work of evangelism is a work that applies to all of us.

But in the realm of benevolence is where you seem to feel that the church cannot participate. For example, the man by the side of the Jericho Road was a man who needed to be helped. We say that if a Christian came along there he should help that man. Now if that is the duty of every Christian to help the man who's been left by the side of the road that way, why is it not the duty of the church? It's the duty of every member of the church, just like it's the duty of every member of the church to preach the gospel where he can. And you say, "Well, we can support that. But we cannot support what is the duty of every individual with respect to this benevolence, because he's not a member of the church."

J. T. Smith – Panelist: The duty as it involves the matter of evangelism is given both to the church and the individual.

Hershel Dyer - Panelist: Uh huh!

J. T. Smith – Panelist: We have passages that clearly indicate from 2 Timothy 2:2 that the individual is to teach others that they may teach other also.

Hershel Dyer - Panelist: Uh huh!

J. T. Smith – Panelist: But we also have authority and instruction to the church in 1 Timothy 3:15, "If I tarry long, that thou mayest know how thou oughtest to behave thyself in the house of God, which is the church of the living God, the pillar and the ground" or support "of the truth." So even though we have passages that discuss and describe the matter of individuals as it involves evangelism, we also have it for the church.

Now the same thing is true with regard to the matter of benevolence. We have the passages that authorize, as you said, those who are individuals to do this as the Good Samaritan. But we also have passages that specifically point out to the church.

Hershel Dyer - Panelist: Uh huh!

J. T. Smith – Panelist: So God makes a distinction and that's the only way and the reason that I can make a distinction, is because God makes one.

And by the way, let me say this while I'm saying. If I'm going to be hindered from using the projector, I'm not going to be able to talk, because Eugene Britnell and I were discussing something one time and I sent him three charts in the letter. And he wrote me back and asked me if I could perform a wedding without charts. (Laughter, whs) So I may have to use those just a little bit.

Neil Abbot – Moderator: No, you can have a panel discussion without charts. (Laughter, whs)

J. T. Smith – Panelist: Well I might could, but I may not want to. (Laughter, whs)

Neil Abbot – Moderator: Well, that may be so. Brother Horn would you like to respond?

Charles Horn – Panelist: Yes, I'd like for us to look back to the head. 1 Peter 2:2ff "Christ also suffered for us leaving us an example that we should follow His steps. Who did no sin, neither was guile found in His mouth. Who, when He was reviled, reviled not again. When He suffered He threatened not but He commended Himself to Him that judgeth righteously." He goes on to tell us how He died for his sins. When did Christ die for our sins? While we were yet sinners. When did Christ go out and heal not only His own Jewish people, but the centurion's daughter? While they were still not…When did he feed the multitudes? Many followed just for the food that He was giving. And yet He taught. That's our head that's our example.

And as I read these scriptures that you brethren have read, I see it's not limited to just the individual action? But this is the action, as Brother Dyer has here pointed out, for not only every individual but every group of individuals as they manifest the love of God. Love God first.

Our mission, the church's mission, is to make known the manifold wisdom of God. Matthew 28, Christ has all authority. By His example and by His life and following His steps we're going to be the Good Samaritan, whether as individual or collectively. And then some of these congregations, in order to handle this problem, they have built the family centers out of individual contribution and not out of the church treasury. Is that acceptable to you brethren?

Paul Earnhart – Panelist: Have you…?

Charles Horn – Panelist: That's it.

Paul Earnhart – Panelist: OK. (Laughter, whs) All right, let me just say…

Charles Horn – Panelist: Be sure and tell my wife about that, that I quit before my time was up.

Paul Earnhart – Panelist: I will by all means do it. Let me say again, what I said before, "That when you establish that every Christian ought to do something, just like we had the case of the Good Samaritan, you have established that the church ought to do it." But that's the universal body which has no collective function. And what concerns me here is the impression that maybe, I'm sure it's not intentional, that if we believe that we should carry these duties out as individuals and that they ought not to be done collectively through the team of the local church, somehow we are unconcerned about it. We don't want to do it; the spirit of Christ is not in us.

Hershel Dyer - Panelist: Uh huh!

Paul Earnhart – Panelist: And that's absolutely not true. The spirit of Christ can as well be carried out in the godly consecrated life of the individual disciple daily taking up his responsibilities, as it can be accomplished by the collective action of the local church. And to say that it must be done by the local church, or somehow God's church is being denied the opportunity to practice these things, is just not true. And I don't know what we need to do to get that across.

I'm troubled by the statements that are sometimes made, "That to interpret this as individual is contrary to the spirit of the gospel." I can't believe that Ephesians 1:22-23 could be limited just to believers in benevolence, and this idea of "it violates the spirit of the gospel." If it violates the spirit of the gospel, we can read in the word of God where the churches did it. We can see when they took care of that.

But if we as individual disciples do our work, there are not going to be anything for the local churches to accomplish in this regard. And that has to do with colleges, and all these other works that have been made the burden of local churches, so that those churches cannot do what God ordained and arranged them to do. Their fragile framework, not fragile in the final analysis, but their simple framework has been broken down because we've loaded them down with every kind of program that should be ours to take care of.

Hershel Dyer - Panelist: Paul, I think I probably didn't clarify myself sufficiently there to you. Both of these brethren in their major speeches emphasized how the work of the church is evangelism, benevolence and edification, and we all agree on that. And what I had reference to when I spoke of a duty that is incumbent upon every, or bound upon every member of the local congregation, I meant every work or service in connection with one of these: evangelism, benevolence, or edification.

Now you brought up the matter of every Christian having the duty to make a living. But I'm talking about duties in relation to these three major things: evangelism, benevolence, and edification. Now if every Christian is obligated in the congregation to do this, in either of these three fields, why is it wrong for these members collectively in the local congregation to join together to do that? It's all right, it's proper; they're commanded to do it as individuals. Why is it wrong for an individual to be rendering service to God in one of these areas when…why is it right for him to do it and wrong for the group collectively to do it, the disciples collectively?

Paul Earnhart – Panelist: Basically my objection is, Brother Dyer, that your argument is a logical argument, in the since that it's based upon a logical statement. And if it can be applied to the three areas you have mentioned, it can be applied to any area. If it's right to say that when in these three areas all Christians are commanded to do these things, therefore the church ought to be allowed to do it. It's right to say that in any area where all Christians are commanded to function it's right for the church to function. And I might add to that, if it can be proved that they are allowed to do that, they are permitted to do that, that it should be said that the churches would be permitted to do that. That's the nature of the logic. And that's the thing that troubles me.

And I think that you'd be in trouble, or I would be in trouble, let me not put you in there. I'd be in trouble in 2 Thessalonians 3:10-12, Ephesians 4:25-28. That's the thing that troubles me with it, has for a long time. And that's the basis for my objection. That's all I had to say.

Neil Abbot – Moderator: Brother Horn?

Charles Horn – Panelist: As I look at the example of Jesus, and as I look at His church, His body, there's one other passage of scripture, for example in Matthew 11:4, where a prophecy about He healed the blind, He gave sight to the blind, healed the lame, the leper, the gospel was preached to the poor.

He goes on to tell many instances, for example John

12:5, when Judas complained about why wasn't the ointment sold that it may be given to the poor. It wasn't that he was interested in the poor but his hand was in the bag. So there was a common treasury of Jesus and His apostles, and they were helping the poor out of that bag.

And I see that as I read these scriptures in the book of Ephesians 1, Jesus is head. In chapter 2 we are built upon the foundation. In chapter 3 it's the, not only the personal mission of Paul, but the purpose and mission of the church, to make known the manifold wisdom of God. In chapter 4 here is council. We talk about individuals and congregations. For example in chapter 5 Paul is counseling, doing some marriage counseling for the wives and the husbands. All men need to know God's law on marriage, whether they're a member of the church or not. That infant child out there needs to be cared for if it's neglected by its parents, whether they are members of the church or not.

The love of God was shown toward lost, frail, sick humanity long before He saved them. And now God's church can go out and follow His steps and His example. They are not a welfare institution, but they may minister benevolent acts of good will, as I understand the scriptures.

J. T. Smith – Panelist: If I… I don't know that I understood your point. Is your point that the church can help those who are not saints, or is that what you're saying?

Charles Horn – Panelist: Yes, uh huh.

J. T. Smith – Panelist: OK. Every passage, and I think this morning in our session, it was clearly pointed out that every passage of scripture that talks about the church and the work of the church, and Brother Warnock did the same thing in his speech, pointed out that every passage of scripture that speaks of the church collectively doing this, speaks of that which was done to those who are saints. Now unless we're willing to accept what the scriptures say about it, and of course that's what, all of us have said that, we believe the scriptures. We believe in establishing authority in the same way; then the passage of scripture needs to be forth coming as to where the church was involved in that.

Because if we're going to take the position that whatever the individual can do the church can do, then I don't think that even you are willing to accept that, as Brother Earnhart has pointed out from Ephesians 4:28. And the matter of the church doing these things to those who are not saints cannot be found. So if we were going to do that, I'm perfectly willing to do it if a passage of scripture can be forth coming.

Hershel Dyer - Panelist: I'd like to come back to 2 Corinthians 9:13 that was discussed in the morning session. And the objection to "all" there referring to men who were other than the saints, or people other than the saints. The objection to that was made with reference to the thanksgiving. That this was the thanksgiving of other saints, the "all" there refers to the other saints who didn't need the material or physical assistance.

But what he's talking about there is that the saints and "all" enjoyed the liberal sharing, if you'll look at the wording. Those who enjoyed this liberal sharing were "them" and "all." He's not talking about the giving of thanks there. He's talking about the sharing in that generosity of these Christians from other places who sent that contribution. So it's the sharing that "them" and "all" are participating in, not the thanksgiving. I'd like to hear some comment on that. Brother Earnhart maybe you'd like to tackle this.

Paul Earnhart – Panelist: Yes, yes. First of all, I think if that happened, it would be the subverting of the purpose that was stated from the beginning for this contribution.

Hershel Dyer – Panelist: Uh huh!

Paul Earnhart – Panelist: They were told to make a collection for the poor saints, 1 Corinthians 16. This statement says that it's for them. Now if it went to others, then it was a rather deceitful thing to say, "we're raising this money to take care of the needs of the saints," but we're going to use it for other things. Now that's on the surface, on the face of it, what I would see as a problem.

The thing about this passage is it seems so tenuous to me. Here we are resting our case in a measure on this passage. It's got to be this one or Galatians 6:10 in concrete terms and yet it's "all" and "we're not sure, it might be." Although it seems to me the circumstances surrounding this collection would say it was not those who were not saints. But if it were possibly that…

Hershel Dyer – Panelist: Uh huh!

Paul Earnhart – Panelist: It's not enough to say "it could be." It's only enough to say, "It absolutely has to be no question about it," in order for us to step out on the solid ground of revelation and say this is the will of Christ.

I want to say again that the work of benevolence is the work of every single disciple. If we have not been doing that, we have been sinning. And I think a lot of us have been. We are so materialistically minded and so comfortable in our situation. Here we're sitting here in this tub of butter. We don't care what's happening to other people. That's the wickedness here, not the fact that the local church is not involved in this.

And as one brother observed, there's not too much benevolence going to those that are not saints, from the local churches. I suspect, I'm speaking about those with which I do not have a personal part, but I think that that might be an accurate statement. You all would know better than I, and perhaps I ought not to be saying anything about it, that's sometime true of some of my statements. But that would be my response Brother Dyer, and I appreciated the question.

J. T. Smith – Panelist: Can I say one thing?

Neil Abbot – Moderator: Sure.

J. T. Smith – Panelist: Also on verse 14 of that same context, when he discusses there your liberal sharing with "them" and "all" "and by their prayer for you" it appears to me that those whom they are helping, the "them" and the "all" were also able to give prayers for those who were at Corinth. Which I think, as Brother Marty Pickup pointed out this morning, that this has to do with the liberal generosity of those who were at Corinth and who were gentiles in assisting those who were Jews. And in doing that, those who were able to share with "them" and the "all" were also able to pray for those who were at Corinth, which would indicate to me that it involved those who were Christians.

Charles Horn – Panelist: I think as we study that passage, and this is getting down to the crux and what we're going to do with it, back up in verses 8 and 9 and 10 particularly, there's a quotation made in verse 9 and 10. "As it is written he hath dispersed abroad, he hath given to the poor his righteousness remaineth forever. And he that ministers the seed to the sower both minister bread for food your food and multiply your seed sown and increase the fruits of your righteousness."

He, even back in the Old Testament, Ruth, not an Israelite could reap the leavings. Glean in the field of Boaz.

That's the reason that I understand and as we discuss when we exegete it and apply hermeneutics to these passages, and I'm not a scholar I'm a practical man, we come out with sincere honest brethren who have come to a different application. And now what are we going to do with this situation?

I believe from my study of the scriptures that 2 Corinthians 9:13; 6:10 apply also as the church to those who are not Christians. I believe in James 1:27, that as Christians keep themselves pure and visit the fatherless and the widows that that's the duty of the congregation itself as well. In 1 Timothy 5 also gives an indication of that. And so how are we going to handle this?

We are to walk in the footsteps of Jesus who committed Himself to be judged by Him, by God. If you have your conviction brethren, don't participate in congregations that are cooperating and sponsoring it. And if we're as equally convinced that we're doing God's word this a way, then be like Michael, "Well I warned you. God's going to have to judge you." Let's get busy then preaching the gospel.

Neil Abbot – Moderator: Excuse me just a second. Time is about up for this section here. And so let each one of you have one more turn, and then we'll date this section.

Hershel Dyer - Panelist: Do you want me to…?

Neil Abbot – Moderator: Yeah. Each one of you has one more turn.

Hershel Dyer - Panelist: I'll just take a moment here. I think, sometimes we get confused with regard to the spiritual and the carnal. We all believe that the church has to deal with carnal matters in order to operate. We all are in flesh and blood bodies and there are flesh and blood needs. So I think it's misleading to say the church must deal with the spiritual and not with the carnal, because we all have to deal with the carnal. I have to receive carnal pay in order to get along, in order to have carnal groceries. So we need to be very careful, I think, about that.

I know what you're saying and I agree with you. Our spiritual mission is evangelism, edification, benevolence, or having heart of compassion for the poor and so on. But I think sometimes we do an injustice by saying, "Well now we're preaching the spiritual but these other people over here are preaching the carnal" because that's creating, I think, the wrong kind of impression. That's all.

J. T. Smith – Panelist: On this matter of, you brought it up and I want to make mention of this before we close this part of it out, because we haven't mentioned it about this new convert and the church could supply the teacher. Could they supply the refreshment? I think they cannot, and the reason I think so is because I do not believe that the church is responsible for social thinks of this nature. And which is generally referred to as fellowship. I have some charts that I'd like to show you on that, and when we get back to Tulsa, if you'll come over why we'll go over that a little more. (Laughter, whs)

Hershel Dyer - Panelist: OK.

J. T. Smith – Panelist: But…

Hershel Dyer - Panelist: He and I'll keep this going when we get back…

J. T. Smith – Panelist: We'll keep this going when we get back to Tulsa. So…but nevertheless, unless there is a time when we can provide, or find authority from the scripture where the matter of fellowship or things of this nature involves the social ... Because a number of years ago I signed a proposition with a brother. And he took the position, he affirmed that the church from its treasury can take funds to build and maintain fellowship halls for the purpose… kitchens and fellowship halls, for the purpose of having social meals.

Hershel Dyer - Panelist: Um hum.

J. T. Smith – Panelist: He believed that. He practiced that. And brethren, of course, many of them still do practice it. But I maintain that it's a violation of the word "fellowship," and that the church is not authorized to provide such things as kitchens and fellowship halls, and or refreshments for anybody simply on a social basis.

Charles Horn – Panelist: It's great to see brethren laugh together. Did you see the cartoon in the paper today? "Boy that was a good meeting, but what did we decide?" May be applicable here.

But it's wonderful seeing the attitudes and appreciate the attitude of these brethren, the sincerity, the plainness with which we've spoken and the honest disagreement that we've had.

Jesus said, "You are the light of the world. A city set on a hill cannot be hid." As individual we are the light, we are the salt. But as cooperate action we are cities, the church and its work is a city.

Perhaps we have surrounded this mountain long enough. Unless every person in every congregation with a commitment to Jesus Christ continue to study these things, love one another, love God, and show this love of God toward a lost and dying world and toward one another.

Let us brighten the corner where we are, individually, in our home, on the job, in the congregation. Let every congregation brighten the city where they are. Show them the love of God and let us continues to be brethren, even though we may come to honest differences on the application of some of these things. If it violates your conscience do not participate in it.

I can go and worship with a congregation that doesn't have Bible classes, but they're teaching on Monday night, Tuesday night, well fine. If I try to bind it and say you have to have it on Sunday morning, I feel that I'm wrong there.

And so in this matter where there are these sincere honest convictions then, James said you know if you warned a brother, be patient, preach the word continue studying. Let's not divide the body of Christ over some of these things.

Let us let God do the judging. If I can face God in the Day of Judgment with the conclusions that I've reached and you've warned me, you've cleared yourself of my blood.

Paul Earnhart – Panelist: Charles, you are my brother.

Charles Horn – Panelist: Amen.

Paul Earnhart – Panelist: That's never been the question in my mind, and I hear your heart talking. And I've heard the hearts of others. And I've tried to listen. I want to hear. And I hope you'll listen to us, too. I agree with what Brother Dyer said. Spiritual and carnal don't mean anything. What means something is "Do we have a Biblical basis for what we're doing?"

Hershel Dyer - Panelist: Yeah, amen!

Paul Earnhart – Panelist: That's the issue. And I want to say again that use of passages which refer to the universal body of disciples, any command given to the universal body of disciples, or the purpose of the universal body of disciples, can be fulfilled by individual action. Absolutely can be done, and I believe it ought to be, no necessity for local church action. I do believe that individuals could have a fellowship hall, the only thing, it ought not to be built on church property that's owned by the church and it ought not be overseen by the elders who don't have any need to be bothered by something like that. They've got enough to do to shepherd the flock, but no problem in my mind.

You've warned me that I should warn and then leave the matter alone. I have to tell you Charles, that warning other people about these things is what got me in trouble. And they didn't want to hear anymore warnings. And I did go away when they told me to go away. And I'm still staying away because they're telling me to stay away, because I will continue out of the earnestness of my conviction, not animosity, but I am a part of the loyal opposition. I love you. And I wouldn't bother with you if I didn't care. And I don't think you'd bother with me if you didn't care. But it was the result of these convictions that moved me to warn.

And I know you can go and worship with the no Bible class brethren, but I can't. You didn't have anything to object to or give your conscience trouble there. But I can't go where they're using a sponsoring church arrangement and where they're involved in using all kind of recreational programs out of the funds of the local church, and where they're involved collectively in things that are contrary, I believe, to the scripture.

Neil Abbot – Moderator: OK. Thank you very much brethren. We appreciate that very much. Our next session will be… the panel will be answering written questions. And so we'd like for you to write out your question and direct your question to a member of the Panelist: so we can get…. Five minute break, let's be back in here.

Work of the Congregation
Question and Answer

Neil Abbot – Moderator: (Beginning not caught on tape whs) the panel answer these written questions and we want to stop the question part about 10 minutes till so that Brother Cosgrove and Brother Warnock can give their 2 minute summation. Panelists, some of the people in the audience have said that they'd like for you to speak into the microphone and scoot up a little bit closer so they can hear. The first question is to Brother Warnock.

Question 1:

Neil Abbot – Moderator: Brother Warnock, are you listening? "If meeting a preacher's needs can include building him a dwelling house, can meeting a sick person's needs include building a clinic?"

Weldon Warnock – Main Speaker: The church may provide for the sick person whatever is necessary. I can't envision building a clinic to take care of your sick people. You'd take them to the hospital, and under the expertise of doctors and nurses. We got many good hospitals operated by the state as well as private citizens, and the church wouldn't have any need as I see, to build a clinic.

Now it can build a house and provide whatever is needed. It might get the doctor. It may have the nurses come to the house. I wouldn't call that a clinic, I... just taking care of some sick people. But it could have a doctor come by once a week and check on a sick person who was in their care, the church's care, or a nurse to come by, have constant care. Whatever is necessary to provide the needs of this sick person that's under the care of the congregation would be scriptural. But I don't know what the church would be doing building a clinic, as I understand the question.

Question 2:

Neil Abbot – Moderator: All right this question is to Brother Cosgrove. "If a church of Christ has a fellowship hall, how do you explain to someone not a member of the church of Christ that that is any different than the Baptist, Catholic, or any other denomination's fellowship hall?"

Owen Cosgrove – Rebuttal Speaker: Lest any one get the wrong impression about this clinic business, this question just asked, and say now that's Brother Warnock's side and Brother Owen is on the other side. I feel just as he does about that clinic, take him to the hospital or give him care. I don't want you brethren to get the idea that we liberals are all in favor of building clinics and so forth. Now, some may be but I'm not. Are you Bob? Bob's not either. Are you John? John's not either. Are you Avery? You're not either? Well, I'll say. Who's turning in those questions anyway? (Laughter, whs)

"If a church of Christ has a fellowship hall, how do you explain to someone not a member of the church of Christ that that is any different than the Baptist, Catholic, or any other denomination's fellowship hall?" Well, if the church of Christ has a restroom, I'm not going to try to explain to someone how it's any different from the Baptist, Catholic or anybody else's restroom.

Yes sir? Oh, I thought you were correcting me for being uncouth. (Laughter, whs)

Question 3:

Neil Abbot – Moderator: All right, this question is directed to Brother Earnhart. "In what sense did Paul bring alms to his nation, Acts 24:17? And then what were offerings?"

Paul Earnhart – Panelist: I think that that passage in Acts must be understood in the light of all the other evidence. And we know what he did. The evidence about that contribution is that he was, and stated several times in Romans, in 2 Corinthians, that it was for the poor saints. It was gathered for them. He states in two other epistles that it was going to be delivered to them. And so bringing alms to his nation was fulfilled. We must understand any statement in light of the total context of scripture. And on the basis of the other passages we understand it. That it had reference to the bringing of alms to his nation. Certainly the Christians in Jerusalem, these saints that were suffering, were his nation. And stating it as he did in front of a Jewish body, these people were not Christians.

He explained to them what he was doing in a way that they might understand it. But anyway, we understand it by reading the total context of the scripture and so interpreting it.

Question 4:

Neil Abbot – Moderator: All right, for Brother Dyer, "Since Brother Earnhart asked for a clear statement on the following point, would you please state clearly whether or not it is unscriptural for the church to finance or oversee the various kinds of recreational facilities we see promoted today by many congregations of the Lord's church?"

Hershel Dyer – Panelist: Let me say this. I will state forthrightly, if something is built and the primary purpose of it is for recreation or social life, and that's the purpose of it, then I would state categorically that it's wrong, it's sinful.

But there are some things churches may do, just as the suggestion I made or the example I gave and raised the question as to whether a church could do that. We probably all do some things in a material way that takes money from the treasury to help the new converts, helps convert the lost, and things like that, that we would say that involve a certain amount of attracting them maybe in a carnal way. We may use filmstrips or something else that engages their attention. That could be called entertainment. But what are we trying to do with those things? We're trying to convert them. We're trying to build them up in the faith. And so I think a lot has to do with your purpose. What are you really trying to do with the cake and the coffee or whatever? What are you trying to do with it?

I sometimes take people to coffee. I'm trying to convert them. I'm trying to lead them to the Lord or up-build them in the faith and my primary purpose is that. I'm not just taking them out to have a little social life with them. So I think your purpose has a lot to do with something like that.

Question 5:

Neil Abbot – Moderator: All right, Brother Smith, "Is the widow kin to a believer, in 1 Timothy 5:16, also a believer? If a believer cannot care for her may the church?"

J. T. Smith – Panelist: "Is the widow who is kin to the believer in 1 Timothy 5:16 also a believer?" Well, I don't know whether she is or not. It just says, "If any man or woman that believeth have widows let them relieve them

and let not the church be charged that IT may relieve those who are widows indeed."

"If believer cannot care for her, may the church?" Well, if she is a widow indeed then she is in fact a Christian, because those things that are said in 1 Timothy 5 that involves the widow, involves those widows who are Christians. That it might relieve them that are widows indeed. So if she was not a Christian, on the basis of what we've already said with regard to the matter of the church not being responsible for those who are not Christians, without any scriptural authority to do so, then no. I would say that the church could not care for her.

Question 6:

Neil Abbot – Moderator: OK, this is for Brother Weldon Warnock. "Could you express is a simply way how all the work of evangelism, edification, and benevolence can be done without sponsoring churches, or orphan's homes organizations and in such a way that all of us can agree on, through both individual efforts and local church efforts?" (Laughter and a lot of crowd noise, whs)

Weldon Warnock – Main Speaker: That's the easiest question I ever had to answer (Laughter, whs) especially the one where all of us can agree on. (Laughter, whs)

My conviction is that the church that God designed can fulfill its mission that He gave it in every area, and it did in the first century. The church evangelized the world in thirty years without a missionary society. It edified itself, equipped its own people, as Ephesians 4 teaches, brought them to maturity. And they were able then to be teachers, and become elders, deacons, etc.

And as far as benevolence, we see in Acts 6 that at Jerusalem they took care of their own widows. And whatever is necessary to take care of widows, the facilities like a house and clothing and food the church may provide that within the charge of the congregation.

And I'll say this about benevolence brethren. We need to not be reluctant in taking money out of the treasury to help those toward whom we're responsible. Now some of our brethren today I notice, want to take everything up individually. Well, that's all right to do it individually. But if we've got a responsibility, we can take it out of the treasury. We give our money into the treasury to be spent for whatever the function of the church is. And here is evangelism, edification and benevolence and any other function that God gave the church to perform, namely worship.

So if we could get back to just let the church do its work and we wouldn't … I think we can all be in agreement on that. I can read in Acts how they did it. We don't have any problem on missionary society. I think all of us oppose that, or most of us are opposed probably to churches subsidizing colleges. Not anything wrong with brethren establishing a school, but not the church subsidize it.

Our problem … a number of problems have been, and are here today, may the church subsidize benevolent institutions? And my conviction is no. Just let the church handle its own, under its eldership, and through its own deacons and members.

Question 7:

Neil Abbot – Moderator: This question is to Brother Horn. "If Jesus did something the church can," that's in parenthesis, "this began as an effort to defend such things as church benevolence to non saints. The same premise is applied now in the new hermeneutic. Jesus was broad minded toward women so churches can use women preachers. Is there any limit to this hermeneutical principle, if Jesus did it the church can?"

Charles Horn – Panelist: There have been clear statements that I whole-heartedly agree with concerning women speaking and preaching to the assembly. And I think there's no disagreement there.

I have no affinity with the new hermeneutics. I simply pointed out that Jesus, the head, did minister to those who were not His immediate disciples, those who were teaching. He fed, he healed the sick. And this was simply a door opener to teach them. And I believe that His body can do the same thing. It's not a welfare institution, but it may extend welfare to those who are in need as God extended His welfare toward us when we were in need, that we might come to know the gospel and to be saved. God would have all men be saved, come to a knowledge…That's the mission of the church. These other things are incidental or fit toward that goal, if it doesn't, concerning the social events, then you know it has no part in it.

The foyer of the congregation or the gymnasium what have you, if it's built for that then our priorities are misplaced, there's abuse there. If it's built for the teaching of God's word … in Acts 2 I find that there's social as well as spiritual. When they in the temple and from house to house they ceased not to teach and to eat and to share. And so the home, the place where they met, was inciden-

tal. And the building where we meet, if we're building a monument, that's wrong. If we're building a building to be utilized to glorify God, to teach His word, where saints can come together to nourish not only the physical, the spiritual, the mental, and emotional needs of mankind though the teaching of Jesus Christ, then there are limits. And I agree with most limits that you say, except the fact that when several congregations cooperate together that's still the church doing it.

Question 8:

Neil Abbot – Moderator: OK, Brother Earnhart, "Is it a social function provided by the church when it builds a foyer where folks can visit before and after service? Is this allowable in the same building we use for worship?"

Paul Earnhart - Panelist: I heard that in 1956 in the Sewell Auditorium at Abilene Christian College, when Hardemen Nichols and Carl Spain first introduced in the lectureships that year the idea of fellowship. And the term was used in that sense, fellowship, speaking about the very thing that Owen said was an abuse, fellowship as a means of evangelism. And the argument was made; we already have a fellowship hall because we have a foyer. I suppose you could make that argument with a porch, or even if there was a tiny little overhang on the outside where somebody could stand out of the drip.

But the purpose of a foyer is to let people come into a building and have some occasion to settle their affairs and get the children's clothes off whatever, and then go into the assembly. The purpose is to facilitate what the church is commanded to do. I don't think that that would justify…I am concerned as I listen to Brother Dyer, and just a moment ago to Charles. I can see that if you build a gymnasium and health spa for evangelism that's all right. Why can't you build a liberal arts college for evangelism and let that be all right? What's the difference?

It seems to me strange that we can't understand the argument of our brothers who use instrumental music when they say, "It's just an aid." We say, "It's something different." And yet we say that a health spa is an aid to evangelism. Something is out of joint there. If one is true the other must be, it seems to me.

Question 9:

Neil Abbot – Moderator: OK, this question is for Brother Cosgrove. "Yes, early churches often met in homes where cooking and eating facilities were already present. Many do so today. Question, were early churches therefore authorized to build and maintain eating facilities out of the collective treasury as is done today?"

Owen Cosgrove – Rebuttal Speaker: I just want to clarify one thing. We don't believe in building health spas. I don't.

Charles Horn – Panelist: Amen.

Owen Cosgrove – Rebuttal Speaker: Anybody else here believe in building health spas?

Hershel Dyer – Panelist: No.

Owen Cosgrove – Rebuttal Speaker: OK. You what? Brethren, we're awful close together on a lot of these things and the implications you know. I look for the day when all of us, in a gathering such as this, are banded more closely together to fight those abuses that we're talking about, because we don't believe in them either.

"Brother Cosgrove, yes early churches met in homes where cooking and eating facilities were already present. Many do so today. The question, were early churches therefore authorized to build and maintain eating facilities out of the collective treasury as is done today?"

Well, the church where I preach pays me and I'm paying for my own house. But many churches have, paid for out of the church treasury, preacher's homes that have eating facilities. They paid for them. Now can the preacher invite a bunch of the brethren over to eat with those facilities that the church paid for? How many of them can he invite over, what percentage? Some one says, "That's individual, that's not the church." Now we get into this business, well if the individuals do it it's OK, not the church. There's some fuzzy areas here.

Individuals come in and build a gymnasium for you and a lot of other things, this is where the incidental use gets into the abuse I think.

Am I through? I'm finished. (Drawing his finger across his throat. whs) I don't know if I even got close to that. Maybe I can get another chance at it.

Question 10:
Neil Abbot – Moderator: OK, Brother Dyer, "Can every church in America cooperate and send funds to one congregation to oversee an evangelistic effort, such as the *One Nation Under God* program of Colyville Tennessee?

Hershel Dyer – Panelist: I'd say J. T. Smith gave that question if I didn't know better. (Laughter, whs) He's already hit me with that.

Neil Abbot – Moderator: I'm sorry it could be. I don't know what it says Cookeville or Colyville. Cookeville.

Hershel Dyer – Panelist: I can remember the question now. This is a program to put a mail out in each home, is it? I'm not that familiar with the program. He hit me with that the other day. Is that a mail out to every home in the country? I don't see anything wrong with helping that church to send a mail out to every home in the country, if that's what it is.

Question 11:
Neil Abbot – Moderator: All right, Brother J. T. Smith, "In 2 Corinthians 8:9 Paul speaks of Jesus becoming poor for your sakes. This is an example for churches/individuals to initiate in the giving of 2 Corinthians 8:9. Was this gift of Jesus limited to saints or was it for sinners?"

J. T. Smith – Panelist: Jesus, as He discussed the matter of giving, and as He talked about the different people such as the Good Samaritan and others, who were to help those who were in need. It was done on an individual basis, every one of them. We do not involve ourselves in the matter of the church doing something along this line because of what Jesus said with regard to the individual Christian. If we can take the passages that involve the individual Christians, and make church action out of them, if we can pervert them in that way, then why can't the denominations do as they've always done and be right about it, in John 15 in talking about the vine and the branches, and take those passages that Jesus used with regard to the individuals and make denominations out of them?

I maintain that they could, and I also maintain from Ephesians 4:28 that the church could involve itself in a pie supper because individuals can do those things as Paul said, "To provide that which is good to those who are in need."

Now I found out this morning form one of the speakers that it would be all right. And that the passages of scripture that we find in the New Testament that involve this matter of visiting, would be all right if we used them over in Africa to build a clinic, but it wouldn't be all right in Dallas. Now what I want to know is where did Jesus make a distinction between the people in Africa and the people in Dallas? I say they're both wrong because we have no authority on the word "visit" to build an orphan home or to build a clinic, because these are the things that Jesus said with regard to the individual Christian and not to the church in building anything.

Question 12:

Neil Abbot – Moderator: OK, thank you. To Charles Horn, "You made the statement that the individual and the congregation are the one and the same. Question, can the congregation have a business?"

Charles Horn – Panelist: Maybe my statement was misunderstood. I used the illustration of the marrow and the bone. They are two different things, but where they join together, does any man have, any doctor have the skill to cut that line of distinction between the individual and the congregational. Many of these responsibilities are overlapping as Brother Owen just said. Now what was the question now? Refresh my mind on that question.

Neil Abbot – Moderator: Pardon?

Charles Horn – Panelist: The question?

Neil Abbot – Moderator: The question is, "You made the statement that the individual and the congregation are the one and the same. Question, can the congregation have a business?"

Charles Horn – Panelist: No. I do not believe the congregation can.

Neil Abbot – Moderator: OK, thank you very much, panelists. This wraps up our question and answer period. Now we are going to have the main speakers, Brother Cosgrove and Brother Warnock, have a two-minute summation speech. Brother Cosgrove.

Cooperation of the Congregation
Summation Speeches

Owen Cosgrove – Rebuttal Summation Speaker

Now brethren, in these repeated discussions I see the issue coming up again and again about individual action and congregational action. It seems to me that things just come back and just settle pretty well right in here.

I'd like to ask this question. I don't know, these rejoinders is this the time to ask questions? Brother Warnock has a chance to answer. If all of the individuals are supposed to do all of these things and the congregation is not supposed to be involved in congregational activities in these things, are the individuals just floating on their own? Are they all just freelancing? Can the elders arrange any program? Can we do anything to organize this? And if we do will it be a church action then or is it still individual action? I'd like to know if we can organize things a little bit, because I find out at home what's everybody's business is nobody's business. We kind of need to arrange the program.

One other thing I'd like to say here. I beg your pardon? One minute. Last time you did that you went like that. OK, all right. So often we justify a thing on some incidental use and then we use that and take advantage of that and build a program on it. I see where you brethren that oppose some of these things, I see your point. I'm looking through your eyes, I think. And we have to stay with the principle. But what we're pleading for is for us to, really before we begin to forbid Christian work, let's make sure that we have the right by the scriptures to forbid something that the Lord has commanded. That we know what we're doing when we make these laws and say, "You can't do it that way." I'll tell you what we don't do doesn't make us anything. We need to get about the work. But I'm not saying that scolding anyone, or trying to judge anyone, because we love and appreciate you. And we hope that you love and appreciate us.

Weldon Warnock – Main Summation Speaker

Well, it's been a pleasure and a joy to have been here and meet some preachers I've read after through the years, never had the pleasure of meeting. There's Brother Banister down there. I've heard of him through the years. Brother Coffman, read his tracts. And Brother Doran, I met him years ago over in eastern Kentucky when he was President of Morehead State University. In fact I had an English teacher who was at Pritchard High School in Grayson, Kentucky who came over to Morehead and taught there for several years, husband was Principal, so we have that connection. And others, it's good to see Brother Ramsey. Of course all these brethren here that stand where I stand, of course I see them frequently and know a lot of them. But it's good to see others that I've known of for a long long time and first opportunity I've had to meet.

Now I ditto what Brother Cosgrove said about binding our own opinions. We need to be careful brethren, you know that we don't bind where God has loosed and loose where God has bound. And I'm aware of that. And I don't want to be guilty of imposing my opinions on anybody. I've been fighting radicalism and extremism from that standpoint through the years. We've got to be balanced.

You know Brother Foy Wallace said years ago, and of course I disagreed with Brother Foy in later years on some things. But he said, "The church is caught in a bind." And I think that's true, and has been. We've got extremism on both sides. We've got radicalism that I don't espouse on one side out in right field, and then you've got ultra liberalism on the other side that we all oppose and object to. And we just need to get back and have the proper hermeneutics and walk in the old paths and try to be balanced and use some common sense in what we're doing. You know God gave us a thinker and we need to use that. And just try to find out what the Bible teaches, and then get back to preaching the gospel and saving the lost.

Thank you so much.

Roy Lanier - Moderator: We owe a great debt of gratitude to all these men that have helped us on this panel and as speakers. I think our experiment of panel speaking and this kind of a format has really turned out well. Our comments at least that have been made to me, with the exception of one or two extremely loud ones (Laughter, whs), were all good. And we certainly are stumbling along trying our best to do what will be of the greatest benefit for those of us who are here to listen and to learn.

I want to thank Neil Abbot on his birthday today for helping us moderate this panel. I'm not going to sing Happy Birthday, but he didn't even know that I knew that. But it's his birthday. I'll not tell you which one, but it's not below 50 folks, I'll tell you. (Laughter whs) It's a good bit above it. But thank you very much Neil for that. I'm sure that he's enjoyed seeing many of his old friends, and you've enjoyed seeing him.

Vick Chase would you please make your way forward... (Tape ends here at this point whs)

END OF SPEECH TWO, DAY TWO

Evening Meal

Day 2 Meal Speeches
Friday, July 13, 1990

Participants

Non-Institutional Brethren	Institutional Brethren
Robert F. Turner — Meal 3	George Bailey — Meal 4

Day 2 Meal Speech 3
Robert F. Turner

Introduction: *Turner, Robert F. He is a native of Scottsville, KY and has been preaching over 54 years. He has done local church work in IL, IN, AZ, TX as well as evangelistic work in 36 states, Australia, Canada and Mexico. He is widely used in lectures and evangelistic meetings and is the editor of Plain Talk. For the last 30 years he has made his home in Burnet, TX.*

I don't feel at all comfortable doing this, but it looks like it had to be done. That's just the case. And I noticed they mentioned this morning they we were going to have some OLDER speakers tonight. (Laughter, whs) And I guess I'm one of those older speakers. Someone asked me how old I was. And I said "Well I've had seven year itch ten times and I'm… (Laughter, whs) and I'm going on the eleventh. I'm pretty far into the eleventh.

I want to say just a word personally here at first. I'm nervous and have been having some problems with my nerves since '86. I hope you'll excuse me if I use notes here that keep me going. I'm going to have to do that, I can't keep my mind on what I'm doing if I don't have something to direct me. I'm easily upset emotionally and so I use notes, please bear with me.

I lived through and preached through the problems that bring us together here tonight. I was brought up in a little church in Scottsville, Kentucky. I don't remember it having the sign Christian Church on the front of it, but I remember very well seeing that Christian Church sign thrown in underneath the church building and we had a new sign on the front that said church of Christ. I remember that very well. I know that that church never had used instrumental music, never had supported the Missionary Society, but they'd called themselves the Christian Church. And I believe E.G. Creasey to whom you just referred, was one of the men that got them to change the sign. My father was an elder in that church. I first took an interest in the church at a very young and early age, and started preaching on in the early '30's. I didn't do any full-time work until 1935, but you can see I have been at it a while.

But my first participation in any sort of a multi-church problem was in Phoenix, Arizona in 1948. And I remember that very well. Two churches were meeting together, the elders met together regularly, and they would try to solve problems they had and try to push the work in the state of Arizona. This was during the war, or just after the war. And one day something came up about some church needing about, it seems to me if I remember correctly, about 400 dollars. They needed 400 dollars for some kind of work, something they were doing, their own work. And one of the brethren suggested, "Well, we'll send them $200, and Westside send them $200." Well the Eastside church brother said "We can't send $200." "We don't have $200. We're still paying on our pews." Well someone else suggested, "Well, why don't Westside send us $200 to pay on our pews so that we can send $200 to Mason?" (Laughter, whs) And that was my first conflict, because I said, "I'll tell you what I think brethren. I believe these two churches need to have a divorce." (Laughter, whs) And some of the brethren didn't like it, but we had the divorce and each church began to operate on its own.

I had not studied in detail the question of multi-church operation. I had not studied that in detail, I freely admit. But I have done a lot of studying in my early years in the history of the church, Restoration History. And I was thoroughly convinced that each church ought to be independent and autonomous. Now I know that's a familiar phrase to you, independent and autonomous. I don't think we pay a whole lot of attention to it sometimes. Maybe we don't really understand what it means and it's a little bit difficult to apply, but everybody seems to agree with it. And that was the reason I wanted to divorce those churches.

But then in 1949 I decided I needed to erase all my previous concepts about church, throw out the old outlines, and sit down and restudy the whole matter. And I did that. I spent three months just doing nothing else, just study day and night. And out of that study, I came to the conclusions that still effect what I believe today and some of the things I'll have to say tonight. I not only studied the New Testament, everything I could find about church, every way I could think to study it. But I also took time to reread a lot of material I had formerly read on the Catholic Concept of church and on the Denominational Concept of church, and I tried to compare these things as I went along.

Then in '52 and '53 I took a sabbatical from my local work, asked the elders if they'd let me be free for a while. And I took off to do some meeting work all over the United States. I did 34 meetings in about 14 months, if I remember correctly, and I was observing. This was when things was just beginning to get hot, just beginning to warm up. And I wanted to observe as I went about preaching. I found that I could go into one community and preach a sermon on the church and they said, "Brother Turner you're just a little liberal on that, I'll tell you that's just not strong enough." Then I'd go into another community and preach the same sermon and they'd say, "Boy you're way too harsh on that, that's just not right." And I could see there were differences developing.

I did not take a stand on the matter myself, really and truly until the late '53's. But in 1953 I walked the streets of Tyler, Texas over and over, back and forth. It was a hard decision. But I had by this time come to some conclusions as to what the scriptures taught and I felt like I had to take a stand. The sponsoring church brethren who loved me so much in those days, would not study with me. And I'm noticing now that many of you are distancing… diting… disting… yourself. My, that's a crazy word to say, you're putting some distance between you and the ultra liberal brethren along this line, and I appreciate that. But I think you're going to find that those whom you have thought loved you so much, won't love you quite that much if you keep on standing like you're standing. I think you're going to find that that's what happened. This is human nature. This is human nature and it's something we have to work with.

I was a participant in the Arlington Meeting and have followed the arguments very carefully since then. I'm giving you a kind of a background here, out of which I'm going to draw my final conclusions here. There's an emotional side and a pragmatic side to this whole matter. The pragmatic side keeps coming back, "Call me 'Lord, Lord' and do not the things that I say." That keeps coming back.

But it has an emotional side too. And I thoroughly appreciate the emotional side. I'm touched easily on the emotional side. But I couldn't help but think as I enjoyed, and I truly did enjoy Brother Camp's discussion at the meal just preceding this, I couldn't help but think if Brother Camp's mountain church had used his money to do something that he thought was very obviously wrong, that he could not agree with it at all and did not want to have any part in, that he would have to either correct that or get out. I don't believe that love for brethren would keep him worshipping, supporting, and putting his money into something that he thought was diametrically opposed to some principle that he believed God taught in his word.

Now, that's my background for what I want to say now. I was asked to use my time to give my impressions of the Institutional Issues, my impressions of the Institutional Issues. Now it's out of that background that I give these impressions.

And the first one and the basic one, the fundamental one is, I believe the basic fundamental issue is collective action of churches. Collective action of churches. Now saints, in order to form a local church, must agree to act as one. I've had to do with forming a number of local churches. Going out, round up some brethren, get them together, convert some more, put them together and get them to agree to function as a congregation. There's got to be an agreement on the part of these saints, a plurality of saints.

Then they've got to accept some common direction and guidance, and I don't mean the scriptures. They've got to accept that to begin with, to be saints in the first place, but in matters of judgment. The scriptures teach us the first day of the week, but there's got to be a time on the first day of the week. Matter of judgment comes into the matter. They've got to accept some kind of common direction and guidance. Eventually the elders can serve in that capacity.

They pool their resources to the end that they may act as one. And in doing this they have to give up some independence. You can not be a member of a local church and not have given up some of your independence. You may think it's best to meet at 9:00, the other brethren may think it's best to meet at 9:30. You give up your independence, that's what I mean by that. You allow the common mind to direct your activity. You couldn't operate as a team if you didn't do that. Now there's scripture for saints doing that. But there is no scripture in my estimation, to my knowledge, for churches doing that.

I find no authority for churches getting together and agreeing to act as one, accepting common direction and guidance, whether it be Sponsoring Elders or the Directors of some institution or a Board of Directors, an Executive Board of some Association. I find no authority for them accepting some common direction and guidance for this activity and then pooling their resources. I find no scripture for them pooling their resources to that end. And I believe when they do so that they also, these churches that enter into that, give up some of their independence. They can no longer claim to be, in the full sense of the word, independent and autonomous.

In fact, when you define local church you define what it really is and how it comes about, then the difference in the individual and the church action will disappear.

Now, there are some other things that need to be said about churches operating together. There's about three big categories to be considered. The Catholic Concept of the matter is that ALL the congregations, ALL the local churches, have a means whereby they can act as one. They have universal oversight in the Pope and the whole Papal system. They have a universal treasury, funds from these various churches pool, in the Vatican City and so on, and they can act as one. The Catholic Church, its central authority, can make a decision, we're going to do so and so and they've got the funds to do it with. That's universal oversight, treasury in action.

Denominations operate a little differently. They do not claim to be the whole. But the Baptist Association is a means for all Baptist Churches, reaching an agreement to do something, working as a team, pooling their resources, accepting a common direction and guidance so they can do so. The Synod of the Lutheran Church does the same thing. The Conference of the Methodist Church does the same. This is the Denominational Concept.

And then there's the independent church. I believe, in an independent church, it operates under its own oversight with its own treasury to the extent of its ability. That's the limit of its action.

Some time ago a doctor in San Antonio asked me to come to his home. And he wanted me to sit down and explain these things to him. He said, "I just like to hear you talk." So I drew that on a chart. I just took a big piece

of paper and put it on the dining room table. And I drew over here the Catholic Concept, tied all the churches together. I said, "What do you think of that doc?" He said, "O that's wrong." I said, "What's wrong with it?" Well, he says, "There's no authority for that." "O, I see."

Well I said, "Let's take this. Here's the Lutheran Synod." And I drew a circle for the Lutheran Synod and put the Lutheran Churches in there, tied them together under an Executive Board of the Lutheran Synod, and the Baptist Association and all. "What do you think of that, Doc?" "Well that's wrong." "What's wrong with it, Doc?" No authority.

Well then I drew some congregations over here by themselves, each one doing its own work in keeping with its ability under its own oversight with its funds. I said, "What do you think of that, Doc?" He said, "That's it. That's the way it is." Well I said, "Doc, how do you account then for this church over here," I marked it, one of them "taking funds from these other churches and allowing their elders to be the Executive Board for the expenditure of that fund so that they operate as one in this particular function, not in everything, but in this particular function." Well he looked at it for a minute. I said, "Haven't you come back over here into the denominational system?" Well he said "I think you can get more done that way." (Light audience laughter, whs) Well, but I said, "Doc, while ago you said, 'There's no authority for it.'"

What about going on back to the Catholic system?" Well he said, "Naaaaww I wouldn't want to do that, no." But he said "You could … in principle it'd probably be alright." Well I said, "Doc, look what you've done. As long as I called it Catholic Church, you said it was wrong. As long as I called it denominations, you said it was wrong. But when I pointed out that you were DOING that through the Sponsoring Church arrangement, you said 'Well, that's alright.'" And in principle we go clear back to Catholicism.

Now please don't understand me to say that I think you brethren are Roman Catholics. Hah (laughing as he talks whs), that you're ready to have a Pope. That's not what I'm saying. That's not what I'm saying at all. I think there are some popular misconceptions that have fueled this problem concerning collective action of churches.

One of these popular misconceptions is we think of the church as composed of churches. THE church, THE church, what is THE church? Well if you're talking about all the saints, just say it. That's saint, they are the saints, all the saints, but not composed of churches. Well of course there are SAINTS that make up CHURCHES, but that doesn't mean that the UNITS of the universal church are CHURCHES. The UNIT of the universal church are SAINTS. We TALK BROTHERHOOD, but we THINK CHURCHHOOD. See what is a hood of brethren? That's brethren considered as one, that's a brotherhood. Now what's a churchhood? Well, when you start putting churches in there and considering them as one you've got a churchhood. Don't call a church… don't call it brotherhood and think churchhood. It would be nice in our discussions if we would identify what we mean by church, just put some sort of identification on that so that we just don't go switching along from the church doing this and the church doing that and not identifying it.

Then the second basic impression that I have, and that's all I'm trying to do here, is that we have got to find a way of determining it seems, the work of the local church. And I believe there are two things necessary for determining the work of the local church.

First, you've got to define an organizational church. An organized church. What do you mean? What do you mean by a local church? It's got to be defined. I think you can go back to what I said in the original statement. That is, "Saints that have covenanted together to work as a team to that end, have accepting common direction and guidance and have pooled their means and abilities." Now when you have defined an organized church, then you go to the scriptures and you seek precepts, approved examples, and necessary inferences for what that kind of thing did. It's just that simple to find out what they did. You know that's right. You've got that.

You said, "Well but can't the church teach on a lot of other things?" Yes of course. They teach on the ethics of the work principle for example, Colossians the 3rd chapter. But teaching on work ethics is not the same as going into business yourself, the church going into business. We teach on the ethics of marriage, but that's not the same as having the church married. I'm talking about a literal marriage of course, we all … that would be ridiculous. We teach on a lot of things that we do not necessarily enter into practice on, that is conducting ourself. For example we teach on government, or respect for civil government. That doesn't mean that we are activist parties going out and trying to change the government as a church, the church trying to change governmental policies and so on.

The intended function of the church, it seems to me, is to do that for which it raises its money and for which it expands its resources. That's these things for which there are Bible examples, precepts, and necessary inferences. Now I'm old fashioned enough to believe that the church is a spiritual institution to meet spiritual needs. I believe there are certain things that God intended saints to do operating as a team. And that he gave us a clue to that in what we can read in the scriptures.

A fire department is allotted funds for a specific work, to prevent and put out fires. If it does spend its fund on an orphan's home, why it's going to cut away from it ability to prevent and put out fires. If it doesn't spend its money on orphan's homes, it doesn't mean that they hate orphans, at least that doesn't mean the fire department hates orphans. It just means that they're doing the function that they were set up to do and funded to do.

Now I believe a local church is funded for specific things. I don't believe we just take our money and just pitch it in there, and no specific. I agree with specific things. I believe we ought to go to the scriptures to find out what the church did and it should be understood when we give of our moneys into this common pool, it is for the work that we are set up to do. I believe that with all my heart, and we shouldn't spend those funds on anything else. The organized church is God's plan for associating saints together to assist one another, to serve the Lord, and go to heaven.

Now, am I pessimistic about the future of God's people? Well I guess I'm very pessimistic if I'm supposed to think that a gathering like this is going to solve all the problems. I don't believe you believe that. But I want you to know that I'm thankful for brethren that will come together and have their say, openly, freely, discuss these matters. I think that's a wonderful thing. And that gives me optimism.

And I'm optimistic about the ultimate outcome of all of this. Not because I think that it's just going to solve all of our problems. I think denominationalism will take its toll from among our number. But faithful brethren will prosper. It may be that their concept of prosperity is different from what others have, but they'll prosper in the Lord's work, and in the Lord's way. Men will arise, as they have in the past, who value truth more than popularity, and will preach it for the Lord's sake rather than for money's sake or for popularity's sake. Men who would rather have heaven than the treasures of earth. And I fully believe, and I surely believe, that some of those men are sitting here in front of me right now.

I believe we have the capacity to do that. It's hard. But I believe we have the capacity to love the Lord more than we do anything else, more than we do our pet ideas. I believe we have the capacity, and many of you have shown that as you've discussed your differences here. You've shown it in a good spirit along that line, and I appreciate that.

But unity is not some sort of a trophy, a static thing to be set on the shelf and admired. Unity is a working process, an ongoing working process. And the only true path to unity is diligent, honest, objective searching for truth. And to the extent that we are doing that in a meeting like this, we are at that very ... in that very process. We're drawing ourselves closer into the kind of unity, the only kind of unity that I believe we are going to have. We are unified in the common desire to serve Jesus Christ above all else.

Whew! Now see that wasn't so bad. (Laughter, whs) Thank you so much (applause, whs). I told you this is not my thing. (Applause, whs).

Day 2 Meal Speech 3
George Bailey

Introduction By Roy H. Lanier: (Beginning not caught on tape whs) … predated us. A number of you here in the room enrolled with me about that time or else you were already there at that time. But there were some rather well known students that have already passed through the hallowed halls of Freed Hardeman College, one of whom was George Bailey. I guess that's the first time I ever heard of you. I will not say what I heard of you at that point, I'll just simply say I heard of you. (light Laughter, whs)

The next time I heard of George Bailey, my older sister and her husband were worshipping in, if I remember correctly, Roseland, New Mexico (George Bailey corrects Roy "Albuquerque," whs) Albuquerque, New Mexico and they raved about this young preacher that was out there that just really was tearing everything up.

Well, the next time I heard of George Bailey my father had invited him. My father was the Head of the Bible Department for the Central Christian College, as it was known when it started in Bartlesville, Oklahoma. And I was preaching up in Iowa and I came down for the lectureship. And they had assigned this young whippersnapper of a fellow from Oklahoma City, I believe at that time, the Culverson Heights church, to speak on the Holy Spirit. Well now, that happened to be one of my father's favorite subjects. And he spent a LIFETIME studying the Holy Spirit. And I said, "Well Dad, what does that guy know about the Holy Spirit?" And he said, "Probably nothing." (Laughter. George Bailey said, "Did he say that before or after?" whs) And so he said, "Let's go early because I want to be sure we get to where we can hear every word he says." Well he hadn't gone but about 5 or 6, 7 minutes into his speech, his sermon, that night at the old Sixth and Hewey congregation building. And my dad turned to me and he said, "Son, you better listen to this guy. He knows what he's talking about." And that was one of the highest compliments my father could pay a man when it came down to talking about the Holy Spirit.

I believe George Bailey's name is a household name among those of us, particularly out here. And the record of his accomplishments through the years has been well known to so many. His involvement in so many of the congregations, and the works, and the campaigns around the world, and we are extremely privileged to have him speak to us tonight. He lives here in Dallas. He is no longer in full-time local work but is still involved in a great deal of evangelism. And we're pleased to have George Bailey. (Polite applause whs)

Day 2 Meal Speech 4
George Bailey

Introduction: *Bailey, George. Nationally known preacher, campaigner, author, and speaker on Herald of Truth. Has been preaching 54 years with works in Weatherford, Lawton and Oklahoma City, OK. Albuquerque, NM, Abilene and Dallas, TX. Presently retired from local work, lives in Dallas, TX and still engages meetings and lectures, over 50 years service.*

Thank you. (Applause whs) Thank you Roy. Now I know how a pancake feels when it had syrup poured all over it. (Laughter, whs) I really appreciate that. And it's an honor to be on the platform with Robert Taylor. You know if he did as good as he could … (George hearing something from the crowd whs). What did I say? (Roy Lanier correcting the name, whs) I mean Robert Turner. Well either one, you know. (Laughter, whs) But if he did that well when he was not feeling well, I said, "What would you say if you were felling well?" So when he gets to feeling better I want to hear him again.

I really don't agree with a fellow… I mean with the fellow who had finished his sermon and people were speaking to him as they left the building. One little lady came up to him and said, "Has anybody ever told you how great you are?" And he tried to be humble and said, "No." And she said, "Well where did you ever get the idea, then?" (Laughter, whs)

So I'll tell you I honestly, I'm nervous. Both of us are nervous but for another reason. His is age and mine is stage. (Laughter, whs) Age and stage, you know. Like somebody said, "Age is a matter of mind. If you don't mind it doesn't matter." (Light Laughter, whs) Or somebody else said, "Age is an attitude. If you didn't know how old you are, how old would you be?"

But isn't this a joy to be with you. I want to express, along with these others, my appreciation to Steve and Roy for a superb job. Do you realize how much is involved in, not only seeing that so many people eat and you don't have to take up the slack, but have you thought about all of the footwork and the paperwork and the telephone calls and all of the other things that it takes to really put a thing like this together? I don't know where we could have found two men that would have done a better job. I really think these fellows deserve a big hand, I tell you. (Applause from the audience, whs)

In addition to the wonderful speech that we've heard tonight, I agree with Roy, that those two today, I think really were worth the whole, whole program. And if we didn't hear anything else, even coming at a distance, and as was mentioned each of us doing it at our own expense, I tell you that was really worth it. Brother R.J.'s brother was a very dear friend of mine. We all loved and appreciated Eldred. I wish Eldred were here. In fact, many a time have I wished that he could be with us, because I would have liked to have asked him some questions, because he and some of us were really concerned, and still are, about the way things, of course, have been going, the trends of the brotherhood. So I really, really am happy to hear R.J.

When Eldred had his debate with Dr. Beavers, a Catholic Priest, Eldred was telling me that Brother O.C. Lambert, that he had gotten to be his Moderator. He thought knew probably as much about Catholicism as any other man in the brotherhood. He said they had studied for months. They had holed up, and they'd studied and they'd studied. And they'd gone through all of the different arguments, and they wanted to leave no stone unturned because this was a historic thing. Because when have we had, other than a written discussion, a debate with a Catholic Priest?

But Eldred said after they had made their preparation, and they were getting ready, just the afternoon before the thing started that night that many of us heard in Stillwater, Oklahoma. He said Brother Lambert gave him a talk that he will never forget. He said, "Eldred we don't want to spare anything when it comes to the issue. We want

to deal with that. We want to deal with it biblically and thoroughly." But said, "We don't want to do anything or say anything or act in such a way that will offset, in our attitude, our spirit as Christians, anything that could be really, the church could be blamed for." And he said, "We want to conduct ourselves as Christians." And he said, "I know, because," he said, "I have been rough at times; I've been unusually rough, in fact, almost mean in handling the truth." And then he said he wished he could have it all to do over and he lay across the bed and he said he just wept like a baby. And I thought, you can't fight the fight of faith and use the weapons of the devil.

And often times in our contention for truth, whether it be with the Catholics, the Baptists, or some brother that has erred. Whether it be on some vital issue like the marriage question, or whatever it might be, remember we cannot fight the fight of faith and use the weapons of the Devil. God's word doesn't need any personal sarcasm on my part, it doesn't need any ugliness.

I think, this week all speakers without a single exception, and I've had the privilege of hearing every one, at the meal times as well as in the big hall where we're meeting, I don't believe anybody could go away saying, "That was a bad attitude." I think these men have really dealt with the issues, and that's what we're here for. And isn't it wonderful, isn't it marvelous, that both of us are willing and anxious to sit down. And these men have gone to great preparation. Isn't it wonderful that we can come together and that we're talking. Because until we talk together we're not going to walk together. But the attitude that's been manifest such as Brother Turner. Brother Turner, I want to be and get that right, his attitude. This is indeed a marvelous thing.

When this split came, some of us of course were sort of targets, because Brother Batsell Barrett Baxter and I were speakers on the *Herald of Truth*. I have heard what was said and have talked very often to the elders at Highland church in Abilene, urging them not to do this, not to do that, this isn't really the right attitude, this isn't the right direction, and over and over. But in all of this, I think that those who have really labeled one another, as brother R.J. mentioned today, have done so, as he so well said. And I have, at times, been guilty and I apologize. And I have before, in maybe making some statement like "Anti's" or what have you, or as R.J. mentioned, "Institutional." Those things really aren't the weapons of the Lord.

And I think this is a great meeting. And may God bless us all. But when this split came some of us were greatly affected. One of my closest friends was Gilbert Copeland. I don't know if you remember Gilbert or not, but Gilbert was a great person. I'd held a lot of meetings where Gilbert was. They used to call him Mr. Atlas, you know. And he, you know, just a little slender fellow. He said, "You ever seen Arm and Hammer soda?" You know. We had a great time together.

I thought Brother Homer Hailey, and still do, is one of the greatest Bible scholars of our day. I was really surprised recently, to hear of his position on the marriage question. I don't agree with that. I feel like I'm sure most of you do, very definitely. I think he is a great scholar. If he were to be in Dallas, if I knew, I'd go to hear him. I have, when he was here the last time that I know of, I went over to hear him.

But Yater Tant preached for the church where my folks went and where my wife grew up. He came after we had married, or just…no, just came just before we were married. But we could just go on and on and mention others.

My roommate in school in Freed Hardeman, Ernest Findley, you know we had known each other a long time before we went to school and purposely chose to room together. And I could just go on down the list and mention men that I've had great love and great admiration for.

But this thing is an individual matter. In fact, Christianity begins with the individual. And if it doesn't begin with the individual, it doesn't begin. Paul said "Each man must bear his own burden" (Gal. 6:5). And each person stands accountable to the Almighty. An eldership won't stand as an eldership before the Lord. But each one individually will stand before the Lord. You won't stand as a group. We won't stand as a brotherhood, or as a city, or as a certain community. But regardless of what we are a part of, whether it be the state, a city, a local congregation, or a brotherhood, one by one, individually we're going to stand accountable to the Almighty. And we go this way but once.

And it has been a sad thing to see brethren divided when you know our Lord so earnestly and so fervently prayed. And this seemed to be upmost in his mind, of all the things he could have thought about before that cross. The thing that really seemed to be pressing Him more was the unity of His people. And He prayed that they may be one even as He and God were one that the world might believe that God had sent Him.

Before Joseph was made known to his father he had been made known to the brothers who went down into Egypt to buy corn. And finally when he was made known to them, Joseph sent those boys back to the old father, who for 22 long years had thought that his boy was dead, and had said he would go to his grave with grey hairs weeping over the death of that boy. Here was news that that man had never heard before, news that would thrill him greatly, news of a long lost boy, news of a boy that he thought was dead. And as Joseph sent those brothers back to tell the father, not only that he was alive, but that provision had been made, wagons were provided for the whole family to come down into Egypt and to live in the land of Goshen.

But here was his parting message, Genesis 45:24. Make a mental note of it. He said, "See that you fall not out by the way." What did he mean? He could have meant, don't falter, because this is important, don't dilly dally, don't tarry, that might be. He might have meant don't faint. I think he meant don't fuss along the way. Time was when they had disagreed. Time was when they had fallen out. They weren't really united as to what to do with Joseph, the dreamer. They all wanted to do something. And so time was they had fallen out. And so that message was very timely. It's possible to fall out along the way.

Some have fallen away from the faith completely. Some have gone the way of error. Some have just surrendered completely. Some have disagreed among themselves and they've become disagreeable. But have you ever thought of why, if that's the meaning, don't fuss along the way, don't fall out, in that sense, have you ever thought of why?

Well first of all, as Abraham said to Lot, "Let there be no strife between us. We be brethren." And if for no other reason, that would be sufficient reason, we're brethren. We're baptized into Christ for the remission of sins. We came into the Lord's body. Our names were written in the Book of Life. We were redeemed in the blood of the Lamb. And because we're brethren, let's see that we fall not out by the way.

But secondly, maybe because they were members of the royal family. See their brother was Prime Minister of Egypt. It would be a shame for any family to fall out, but especially for the royal family. You think of all the harm that would result. Do you realize that we're called a royal priesthood? And let's be loyal to the royal that is within us. We are brothers and sisters of the King of Kings and the Lord of Lords. The one who is heir of all things, and if we're joint heirs with him, that means all of this and heaven too. And if for no other reason, let's not forget who we are and let's not forget whose we are. We belong to Him. We were bought with a price. We're a part of the royal colony of heaven. As Paul mentioned to the Philippians, "Our citizenship is in heaven."

But then maybe another reason they were asked not to fall out along the way, was because of the irreparable harm that would be done. You know Solomon said, "The beginning of strife is as when one lets out a water: Therefore leave off strife, before it is meddled with" (Prov. 17:14). And 2 Samuel 14:14 says that water spilt cannot be gotten up again. Have you ever thought that whether it be in the family, in the church, in the brotherhood, in the community, that anytime there is disharmony, anytime there is a division, in all probability somebody is going to lose a soul.

And I've wondered, really I've wondered, how many might have lost their souls. There are those who lie sleeping beneath the sod now, one in Oklahoma City that I know, so far as I know he never did come back. And because of some division in the church, the man gave up and quit completely. Somebody is going to be held responsible. We do go this way but once. And some day I and you and all of us will have to stand accountable to the Almighty. I'm not responsible for our brotherhood. I can't speak for anybody but myself. Each man bears his own burden. But I can be responsible for my own self.

If you don't remember anything else remember Song of Solomon 1:6. Maybe you've thought a lot about this. Maybe you've preached on it. But it hit me not long ago. And Solomon said, "They made me keepers of the vineyard, but mine own vineyard have I not kept." And I've often said that while preachers are saving others, they might well lose their own. And how many preachers have lost their own children? I've often said to elders, "While you are shepherding others you might fail to shepherd your own." Bible teachers, and couldn't we also say to the whole brotherhood, that while we're trying to save others we might lose our own? We might lose those that are among us.

Let's be sensitive and let's be really deeply concerned. That doesn't mean we glide over, sweep under the rug, lightly esteem anything. Anything that's big enough to

divide us is big enough to talk about and it's big enough to really give attention to. But let's be sure that when we fight that fight of faith we use the right weapons. Let's not use the weapon of the Devil. You can't get peace with God without picking a fight with the Devil. And you can't be at peace with the Devil without being at war with God. But let's be sure that while we're keeper of the vineyards, our own vineyards we're also keeping. It's not enough to save the lost; we've got to keep the saved, saved. And let's be sure that we're doing everything that we possibly can to do that. Let's not fall out along the way.

But maybe one more reason, in addition to being brethren, being members of the royal family, and in addition to all the harm that will be done, water spilt cannot be all gotten up again. Some will immediately evaporate. Some will go into the pores over which it goes. I doubt seriously that after any church trouble you can ever get it ALL back together exactly as it you had it before. It leaves its mark and it leaves its scare. And unfortunately this thing has left some ugly scares. Frankly, among our own people I've seen some ugly spirits. Maybe you've seen, among those that you work with, maybe you've seen the same thing. Two wrongs don't make a right. Let's be sure that while we're dealing with issues, let's be sure while we're dealing with the way to do a thing, that our spirit, our attitude, our motive, our disposition, our attitude, that real genuine concern for somebody's soul, that that is everything that God wants it to be.

The late Sir Winston Churchill said, "Never have so many owed so much, to so few." Have you ever thought about those to whom we're greatly indebted? Those that have blazed the trails, those who have fought, those who have debated the sectarians, those who have by burning the midnight oil, of burning the candles at both ends, they've worked out, studied, they've brought things to our attention that maybe we never would have really seen had it not been for their untiring efforts and they're great love and zeal as Roy's father and R. J.'s father, and so many others that we could just mention. While we owe so much to those who now lie sleeping beneath the sod, don't ever forget that we also owe a whole lot to those who will come after us.

We're in debt to the past, but we're even more greatly indebted to the future. And the only way we can pay our debt to the past, brethren, is by making the future indebted to the present, by making future generations indebted to the present. And let's be sure that while we disagree, while one person takes a position on this and another on that, regardless of how important it might be, let's be sure that we're not standing where we stand because of a group, a brotherhood, peer pressure, the one's we work with, or what have you. Let's just be sure that we have the right attitude. And since it is an individual thing and it won't happen as a group, it will be one by one. And that doesn't means you have to wait till the whole group with whom you are aligned makes the change. In other words, if I see I'm wrong, honestly I want to go to heaven when I die.

I started preaching at the age of 14. I don't know what I said, probably a lot of things that had no meaning at all. I noticed in an old Bible I gave one of my sons, I had put in the margin, now this shows the depth boy, of a 14 year old preacher. I had in boldfaced type, "Sin is wrong!" exclamation point. (audience Laughter, whs) Well he laughed. I said, "That's right son it is." He said, "I know, but that's sort of silly." you know. But now that's the Devil. But I don't want to spend my life preaching and then lose that soul eventually. I think that's the thought and the wish of everybody here. I don't believe there's anybody here, have you ever heard anybody say? "I want to go to hell. I can't wait. I'd like to die right now. I'm just looking forward to it." No. Nobody wants to go to hell; we all want to go to heaven.

Let's be sure that regardless of what we do, EVERY-THING we do, EVERY position we take, is from the heart. And as Paul, though he persecuted the Christians, and the Lord had said, "the time would come when men would put others to death and in so doing think they would do God a service" (John 16:2), and that was Saul. He thought he was right. And he stood there until he was convinced otherwise. Conscience is a safe guide only when conscience is safely guided, but it might not be safely guided. But when he found that he was wrong, he could have thought of his parents, he could have thought of his background, he could have thought of his peers, he could have thought of … but when he found out he was wrong, he didn't wait for a group to make a move. He immediately did it. And it will be one by one. God left a plan for saving the world, but he never left a plan for saving the world in the masses. The world will be saved one by one, individually. Let's be sure that in all of our efforts that we fall not out by the way.

I tell you this meeting Roy and Steve, and all the others who've helped, I think has given us a greater appreciation for each other. I know that some felt that maybe others have turned a cold soldier, or ignored, or what have you. And I'm sure you have, those of you that have different views on the issues that we've talked about, you probably have in your own ranks some difficulties. I would not ascribe to you what some other congregation among you is doing, unless you yourself believe that. And as Brother Cosgrove and others have mentioned, there are many of us that are not for gymnasiums, many of us that are not for this, we're not for that, we're not for the other, there are many of us. We're probably closer than you think. I believe the things that unite us are a lot more than the things that divide us.

Let me mention three passages, not teaching you but just calling them to your attention, because you know them well. In all of our change, there are some things that don't change. Here is one of them. 1 Corinthians 1:21, "It is God's good pleasure through the foolishness of preaching"—not the preaching of foolishness, there's a difference, but the foolishness of preaching—"to save them that believe." And still in the 20th century "it is God's good pleasure through the foolishness of preaching to save them that believe."

And then Paul said in Romans 1:15, "I am ready to preach." Bob, I know that you have students that have taken certain courses, graduation comes, they feel they're ready to preach. Brother Turner and I, others of you have … we've been at it quite a while, but it doesn't matter how much training, how much experience, how much expertise, how much ability, how much talent, how much knowledge, how much wisdom, how much personality, no man is ever ready to preach until he believes that gospel with all of his heart. And nobody is ever ready to preach until it means more to him than anything else. No man's ever ready to preach unless he is ready to live to the best of his ability up to its sacred precepts. And nobody is ever really ready to preach unless the people to whom he preaches mean more to him than the mere art of preaching. Some people just like to talk, they like to speak.

But the other passage is 1 Thessalonians 2:4. Paul said "God allowed me to be put in trust with the gospel." Have you ever thought of what a sacred trust we have? Let me ask you a question. I was in New Zealand standing on the beautiful hill, and on the top of the crater. And we were looking down upon the beautiful city of Oakland, on the north island. There were two preachers between whom I was standing and for some reason for the first time that passage just came to mind. And I said, "Brethren can you be trusted with the gospel in New Zealand?" Then I got to thinking, can I be trusted in Dallas, Los Angeles, Miami, Tampa? Can you be trusted with the gospel of Jesus? Is it trustworthy? Can the messenger be trusted? Can the message be trusted? Can the meaning of the passage that you put, can it be trusted? Can the method, the manner?

Suppose you were the only preacher in the world. Would the gospel be safe in your hands? Would it really? Suppose the congregation of which you are a member were the only congregation of the Lord's people anywhere in the world. Would the gospel be safe in the hands of that congregation? It's still "God's good pleasure through the foolishness of preaching to save them that believe." But each person has to really answer, "Am I really ready to preach, not just ability wise, but am I really ready to preach?"

But finally, is the gospel safe in my hands? Someday when we stand before the Almighty, there's another chapter. We will be held accountable for the way we preached it. We will be held accountable for the way we handled that great word. It's a precious jewel. Somebody said, "When one member of the team fumbles the ball the whole team loses ground." The Dallas Cowboys learned that. They've learned that several times.

Is that true in the brotherhood? Wasn't that true in Achan's case? When Achan sinned in Joshua 7, the whole team lost ground. And brethren, some of us have fumbled that ball and the whole cause of Christ has lost some ground. But you can't call time back in this life. I wish we could live those days over. I've often wished that we could. But we can do the next best thing. We can start from where we are now. And let's be sure that we don't fumble that ball. We're going to make some mistakes. We've made some. We're going to continue to make them. Let's make as few as we can. But let's be sure that we're most sincere when we make them. And when we find out we're wrong, let's be big enough, let's be earnest and sincere enough and Christian enough. We're ready to say I was wrong, I made a mistake. May the Lord bless us.

There was a little boy, just before the wheat harvest, that was lost. They'd search everywhere for the little fellow. Finally, it was said maybe he'd wondered off into the wheat field, because the wheat was high and ready for har-vest. And so they began to search, and they searched, and searched. And finally somebody came up with the idea. Maybe if we just join hands and… and comb the whole field we'll find the child. And after they joined hands, finally but too late, they found the lifeless form of that little boy. And the father, heartbroken, fell upon his boy and said "Would to God that we had joined hands sooner." Thank you. (Applause whs)

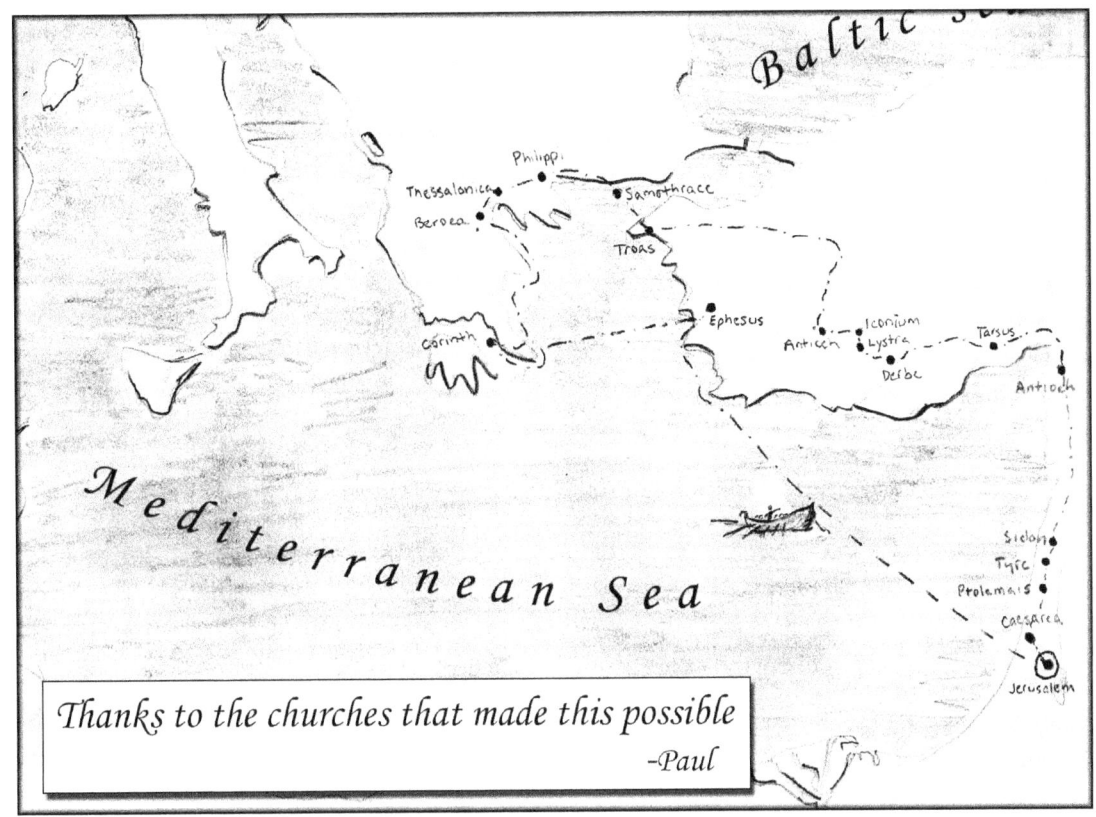

Thanks to the churches that made this possible
-Paul

Cooperation of Congregations

Day 2 Cycle 3
Friday, July 13, 1990

Participants

Non-Institutional Brethren	**Institutional Brethren**
Tom Roberts — Rebuttal	Bobby Duncan — Main
David Tant — Panelist 2	Lewis Hale — Panelist 1
Harry Osborne — Panelist 4	C. W. Lincoln — Panelist 3

Cooperation of Congregations
Day 2 Speech 3 Main
Bobby Duncan

Introduction: *Duncan, Bobby. Noted author, preacher for 39 years, lecturer throughout the southeastern states particularly, now in his 23rd year at Adamsville, AL. Also preached in Munford and Jasper, AL.*

I want to express my gratitude to Brother Steve Wolfgang and Brother Roy Lanier for the work that they have done in putting this program together and to those who bore the expense for getting the materials printed to advertise it and the programs printed. And I certainly want to express my gratitude for the opportunity of having a part on this program. If I live until next May, I will have been preaching the gospel forty years. I do not remember a single time when I have felt more keenly the weight of the responsibility than I feel tonight.

I'm honored to be able to stand on this platform with Brother Tom Roberts. I did not meet him until this morning. And I received a letter from him several weeks ago. It was a very kind letter and he is a very courteous person. And I know that the speech that he is going to present will be one that you will want to listen to very carefully. I think he's wrong of course, but I want you to listen to him very carefully. He thinks I am wrong. If that were not the case, then we would not be having this meeting.

I think it's good that we can get together and discuss our differences. And I am a great deal more optimistic about accomplishing something in meetings like this, than I am in accomplishing something with those who use the piano in worship. I believe that we have a ground upon which we can come and meet. We have the same attitude toward the scriptures. We believe what we do in religion has to be authorized. We believe we have to be governed by the Bible, that it's God's book, and that we're going to give an account in the judgment for the way that we treat it.

The subject with which I am to deal tonight is the subject of church cooperation. And I want to make mention in the very outset of our lesson that the differences that we have over this subject are not differences over whether or not churches can cooperate. So far as I know, every body

here tonight believe that churches of Christ can cooperate one with another. So far as I know, we are in agreement on a number of different ways that churches can cooperate, if I understand brethren who differ with me. And I want to say, that if I misrepresent any thing with reference to what these brethren believe, I do not do it intentionally. I have never, to my knowledge, intentionally attributed a position to a brother that he does not hold, or did not hold. Now I may make a mistake.

But if I understand our differences, all of us here tonight believe that churches can cooperate by announcing each others gospel meetings, announcing singings, and other church activities. We believe that churches can cooperate with each other by allowing their preachers to go from one congregation to another to preach a meeting, and to fill in, in cases where there is a need for that. We are in agreement that a church can cooperate with another church by allowing that church to use its baptistery. I remember when I first moved to Adamsville. We had a baptistery, but we didn't have a heater in it. And in the wintertime we would go over to north Birmingham and use the baptistery of that church building. Those brethren had a good heater in that one. We believe in cooperation. Nobody, so far as I know, believes that that would be wrong. I think all of us are in agreement that churches can cooperate by lending chairs, or songbooks, or even by giving pews to a church that may need them.

Here's a congregation that's built a new building, or maybe remodeled their old building, they have some pews that they're not going to use. Here's another congregation that's just started, maybe in another section of town, or in another town. I doubt that anybody here would oppose that church's giving those used pews to the church that's just beginning. That's church cooperation. I believe that's church cooperation in evangelism. I think all of us here tonight would agree that it would be scriptural for one church to give another church some copies of the New Testament, if there was a need for that sort of thing.

Now listen carefully folks. If I understand our differences on the subject of church cooperation, our differences are this. We have a difference with reference to whether or not one church can contribute money to another church to help that receiving church do evangelistic work. Now that may be an over simplification, but I don't believe that it is. It's not a matter of can one church contribute to another church. It's not a matter of can one church contribute money to another church. It's not a matter of can one church help another church do evangelistic work. It is a matter of whether or not one church can contribute MONEY to another church to help the receiving church do evangelistic work. And that's what I want to talk about tonight.

Now if those brethren who differ with me with reference to this say that the Lord's congregations must maintain their local autonomy, I will say amen. If they say that a congregation has no right to be in control of funds that belong to another church, I will say amen, in evangelism and in benevolent work. One congregation has no right to be in control of funds belonging to another church. If my brethren say that no congregation has a right to exert undue pressure on other congregations to get them to contribute to a certain work, I will say we are in agreement on that. And if my brethren say that some brethren have abused certain scriptural principles, I would not argue with that. I think perhaps, if I would think about it, I don't have anything in mind, if I would think about it, I probably could tell you about some abuses of what I believe to be some scriptural principles, and you know that sort of thing.

But the thing over which we differ is whether or not one church can contribute money to another church, to have the receiving church do evangelistic work. Now the kind of authority which the Bible furnishes for church to church contributions in evangelism is the same kind of authority that it furnishes for paying the preacher out of the treasury which was maintained by taking up a collection on the first day of the week. That's the kind of authority I hope to offer.

I cannot find an example for everything that I believe is authorized. I believe it has to be authorized but there are some things that are authorized in a generic way. And now the kind of authority that I'm going to suggest to you is that same kind of authority that a church would have for building and maintaining a meeting house with money that it collects on the first day of the week, according to 1 Corinthians 16 verses 1 and 2. That's the kind of authority. When I've done this then I will have shown that no scriptural principle is violated when one church contributes money to another church to assist that church in doing some evangelistic work.

Now then, notice with me some passages. In Acts 11:22-26, the Bible tells us that the church at Jerusalem sent Barnabas down to Antioch. And the Bible tells us that Barnabas taught and exhorted the saints at Antioch to cleave to the Lord. And then some time later, "Barnabas went to up Tarsus to seek for Saul. And the two of them taught much people at Antioch." Here's a case where one church, the church at Jerusalem, helped another, the church at Antioch, in the business of edification and evangelism. Later on in Acts 13, this very same Barnabas was sent along with Saul by the church at Antioch under the direction of the Holy Spirit on what we sometimes call the first missionary journey. Now since the church at Jerusalem had sent Barnabas down to Antioch, and then the church at Antioch sends Paul and Barnabas, or Barnabas and Saul, on this first missionary journey, then could we say that Jerusalem assisted Antioch in preaching the gospel in the places where Paul and Barnabas went on that first journey?

In Acts chapter 15, the church at Jerusalem helped the church at Antioch in dealing with a problem, which was created by Judaizing teachers. Growing out of this, two men from Jerusalem were sent with Paul and Barnabas to Antioch, Acts 15 and verse 22. And they went with a message of divine instruction to the church at Antioch. But it didn't stop there. From Antioch the message was to go into the churches in Syria and Cilicia, according to verse 23. Now here's Jerusalem, assisting Antioch, in connection with a matter of edification and evangelism. And they were assisting them in getting this message out to other churches. And so far as I am able to determine, the work that was being done was a work concerning which Jerusalem and Antioch sustained the very same relationship.

In Acts 11:27-30, the Bible tells us that some prophets came from Jerusalem down to Antioch. One of them delivered an inspired message to the church at Antioch concerning "a great dearth that was to come upon all of the world." Antioch took up a collection, sent relief to the brethren in Judaea; the Bible tells us that this relief was sent to the elders of the church. Now I heard somebody say (chuckling as he spoke, whs), that that passage said, "Every man according to his ability determined to send relief unto the brethren, which dwelt in Judaea," therefore this was individual action not church action. Seems to me, that when every man in the church does something, unless they all sent their contributions separately, they didn't, they all sent it by the hands of Barnabas and Saul, that this would be an action of the church. They sent it to the elders of the church in Jerusalem. Now notice my friends, the autonomy of the church at Antioch was in no way violated by the fact that they sent this contribution from Antioch up to Jerusalem and gave it to the elders of the church to be used in taking care of that particular situation. The Jerusalem church was not controlling funds that belonged to the church in Antioch. They were controlling funds that the Antioch church had sent to THEM to USE as the elders of that church saw fit. In this case, the need was a physical need.

In 1 Corinthians 16:1-2, 2 Corinthians chapters 8 and 9, Romans 15:26 and other passages, we learn that under the direction of the inspired Apostle, a number of churches collected funds to send to Jerusalem. This collection was taken to Jerusalem by Paul and evidently from Acts 21:17-20, it was delivered to the elders of the church. I believe that all of us here would agree that that's where it was delivered. And I especially believe, that those of you who may differ with me on this matter, would say that that's where it should have been delivered, because it had to do with a matter that was benevolent in nature. So these churches sent their funds to Jerusalem. Paul delivered it to the elders. Now then, I want to ask you a question. "Did the contributing churches loose their autonomy? Did the church at Jerusalem exercise undue control over the church down at Corinth, the churches up in Macedonia, and other churches that had a part in this collection? Was this a case of centralized control?"

In Colossians 4:16, the church at Colosse is commanded to send a book of the New Testament to Laodicea. They were also to get a letter that Paul wrote to Laodicea and they were to read that letter to the Colossian church. Now, question, "Can a church send a book of the New Testament to another church?" Well, I said in the very outset we all believe that it would be right for one church to send a New Testament to another church. I believe that we would agree that one church could buy some New Testaments and send them to another church, if that church needed that kind of help. But if I understand now our dif-

ference, there are some who say that one church could not send money to that receiving church and let that receiving church buy these copies of the New Testament. If I am wrong in saying that that's what my brethren believe, and I want you to know I'm sincere in that, and all that somebody will need to do whenever the panel gets up here, just say, "Duncan you missed it on that. We believe it's all right for one church to send money to another church so that that receiving church can buy New Testaments with it." You just correct me on that if I'm wrong.

In 2 Corinthians 11:8 the Apostle Paul says, "I robbed other churches taking wages of them to do you service." Now here's a case in which a plurality of churches supported Paul to enable him to preach the gospel in Corinth. This is cooperation in the field of evangelism.

Now folks I want you to notice something. We have shown these things from these passages. We have shown that it is scriptural for one church to assist another church; nobody differs with that. We have shown it's scriptural for one or more churches to send money to another church; we're all in agreement on that. We have shown that it's scriptural for one church to assist another church in evangelism; I don't believe anybody would deny that. I think we have shown conclusively, that one church does not loose its autonomy whenever these things take place, or that the giving churches do not lose their autonomy when these things take place. In other words, when one or more churches contribute money to another church to assist the receiving church in some evangelistic effort, every element of this arrangement is in harmony with the scriptures. And therefore the entire arrangement is in harmony with the scriptures.

It's scriptural for the church to assist...for one church to assist another. It's scriptural for one or more churches to send money to another church. It's scriptural for one church to assist another church in evangelism. Therefore, it is scriptural for one church to send money to another church to assist that church in evangelism. That's the same kind of authority that you use to show that the collection, which is taken on the first day of the week, can be used to pay the preacher, or build a meeting house, or do anything else for that matter, other than helping those who are in need.

Another way of saying the same thing is this. If no element of an arrangement violates any scriptural principle, then the entire arrangement violates no scriptural principle. What scriptural principle is violated? We've shown that every element of this arrangement is in harmony with the scriptures, violates no scriptural principle. Therefore the entire arrangement is in harmony with the scriptures. If that's not true, then there's not a man here who can find authority for paying the preacher out of the first day of the week collection.

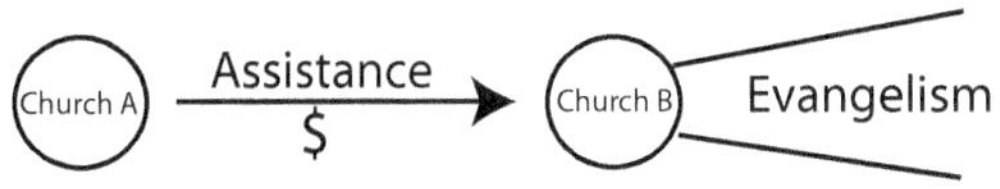
Church A
Assistance
$
Church B
Evangelism

1. Q. Can Church A assist Church B?
   A. Yes. Acts 11:27-30; 1 Cor. 16:1-3; Acts 11:17-19
2. Q. Can Church A contribute money to Church B?
   A. Yes. Acts 11:22-26; Col. 2:16 (sic); Acts 15:22-23
3. Q. Can Church A assist Church B in Evangelism?
   A. Yes. Acts 13:22-26; 1 Cor. 16:1-2; Col. 4:16; Acts 15:22-23

What Part of this arrangement is unscriptural? (scriptural references not clear)

What Scriptural Principle is violated? If all the parts are scriptural then the Whole arrangement is scriptural.

Now, look at this. (Chart #1) I'm not an artist. I hope you can see that. Can church "A" assist church "B"? And the answer is yes and we've given those passages. Nobody would differ with that. Can church "A" contribute MONEY to church "B"? Well, we've already seen that church "A" can contribute money to church "B" from those passages. Can church "A" assist church "B" in evangelism? Now those passages that we've seen show, and I don't think anybody here would say, "No church 'A' can't assist church 'B' in evangelism." Now look at it. What part of this arrangement is unscriptural? What part of it violates some scriptural principle, and what scriptural principle is violated? If all of the parts are scriptural, then the whole arrangement is scriptural.

In the remaining part of my time... how much time do I have? 9 Minutes. In the remaining part of my time I want to show that what I've said thus far is exactly what faithful brethren in general believed and practiced and de-

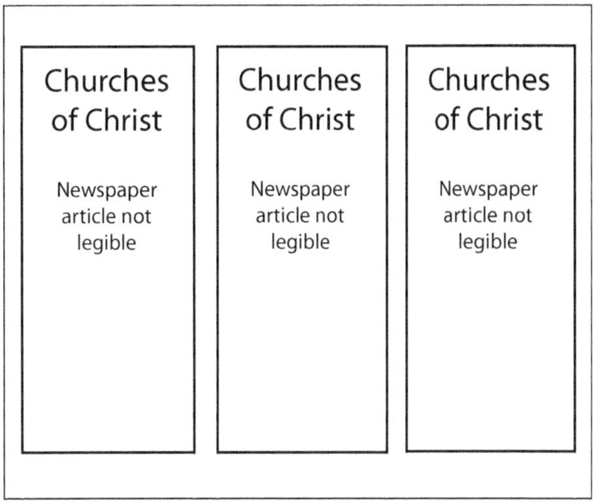
Churches of Christ
Newspaper article not legible
Churches of Christ
Newspaper article not legible
Churches of Christ
Newspaper article not legible

fended up until the last half of this century. (Chart #2) Here is a copy of some cooperative advertisements, and I...I'm sorry you can't read them any better than that. But you can take my word for it; these are cooperative advertisements that appeared in the *Birmingham News.* One of them appeared in 1945. There were thirteen churches that cooperated in paying for this advertisement, and you can see the names of them there. Some of you might recognize some of those names, but I will suggest to you that there were a number of those churches that participated in all of these ads. The middle one was in February of 1950 and then this one was as late as August the 28, 1954. I believe this the last one of those ads that appeared in the *Birmingham News.*

But in every case they have churches in the Birmingham area (that's the area that I'm familiar with; I'm sorry I don't have anything from Dallas; that's where I've done all of my preaching, in the Birmingham area), but brethren were practicing the same thing in this area that they were practicing in Birmingham. And some months ago we had a meeting somewhat similar to this, with not nearly this many people present, on a local level in Birmingham. And I presented some of this very same material, and Brother Yater Tant was present and he's here tonight. And when I finished Brother Tant told me privately, "Brother Duncun, there are some of those things that you have presented that were done by the churches in Birmingham that I would not oppose." Now Brother Tant, if I've misrepresented you on that, you're here and you can tell us wherein I've done so. But if you'll talk with Brother Tant, I think that he'll tell you that that's the case. But these churches took care of this radio progr...these newspaper ads in the very way that we're defending tonight. One church would be in charge of those ads, and then other churches in the area would send their money to that church who would in turn pay for those ads.

I'm not going to take the time to present a copy of a letter I have here from the 77th street church (holding up a transparency whs) from the elders of the 77th street church in Birmingham, which now says of course that this arrangement is unscriptural. Have a letter in which they're describing that and asking brethren in the area to send their contributions to them so that they can take care of paying for the bill.

Elders of the 77th Street Church of Christ	
First Avenue, South	
Birmingham 6, Alabama	
Brethren:	
Referring to your Memorandum of August 6th concerning the effort to teach the Gospel through the Birmingham New and Post-Herald.	
The Insley Church of Christ hereby pledges ?.00 per? For carrying on this work during the period covered by contract to the ? September 1,?.	
Please advise if we are correct in assuming that?? Contract will cover a period of 12 months.	
? ? Appreciate your advising (the rest illegible).	

(Chart #3) Now I have…I do want to show you this. Here is a reply to that letter from the 77th street church. You can see it's addressed to the elders of the 77th Street church of Christ in Birmingham. And the question is asked concerning, "Tell us who this contribution is to be sent to, who the check is to be made to," and so forth. And you can see of course that Brother John T. Lewis was the Minister of the Insley church of Christ in Birmingham. That letter was signed by Brother O.E.M. Stag.

Now in response to that letter, a letter was mailed out from the 77th Street church, telling them just exactly how that was to be done. (Chart #4) And I'm sorry you can't

77th Street	50.00
Central	75.00
Woodlawn	35.00
North B'ham	40.00
Berney Pairata	10.00
Cusley	25.00
Featherdale	10.00
Total	$245.00

Checks from various congregations to be mailed on the 25th of each month to reach 77th st Church not later than the first of the month.
Checks to be payable to the 77th Street Church of Christ.
Checks are to be mailed to Morris F. Hide. (the rest not legible.)

read it any better than that. But this paragraph here says, "Checks from various congregations, to be mailed on the 25th of each month to reach 77th Street church not later than the first of the month, checks to be payable to the 77th Street church of Christ. Checks are to be mailed to Morris F. Hide," and then gives his address. And that letter was signed by Brother H.S. St. John, Sewell St. John. Some of you may remember Brother St. John, some of you who lived in that area. Brother St. John still believes today what he did then, but he is no longer in fellowship with the 77th Street church. Now this does not prove that it's right. But it proves that all of us at one time believed it was scriptural to do the thing that some of us are still doing.

Let me give you another example. (Chart #5) I think you can see this a little bit better. This is from a paper called *The Way of Life;* the date on this is October 1946.

Time Keeper: 5 minutes.

Bobby Duncan – Main Speaker: Thank you.

An article written by Herschel E. Patton and he says in this article, second paragraph, "Although the Woodlawn church signed the contract, it is not necessarily their program. The churches of Christ in Birmingham have always presented a untied front and it is desired that this program be the program of the churches of Christ in Birmingham. Other congregations in Birmingham will contribute to the support of this program and the various preachers in this area will take week-about preaching." Here is a work

Radio Program - Herschel E. Patton

A radio program has finally been secured for the Churches of Christ in Birmingham. For a number of years the Churches of Christ have been unable to purchase time on any of the radio stations in the city. However, now that the new station WTNB (1400 on your dial) is in operation, we have been successful in purchasing some time. Tuesday morning, October 1, 1945, John Harton (?) and Herschel E. Patton arranged for a year's contract with this station for the Woodlawn Church of Christ. Although the Woodlawn church signed the contract, it is not necessarily their program. The Churches of Christ in Birmingham have always presented a united front and it is desired that this program be the program of the Churches of Christ in Birmingham. Other congregations in Birmingham will contribute to the support of this program and the various preachers in this area will take week-about preaching.

(Top Portion Not legible)

Brother jack Meyer and the Heights Church were asked to plan and supervise the advertising of the meeting and that they did their work in fine fashion was simply evidenced by the widespread interest and attendance provoked. Brother F.F. Coalley and the Milley Church supervised the ushering at all of the services and received splendid cooperation from the other churches of the city in that work and the large audiences were handled in a fine way. Brother Frank Smith and the church at P? and Baldwin had charge of the entertainment of visitors from out of the city and homes were provided for all while attending the meeting. Never has an effort of this magnitude been carried to completion with any better cooperation, finer spirit of unity, or less friction than this was. That was an outstanding feature of the meeting. Twenty churches worked together as one throughout the cities and the Churches of Christ in Houston demonstrated the practical side of Christian unity and above the all sufficiency of the Lord's church in the accomplishment of His work without the interference of human organizations. ***All of the funds were handled through the Norhill Church and all bills incurred paid out of that treasury, with a complete report furnished, each church assisting.*** That this arrangement worked to the satisfaction of all is attested by the fact that in a city wide gathering of ? After the meeting was over, the unanimous request of the church operating in the first meeting was that Norhill congregation ? The second meeting to be held the coming year. (Bottom portion not legible)

to which all of the churches in Birmingham were equally related. Some of you recognize the name of Brother Herschel Patton. He would not do this now. He believes that this would be centralized control. He believes this would be one church exercising oversight over other churches.

Now all of these examples that I have given, are from the area of the country where I've spent all of my time, because that's the area of the country that I know about. And I'm showing you these to let you know, and of course you're familiar with this. (Chart #6) Brother Roy E. Cogdill, in the introduction to the original edition of *God's Prophetic Word*, he said, "All of the funds were handled through the Norhill church and all bills incurred paid out of that treasury. With a complete report furnished, each congregation assisting." That doesn't prove it's right. It just shows that we believed back in those days prior to 1950 and on into 1954, what I have preached tonight. That whenever the Bible shows that it's scriptural for one church to contribute money to another, whenever one church can assist another in evangelism, that that's what we all believed and practiced back then and we believe that that was the way that it ought to be done.

Now, it's not like the instrumental music thing. The church divided over instrumental music when instrumental music began to be used. (A faint AMEN is heard from somewhere, whs) (Bobby Duncan responds to the man,

whs) Thank you. The church divided over this after we had practiced what some of us are practicing today, for years and years. And I'm afraid. I'm afraid brethren, that it divided over a scriptural principle but because there was opposition to a specific program. If you're interested in knowing, we don't support the *Herald of Truth* at Adamsville, we haven't in years. But we defend the principle by which it is supported.

Now in the remaining two minutes that I have, "Can we be united on this matter?" Well, of course I could be ugly and I could say, "Yea we can be united if all of you folks would just come on back and start believing what all of us at one time believed and practiced." But I know that you can't do that. I know that you've got scruples about it. You can't conscientiously do that, I understand that. And I don't think you ought to violate your conscience. How can we be united? And I know you're tempted to say, "Well, you brethren just give it up like we did back yonder in the '50's and we can be united." Now there are some of us who have scruples against giving it up, because of such passages as 1 Timothy 4:1-4 and Galatians 2, where the Apostle Paul said, "Titus was not required to be circumcised. That we did not give place to those brethren who came in privily unawares to spy out our liberty, no not for a moment, not for one day, lest the truth of the gospel be hindered." We can't allow ourselves to give IN, any more than we can give in to those who say, "Give up your Bible classes and we can be united. Give up your individual communion cups and we can be united."

How can we be united? Let me tell you. When I was a boy growing up in Calhoun County, Alabama, Brother Cecil Abercrombie and Brother Gus Nichols held a debate out from Piedmont, Alabama at a little place called Lebanon. They debated the Bible class question. When the debate was over, the brethren at Lebanon still held their anticlass position. But they realized that they did not have a right to bind their scruples on their brethren. They said to the brethren in that area, "We don't believe we're wrong about our position on classes. We choose not to have Bible classes, but we will give you brethren the right to make YOUR choice about it. We will announce your meetings, we'll attend your meetings, we'll fellowship you if you will fellowship us." I believe that's the answer.

I want you to listen very carefully to Brother Tom Roberts. He's a gentleman. He has a good speech.

Cooperation of Congregations
Day 2 Speech 3 Rebuttal
Tom Roberts

Introduction: *Roberts, Tom. He is a native of Gladewater, TX and presently works with the West Side church in Ft. Worth, TX. He has been preaching 34 years with works in Whitesboro, Sherman, and Crockett, Texas along with twice working with Newport, North Carolina. He is staff writer for several papers, experienced radio speaker, and respected author.*

Someone said not long ago, that a lot of great things have happened in Dallas, and probably this meeting will not be one of them. (Laughter, whs). I would like to differ with that. And I do believe some great things can happen, in the sense that we are here, we're studying, we love the Lord, and we pray that much good can be accomplished by those who do love the Lord.

In the area of church cooperation, non-institutional brethren have been falsely labeled as non-cooperative, when in fact we believe and practice church cooperation. Institutional brethren on the other hand have claimed to practice church cooperation, when I believe you practice a form of centralized control. Adding to the difficulty is the fact that church cooperation is not a Bible phrase but one that has been discussed widely among brethren since the time of Alexander Campbell and the *Millennial Harbinger*. I believe the concept to be authorized if properly defined and limited by the Biblical principles. However it must not be allowed to become a catch-all phrase, which is stretched to include every kind of centralized control.

I'll be making two major arguments that I'll ask you to consider, that will establish the principles and limits of church cooperation: first, an argument from design or structure; secondly, an argument from the restraints of the Biblical pattern. There'll be nothing new from a Biblical standpoint in these arguments. But I believe they'll be an affirmation of things that are being denied by many in our generation.

In arguing from design or structure, I take the position that the church as God designed it is perfectly and sufficiently able to fulfill the mission and the purpose for which it was designed. Ephesians 3:10-11 states that the church by its existence "makes known the manifold wisdom of God according to the eternal purpose which He purposed in Christ Jesus our Lord." This eternal purpose provides the ideal body of Christ in the scriptures by which we measure ourselves and our labors. To illustrate, we understand that the human body has design that imposes limits upon man in keeping with God's purpose for him. Man lives in an oxygen atmosphere because that's the way God made him, with lungs. He does not live underwater because God did not give him gills. Thus, design implies both function and limitation. Even so, the church of Christ has certain design, and the structure of that design suggests the operation of the church as well as the limitations in keeping with that design.

How did God design the church? It's structured in two senses: the universal or general and local. The church general is described in Hebrews 12:23 where we read, "to the general assembly and church of the first born who are enrolled in Heaven." This is evidently the church of which Jesus spoke when He promised to build it in Matthew 16:18. Likewise, Peter had the same church in mind when he said in 1 Peter 2:17, "Love the brotherhood." In these instances, no local church is under consideration, but all the saved of God considered as brothers in the distributive sense. This use of church speaks of relationship only. (Chart #1) It suggests fellowship. The general assembly of saints has no earthly headquarters, no treasury, no corporate work. It can never meet on earth.

When one sees the universal church as composed of churches (Chart #2), the result is a church-hood instead of brotherhood, which would require overseeing elders more than the local church, a treasury larger than a local treasury, a corporate work for the universal church and some arrangement to tie the churches together, voluntarily of course. Failure to understand that one can not harness or make operational the universal church, has led to the

The Structure of the Church
A Brotherhood Fellowship
A Spiritual Relationship Only

No Earthly Headquarters

No Treasury

No Corporate Work

monstrous hierarchy of the Catholic Church. Likewise the American Christian Missionary Society has made the same mistake. The Restoration began to flounder on this point. There should be no doubt that the sponsoring church is no less than the same tragic mistake, seeking to organize the church universal from brotherhood to church-hood with the attendant overseeing eldership and pooled treasuries of many churches. Such can not be done without restructuring the church and denying God's structure even as the Disciples of Christ have done.

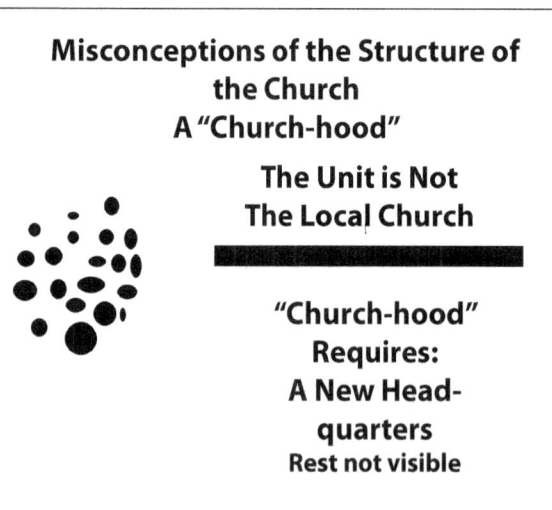

Misconceptions of the Structure of the Church
A "Church-hood"

The Unit is Not The Local Church

"Church-hood" Requires: A New Head-quarters
Rest not visible

It should come as no surprise, to see the Boston Cross-roads Discipling Movement carry the sponsoring church to its logical conclusion, by creating a hierarchy of churches, the Country, City and Pillar Churches. The Pillar Church, I believe, is only the sponsoring church spelled differently. It would be interesting to hear a sponsoring church advocate debate the Pillar Church advocate. How would you prove a Pillar Church to be unscriptural? I know that you believe it to be wrong, but how would you prove it to be wrong when you occupy the same ground in the sponsoring church. Boston is more willing to accept the consequences, and preach against local autonomy, while the sponsoring church takes away local autonomy while claiming to believe in it. Whether one calls it a Diocese, a Pillar Church, or a sponsoring church the difference is degree and not kind.

The essential elements of a sponsoring church include these things. #1. Many contributing churches send to a sponsoring church. #2. The sponsoring church has exclusive control of the work by its overseeing eldership. #3. Thus the work of many churches is supervised by the elders of one church, and equality is destroyed. The arrange-

The one church is composed of many local congregations

Sears & Roebuck Co.	Shell Oil Co.	Church of Christ (Rom. 16:16)
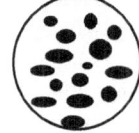	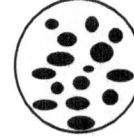	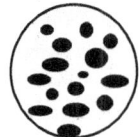

Local congregations are not different denominational

The local units are to be united (Spiritual Twins)

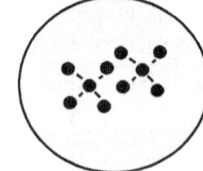

ment is one of church-hood, a collectivity of churches. It parallels the Boston plan. (Chart #3) One example of this concept being currently taught is material used by the Whites Ferry Road church in Louisiana, which likens the general assembly to a corporation like Sears or Shell, with all the attendant levels of control. It is impossible to have that arrangement without levels of control.

Brethren whether it is the cooperation board, the Diocesan Bishop, the Pillar Church, or the sponsoring eldership, it is centralized control by definition and practice and a violation of design. This is not the structure God gave the general assembly of the saints. (Chart #4) On the other hand, the only functional arrangement whereby the church operates collectively is the local church, with elders and deacons. I cite Acts 14:23; Acts 20:28; 1 Peter

---

The Structure of the Local Church:

The Local Church

Is the Only

Functional Unit

To do God's work

---

5 and verses 1 and 2. Each church is to be independent, equal, sufficient, and autonomous or self-governing. This is God's design, God's structure, God's collectivity, God's team; God's working arrangement to do the work of the church. The design implied both function and limitation.

This is in the words of Robert Turner "The harness which God made and the church is to work for God." He said, and I'm quoting from Brother Turner's article, (Chart #5) "But a team of horses can not be worked with a single harness. The size or scope of oversight, the scope of the organizational structure, must equal the size and scope of the overseen. When two or more churches are linked together in any project, that is act collectively, the elders who direct the project must act as double or multiple harness with respect to that project. Calling them local elders, as indeed they may be in one capacity, does not alter what they're doing in their roll as overseers of the larger working unit, nor have we changed what they're doing by giving them this position voluntarily." So we have changed God's plan for government or polity. We have made diocesan elders.

"But a team of horses can not be worked with a single harness. The size or scope of the organizational structure must equal the size and scope of the overseen. When two or more churches are linked together in any project, act collectively, the elders who direct the project must act as double or multiple harness with respect to that project. Calling them local elders, as indeed they may be in one capacity, does not alter what they're doing in their roll as overseers of the larger working unit, nor have we changed what they're doing by giving them this position voluntarily. So we have changed God's plan for government or polity. We have made diocesan elders."

Brethren, God did not design both the local church and the sponsoring church. (Chart #6) The structure is different and antithetical. The local church is independent, equal, autonomous, and sufficient. The Sponsoring church is dependent, unequal, central in government, and insufficient. Though the local church has fallen into disfavor by those who think in terms of national and international projects, the scripture clearly defines the local church as God's choice to do His work. Paul declared that the Gospel was preached to every creature under Heaven, Colossians 1:23, without a single Sponsoring Church, without a Pillar Church, or overseeing eldership. God's way works if we will use it.

The Structure of the Church

God's Harness	A New Harness
Local Church	Sponsoring churches
Local elders	Overseeing elderships
Acts 14:23	A Team Harness
1 Pet. 5:2	
God's design	Unknown to the Scriptures

Now the other major argument which I hope you'll consider carefully is one of authority, the Biblical pattern. (Chart #7) Coming under increasing ridicule in this age of new hermeneutics, the pattern principle is eminently scriptural. A denial of patterns has far reaching results. I

The Biblical Pattern

ask brethren, "Are you really ready for patterns to be forsaken?" Are you really aware of the consequences of saying, "There is no pattern?" Listen carefully. Where there is no Biblical pattern, there can be no sinful practices, no limitations, anything goes. Are we not seeing the results of this in our midst today with the new hermeneutics, with the denial of binding examples or necessary inference, with the jeering at the silence of the scriptures, with compromise on every doctrinal position, and unity summits with sectarians? The distinctiveness of the Lord's people is tied to the Biblical pattern. Do away with it and you do away with God's people in this generation.

Pattern Principle
Does A Pattern Exist?

The New Testament Teaches:

Hebrews 8:5	Philippians 3:17
2 Timothy 1:13	Philippians 4:19
Titus 2:7-8	1 Corinthians 11:1

Some Brethren Teach:
No Patternism
"How May A Pattern Be Violated That Does Not Exist?"

Compare modern attitudes with that of the writer of Hebrews. (Chart #8) Even as Moses is warned of God when he was about to make the tabernacle, "For see, saith He, that thou makest all things according to the pattern that was showed thee in the mount" (Heb. 8:5). Again, Philippians 3:17, "Brethren join in following my example and note those who so walk as you have us for a pattern." Or, 1 Corinthians 11:1, "Be ye imitators of me even as I also am of Christ." Or Philippians 4:9, "The things which you both learned and received and heard and saw in me, these things do, and the God of peace shall be with you." Consider 1 Corinthians 4:17, "For this cause have I sent unto you Timothy, who is my beloved and faithful child in the Lord, who shall put you in remembrance of my ways which are in Christ, even as I teach everywhere in every church." Not the least of things to consider are the words

of Jesus in Matthew 28:20, "Teaching them to observe all things whatsoever I have commanded you." Thus, a pattern consists of all of that God has stated on a subject and is put there through divine wisdom to be followed.

But no patternism is a two edged sword that those who would use it must learn to their sorrow. When brethren deny there's a pattern, they make themselves vulnerable to and every denominational type. If one claims no pattern for church cooperation, he can no longer deny the practice of the Catholic Church, or the Christian Church, or the Boston Church. Deny there's a pattern in worship, and the Christian Church will take you apart on the music question. Deny there's a pattern in the work of the church, and someone will build a theme park, like Jim and Tammy, or Six Flags as a work of the church. Would it be sinful?

> "We are to have fellowship one with another, and the Lord gave no pattern for congregational cooperation. How then can one violate a pattern that does not exist?" (G.K. Wallace, *The Gospel Advocate*, 1956)

(Chart #9) That some do indeed reject patterns is proved by the following quotes, "We are to have fellowship one with another, and the Lord gave no pattern … pardon me…gave no pattern for congregational cooperation. How then can one violate a pattern that does not exist." That's from G.K. Wallace, the *Gospel Advocate*, in 1956. Brethren remember that no patternism is a two edged sword. If there is no pattern, there is nothing sinful. So where is the SIN of the Missionary Society, where is the SIN of the Pillar Church, where is the SIN of the Catholic Church?

(Chart #10) Another quote, "Those within the Restoration Movement who've written on the subject usually have assumed that at least some of the New Testament examples are binding. In contrast, the New Testament seems to provide no basis for this conclusion. Neither churches nor individuals in the New Testament are presented as patterns to be identified in specific details. There is no evidence that New Testament writers exercised selectivity in choosing particular actions or patterns to be copied," by Milo Hadwin in his Masters Thesis, if I remember correct-

> "Those within the Restoration Movement who've written on the subject usually have assumed that at least some of the New Testament examples are binding. In contrast the New Testament seems to provide no basis for this conclusion. Neither churches nor individuals in the New Testament are presented as patterns to be identified in specific details. There is no evidence that New Testament writers exercised selectivity in choosing particular actions or patterns to be copied" (Milo Hadwin, *The Role of New Testament Examples as Related to Biblical Authority*).

ly while he was at ACC. No basis for any New Testament example to be binding? Neither churches nor individuals are presented as patterns to be identified? Brethren are we even in the same ballpark, or reading the same Bibles? This is no patternism gone to seed. What about Paul telling Titus to "show yourself to be a pattern of good works; in doctrine, showing integrity, reverence, incorruptibility, sound speech that cannot be condemned" (Tit. 2:7-8).

> "We have approached the area of hermeneutics with the idea that they had a complete set of documents, which we know as the New Testament, and that they searched these scriptures to determine God's pattern in church organization, structure, and practice. I submit to you that is an incorrect assumption" (Bill Swetman, The Nashville Meeting).

(Chart #11) Another quote, "We have approached the idea, the area of hermeneutics, with the idea that they had a complete set of documents, which we know as the New Testament, and that they searched these scriptures to determine God's pattern in church organization, structure, and practice. I submit to you that is an incorrect assumption," Bill Swetman, *The Nashville Tapes*. So now we learn that it is incorrect to work…to look for patterns in church organization, or structure and practice. Brethren, what about elders? What about local autonomy? What about the Lord's Supper on the first day of the week? What about singing? What about the reign of Christ, and other distinctive marks of the Lord's kingdom? This writer says that not only do we not have a pattern, but that the early church, the New Testament church, did not have any patterns. Again I say, if there is no pattern, there is nothing

sinful. We might as well stop being the church of Christ and join the nearest denomination. No patternism is alive and well on the planet earth and in the church of Christ. It is wrong and sinful, but it is with us to this day.

Now is there a pattern in church cooperation? I maintain that there is, that it's identifiable, and understandable. (Chart #12) We want to begin our search for the pattern

> # Defining Terms
>
> Cooperate: (1) To act or operate JOINTLY with another or others, to concur in action, effort or effect (*Webster's Unabridged Dictionary*, Emph. Mine, tr).
>
> ### Note: Two kinds of Cooperation
> Joint - Collective
> Concurrent - Independent

by defining some of our terms to be sure that we don't assume that which needs to be proven. The word before us that give us so much trouble is the word "cooperation." It means, "To act or to operate jointly with another or others, to concur in action effort or effect." Please note that two kinds of action are defined under cooperation, whereas modern day advocates try to limit to one. There is joint action, that which is collective action. However there is also concurrent action, which is independent action. The Bible teaches independent action of churches and NOT collective action.

A parallel can be seen in the word "music." There are two kinds of music, vocal and instrumental. "Do you believe," someone asks, "in music in worship?" "Yes, but vocal music not instrumental." "Do you believe," someone asks, "in cooperation of churches?" "Yes, but independent action, not collective action." Collective action is "The characteristic of the experience in common or united action of the members of an aggregation or group, distinct from that of individuals." Thus collective action of churches suggests church-hood with a new harness larger than local elderships. The sponsoring church and the Pillar Church is collective action, not independent action.

> ### Collective Action
> "3. Characteristic of the experience in common or the united action of the members of an aggregation or group distinct from that of individuals" (*Webster's Dictionary* (Emph. Mine, tr).

(Chart #13) Brethren I call to your attention that many of you are defining cooperation only in the collective sense with no consideration that this does not fit the Bible principles or design of church cooperation. Rather the Bible idea is concurrent action, independent action. (Chart #14)

> ### Coordinate:
> "One that is Equal in importance, rank, or degree…adj. Of equal importance, rank, or degree, Not Subordinate" (*Grolier International Dictionary*, Emp. Mine, tr.).
> **Coordinate** – "1. Of the same order, equal in rank, degree, or importance (with); Opposed to Subordinate 3. Involving coordination: Consisting of a number of things of equal rank, or of a number of actions or processes properly combined for the production of one result…B. One who or that which is co-ordinate, or of the same as rank, an equal , A CO-ORDINATE (rest not visible)

This recognition of independent action among churches is fully acknowledged by another word not so common among us but worthy of consideration, it is coordination. A "coordinate" is "one that is equal in importance, rank or degree, no subordinate. "Coordination" is consisting of a number of things of equal rank or the number of actions or process properly combined for the production of one result." Brethren THIS describes the Biblical pattern of churches working together. It respects the autonomy, independence, and equality of each church. It is the same as concurrent action, the definition of cooperation, but NOT the same as JOINT action of definition. This drives,

I believe, to the heart of our controversy. We must speak as the oracles of God, and the use of cooperation as to allow joint collective action is not Biblical in precept. Independent, concurrent, coordinate action is Biblical.

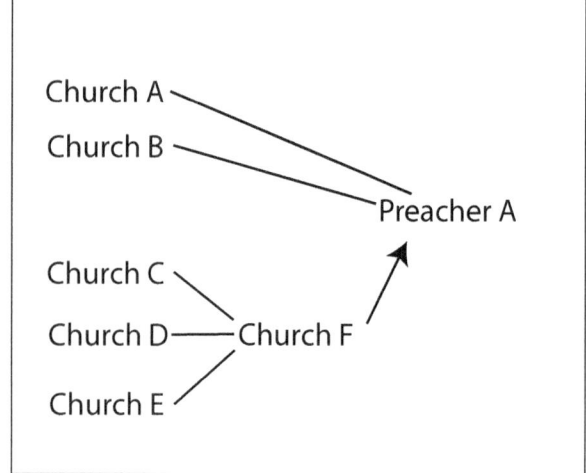

Let me show you the practical use of definitions as we've considered them in the chart (Chart #15) on cooperation in evangelism. We have 6 churches that are engaged in evangelism and all are cooperating. Churches "A" and "B" are cooperating concurrently, independently, by coordinating their efforts as equals by sending wages to preacher "A." But churches "C," "D," "E," and "F" are also practicing cooperation according to definition. They are collectively pooling their funds under the oversight of church "F" in an unequal, dependent, non-autonomous arrangement. By using this arrangement, churches "C," "D," "E" and "F" could just as easily be identified as a Missionary Society if church "F" were called…changed to a board. We could call churches "C," "D," "E" and "F" the city churches and the Pillar Churches under this arrangement. If three churches can pool their resources under one eldership, why not 300? Why not 3000? Why not every church? It took 600 years to build the Roman Church, but the principle began exactly the same and I believe history is repeating itself in front of our eyes.

(Chart #16) The Biblical pattern that applies to evangelism is plainly taught in the scriptures. Note that it incorporates the equality and independence and autonomy of every church. The pattern permits: #1 A church sending teaching to another church. No loss of autonomy is involved since each church has the equal responsibility to teach the gospel to the whole world. The fact that one

---

Autonomy – Cooperation Among Churches For Evangelism

1. A Church May Send Teaching To Other Churches –
   - Acts 11:22-23; 13:1-3;
   - Acts 14:21-23; 14:26-28; 15:22-31
   - Acts 15:40; 18:22; Colossians 4:16
2. A Church May Send Teaching Anywhere –
   - 1 Thessalonians 1:8; Acts 13:1-3
3. A Church May Send Teaching Anywhere –
   - 2 Corinthians 12:13 (3. not visible derived from speech)

---

church teaches another church, does not diminish its ability or responsibility, does not diminish its equality, or independence or autonomy. However, if one church gives up its funds to another church to do what the first church should be doing, there is a loss of equality, and independence and autonomy. Acts 11 verses 22-23 shows that a church may send teaching to another church, because Jerusalem sent Barnabas to Antioch, Acts 13 and 14 of the Missionary Journeys of the Apostle Paul and his companions. Acts 15, Jerusalem sent teaching to other churches. Colossians 4:16, the epistles went from church to church.

2ndly, a church may send teaching anywhere as evidence by, first of all, 1 Thessalonians 1:8 where "The word was sounded forth everywhere," and in Acts 13 and 14 again the Missionary Journeys.

#3 A church may support its own evangelist as 2 Corinthians 12 and verse13 points out, that only Corinth among the churches did not support Paul. (Chart #17)

#4 One church may support a preacher elsewhere as

Autonomy – Cooperation Among Churches For Evangelism

4. One Church Alone May Support A Preacher Elsewhere –
   - Philippians 1:3-5; 2:25, 30
   - Philippians 4:14-18
5. Several Churches May Independently And Directly Support A Preacher Elsewhere – 2 Corinthians 11:8-9

Philippians 1:3-5 shows that Philippi had fellowship with Paul, as also states Philippians 2:25 and 30, and Philippians 4:14-18.

#5 Several churches may independently and directly support a preacher anywhere, 2 Corinthians 11 verses 8-9 says that "Paul took wages of churches." Note however, no principle permits collective action. No principle permits pooling of funds.

The sum total of all these scriptures teaches concurrent independent autonomous actions that is coordinated between churches that are equal.

Also please note every church in the world is equally related in evangelism and can never have an abundance which it may surrender to another church. However in benevolence, one church may be unequal to another because of greater need and may require sending funds in order that there may be equality. This leads to the distinctive pattern for benevolence. God foresaw that tragedy sometimes destroy the desired equality among churches, such as famines. (Chart #18) Therefore He provided a plan for

---

Autonomy – Cooperation Among Churches For Benevolence

1. Each Church Raises Its Own Funds By Free Will, 1st Day Of The Week Offering Of It's Own Members –
   - 1 Corinthians 16:1-2
2. Each Church Selects Its Own Messengers –
   - 1 Corinthians 16:3-4;
   - 2 Corinthians 8:19, 23
3. Each Church Sends To The Church In Need
   - 2 Corinthians 16:6
4. Churches May Send To Another Church When The Needy Church Cannot Care For All Its Own Members – Acts 11:27-30

---

benevolence to restore that equality, 2 Corinthians 8:13. Such does not permit a permanent sponsoring church that becomes an international receiving and dispersing church for the church-hood. This is planned inequality for which there is no Biblical authority.

Note the pattern for church cooperation in benevolence: #1 Each church raises its own funds by a free will first-day-of-the-week offering by its own members, 1 Corinthians 16:1-2. #2 Each church selects its own messengers, 1 Corinthians 16:3-4, 2 Corinthians 8:19, 23. Each

> ### Autonomy – Cooperation Among Churches For Benevolence
>
> 5. Churches May Send To Other Churches When The Needy Churches Cannot Care For All Their Own Members –
>   1 Corinthians 16:1-4;
>   2 Corinthians 8:9; Romans 15:25-28
> 6. The Purpose Of Sending From One Church To Another Is "That There May Be Equality" –
>   2 Corinthians 8:13
> 7. No One Church Ever Acted As A Receiving And Dispersing Church For Other Churches Beyond Its Own Local Needs (7. Not visible derived from speech)

church sends to the church in need, 1 Corinthians 16:3. Churches may send to another church when the needy church can not care for all its own members, Acts 11:27-30. (Chart #19) #5 Churches may send to other churches when the needy churches can not care for its own members, 1 Corinthians 16:1-4; 2 Corinthians 8 and 9; Romans 15:25-28. The purpose of sending from one church to another is that there may be equality, 2 Corinthians 8:13. #7 No one church EVER acted as receiving and dispersing church for other churches beyond its own local numerical needs. However, it was temporary to restore equality. The receiving church was in need, and the need was among its own local numerical membership. There

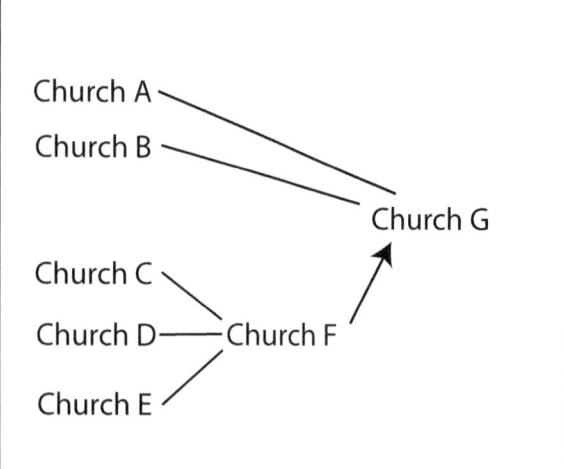

was no pooling of funds. This teaches cooperation. Independent, autonomous and equal action, a coordinate effort, not centralized control.

(Chart #20) To illustrate the pattern on benevolence, churches "A" and "B" helped needy church "F" by concurrently equally and autonomously coordinating their efforts of church cooperation. Churches "C," "D," and "E" helped needy church "F" (sic, he meant "G") but unequally, dependently, collectively and with the loss of autonomy, since church "F" (sic, he meant "G") takes the oversight or harness of funds from many churches. All six churches are cooperating in the broad sense of the word.

Alien Sinner	Erring Christian
Repent	Repent
And	And
Be Baptized	Pray God

Churches "A" and "B" are cooperating concurrently, the others are acting collectively.

Some have asserted that there are examples of churches sending to churches, so why not make it…what does it matter if it's in evangelism or benevolence. (Chart #21) I would reply there are examples of aliens being baptized, so why not baptize both aliens and erring Christians? This is a classic case of mixing apples and oranges to come up with a bad case of confusion. There is a pattern for salvation for the alien. There is a pattern for salvation for the erring Christian. We don't baptize the erring Christians, nor teach the alien to repent and pray. Such is mixing the patterns, like apples and oranges. There is a pattern in evangelism, and a pattern in benevolence. We should no more mix the patterns here than in the plan of salvation. As is stated so often and so deeply felt, "We be brethren."

But just as the past has revealed departures from the faith of God, we must labor to keep this from happening again. Cooperation among churches of Christ is possible so long as we understand the Bible definition and usage. Let it be clear though, that those who believe in and practice collective action of churches with overseeing elderships, can never logically object to ANY FORM of collective action. Open that door, and in walks the Christian Church, the Missionary Society, the Boston Church, and the Catholic Church, again it is a matter of degree and not kind. Already as we speak, the One Nation Under God plan for evangelism, sponsored by a church in Tennessee, would harness all of the churches in America together. When will ONE WORLD UNDER GOD be planned by a single church?

In contrast, local churches across the country are conducting thousands of Gospel Meetings, independently and concurrently, requiring no such central oversight of pooled funds and yet converting the lost as Jesus has taught. God's way works. Let's use God's design in both evangelism and benevolence according to the pattern set forth in God's word, so that we may pray "Thy will be done on earth as it is in Heaven."

Cooperation of Congregations
Day 2 Speech 3 Panelist 1
Lewis Hale

Roy Lanier – Moderator: (Beginning not caught on tape) Now we're going to have a panel discussion. It is designed that now (the recording ends)

Introduction: *Hale, Lewis. Presently in his 35th year with the Southwest congregation in Oklahoma City, well known for his writings and debates. Preaching for 46 years includes Stigler, OK and Lorenzo, TX.*

Thank you Roy, and thank you for your kind audience. In the speech that was just given by Brother Roberts, he was talking about mixing apples and oranges. I want to read to you from page 105 of the *New Testament Church* by the late Roy Cogdill. In commenting on 1 Corinthians 16:1-2 he said, "Sometimes it is argued that this is the plan for raising money only for benevolence in the church. It remains however, that divine wisdom led Paul to give this plan to Corinth for raising money and GOOD REASONING will convince one that if it will work for raising money for one righteous cause, it will work for another and for all." Now that was before you brethren began arguing that there was ONE pattern for benevolence and another pattern for evangelism. Now you see Brother Cogdill didn't know that and so HE believed that this was a pattern for raising money for EITHER ONE.

Let me ask you, if it's a pattern for how you can raise money for preaching, even though it's not in the verse, why isn't it a pattern for how you can cooperate in using that money once you get it? Why can't you SPEND it the same way they did, if you raise it the same way they did? A plurality of churches got together to relieve the need of saints in Jerusalem from that collection. Why couldn't they have done the same thing is PREACHING in Jerusalem from that same collection? IF that authorizes paying preachers out of that collection, and it does, I don't believe it's mixing apples and oranges.

And then in that same way, an illustration was given of churches on a chart. It's not up there now, but you'll remember it, churches "C," "D," "E" and "F" and how that they make a collective decision to pool their resources

under the oversight of congregation "F." And he said that destroys autonomy. Let me ask you. Let's let church "C" be the churches of Galatia. Let's let "B" be the churches of Macedonia. Let's let "E" be the churches of Achaia, and "F" of course would be Jerusalem. Now let me ask you. Did Galatia, Macedonia, and Achaia personally supervise and administer the help in Jerusalem? Or did they take the help to the church in Jerusalem? I heard you brethren up here saying over and over again, they sent it to the church in Jerusalem. So in that illustration, your OWN illustration, church "F" would be the Jerusalem church. Oh, you had it there for evangelism I know, but just apply it what happened in benevolence. And according to you its autonomy was destroyed.

What kind of logic is it that will tell us that autonomy is destroyed when a church…group of churches get together and pool their resources in some way and work through a local church for evangelism, but it doesn't destroy their autonomy if it is for benevolence? That's very strange reasoning

And then we've heard a lot about the all sufficiency of the church. I believe the church can do what God intended for it to do. But the question is, "What did God intend for it to do?" I remember when Brother Yater Tant, who is here and the father of course of David, say when he had *The Gospel Guardian*, the masthead said it was "Dedicated for the propagation and defense of New Testament Christianity." When did God ever give that responsibility to a human organization called *The Gospel Guardian*? I don't believe they were out of place. But according to the kind of reasoning we hear on the all sufficiency of the church, if that's true, then the church was not all sufficient to defend itself and propagate the gospel. If not, why not? I don't believe that infringes on the autonomy of the church, nor the all sufficiency of the church. Thank you. You said I had one minute?

Roy Lanier – Moderator: No! That's it.

Lewis Hale – Panelist: OK.

Cooperation of Congregations
Day 2 Speech 3 Panelist: 2
David Tant

Introduction: *Tant, David. He is a native of Fr. Smith, AR with both father and grandfather as preachers. He has done local work in Oklahoma, New Mexico, and Georgia. Served three congregations in the Atlanta area for 28 years, has been with Roswell, GA for 16 years, also serves as a pastor.*

I express my thanks to those who are the powers that be that had confidence in me to invite me to participate in this discussion. I appreciate the opportunity.

At the outset, I would like to disabuse the rumors that are circulated with my relationship to Yater Tant (a low crowd rumble is audible, whs). I have heard that he is my grandfather (Laughter, whs). That either means that he looks very old or I look very young. I prefer that. He is my father and I am glad that he is. People often confuse members of the family. Twenty-five years ago I was preaching at Ft. Smith and a little dear old sister, about 90 years old, came hobbling out of the building with poor eyesight. (Speaking in a shaky voice to simulate old age, whs) "So you're Brother Tant. I've heard of you all my life, but never met you until tonight." (Laughter, whs) And to confuse further, I have a son who is J. D. Tant the IV, and now a seven-week-old grandson who J. D. the V and that just blows people away.

Brother Duncan in his presentation among other things, sought to prove that Jerusalem was a sponsoring church, with respect to the funds that were sent for relief of the famine in Judaea. I appreciate my brother's appeal to scripture, for without this we have no hope of dwelling together in unity, or being found pleasing to God. Thank you brother for this. But as I read, listened to and considered his speech, there was some things about this and other matters, that struck me as being out of hand. Particularly I refer to comments that he made in his manuscript on page 3, paragraphs 3 and 4 of the printed text.

One thing that bothers me about this is that he is mixing benevolence and evangelism and they're not the same thing. The second thing that bothers me is that there is absolutely no evidence that Jerusalem was a sponsoring church. And this good brother is not the first brother in this discussion this weekend that has made that assertion. This has been made for many years that Jerusalem was a sponsoring church, and the argument goes somewhat like this. (Chart #1) That Barnabas and Saul delivered relief

---

Sponsoring Church
Argument From Acts 11:27ff

Barnabas and Saul delivered "relief unto the brethren that dwelt in Judea… which was sent to the elders."

But Paul told the Galatians he was "unknown by face unto the churches of Judea" (Gal. 1:22)

Therefore Paul had only delivered the relief to the Jerusalem elders who then made further distribution

---

unto the brethren that dwelt in Judaea, which was sent to the elders, that's what the text says, "to the elders." Brother Duncan in his presentation quoted this passage and he said, and I wrote it down and asked another that "it was sent to the elders in Jerusalem." Now I believe that's what he believes, that's not what the text says.

But Paul told the Galatians he was unknown by face unto the churches of Judaea, Galatians 1:22. The argument, therefore, is that Paul had only delivered the relief to the Jerusalem elders who then made distribution throughout Judaea, thus Jerusalem was a sponsoring church, a sponsoring church. They maintain that Paul and Barnabas could NOT have delivered this among the brethren in Judaea since he was unknown by face, and he couldn't have said that if he had traveled among them. And this was true at least until the time of the Jerusalem conference in Acts the 15th chapter, see also Galatians 1:22–2:1.

(Chart #2) Well, the fact is that the record reveals Paul made only five trips to Judaea after that he became a Chris-

---

Paul's Visit To Judea

1. 15 days in Jerusalem with Peter
   Gal. 1:18-20; Acts 9:26-30 Ca. 35 A.D.

2. Delivering Antioch's relief during famine
   Acts 11:27-12:25; Visit lasted possibly 6 months
   Ca. 41-42 A. D.

3. Jerusalem (rest illegible)

4.

---

tian. The first trip he spent some fifteen days with Peter in Jerusalem, about 35 AD. The second trip was the occasion of the famine…Time? That's 4 minutes? Boy! OK, I'll get to it later. I'll quit on time finished or not. Thank you.

Cooperation of Congregations
Day 2 Speech 3 Panelist: 3
C. W. Lincoln

Introduction: *Lincoln, C.W. Noted preacher for years in congregations in Cedar Rapids, IA, Colorado City, Fort Worth, and Odessa, TX, as well as overseas in Port Elizabeth, South Africa. Longtime teacher at Sunset School of Preaching in Lubbock, TX, presently preaches also at Seminole, TX.*

As Paul said in 1 Corinthians 1, "I thank my God for His grace that's come to each of us." I regret that we don't have four hours rather than four minutes. And if you want to stay up all night, I'll be here.

In our lesson tonight from our Brother Tom, there were a number of assumptions made from God's word. Let's turn first to Acts chapter 11. The first reference we have of one church sending to another church is back in Acts 8. The church in Jerusalem sent Peter and John. I do not read that the saints in Samaria asked him to come. But they sent these brethren; we know the purpose for which they came in Acts chapter 8. Here in Acts chapter 11, the church in Jerusalem heard that disciples were now over in Antioch and so verse 22, they sent Barnabas off to Antioch. I don't read of Antioch and Syria asking this brother to come.

I want you to see the spiritual concern that the brethren in Jerusalem had for God's service, no violation of autonomy. And brethren, everything I've heard since yesterday with regard to autonomy has been with regard to the elders. The church is independent and autonomous whether you have elders or not brethren. Here in Acts chapter 11, Antioch didn't have any elders, but they got together and determined to send relief, verse 19. That's the autonomy of each church.

What Brother Tom said tonight may have reference to someone in Dallas, but it didn't have any reference to Brother Lewis and myself with regard to going beyond a pattern. We believe in the pattern just as you do. And so much of that material was a straw man insofar as I'm concerned. Has absolutely no reference to my conviction and to my practice.

But notice Agabus came from Jerusalem. And the brethren, after they took the collection, returned from Jerusalem (Acts 12:25). And so they allowed Agabus to speak. And he got up and told of the need, and the brethren "determined," that means agreed, decided, that's the work of the local church. We must never give up the right to agree or to decide what we're going to do. No elders, they just agreed to send relief. Now the word "relief," if you look in the margin in the New American Standard Version, it says "service." In the American Standard it says for "ministry." It is the very word that Paul used in 2 Timothy 4:5 to describe the evangelist's work. "Fulfill thy work, do the work of an evangelist, fulfill thy ministry," same word. It's used in Ephesians 4:12, we are to "equip the saints" in order that they might be engaged in their ministry, equipped for their service or *ministry*. Brethren that's not benevolence, Ephesians chapter 4, and neither is benevolence found in 2 Timothy 4, same word.

One church had the right to send to another church for service. I want us to see that. We have assumed that it's only for benevolence. It doesn't say that, it said for service. So one church determined or decided to send, that's the work of every church. The receiving eldership, it was not their design and effort to oversee Antioch's work. It was Antioch's work through the hands of Barnabas and Saul to receive the support and then to oversee the spending of the money. So the assumption is that this is just for benevolence.

We'll see further on in our study, assumptions that they sent directly to Paul. I'm amazed how you brethren insert in the word of God, the word "directly." And we'll talk about the meaning of that word as we progress.

Cooperation of Congregations
Day 2 Speech 3 Panelist 4
Harry Osborne

Introduction: *Osborne, Harry. Presently works with the church in Alvin, TX, native of Pampa, TX and has done local work in Texas, Missouri and Florida. Has been preaching for 14 years.*

I too want to start out by thanking you for the invitation to be here. I must admit that when Steve called me a few months ago, I was a lot more thankful than I am right now to have been asked. But at any rate I am thankful and

---

"Supporting Passages"?
Passages Used Fail To Prove Proposition
1. Church May Support Preacher:
    Acts 11:22-26
    Acts 15 (specified vs 22-23)
    2 Cor. 11:8
2. Churches May Send Teaching To Another Church:
    Col. 4:16
3. Church May Give Benevolent Aid To Another Church In Need:
    Acts 11:27-30
    1 Cor. 16:1-3
    2 Cor. 8 & 9
4. Unrelated Passages Fill Space:
    Acts 21:17-19
    NO SPONSORING CHURCH FOUND!

I'm glad to have the opportunity.

(Chart #1) I want to give my attention to a few things that were stated in Brother Duncan's address, so as to help frame the discussion that we're going to have. It was suggested that the only difference that we have in this area is with regard to one church sending to another church for evangelism. Our problem in this area is not that. Our problem is one of centralization. It is a centralization that happens in the sponsoring church, whether that be with regard to the work of evangelism, or the work of edification, or the work of benevolence. It is wrong through

and through because of the principle of centralization. The same thing is so with institutions to be talked about tomorrow.

But that fourth one on the list there, that we have among us a practice of big churches overseeing smaller churches is nothing less than pure centralization, and purely that which is against the will of God. Now in effort to defend this, Brother Duncan pointed out several passages of scripture. And what the passages of scripture taught us, was not what was told that they would teach us. What they taught us was that a church may support a gospel preacher. I don't know of anybody who differs with that. But is that a sponsoring church arrangement? No! What Colossians 4 teaches is that a church may send a teaching to another church. Is that a sponsoring church arrangement? No, it is not. And what's taught to us is that one church may give benevolent aid to another church in need. Is it a sponsoring church arrangement? No, it's not. And the last passage that was stated was Acts chapter 21:17-19. Open your Bible and see if you see anything about one church giving to another one in there. It's totally unrelated. I don't know what it has to do with it.

MISSING "ESSENTIALS ELEMENTS"
Darwin & Duncan Both Have Missing Links
1. One church sends to another for evangelism
2. Elders of one church exercise degree of control that other churches and elders cannot
    a. Who or what supported?
    b. How much and how long?
3. Church without essential need soliciting other churches
4. Plurality of churches pooling resources through one church
5. One church acting as agent and other churches in subordination to aid agency
6. Right to assume oversight to which all other churches (rest illegible)

(Chart #2) Now we don't differ about the matter of looking at elements and seeing whether all of them are so and their argument being true. The problem is that he didn't get all the essential elements. That's the problem. There are missing links in the Theory of Evolution and Darwinism and there were missing links in what Brother Duncan said. Now that's what we need to look at. The essential elements of one church sending to another for evangelism, for them having a pooling of resources, for them taking an oversight that's not given to them. These were all listed in Brother Roberts's speech; I'll not go back

---

Acts 20:28

"Take heed therefore unto yourselves, and to all the flock, over the which the Holy Ghost hath made you overseers, to feed the church of God, which he hath purchased with his own blood."

Over Which Church Did The Holy Spirit Give Sponsoring Church Authority?

---

over them. (Chart #3) But I'll tell you what wasn't pointed out in the pattern that Brother Duncan tried to bring before us, Acts chapter 20:28, where it says, "Take heed unto yourselves and to all the flock in which the Holy Spirit made you bishops, to feed the church of the Lord which He purchased with His own blood." The elders what? "In the church in which the Holy Spirit made you bishops."

---

1 Peter 5:2

"Feed the flock of God which is among you, taking the oversight thereof, not by constraint, but willingly; not for filthy lucre, but of a ready mind."

How Are Solicited Churches "Among" The Sponsoring Church Eldership?

(Chart #4) Or as Peter stated that, "the flock which is among you." Now brethren I want to ask something. How in the world are solicited churches among the sponsoring church eldership? How is it that those ones who are the sponsoring elders are OVER IN ANY SENSE, IN ANY WORK that which has been solicited?

Church Of Christ Riverchase Flyer
(Entire chart Illegible)

(Chart #5) Let me tell you where that leads. The Riverchase church in Birmingham, I suggest Brother Duncan might be familiar with this, is one that sent out a little flyer in introducing it that says, "We want you to know about our autonomy." And they said in speaking about their autonomy, "The Riverchase work will be under the supervision of the Central church of Christ elders until such time as it becomes self supporting." I'll tell you about the autonomy of that, it's non existent. And I'll tell you what else happens. (Chart #6) In *The Firm Foundation*, you can find

---

Firm Foundation
October 27, 1987 – p. 22
Wanted:
Church of Christ desiring to sponsor Mission Work. Must be willing to locate, train and support fulltime evangelists
(rest illegible)

---

cases of this over and over again, of one church advertising "Church of Christ desiring to sponsor mission work. Must be willing to locate, train and support full time evangelists" and part of the work is "to oversee the work of the current membership." That is unlawful centralization.

Cooperation Of Congregations
Panel Discussion

Roy Lanier – Moderator: Now that we have agreed on everything we'll go ahead with our panel discussion (Laughter, whs). We'd love to let these men now do a little free wheel discussion among themselves. And who wants to begin? These particular parts of our discussion are limited to two minutes and our time keeper will just simply hold up your hand and wave it at them and touch your throat and so forth. Who wants to speak first? Abe Lincoln.

Panel Discussion

C. W. Lincoln - Panelist: Be glad to. Brethren say that the support that was sent to Paul was sent directly. We saw it on the chart. Brother Tom in his manuscript that we received used the word, if I recall, four times. And that's adding to God's word. It doesn't say "direct" brethren. It's not in any version, not in any text. And to assume that Paul robbed other churches taking wages from them, and even got from Epaphroditus something "direct" is not in the text. They did not send to the needy in a direct way in Acts chapter 11, sent it to the elders. And we'll look at Philippians 4 in a moment to see what verse 15 has to say concerning Paul's unique relationship with the church at Philippi.

But the word "direct," I looked it up, I thought since it's used so repeatedly . . . Webster says, "Leading from one point to another in time and space, without turn or stop, straight, operating without any intervening agency or step." Now how direct do you brethren support a man? If I understand it, you deposit the first day of the week contribution in a bank and you write a check and use the Post Office, and they use the airline. And we were over in Africa, you're involved in the government, they look at every document that comes in to see whether they want to open it or not, they inspect it. And then you finally get it in your Post Office. Now that's "direct" brethren, five agencies.

And I believe that you don't have to bypass elders or the Lord's church in evangelism. I've been 10,000 miles from the eldership and there is no way that the overseeing elders…they oversee the sending of you and the money. They don't oversee you after you get on the boat. You're a part of the local church in Africa, and the elders have absolutely NO oversight of you when you get over there. Have oversight of the sending of the money.

David Tant – Panelist: Brother Lincoln, I'm sorry I fail to understand how money put in the bank, which goes to the Post Office, which goes to the airline, which goes to the receiving Post Office and or bank in Zimbabwe or wherever, I fail to understand how that authorizes a sponsoring church.

C. W. Lincoln - Panelist: Well now I…

David Tant – Panelist: I just don't understand the connection there.

C. W. Lincoln - Panelist: I wouldn't even use the word sponsoring, just receiving church. Could a church in Zimbabwe receive that check for my support? Yes or no! You can use the bank and the Post Office…

David Tant - Panelist: I'd prefer…

Harry Osborne – Panelist: There is no Bible authority for that.

David Tant - Panelist: I'd just prefer to use it the way the scriptures do, the money was sent to Paul, or to whoever was there.

C. W. Lincoln – Panelist: But it doesn't say "directly." And when they sent to the needy in Acts 11, they sent it to the elders, didn't send it directly to the needy. That's my point. We have the concept in Acts 11 of sending to the elders. They didn't bypass the church or the elders in order to get to the needy. Paul and Barnabas gave the contribution to the elders and they distributed it to the needy.

Harry Osborne - Panelist: Well, let's go to a case of evangelism, if that's what we're going to talk about, and that's found in Philippians chapter 4 and verse 15. "And ye yourselves also know you Philippians, that in the beginning of the gospel, when I departed from Macedonia, no church had fellowship with me in the matter of giving and receiving but ye only." Now my question to you would be this, Brother Lincoln. If somehow that bank receiving it and the airline receiving it and the telegram office and all of that receiving it, made them have fellowship with one, I'd like you to state that. If not the case is still the same. That this one sent, this church at Philippi, to Paul, we put the modern inconveniences in the middle, no problem there. We still don't have a sponsoring church arrangement like you have.

C. W. Lincoln – Panelist: Now...

Harry Osborne - Panelist: Now what needs to be proven is the sponsoring church arrangement in which there is multiple churches giving to one church. Them having an overseeing right that these multiple solicited churches have no right to. They come along now, oversee the entirety of that. Send out to this fellow, make all the decisions with regard to that, how much, how long, just exactly where he's going to be, what's going to be done, that kind of thing. That's under the oversight of that sponsoring church.

C. W. Lincoln – Panelist: That...

Harry Osborne - Panelist: When you prove that, then you'll have proven all the essential elements, and not until then.

C. W. Lincoln – Panelist: All right, in Philippians chapter 4, the passage that you refereed to, the subject here is the church. Not Paul and the church in verse 15. No church after I departed from Macedonia, and of course he went to Corinth after he left Macedonia. "No church shared with me in the matter of giving and receiving but you alone." So Paul is discussing the unique kind of fellowship that he had with the church at Philippi. They had started from the first day, Philippians chapter 1. Sent to him time and time again, even in Thessalonica they sent, and even after he left Macedonia. But he robbed other churches. The only way that you can reconcile 2 Corinthians 11 with this passage is that the brethren determined to send to Philippi and they oversaw the sending of the money. (There is an audible buzzing as the audience converses among themselves. whs)

Harry Osborne - Panelist: Who oversaw the sending of the money? What are you saying?

C. W. Lincoln – Panelist: The church at Philippi! He said

"you were the only church," church is the subject. "No church but you were involved in the matter of giving and receiving unto me."

Harry Osborne - Panelist: You have two entirely different times when Paul was helped. This occasion is one in which at the beginning that was done. Later on was the occasion on which the multiple churches, 2 Corinthians 11 verse 8 was there, and a harmony of the book of Acts, when those messengers came, fully show that they were the messengers from those churches that brought the funds to him. He robbed other churches, plural, taking wages of them. They did not act through Philippi. You go back and prove that...

C. W. Lincoln – Panelist: What messengers are you alluding to? What messengers are you referring to?

Harry Osborne - Panelist: I have a chart here can I use it?

C. W. Lincoln – Panelist: Naugh, now Epaphroditus came, but who are the messengers? You referring to Acts 18, the brethren that came from Macedonia, and Paul then devoted himself exclusively to the preaching because he got support?

WAS PHILIPPI A SPONSORING CHURCH?
ORDER OF EVENTS

1. (Text illegible).
2.
3.
4.
5.
6.
7.
8.

Harry Osborne - Panelist: (Osborne Panel Chart 1, whs.) This is the order that I am talking about, of events in which Paul established the church at Philippi, Thessalonica, and Berea in Macedonia. There are the passages. When Paul left Macedonia from Berea, only Philippi assisted him, that's Philippians 4. Silas and Timothy remained in Macedonia at Berea. From Athens, Paul sent for Timothy and

Silas. Timothy came while Paul was in Athens. Paul sent him back to Thessalonica in Macedonia. Paul went from Athens to Corinth. Then there was Silas and Timothy that came to him from Macedonia, these were evidently the brethren which came from Macedonia. This record gives no support of your sponsoring church either. You have two different occasions which Paul received support.

Roy Lanier – Moderator: Let me break in just a moment. You need to speak into the mic there Harry.

Harry Osborne - Panelist: Yes sir.

Roy Lanier – Moderator: So everybody can hear you. Go ahead.

Harry Osborne - Panelist: Uh huh, yes sir. All right, appreciate it.

Roy Lanier – Moderator: You're behaving pretty good. I think you're doing all right. (Laughter from the audience. whs)

Harry Osborne - Panelist: Thank you, I appreciate that. I need a vote of confidence now and then (Laughter, whs), being the youngest one on the panel that's always needful.

Lewis Hale - Panelist: Harry?

Harry Osborne – Panelist: I'm through.

Lewis Hale - Panelist: All right. We heard the expression that in cooperation there had to be coordinate action and it had to be equal. I just wonder if the church in Jerusalem was coordinate with the churches of Galatia, Macedonia, and Achaia, when they sent funds to Jerusalem. Some of them were sending churches, one was a receiving church, and that doesn't sound like coordinate to me. And was the collection, this isn't intended as a pun, was the collection for Jerusalem collective action? Was the collection collective action? I believe that it was. If not, you have a contradiction of the same term.

Now in cooperation, he said the purpose was to create equality. And yet we have this strange statement made by Brother Roberts, and that was that if a church sent money to another church to cooperate in evangelism it would destroy equality. Now do you notice what's strange in that? To cooperate in benevolence creates equality; to cooperate in evangelism destroys equality. What kind of logic is that? It may be excellent, but if it does it escapes me. If so, why?

Now let me ask this question. "A team of horses cannot be worked with a single harness," it says. If the Highland church completely and single handedly funded the Herald of Truth, would they need a different harness than they have now. (Could not tell exactly what was said in the next sentence, but think this is what was said. whs) Some would say, but they don't. That's not my question. If they funded it alone, what would they need to change in the way they set the program up, their filming of it, their staffing of the people who work on the program? They wouldn't need to change a thing, except some secretaries and some mailing out of fliers asking you to support the thing. That's all they'd need to change. Thank you.

David Tant - Panelist: Well Brother Hale, on the fact of creating equality or inequality, in respect to benevolence the brethren in Judaea or in Jerusalem were not equal. They were in need they were hungry. Other brethren had more than they did. Granted, those in Macedonia were in deep poverty, but they gave so that there might be equality. That's what Paul said, they gave that there might be equality. When they received sufficient, then there was equality.

But when you have a sponsoring church, where the Highland church receives funds from thousands of other churches … and I've known of situations where a church that could not afford its own preacher, but was pressured to put the Highland program in the budget, so that they could do this. That doesn't create equality. That creates one super church, and other churches out here that may not have enough funds to carry out their own work, that's not equality.

Both are equally related to preaching the gospel to the whole world. They already have that equality to start with. Now then, when one assumes something that the other has to support it to do, then you don't have equality there. And that destroys the very thing that we're trying to find, that we're trying to establish.

And I still don't see how the churches out here, even sending to Jerusalem there, how that equates to make a sponsoring church.

And Brother Lincoln, back on Philippians the 4th chapter. I'll tell you what, if as you contend that these other churches were sending money to Philippi who in turn sent it to Paul, I'd be upset. Because here the church at Roswell, where I am, we sent money to Philippi, and Paul says, "You only had fellowship with me, you brethren at Philippi," and I'd feel kind of left out.

C. W. Lincoln – Panelist: In what? Fellowship in what, David?

David Tant - Panelist: I don't care what.

C. W. Lincoln – Panelist: Well, it says giving and receiving. How in the world could they have received?

David Tant - Panelist: How could they give if I hadn't given to Philippi?

C. W. Lincoln – Panelist: Naugh, naugh, you're assuming that this verse is saying that Paul received and they sent. That's not what he says.

David Tant - Panelist: Well, but…

C. W. Lincoln – Panelist: It says no church but you were involved in giving and receiving.

David Tant - Panelist: But…

C. W. Lincoln – Panelist: How was Philippi involved in receiving?

David Tant - Panelist: Regardless…regardless…regardless of that…regardless of that matter, we're talking about two different occasions as Brother Harry pointed out on his chart, that they're separate occasions.

C. W. Lincoln – Panelist: He said in the matter of giving and receiving. They had received as well…

David Tant - Panelist: Had they received the gospel from Paul?

Harry Osborne - Panelist: Your argument on giving and receiving…

C. W. Lincoln – Panelist: Talking about the matter of finances there on the account he said.

Harry Osborne - Panelist: I'm not sure I understand, Brother Lincoln, what the point is; maybe you can correct me if I don't. But Philippians chapter 1 and verse 5 is another occasion of him talking about this in the same letter, for your fellowship. There! It doesn't talk about it in the matter of giving and receiving, if that's the problem with that particular phrase that's not present in Philippians chapter 1 and verse 5. It's obvious that they sent and he received. "For your fellowship in the furtherance of the gospel." They had supported him in furthering the gospel.

That shows nothing of the nature of what we're talking about.

But one thing that I would like to notice is, that if the sponsoring church arrangement is what you say that it is, just a means of function and it doesn't mean any loss of equality or anything like that, then why are not the Boston brethren? Same thing. All they've decided is to take over the whole work. Now I'm not talking about their theology. I'm talking about the structure. It's peas in a pod of centralization. You claim that the Boston church is something that's just an illegitimate child, but I think it was born in the wedlock that y'all have with the sponsoring church. What's happened is you've just taken many and doing a lot of the work, and you've made it all of that work. That's where it came from. That's the background from it and I'd like to know what the difference is, ORGANIZATIONALLY. What's the difference? If your sponsoring church arrangement is right, then the Boston church is right in their organization, pure and simple.

C. W. Lincoln – Panelist: I'm not acquainted…I don't get any Boston publications and I've heard that they think that they're over the other brethren, whoever they send out and even over other churches. But in the New Testament, anytime a church had the oversight of sending a man out that's all they had oversight of brethren. You don't have oversight of a man 10,000 miles away. I've been there.

Harry Osborne - Panelist: All right, how about the case…

C. W. Lincoln – Panelist: You're a part of that congregation.

Harry Osborne - Panelist: How about the case that I brought up? I think we might be moving toward some area of agreement here that we can kick out some of the problem. The one that I brought up from *Firm Foundation*, one church soliciting another church to oversee mission works. Churches out there, where one eldership oversees this church. Or the Riverchase Church in Birmingham says this church has the authority, the Central Church and their elders, have authority over us. They oversee us.

C. W. Lincoln – Panelist: I think that's unscriptural. I've talked to elders who made decisions…

Harry Osborne - Panelist: Is it sinful?

C. W. Lincoln – Panelist: Sure, certainly it's sinful.

Harry Osborne - Panelist: Would you have any fellowship with people who do that?

C. W. Lincoln – Panelist: I sure don't. I don't.

Harry Osborne - Panelist: Not at all?

C. W. Lincoln – Panelist: No!

Harry Osborne - Panelist: So the *Firm Foundation* and that crew are not in fellowship with you in regard to that?

C. W. Lincoln – Panelist: Well not on that point. Any more than one of you brethren, you believe the universal church can work through a preacher. You believe that a thousand churches can send to you and to the radio station and the TV station. And so you get one Diotrephes among you you'll have a Pope, according to your reasoning, because you could enlist the universal church through a preacher.

Harry Osborne - Panelist: No sir. I don't see how…

Lewis Hale - Panelist: How many churches can he receive from?

C. W. Lincoln – Panelist: How many churches can he get money from for a TV and radio program?

David Tant - Panelist: How many could Paul have received money from when he said "I robbed other churches?" How many could he have done it from?

Harry Osborne - Panelist: As many as it took to support him.

C. W. Lincoln – Panelist: Yep.

Harry Osborne – Panelist: Now you know, I've been accused of a lot of things, but one of them isn't being a rich preacher that got too much. And I don't know of any of us, among us … (Laughter, whs), as far as I looked at salaries, y'all are getting more than we are, the last time I checked. (Laughter, whs) So this matter of a bunch of us all receiving one thing, I don't see where that's being done, or where the possibility…

Lewis Hale – Panelist: Brethren I think we need to observe the two-minute…I don't think that one interruption constitutes a new start of two minutes.

Harry Osborne – Panelist: I'm sorry; I was asked a question, so I answered it.

Lewis Hale – Panelist: I know. But I really do believe that we ought to do that.

Harry Osborne – Panelist: OK. I'll do it.

Lewis Hale – Panelist: I think that's the only fair procedure. I…sorry Roy, I didn't mean to take your place.

Roy Lanier – Moderator: That's all right.

Lewis Hale – Panelist: But I do not believe that that's the way that it ought to be done.

Roy Lanier – Moderator: Go ahead with it.

Harry Osborne – Panelist: You wave at him when you want me to do it and that'll be fine.

Lewis Hale – Panelist: But I think we ought to each take turns and each one take his two minutes.

Harry Osborne – Panelist: That'll be fine.

Roy Lanier – Moderator: Who's speaking now?

Lewis Hale – Panelist: Abe go ahead.

C. W. Lincoln – Panelist: Naugh it's your turn.

Lewis Hale – Panelist: OK. (Laughter, whs)

C. W. Lincoln – Panelist: I'll be glad to speak.

Roy Lanier – Moderator: They're starting to misbehave; I'm sorry fellows. (Laughter, whs) OK, Lewis it's your turn.

Lewis Hale – Panelist: Been a statement made about the sponsoring church. You can give the dog a bad name and become prejudicial toward anything you want to. Let's just talk about a church receiving funds from another church.

But anyway, we had a statement about a sponsoring church and what const… what the description of a const…of a sponsoring church was. And if Brother Robert's definition of a sponsoring church is correct, I want to go on record as saying that I don't know of a sponsoring church among us.

C. W. Lincoln – Panelist: That's right.

Lewis Hale – Panelist: He talks about assuming control over other church; he talks about loss of oversight. I don't know of a church that does that, not a single church. I know that we send support to the *Search* program in Edmond, Oklahoma. We help them fund it. We do not… It's not a matter of overseeing it, it's there work, we're just helping them with it.

If it was a matter of a child that needed support in that

congregation and we sent them money, we wouldn't expect to administer it. It wouldn't be the loss of autonomy in either case when you send funds and they oversee it. And so, to me, this matter of autonomy has become a sort of straw man.

Let me ask you, when Paul in a matter of judgment… Is it a matter of judgment what a church uses its money for, once it's collected? What preacher they would support, and what people they will help benevolently? Paul ordered the churches of Galatia to help the poor saints among Jerusalem. Paul ordered the church at Corinth to help the poor saints among Jerusalem. If somebody would come into your congregation today, and order your elders to support any certain work in our brotherhood you'd throw them out.

David Tant - Panelist: Well, Paul was an Apostle.

Lewis Hale - Panelist: That's true.

David Tant - Panelist: I believe Paul had some rights that you and I may not have. But here again if we're discussing a sponsoring church, we talk about cases that you're citing there, are one kind of a sponsoring church where somebody's sponsoring something right there or whatever, one church contributing to another.

But when we have these huge organizations of a church that receives funds from many, many churches, and then this church sends the money off to Africa or to China or wherever, and or the *Herald of Truth* where the money is received that goes to a separate organization with its own Board of Directors, its own setup to do another work. That's something I still, when I look in the scriptures, I find nothing, nothing like it. I find no scripture implied, stated, example or whatever. And I've read much on this.

And I'll confess brethren, you know, that I've changed on this. When I was young, and when I was in college, and when I played with John Banister's son, when Bill and I were friends together, I tried to find some way to justify this, because that's where my friends were from, Abilene, where I was in school. I couldn't find it. There's no scripture there top side nor bottom, inside nor out. There is no scripture that authorizes this type of arrangement for one church to receive money from many churches to send it off somewhere else.

C. W. Lincoln – Panelist: I don't have fellowship…I was trying to think if I have fellowship with any brethren that receive funds and send it to a board or something other than the church. If I do I want to repent of it quickly. I don't know of that. I know of brethren who have the oversight of receiving funds from other brethren to do the work of the Lord, just as they did in the first century.

The point I wanted to make is we have assumed that Acts 11 is for benevolence only. And that word doesn't mean just benevolence; it's for service and for ministry. And you brethren need to look again at Philippians 4 and be honest with that verse. Paul says again, that you are "the only church that shared with me" in the unique kind of fellowship "in the matter of giving and receiving," and in classical Greek that means "receipts and disbursements." And so Paul said "you are the only church that received and sent." "You shared with me," that's… the subject is the church, not Paul and the church in verse 15.

I want to ask a question. I get the impression brethren, and I don't want to misrepresent brethren who forbid what God authorizes, but I get the idea that, in your concept of wanting to be autonomous and independent, and that's our desire and purpose.

Lewis Hale - Panelist: That's right.

C. W. Lincoln – Panelist: That you could not, or it would be difficult to, send any money for any purpose to another church. When was the last time that the church where you brethren preach sent money to another church?

Roy Lanier – Moderator: This is going to be the last comment before we take a break.

David Tant - Panelist: Is that…

C. W. Lincoln – Panelist: Yes, to both of you.

Roy Lanier – Moderator: No just one. Harry Osborne.

Harry Osborne - Panelist: As I recall, it had to back when I was in Corpus Christi about 10 years ago or so, with a regard to relief due to some people who had been hurt in a natural disaster and the church was unable to fully meet that need. That's the best of my recollection, I could be wrong it could be another.

But let me do two things. First off, the chronology of the book of Acts simply will not permit your interpretation, Brother Lincoln. That's all there is to it. Besides that, the passages of 1 Peter 5:2 and Acts 20:28, there was a work there that they assumed the oversight of in the sponsoring church arrangement that is not among them. That's the problem that we've got, it's one of centralization.

Now what Brother Hale said, "Well, I don't know of anybody who ordered them, therefore we're all autonomous," if every church under the Boston arrangement said that we of our own free will submit to this one world church, Boston, does that make it all right? Does the fact that they submit to it make it no loss of autonomy? I submit it doesn't.

C. W. Lincoln – Panelist: That's true. I agree

Harry Osborne - Panelist: The violation has still taken place of Acts 20:28, and I'm glad we agree, and 1 Peter 5:2, therefore that argument is not correct. That won't hold water. The idea is that when one oversees the work of another, one takes the place of being that centralized agent through which many act, pool their funds, and have the oversight of everything that has to do with the doing of that work. That's what a sponsoring church is. That's what's not authorized in the word of God.

Roy Lanier – Moderator: All right, let's take, at this point, a little bit of a break. With just before you leave, if you have questions, please write them down and get them into me or to Jamie Sloan… (Recording ends at this point whs).

Cooperation of Congregations
Question and Answer

Roy Lanier – Moderator: (Beginning not caught on tape whs) able to get to all of the questions. We've had a multitude of questions turned in on these sessions and we just cannot get around to all of them. So we're trying to pick up the ones that, not necessarily turned in first, well just to tell you the truth, I use the ones I like. (Laughter, whs)

Lewis Hale – Panelist: Amen? (Said as if asking for an "amen" response from others. whs)

Roy Lanier – Moderator: No, not really. We're trying to get as much as is representative of what it's all about. Because our speakers are the featured men, I think it would be fair to give questions to them first, our two major speakers.

Question 1:

So Brother Duncan, "You labored to prove that brethren were united in cooperative work a few decades ago. One can likewise argue that in the 19th century brethren like Tolbert Fanning and Benjamin Franklin and others were united in support of the Missionary Society during the seeming innocence of its infancy. Did this prove the Missionary Society scriptural and should Fanning and Franklin and others have changed, or should they have remained involved in the society, why or why not?" I'm glad I turned that over, I thought I'd misread that and just had a statement. Brother Duncan, two minutes.

Bobby Duncan – Main Speaker: I don't think it'll take me that long on that. I made the statement that I was not proving the scripturalness of church-to-church contributions by what we had practiced in the past. But from the very beginning there were some brethren who recognized the evils of the Missionary Society. It took our brethren years and years of practicing what they defended as being scriptural by one church contributing to another, until the Herald of Truth started. And then some brethren decided, well it's wrong for one church to contribute to another, and I've shown that it was right. But I don't think any of us would defend what some of these brethren are opposing, that is centralized control, one eldership overseeing other churches.

C. W. Lincoln – Panelist: Amen.

Lewis Hale – Panelist: Amen.

Bobby Duncan – Main Speaker: None of us defend that. It's a question of can one church contribute to another church in evangelism.

Question 2:

Roy Lanier – Moderator: Brother Tom Roberts, "Did the contribution of Acts 11:27-30 go to the elders in Jerusalem? Was not the assistance given in Acts 11:27-30 and the one spoken of in Romans 15, 1 Corinthians 16, 2 Corinthians 8 and 9 two different ones, separated by some 10 or 15 years"? Please comment.

Tom Roberts – Rebuttal Speaker: Those were two separate times, separated by somewhat like a decade. The contribution of Acts 11:27-30, it is not stated that it went to the elders in Jerusalem, it went to the elders of Judaea. Now if the elders of Judaea form a diocesan eldership, then we've really got a problem. Now if that's what the Bible teaches, and we want to have a diocesan eldership, that that's what we're going to say that Acts 11 is teaching, then we need to stop all talk about local autonomy and restructure like the Christian Church has, because the need, the funds, the support, went to the need. There were needy churches in Judaea, the churches had elders, therefore the elders in the needy churches were in control of those funds that were sent to them.

And with regard to Acts 11, with regard to the word "service" that is used, the word "service" is a very generic term that can be used in different verses with regard to different things. But in Acts 11, beginning in verse 27, the word "service" in the context of that chapter is the famine. It was not ministry, it was not in the sense of evangelism, it was ministry in the sense of benevolence. It went to take care of the need created by the famine. That's the way that's used in Acts chapter 11, it went to the needy churches who were affected by the famine. It did not go to the church at Jerusalem.

Now brethren if you want the elders at Jerusalem to be a diocesan elders, then we've got another ballgame to play. We've got something else to deal with. And when you begin arguing that the Jerusalem elders oversaw the distribution for all the funds that came into Judaea, you've got Judaea Diocesan elders. Now let's talk about that and think about that. Are you ready for it? I don't believe you are, but I believe your argument will drive you to diocesan elders. You couldn't ask for an argument that would establish diocesan elders anymore than to argue it from that point.

Roy Lanier – Moderator: Would you men please speak a little more bluntly so I can understand what you're talking about? (Laughter, whs)

Harry Osborne – Panelist: Since you asked. (Laughter, whs)

Question 3:

Roy Lanier – Moderator: For Abe Lincoln, "Does each contributing church have the same oversight and control of the preacher being supported as the receiving, sponsoring eldership has?" Do you understand the question Abe?

C. W. Lincoln – Panelist: I think so.

Roy Lanier – Moderator: All right.

C. W. Lincoln – Panelist: The work of each church is to decide or determine, look at Acts 11, whether or not you will send a contribution to another church or to an eldership. Now that's the extent of the work of that church. Agabus didn't say, "We had a business meeting over at Jerusalem and decided you're going to send some money." That would have been wrong. All churches were equal and there was no coercion and pressure at all. They allowed him to tell of an opportunity to give and the brethren decided, they agreed to send relief. That's the work of the church, deciding whether or not to send. A church that receives, or an eldership, and it could be a church, the concept is there. The church is autonomous whether you have elders or not. They have the oversight of receiving the funds and spending it, and that's it.

And Brother Tom's first publication that we looked at, which was much longer than the speech that we have here tonight, dealt with that idea that the church, if it were to send to another one, would be losing its oversight. You don't have oversight brethren. We went 10,000 miles away. The church in Texas had the oversight of sending me and sending the money. I became identified with a little church in Africa the first Sunday there, and they had no oversight of that church.

Question 4:

Roy Lanier – Moderator: This question is to Harry Osborne, "Is the oversight over the sending churches or the ones being helped?" (Laughter, whs) You guys are the experts I'm not. (Laughter, whs) "Is the oversight over the sending churches or the ones being helped?" I assume…

Harry Osborne – Panelist: Uhuh.

Roy Lanier – Moderator: that that's referring to a benevolent question where if one church sends to another church for benevolence, then do they lose the oversight over the church or over the ones being helped?

Harry Osborne – Panelist: OK, I'll answer that.

Roy Lanier – Moderator: I think that's what's being asked.

Harry Osborne – Panelist: I'll answer that.

Roy Lanier – Moderator: There's no name on it so I can't find out who it is.

Harry Osborne – Panelist: Ok. We have to understand the area of need in the matter of benevolence. The problem was that one church had so spent its resources that it could no longer take care of the needy, therefore the problem was that they had no ability to meet that need. Now what the sending churches did, was sent to bring about the possibility of them meeting that responsibility. The need was they had not sufficient to feed those people who were impoverished.

Now where is the need with regard to evangelism? The need with regard to evangelism, of how these brethren are using the word, is supporting a gospel preacher. Now what they're saying is, "We send to a church so that they can meet the need." The sending to the church in benevolence was meeting the need. What they're doing is sending to a church, allowing that church to have oversight through its elders. That set of elders being the ones who make all of the decisions with regard to how much, how long, for what. All of that is under the oversight of that church.

Now nothing of that nature takes place in benevolence. It was sent for a reason. To make them able to meet the need of helping to feed those who were poor. That's not an equivalent case with regard to evangelism, it's just not in any shape, fashion or form. And besides that, even if you had an equivalency there, you do not establish the sponsoring church. And I'm just going to keep trying to drive home, these brethren need to establish what their practice is, a sponsoring church that has authority that extends beyond that which God has given them in 1 Peter 5:2 and Acts 20:28. And them saying, "well we don't" doesn't answer the point. The fact is they do, and that's what needs to be seen.

Time Keeper: Time.

Question 5:

Roy Lanier – Moderator: Lewis Hale "did the churches of Macedonia, Achaia, or Galatia ever form the sponsoring church arrangement for evangelism?" And the word evangelism is underlined. "If so where?"

Lewis Hale – Panelist: As far as those all going together to do so, I know of no record whatsoever. Could I use the rest of my time in answering something else?

Roy Lanier – Moderator: Sure, yes.

Lewis Hale – Panelist: All right, if cooperation as Brother Roberts defined it means that really its just a matter of acting in conjunction with others, like you clean up your yard and I clean up mine, therefore we keep a clean neighborhood. That's in … somewhat in his speech that was printed first. If that's really what's meant in cooperation, you do your job and I do mine, even though you don't know what mine is and I don't know what your doing, if that's really true, then all of you who help anybody is cooperating just as much with a Baptism, or a Methodist, or a Muslim, or a Hindu that takes care of theirs. If not, why not? You're all doing it independently, separately from each other, but you're all doing it at once. Now if that really constitutes cooperation, your cooperation is with all sorts of religious groups and you don't believe that, and I don't either. That's not the kind of cooperation the Bible's talking about.

Now, if a church can only do what its peculiar obligation is, what about Macedonia? What was its peculiar obligation to pay Paul to preach in Corinth? In the same chapter, Paul says that Corinth (sic, meaning the churches of Macedonia while referring to 2 Cor. 8:1-2, whs) was in deep poverty. Corinth had an abundance, a poor church supported the preacher for a well to do church, and at the same time required Corinth to send funds to Jerusalem. Now, we've heard that sort of thing criticized for years

and years. I've been in this same argument for over 37 years. And I've heard the argument, "think how ridiculous it is for Broadway to be receiving funds for a children's home, same time sending funds to the work in Germany." Corinth let another church pay her preacher, and it was a church in deep poverty, and Corinth had an abundance, and Corinth was supporting saints in Jerusalem. Thank you.

Question 6:

Roy Lanier – Moderator: Brother Duncan, "When a church in the United States owns the land and the church building of another church in a foreign land, has not that church in a foreign land lost its autonomy?"

Bobby Duncan – Main Speaker: NO!

Now then I want to take the rest of my time (Laughter, whs) to comment on whether or not a contribution was taken from churches to Jerusalem and given to the Jerusalem elders. Paul wrote in Romans 15:26, that the collection that was made up from the churches in Macedonia and Achaia, was for the saints in Jerusalem. In Acts 21 he went to Jerusalem, and in verse 17 the Bible says, "And when we were come to Jerusalem the brethren received us gladly and the day following Paul went in with us unto James and all the elders were present."

Now is that all of the elders all over Judaea? Is this a meeting of the eldership of all of the churches in Judaea, or is this the elders of the church at Jerusalem? But in Acts 24 and verse 17 Paul said, "I brought a contribution to my nation." He brought that contribution from these churches, delivered it to the elders of the church in Jerusalem for that nation. I don't believe that that was what these brethren are opposing. Well, I think it is what they're opposing. If we practice that today, they say it's the sponsoring church arrangement, it's centralized control, it's elders of one church overseeing another.

Roy Lanier – Moderator: There's one man here that, I guess, just answered everything, because no questions were directed to him by name. But I'm going to give him two minutes to make any miscellaneous remarks that he chooses to, David Tant.

David Tant – Panelist: Something that I thought about as I was eating supper today, going back to a conversation I had earlier with some of the people that are here, and that is to my brethren, where are your young men? Someone revealed or remarked about Brother Marty Pickup and I would say the same about Brother Harry here, that they were surprised to see young men taking stands and having convictions on these matters. They said, "it was very unusual, because" they said "among those brethren that they didn't have many young men."

And the problem is that the young men have been sent to Abilene, to Harding, to Lipscomb, to places where they're taught a different understanding of the scriptures and of authority. The young men are missing in a generation.

I've talked to some young people here today who said that they had never heard of these questions until just recently. Had never heard them, had no idea. When we raise a generation in the church that is untaught on any subject, we're inviting apostasy. We taught them what's wrong with instrumental music after the last division. There hasn't been a lot of teaching on what's wrong with the Missionary Society. We don't have much problem on instrumental music, we've got all kind of problems on Missionary Societies, sponsoring churches, and other same of the same nature with different names.

We've got to preach the truth. And if you brethren believe what you believe on these matters, teach them to your young people. Let them examine them, let them search the scriptures to the law and to the testimony. Don't raise up a generation that's ignorant on any Bible subject. We're inviting apostasy and departure. It's happened before; it's going to happen again, it IS happening again. Why aren't these people being taught on these things? Is it because it's difficult to establish your practice, because the scriptures do not clearly teach these things? I wonder! Thank you.

Question 7:

Roy Lanier – Moderator: Brother Lincoln, "In Philippians 4, what did the Philippians receive? Was it money from other congregations, or instruction from Paul? If money from other churches, then how does Paul share in that fellowship?"

C. W. Lincoln - Panelist: Well let's read the verse again. In the context, he is discussing the gift that the church at Philippi had sent to his needs, Philippians chapter 4. Brethren have assumed that Epaphroditus sent it directly to Paul. You base that as an assumption, because in Acts 11 they didn't send it directly to the needy, they sent it to the church, sent it to the elders. And so Paul said, "Not that I seek the profit or seek the gift itself, but I seek for

the profit which increases to your account." So Paul said, "No church after I departed from Macedonian," subject is the church, "shared with me in the matter of giving and receiving." And it's still there brethren! That Philippi had a unique relationship with Paul. And in the matter of giving and receiving, the church at Philippi was the only one involved in that particular kind of fellowship, Philippians chapter 4 and verse 15.

And may I respond to what our Brother David said. I appreciate the warning, but I've had the privilege of touching the lives of 1800 men in 25 years who are out preaching Christ. And we take Brother Homer Hailey's outline *The Problems of the Local Church* and we deal with all types of forbidding brethren. We deal with those who forbid the use of Bible Classes and local preachers, and church cooperation, we deal with all of it. So whether we do a good job of it or not, we are making them aware of these things. I know 1800 men have heard it, I don't know about the other young men.

Roy Lanier – Moderator: Is there a Scott Powers here? Please meet Brother Wolfgang at the back door please. Scott Powers I believe is the name, for a message.

Tom Roberts needs two minutes anonymous at this time. Not a question, he… but I have no more questions directed to him by name, but he needs two minutes.

Tom Roberts – Rebuttal Speaker: Comments were made about the fact that instrumental music split the church immediately when it was introduced, but that the things with regard to the sponsoring church did not split the church immediately. It's sometimes very simple to see a thing clearly on one occasion and another time you see a seed slowly and you don't really understand the whole thing until it bears its fruit. I'm persuaded that that's the case with regard to some of the institutions and the sponsoring church arrangements.

Good and honest brethren who sometimes have been quoted as participating in those things, because they later changed, we say well then that must make it all right. It does not mean that it's all right because they didn't see it wrong from its inception.

What is the fact, that the cooperation problem, in fact I wish I had more time to go back to the cooperation word and show the history. You go back to the *Millennial Harbinger* in 1841; brethren were discussing with Alexander Campbell from the first series of articles he started on cooperation, with their disputes as to what he was saying. Brother Campbell used the word "cooperation" and saddled us with that word. I don't think it's a good word so far as its description of what the church ought to do unless you understand "cooperation" of concurrent action, independent action.

But he saw a church-hood. His quotations are very clear. He saw an arrangement of church-hoods together, whereby the whole church could be made to operate. And when he wrote his first article about that, there were brethren who objected to it.

Now we're still talking about it today and I suppose every generation's going to have to work with how we learn to get along and cooperate together. But the fact that some are slow in seeing the problem does not mean that it's all right to practice it. We'll just have to learn when we do see something wrong though we've been slow, then change because true repentance requires that.

Lewis Hale – Panelist: Amen.

C. W. Lincoln - Panelist: Amen.

Question 8:

Roy Lanier – Moderator: For Lewis Hale, "Do you believe churches can send to boards, such as those which oversee Christian camps, or benevolent work?"

Lewis Hale – Panelist: I've had more than one public debate on the question of the church support, for example of children's homes. And I defended that principle and I would again. Yes, I do believe that they may. I have in those discussions brought up the matter of the church using intermediate agencies. If the church wants to have a local preacher there for a meeting, they do not mind going down and hiring a motel to feed their preacher, to bed him, and to take care of those needs while he is there. If they had a dozen preachers like that to take care of, could they do that through a human institution? Somebody says, "But that's paying the bill." And I said in that debate and I'll say to any of you. If you'll show me one example, one New Testament command, one necessary inference where any New Testament church, you can show me, prove to me where any New Testament church ever bought the service a human institution, I'll take down my flag. I'll throw in the towel.

Brother Keith Sharp said, "Oh they paid Paul's board… way on board ship." Of course (laughing as he is speaking

whs) he couldn't produce any such scripture and he realized it immediately, and you can't either. You'll never find me an approved example, a command, or an inference where a New Testament church ever bought the services.

Now if we're going to demand those things for anything we practice, then the church is either going to have to find that in the Bible, or quit buying human services from a human institution. Thank you.

Roy Lanier – Moderator: Harry would you like to respond to that, or David?

Harry Osborne – Panelist: Yeah.

Roy Lanier – Moderator: Since I have no more questions.

Harry Osborne – Panelist: I'd like, I'd like to.

Roy Lanier – Moderator: All right.

Harry Osborne – Panelist: Would you…

Roy Lanier – Moderator: You can use two minutes.

Harry Osborne – Panelist: OK.

Roy Lanier – Moderator: If you want to respond to that, you can have two minutes on that.

Harry Osborne – Panelist: Yeah, I want to respond to that because it scares me to death. What I see happening is more and more during this discussion…I was so encouraged brethren on Thursday evening when Brother Winkler got up, I told him so afterwards, and said, "We don't believe in no-patternism." But all I've been hearing today is more and more of the same under a different guise. What you just got through hearing was the idea, "We can't show that this is done but we're going to do it because we're doing it anyway and we're going to continue to do it." What is that but to say, "Well we don't have authority for it but we'll continue to do it, you can't show that it's wrong so everything's OK."

Now I want you to think about something just honestly. If I'm wrong, I want to know it. But honestly think about something. What kind of respect for a pattern does that teach people? How in the world are you going to instill in them that there is a pattern for what is done and how it's done in the word of God? And expect them to believe that in matters with regard to music and with regard to other things that would deny women preachers…You got fellows in this city who are saying, "You ought to have them." Now what you're denying in this sense is that the pattern's not all that plain.

They're going to throw the same thing back on you. And they're going to say, "Well if it isn't all that plain and there's plenty of teaching on this, then we can disregard 1 Timothy chapter 2 and we can disregard some other things that don't seem to them to be too plain. That's exactly how denominationalism developed. That's exactly how you found the broadening kind of thing to where no longer was there any authority that was seen, no authority which was respected.

I worry like crazy when I hear that kind of thing. Whether it be from Brother Hale or whether it be from David Tant, wouldn't matter to me one wit. It's that logic that bothers me. And I've heard it in each of the panels today. That what will happen in individual versus church, or whatever else, we don't see a real plain passage, we don't see a plain pattern we'll do it anyway.

Lewis Hale – Panelist: Brother Lanier, I want to ask him a question. Since that bothers you, doesn't it bother you more that you can't find what I asked for?

Roy Lanier – Moderator: We have time now (laughing as he is speaking, whs) for one more question and then we will have the two responses from the…

Harry Osborne – Panelist: I'll talk to you afterwards.

Lewis Hale – Panelist: OK.

Roy Lanier – Moderator: Yea, y'all can have that later (Laughter, whs), because our time is out.

David Tant – Panelist: Saying something unintelligible.

Roy Lanier – Moderator: I tell you what. I'll ask Abe Lincoln which is addressed to him, the last question. I'll let you have a half a minute to say something on that or whatever you want to and then it's time for our two speakers to give their wrap up declarations.

Question 9:

Abe Lincoln, "Does not the church need the experience of planing and overseeing its own work?" I'm assuming that means does…yes "does not each church, each congregation need…"

C. W. Lincoln - Panelist: Read that again. Read that again.

Roy Lanier – Moderator: "Does not the church, or does not each church need the experience of planing and overseeing its own work?"

C. W. Lincoln - Panelist: Why, certainly. I can't imagine any brethren not wanting to get together and discuss and determine the nature of their work. There were 13 of us when we arrived in Africa, our family of 4. And we became a part of them that Lord's Day. And we met, you know, soon after we were there and we talked about the work that we need to do in a city of half a million. And so they need to do their own work and planning.

Let me say also quickly Brother Roy. That it really disturbs me when YOU brethren take 1 Corinthians 16, I know its been cited but it's still there, and get every kind of needed support from a benevolence pattern. Now if I believed that there is a pattern between benevolence and evangelism, if I know my heart I could not use 1 Corinthians 16 for evangelism. Now that's benevolence brethren. And you just observe the Passover with regard to that passage. You just pass over and gloss all of the pattern arguments on benevolence and evangelism and get everything that you want in that first day of the week contribution. Now, that smacks me, as Jesus said in Matthew chapter 23 of "straining the gnat and swallowing the camel" I mean hairy legs, hump and saddle. (Light Laughter, whs) That here, you would strain out the benevolent pattern and evangelism pattern and get all of your support from a benevolent pattern.

Roy Lanier – Moderator: David, do you want your two minutes?

David Tant – Panelist: Five or six things I'd like to deal with, (Light Laughter, whs) briefly this. The Bible authorizes the church to spend money for benevolence. The Bible authorizes the church to spend money for evangelism. I don't any other way for the church to get its money. If you have another way from some other passage than 1 Corinthians 16, I'll be glad to hear it.

Some things I wanted to come up on but… I want to refer back to something; I turned in a question to the earlier panel. Brother Dyer had said, "Is it wrong for a congregation to do what every member is obligated to do?" In showing that there really is no distinction between individuals and the congregation. It was cited Ephesians 4:28. Individuals are required to go and to do work, run a business, whatever. I think that's a valid argument.

Another consideration on that is 1Corinthians, written

to the church of God at Corinth, 1 Corinthians 7:3 which says "Let the husband render unto the wife her due benevolence, and likewise also the wife unto the husband." I've known of congregations that were composed entirely of a few couples. How in the world is the church going to render sexual favors upon the various members? I don't know how that would take place.

Cooperation of Congregations
Summation Speech Ground Rules

Roy Lanier – Moderator: Now we'll have our final two wrap up speeches by our major speakers. Brother Tom Roberts now has his two minutes.

Cooperation of Congregations
Day 2 Speech 3
Summation Speeches

Tom Roberts – Rebuttal Summation Speaker: I wouldn't want to have brother Abe leave with indigestion over a hairy legged camel hump and all (laughter), so I do want again to refer again to 1 Corinthians 16. There are passages that teach, like 2 Corinthians 11:8 how we pay preachers, and the idea they robbed churches paying them wages. "Wages" is a stipulated amount over a regular course of events. And that shows that the church had access to funds which were regularly contributed in order that they might have that fund available to pay the preacher the wages. 2 Corinthians 11 and other passages show that churches did pay the preachers. It shows how they paid them; it doesn't show how they raised the money. The ONLY passage that shows how churches raised the money were 1 Corinthians 16. I don't use 1 Corinthians 16 to prove that we pay preachers; I don't know other brethren who do. So I'd like to cure his indigestion. We don't use 1 Corinthians 16 to authorize paying the preacher, other passages do that. We show how churches raised the funds.

Now for the remainder of the time… When I was a young boy in Gladewater, Texas growing up, brother Foy L. Smith, whom I have not seen in many years, preached a series of sermons on Catholicism, and what was wrong with Catholicism. And as a young boy that marked my mind. And when I began to see the Herald Of Truth begin to emerge, I began to talk with brethren, "What was the *Herald Of Truth?*" When they described to me the arrangement in Catholicism…of churches in the *Herald of Truth*, the first thing that popped in my mind was Foy L. Smith's sermons on Catholicism, and I've not changed on that at all. There is a sponsoring church arrangement in the *Herald of Truth* arrangement and sponsoring churches that mirrors the Catholic Church. It is just undeniable so

far as I am concerned and we must deal with the fact that when you have the sponsoring church arrangement, your taking steps toward Rome because churches are no longer equal. That is something we must learn to deal with, because once you open that gate there is no stopping place until you get to Rome.

Bobby Duncan – Main Summation Speaker: In this next half hour (laughter), I want to mention two or three things. One, I believe that what we do in religion has to be authorized by direct statement, by approved apostolic example, or by necessary inference or implication. But I believe that the Bible authorizes in a generic way. All of us believe that. It's not whether or not we have to have a pattern; certainly we have to have a pattern. But the pattern doesn't always spell out all of the details. Some of these things have to be supplied by human judgment. Now you believe that in the Bible class arrangement, in building your buildings, and including a baptistery. You believe those are authorized under generic authority. But that doesn't mean that you're saying there is no pattern.

The second thing I'd like to say is… It's a little bit alarming, disturbing to me, whenever a preacher is not working under the direction of an eldership, whenever he receives his support from a plurality of churches. When Paul took up a contribution from a plurality of churches, he wrote in 1 Corinthians 16 that when I come to Corinth you select some men to go to Jerusalem and take this contribution. You want me to go with them, I'll go. That shows that even the Apostle Paul didn't want a plurality of churches to turn those funds over to him. Men need to be overseen by elders.

The third thing I want to say is… Brethren, let us not be divided over a matter of judgment. You brethren can practice what you practice, let us practice what we practice, but let's be brethren. Let's be in fellowship over this now.

Jamie Sloan - Moderator: If I could take just a moment please and make an announcement. Brother Chuck Durham is the preacher for the Reel Road church in Longview and he's been here with us this weekend, and he received an emergency phone call. He and his wife Wilma have a four year old son, Jonathan, who has been in fragile health since he was born. He had a serious operation when he was a baby and has a drainage shunt in his head. And they've had to take him to… rush him to the hospital here in Dallas. And that may not be serious, we don't know, but I ask that you remember them in your prayers.

END OF SPEECH THREE, DAY TWO

END OF DAY TWO

Congregations and Institutions

Day 3 Cycle 1
Saturday, July 14, 1990

Participants

Non-Institutional Brethren
Pat Farish — Main
Foy Vinson — Panelist 2
Robert Gabhart — Panelist 4

Institutional Brethren
Furman F. Kearley — Rebuttal
Sidney Ellis — Panelist 1
H. A. Dobbs — Panelist 3

Congregations and Institutions
Day 3 Speech 1 Main
Pat Farish

Introduction: *Farish, Pat. His is a native of Columbus, MS and presently resides and works in Lancaster, TX. Other local works include Concord, NC, Corpus Christi, Ft. Worth, and Mt. Pleasant, TX churches.*

I took my glasses off and now I can't see who I'm looking for. Brother Kearley, Brother Lanier, Brother Wolfgang, Brother Sloan, brothers and sisters, I've enjoyed these two days up to this point. But I believe that it has been good for us to be here. I've met folks that I haven't seen, some in 30 years or more. Some with whom I was in school who have gone a different way than I have, so we haven't had the communication.

And I don't know much about the prospects of great changes being affected by these meetings. But I know that without our getting together, and without our talking, without our opening the Bible in a candid way, endeavoring to determine what God has spoken, we're not ever going to get closer together. And so I think that it is good for us in efforts like this, or perhaps less elaborate efforts, to be searching each other out, opening the Bible and studying together God's word.

Our study this morning of "The Church and Institutions" is going to approach the subject from a consideration first of all of the church, and organization; then the church, the local church as an adequate functional unit; and then finally the local church and human institutions.

The word translated "church" is used in the New Testament of saved people in two senses. (Chart #1) It's used in a local or congregational sense, in which it describes the saved ones who have agreed to work and worship together. We find it used that way by the apostle Paul several times in Romans chapter 16. Probably the most familiar of those several references is the statement of verse 16, all "the churches of Christ salute you." The church in that sense, obviously composed of people, of those who have responded to the invitation of Heaven, but who have

> ## THE CHURCH AND ORGANIZATION
> A. "Church" in New Testament
>   1. Local (Rom. 16:1, 4, 5, 16, 23)
>   2. Universal (Matt. 16:18)
> B. Only "local" church has organization revealed (Phil. 1:1)
>   1. This organization for every church (Acts 14:23)
>   2. Qualifications for elders, deacons (1 Tim. 3:1-13; Tit. 1:5-9)
> C. Review (Acts 20:28; 1 Pet. 5:1, 2)
> **Oversight excludes donations, demands buying of services and products**

moreover agreed to work and worship together.

The word is used also of the saved people in a universal or brotherhood sense. It's used there to refer to all the saved people everywhere. Jesus used it that way in Matthew chapter 16:18 when he said, "Upon this rock I will build my church and the gates of Hades shall not prevail against it." And the church as used, or the word *church* as used in that sense, is possessed of the same composition that it is when it's used in the local sense. It's composed of people, of those who have been called by the gospel of Christ, and whose response to that call has been to yield to it.

But in consideration of the church in these two senses, we're impressed with the fact that only for the local church is organization revealed. The apostle Paul in writing to the church at Philippi begins by saying, "Paul and Timothy servants of Christ Jesus to all the saints in Christ Jesus that are at Philippi with the bishops and deacons." The church of Christ in Philippi was composed of saints, that is, of people who had been responsive to the word of God and who had been separated or set apart unto God by that responsiveness. Some of these saints, by virtue of qualifications revealed in 1 Timothy chapter 3 and Titus chapter 1 and their appointment thereto, serve in the capacity of bishops, elders, pastors; they have the oversight of the local church. Some other of those saints, by virtue of the qualifications revealed in the same places, other qualifications, serve as deacons in the local church. And this organization is for every, and it will be found in every mature local church of Christ. "They appointed for them"… Acts 14 and verse 23 says "they appointed for them elders in every church."

Now, the functional limitation of this organization is also a matter of revelation. It's not a matter of some men getting together and deciding well this might be a good way to do it, or that might be a good way to do it. No! God said this is the way you do it. He said this in passages like Acts 20:28, where the apostle Paul in talking to the elders of the church in Miletus, or of the church at Ephesus in Miletus, told them "take heed unto yourselves." I want you to listen, I know you've heard this probably in every speech this week, but listen to it one more time. Elders of a local church are responsible for "taking heed" first of all "to themselves." And then they are responsible for taking "heed to themselves and to all the flock in which the Holy Spirit has made you bishops."

If you want to find authority for elders to take heed to some flock other than that which the Holy Spirit has made them bishops, you have to find another verse. If you want to find authority for elders being responsible for some institution other than that "which the Holy Spirit made them bishops," you have to find another verse. If you want to find authority for elders having the oversight, "taking heed" to anything else in their capacity as elders than "the flock in which the Holy Spirit's made them bishops," you have to find another passage. The only other passage that I know of that speaks to the oversight of elders is 1 Peter chapter 5 verses 1 and 2. We'll have occasion to look at that as we proceed.

But for now, we turn to talk about this local church, an adequate functional unit. (Chart #2) God ordained the church, arranged the church, gave it its responsibil-

---

THE LOCAL CHURCH AN ADAQUATE FUNCTIONAL UNIT

A. Work of the Church
1. Evangelism (Phil. 1:5; Col. 1:23)
2. Edification (Eph. 4:11-15; Acts 9:31)
3. Benevolence (Acts 4:32-35; 6:1-6)
B. Divine Provision for emergencies (Acts 11:27-30; Rom. 15:26; 1 Cor. 16:1ff.; 2 Cor. 8, 9)

(rest not visible whs)

---

ity, and created it, capable of discharging the responsibility that He assigned. The work of the church, as the scripture reveals it, is set forth in three areas. Someone divided it into two, spiritual and temporal, I like that. But I've got it divided into three here; we're going to leave it like that for right now.

The responsibility of preaching the gospel. The apostle Paul told the Philippians that "he gave thanks to God for them," Philippians chapter 1 and verse 5, "for your fellowship in furtherance of the gospel from the first day until now." The church at Philippi had fellowship with the apostle Paul, was accomplishing their responsibility in the matter of evangelism, and the church is adequate to accomplish this. By the time the apostle Paul, in the 60s, gets around to writing the letter to the church at Colosse, he's able to say, Colossians chapter 1 and verse 23, that "the gospel was preached in all creation under Heaven whereof I, Paul, was made a minister."

By the time Mark lays down the pen of inspiration, his last words, Mark chapter 16 and verse 20, are able to be that "they went forth and preached everywhere the Lord working with them and confirming the word by the signs that followed." The arrangement that God has given, as far as the matter of evangelism is concerned, was adequate in the first century to accomplish the preaching of the gospel to every creature under Heaven. They didn't have the conveniences that we have. They didn't have the printing presses. They didn't have the mass media that we enjoy or are afflicted with. They didn't have the other things that enable us to get around and to spread the word widely. But by working God's plan they got the job done, and so can we today.

The responsibility of the church involves also the matter of edification. In the 4th chapter of the Ephesian letter, the apostle Paul is describing the provision that God has made for edification. Beginning with verse 11, "And He gave some to be apostles; and some prophets; and some evangelists; and some pastors, and teachers; for the perfecting of the saints, unto the work of ministry, unto the building up of the body of Christ. Till we all attain unto the unity of the faith and of the knowledge of the Son of God, unto a full grown man, unto the measure of the stature of the fullness of Christ." For what reason? To what end? "That we may be no longer children, tossed to and fro and carried about with every wind of doctrine by the slight of men in craftiness after the wiles of error, but speaking truth in love may grow up in all things into Him who is the head, even Christ." Here is the arrangement, here is the purpose of bringing Christians to a level of spiritual maturity, to be accomplished by the arrangement that God has given in the local church, and the scripture abundantly indicates its adequacy to that end.

But there is also a responsibility in material things that the local church has, a responsibility in the realm of benevolence or charity. We could cite many passages to call attention to that. We'll turn to Acts chapter 4 and begin reading with verse 32, which says that "the multitude of them that believed were of one heart and soul: and not one of them said that ought of the things which he possessed was his own; but they had all things common. And with great power gave the apostles their witness of the resurrection of the Lord Jesus: and great grace was upon them all. For neither was there among them any that lacked: for as many as were possessors of lands or houses sold them, and brought the prices of the things that were sold, and laid them at the apostles' feet: and distribution was made unto each according as anyone had need."

The matter of responsibility that the Lord has assigned the local church in the realm of benevolence or charity is also something that the local church with the arrangement that God gave is adequate to discharge. Turn with me to the 6th chapter of Acts beginning with the 1st verse. "Now in those days, when the number of the disciples was multiplied, there arose a murmuring of the Grecians Jews against the Hebrews, because their widows were neglected in the daily ministration. And the twelve called the multitude of the disciples unto them, and said it is not fit that we should forsake the word of God and serve tables."

It's important of course, to interrupt, it's important that hungry people be fed. But you notice the emphasis

that I'm sure we all understood before we began to read this, that the apostles give, that there are things that are MORE important. They say it's not fit for us to turn away from that which has ETERNAL implications to occupy ourselves, to tie our time and our other resources up in things of serving tables. "Not fit that we should forsake the word of God and serve tables. Look ye out therefore brethren from among you, seven men of good report full of the spirit and of wisdom whom we may appoint over this business." And that's what they did. And the need was met. The arrangement that God gave with these seven men, that are easily comparable of course to our deacons, these seven men who were selected and set over the job, they got the job done. They had the things that were causing the problem, the need that was present was met by this arrangement that God gave.

The things that we've looked at, in terms of the work of the church, are things that obligate a local congregation to the extent of its ability. The church does not have responsibility in terms of evangelism beyond that which it is able to do. God didn't put upon us any responsibility that we don't have the corresponding ABILITY to tend to in the matter of evangelism. God didn't put upon us responsibilities that we can't attend to in the matter of edification. When it comes to a consideration of charity or benevolence, recognizing that circumstances sometimes conspire, as it were, to create conditions in which the resources of a local fellowship are inadequate, God, anticipating that, made the provisions for benevolence in a greater sense, or beyond the capacity of a local church. Which provisions are set forth and looked at as passages such as Acts 11:27 through 30, Romans 15:26, 1 Corinthians chapter 16:1-2, and 2 Corinthians chapters 8 and 9.

Now then, let's come to a consideration of the local church and human institutions. (Chart #3) And we begin with the observation that we must have authority, the right to command or act or permission. We must have authority for all that we do. "Whatsoever ye do," Colossians chapter 3 and verse 17, "whatsoever ye do in word or in deed, do all in the name of the Lord Jesus, giving thanks to God the Father through him." As we read the New Testament, which is the revelation of the mind of God provided by the Holy Spirit to select men who were governed by Him in what they wrote, we discover of them revealing the mind of God. Revealing what God would have us do, first of all, by way of command. The apostle Peter commanded the household of Cornelius, commanded them to be bap-

---

THE LOCAL CHURCH AND HUMAN INSTITUTIONS

A. Must have authority for all we do (Col. 3:17)

　1. Authority established by

　　a. Command, statement (Acts 10:48)

　　b. Approved apostolic example (1 Cor. 11:1)

　　c. Necessary inference (Matt. 22:31-33)

　2. KIND of authority

　　a. General, implicit, inclusive (Matt. 28:19, "go" -- how?

　　b. Specific, explicit, exclusive (Mark 16:15; Eph. 5:19) (rest blocked whs)

---

tized in the name of Jesus Christ. Command is obviously one of the ways that the mind of God is revealed and our obligation or our permission to act is set before us.

Another way that is set before us, in numerous passages, we'll read just one, is that of approved, apostolic example. As these men directed by God in what they preached and wrote, behaved in response to that will. Paul is able to write 1 Corinthians chapter 11 and verse 1, "Be ye imitators of me even as I also am of Christ." We discover the things that we need to be doing in terms of our relationship to God. One of the ways we discover that is by the information provided for us through approved apostolic example.

Then another way in which we discover the will of God is by or through the means or the use of necessary inference. In Matthew chapter 32…chapter 22, just rewrote it. In Matthew chapter 22 the Sadducees who believe there's no resurrection, came trying to trap Jesus. And they gave Him this hypothetical case and expected Him to try to untangle it. He did not try to untangle it. He explained the reason for their problem as being their ignorance of the word of God. And then He went on to say, verse 31 of Matthew chapter 22, "But as touching the resurrection of the dead, have ye not read that which was spoken unto you by God, saying, I am the God of Abraham, and the God of Isaac, and the God of Jacob?" Quotation from

Exodus chapter 3. Jesus then said, "God is not the God of the dead, but of the living."

Jesus provided information for them. They would have been much more familiar with the chronology, probably, than at least I am. They would have understood that the passage that He quoted, from Exodus chapter three, was one which was many years after the death of Abraham, of Isaac, and of Jacob. And yet Jesus speaks to them, suspends an argument on the tense that's being used, "I am," present tense, "I am the God of Abraham, Isaac and Jacob." And then says, "God is not the God of the dead but of the living." And with those words, Jesus implied that which He expected the Sadducees to conclude, or to infer. And there was no other possible conclusion that they could draw. The information that He gave, was information which could lead them to draw only the one conclusion.

Someone says, "Well I don't object to Jesus using necessary inference. What I object to is you using it." (Light laughter whs) While that's generous (more laughter whs) the point is that the use of necessary inference is still… we're just in the position of the Sadducees if you will. Jesus is still doing the implying. Jesus is still saying to us, without speaking a word in this matter, in the specific things under consideration, without speaking a word He is saying to us that there is life after death. And the Sadducees understood what He was saying. "When the multitude heard it they were astonished at His teaching."

In consideration of authority, we note the kind of authority as well. Authority may be general, generic, or specific. General authority is inclusive; it is recognizable by options. For instance, Jesus in Mark chapter 16 and verse 15 said, "Go." "Go ye into all the world." Now the instruction to go, put those to whom He spoke those words under an obligation to go, but left them with the option of choosing the way of going which was best suited to their circumstances and to the need there. He didn't have to say, "you walk, you ride, or you fly." He didn't say that. He told them "you go." And without saying a word He instructed them, authorized for them, the manner of going, whatever suited their needs and their circumstances. Specific… generic rather, generic authority is inclusive.

Specific authority names and excludes. Jesus went on to say in Mark chapter 16 and verse 15, "Go ye into all the world, and preach the gospel." "Preach the gospel to every creature." That left them, who would walk by faith, who would yield to the instruction of Jesus, with only the option of preaching that message. They had no authority, they had no direction, to preach any other message. That which they were to preach was the gospel. Specific authority names and excludes. Ephesians chapter 5 and verse 19 Paul writes, "Speaking one to another in psalms and hymns and spiritual songs, singing and making melody with your heart to the Lord." The instruction was not general, making music and making melody with your heart. If it had been thus general, to make music, anything that was music would have been authorized. But the instruction was specific, you sing, and thus excluding those who would follow Him in worship to Him from any other worship in song than sing.

We turn to look now at the authority for the church to use human institutions. (Chart #4) The church uses human institutions. First of all, the activity must be authorized. 2 John 9 says it, "Whosoever goeth onward and abideth not in the teaching of Christ, hath not God. He that abideth in the teaching the same hath both the Father and

---

THE LOCAL CHURCH AND HUMAN INSTITUTIONS

B. Local church uses human institutions
1. The activity must first be authorized (2 John 9)
2. The institution used flows from the authorized work undertaken
   a. Hebrews 10:25, assemble – realtor, utility, contractor
   b. I Timothy 5:16; relieve widows – realtor, grocer, doctor, convales cent home
   c. Matthew 28:19, teach - Publishing company
C. (blocked, whs) Acts 20:28; 1 Peter 5:1-2 (rest blocked, whs)

---

the Son." This aspect of the subject has been developed and worked upon at length already; we'll have no more to say about it than that. If we're going to be legitimately involved in the use of a human institution, we must be doing that for which we have authority in the first place.

The authority for the church to use human institu-

tions flows from the thing required. I read, for instance, Hebrews chapter 10 and verse 25, "Not forsaking our own assembling together, as the custom of some is; but exhorting one another: and so much the more, as ye see the day drawing nigh." Christians have the responsibility to assemble. Now there is no way that we can assemble without a place.

Someone says, "Well we do many things for which we do not have authority, and what about the church building?" Well, you figure out a way that we can assemble without a place to assemble and then we'll have something to talk about. But until we're able to do that, as long as we're under obligation to assemble, while we're under obligation to provide at our best judgment a place to assemble. We may rent a place. We may borrow a place. We may buy a place already built, or we may build a place ourselves. But whatever seems best to us, in our judgment, God has left it to us in the carrying out of this thing that He's required, that we assemble.

Now that may mean that we use… WILL mean that we'll use various human institutions. It might mean, depending on the way we go, that we use a contractor or a realtor. It will involve us in the use, in a relationship with utility companies. But in all of these transactions, the thing that will be happening is that we'll be ordering the product, ordering the service, or the elders of the local church will be ordering the product, ordering the service and paying for it. Not a matter of making a contribution to it. I need to move on.

We need to look at, and to make the bottom line emphasis, the limitation that God provided. Let's not talk about a stifling autonomy, as I've heard some say, not here but I've heard it said. The autonomy that God has revealed and required is not stifling. The apostle Peter, 1 Peter chapter 5 and verses 1-2 told "the elders among you" from himself who was "a fellow elder" that the responsibility is to "tend the flock of God, which is among you, exercising the oversight." That's the obligation that elders have, no more and no less, the flock of God which is among you.

We PLEAD that the sufficient arrangement of God be RESPECTED in DEED as well as in word. If we do what He said, within the framework He revealed, we will not be applauded by the world. And we will not be able to undertake the spectacular extravagances of the denominations. But HE will be pleased and His WILL BE DONE, and what else matters.

Congregations and Institutions
Day 3 Speech 1 Rebuttal
Furman Kearley

Introduction: *Kearley, Furman. Presently local preacher at Monahans, TX congregation, editor of Gospel Advocate, noted for his 40 years of preaching and his professorships at Alabama Christian, Alabama School of Religion, Lubbock Christian and Abilene Christian colleges, frequent speaker on many lectureships and unity forums.*

Thank you so very much and we're delighted to be here. And as others have noted, we certainly feel the responsibility and the importance of dealing with these matters. I do a good bit of marriage counseling, and I suppose the thing we emphasis more in that area is communication. If a husband and wife are communicating, then there is the possibility of progress. When there is no communication, all the way from they're not even talking to or speaking with each other, to the type of communication that is screaming and yelling at each other which is no communication, then there is no progress. But when there is meaningful communication going on, there's progress. And I believe that's the value of the Nashville Meeting and this meeting, and other meetings, is that there is communication going on.

I have many mixed emotions as I come before you, and these have run the gauntlet throughout being here. I am both hopeful and in other ways hopeless with regard to some of our problems. I am encouraged on the one hand about some things and very frustrated on the other. I am downhearted about some aspects of this and uplifted about others. I believe that thus far the highlight of this meeting, at least for me, was the noon luncheon Friday and the great messages brought by Brother Camp and Brother R.J. Stevens. The attitudes and actions of these men, maybe even more so than certainly the delivery, necessarily, of their lessons and even beyond the content of that which they said. I believe that they manifested the right attitude, the right spirit, that is necessary to bring us together.

I guess I feel hopeless that we are ever going to approach these matters exactly the same and have exactly the same understanding about them. But I am hopeful on the other hand, that I can allow you your conviction and you can allow me my conviction and we can work together as BROTHERS in the great cause of Christ. And I believe if there is not hope in that direction, then indeed it is hopeless. I am hopeful that we have grown in love and understanding and respect for one another, and can do so the more we COMMUNICATE rather than scream and holler. I'm afraid that a lot of what happened in the '50s was screaming and hollering and no meaningful communication. But I believe that as we can have meaningful communication that we can grow in respect and love for one another.

I am encouraged that we both believe in many things in common. And I think this is where we need to put a lot of emphasis, that we do believe in many things in common. We believe in God, in Christ, in the Holy Spirit. And though you may have some differences yourselves about how the Holy Spirit dwells and works, and we among us have some differences about how the Holy Spirit deals and works, we all believe in the Holy Spirit. And we've not divided over those differences about how the Holy Spirit dwells and works and such like. And so I'm encouraged that we share so many things in common. We believe in the inspiration, the infallibility, the inerrancy, the authority of the Bible, and we believe that the New Testament is a pattern, a constitution, a covenant.

I told Brother Parish as he began, I'd read his paper. I did not find a thing in his paper or in his speech with which I disagree in principle. I would only see the application of these things in some different directions and more extensive directions. But I do not disagree with A THING in his paper or in his speech that he has presented. But, while encouraged, I am frustrated that we are so far apart in sometimes agreeing as to what the pattern is; though we believe the New Testament presents and teaches the pattern. And though we agree that the New Testament teaches by command, and by example, and by inference, we at the same time seem to be, in many instances, far apart in interpreting these examples and these inferences.

I am downhearted about our human predicament and perhaps discouraged that, in our human predicament, we may never come to perfect understanding. But I am encouraged about how, if we have the right attitude and the right love, that God can help us to work together and overcome and move even beyond our own limitations.

I have somewhat the spirit of the apostle Paul in 2 Corinthians 4 and verses 7 through 15 about these matters. Paul said, "But we have this treasure in earthen vessels, that the exceeding greatness of the power may be of God, and not from ourselves; we are pressed on every side, yet not straightened; perplexed yet not unto despair; pursued yet not forsaken; smitten down, yet not destroyed; always bearing about in the body the dying of Jesus, that the life also of Jesus may be made manifested in our body. For we who live are always delivered unto death for Jesus' sake, that the life also of Jesus may be manifested in our mortal flesh. So then death works in us, but life in you. But having the same spirit of faith, according to that which is written," from Psalm 116, "I believed, and therefore did I speak; we also believe, and therefore we also speak; knowing that he who raised up the Lord Jesus shall raise up us also with Jesus, and shall present us with you. For all things are for your sakes, that the grace, being multiplied through the many, may cause the thanksgiving to abound unto the glory of God."

And so though I have mixed emotions. I believe the bottom line is that if we can move to respect one another's consciences, and to work out compromise in the application of many of these things, we can come to a greater unity and move back to where we ought to be.

I would like to emphasize, as some other speakers have, that we are brethren, and that I have always considered those who have differed to be my brethren. Brother John T. Lewis was a great influence and impact on my life, a lot of that direct but much more of it indirect through the people that he impacted, such as Dr. Rex A. Turner. But I, through at least my younger years, heard Brother Lewis in gospel meetings three to four to five times a year. And read many, many things, if not most of the things that he wrote. And though we differed in certain areas, I feel certain that John T. Lewis is basking in the sunshine of the glory of the Father in Heaven. And have no question, at least so far as these issues are concerned, there may be

things I don't know anything about, you know, but from all that I know, I think John T. Lewis will be in the presence of God and in Heaven.

Brother Ed Holt, I don't know how many of you know Brother Ed Holt, but he was my teacher up at the old Montgomery Bible College, or the Alabama Christian College. Brother Ed Holt is dearly beloved to me. And though we later parted and separated on these issues, I have no doubt that Ed Holt, who is dead now, also will be saved. One of my dearest friends through…all the way through elementary and high school and college, and in Sunday school together, and playing basketball together, and we were in each other's weddings, and all of these things. We later differed over these matters, but I never broke fellowship with him.

I don't know if any of you can help me to understand some things that happened. But I remember somewhere about 1958 after a lectureship, we were at our house and discussed these issues till some two o'clock in the morning. He and his wife with whom we'd been friends and as I said, in the weddings of each other for all of these years, they left our home. From that time until his death of cancer some few years ago, he never had any further contact with me. My wife always sent New Year's cards to them, and we always sent Anniversary Cards to them for more than twenty-five years after that, until he died. The only thing I could ever figure is that somehow he literally shook off the dust of his feet against me. But I never broke fellowship with him. And I never understood it, and do not understand it to this day. But I still believe that he, unless there's some other things about attitudes, but as far as the issues are concerned, I don't believe the issues will keep him out of Heaven.

My topic has to do with institutions. And though, I guess, I'm more hopeful in talking about (Lightly chuckling as he talked, whs) the things I've talked about up to this point, than I am in our agreeing on anything I'm going to say about institutions. In other words my hope is in attitude, not on issues. I will move to talk about the assigned topic of institutions.

Concerning institutions, I believe there is a vast area of agreement between us with regard to that. We all use institutions to assist the church in doing its work, you do, we do. We use construction companies, repair companies, publishing companies. The question then simply has to do with some things about HOW, and WHICH, and maybe the legal constitution, of some of these institutions. Institutions were used in the New Testament. The Good Samaritan used an institution. He used the Inn, and he used the Innkeeper in Luke chapter 10 verses 34 and 35. Paul used institutions. He used ship companies at the very least. Now much of this, it seems, to relate to more the problem we have about what individuals can do and what congregations can do.

I mentioned to some yesterday, I believe that we could be united in Florida College. You all believe that Florida College can exist as an institution. You all believe that it can do the work of evangelism. It can send teachers anywhere in the world, to teach and preach the gospel, and so it can be a missionary society. Florida College can fulfill the edification work. It can send teachers anywhere in the world to teach people more about the gospel, to teach all things Jesus commanded. Florida College can build gymnasiums and can provide recreation for children. You just believe it has to be supported by contributions from individuals and not by the church. And so there's no disagreement with us, except about one little thing, I mean, why, maybe it's a big thing, but I mean one little aspect, and that is, can that money, or any money, come out of a CHURCH TREASURY as opposed to out of the individual pockets?

Well instead of my putting 10% into the church contribution, I'll put 10% into Florida College and 1% into the church contribution. But we can do EVERYTHING IN THE WORLD that I believe the church can do through Florida College, but we can't do it through the church according to the way that we work it out. So I would say let's organize as individuals, or cooperate as individuals. But you see what that does, to me is, it puts the church down here as just a little insignificant organization instead of making the church the MAIN THING that can really do all of this great work that needs to be done.

Institutions, in maybe the sense that we talk about the magnitude, are not mentioned in the Bible in detail. As I said, the germ idea is there in the Good Samaritan and the Inn. The Inn was a hospital. The Inn was a nursing home. But in the expanded sense of it that we're talking about, it's not there. If they then are authorized, they're authorized under generic authority, by necessary inference, or the law of inclusion, or the principle of expedient. The institutions are in direct relation to the churches—are not discussed in the New Testament. But neither are newspapers, radio stations, printing houses, yet we use them. Institutions then must be considered under either: institutions allowed by the law of inclusion, necessary inference; institutions prohibited by the law of exclusion; or institutions allowed by the law of incidentals. You all know that chart well enough that I don't have to put it up here. But you know the first column is the law the command, the second column the law of what is included, the third column the law of what is excluded, and the forth column the law of incidentals. Institutions must be viewed then in relation to the whole structure and this is wherein somehow, I think, we need to communicate more.

But Christian work can be done by individuals, we all agree. Christian work can be done by two or three or four individuals working or cooperating together. If one of you finds that there is a family in need, you feel that you can share this with two or three other brethren and you can go to the grocery store and buy groceries and take it to this family and you can work together in a NON-INSTITUTIONALIZED form. Three, five, ten, a hundred of you can work together in an individual form, but something happens if you become legally chartered that stops this process to a certain degree, or limits it to a certain degree.

And so we have the individual level, the group of individuals together, and then there is the home, and then there is the Para-home if we want to use that term. The home can work through the school. The home can work through the playground, the recreation and so on, the Para-home, the YMCA, the Para-home or whatever. And then there is the church. And then there would be the Para-church organizations, which is really what we are talking about principally in this situation, institutions such as orphan homes, or Christian schools, though they might be Para-home as well as Para-church. Para-home in terms of general education, Para-church in terms of training and preparing preachers to preach the gospel. And then there are private businesses that… whose sole concern such as the *Gospel Advocate*, or I take it *Guardian Of Truth*, whose sole concern… and I'm not sure if *Guardian Of Truth* is a private business or if it is a non-profit foundation. I believe…is it a non-profit foundation?

Someone answers: Yes.

Furman Kearley – Panelist: All right that's…so, a little bit different here, it goes in the PARA-CHURCH category instead of the PRIVATE BUSINESS category. And then there are private businesses that are principally secular, but through which we work to do some work of the church, such as newspapers, and teaching adds, or printing companies, and things of that nature.

But we agree that we can use institutions to carry out the command to assemble, for example. The law is to assemble. The incidental is we may use a rented agency. We may use a Real-estate agency to locate and buy property. We may use a architect or architect agency to draw the plans. We may use a contractor to do the building of the building. But what about some marginal things? What about a contractor, say some retired member of your congregation who is spending all of his time in building church buildings for mission churches? Or maybe not all of his time, but as a mission church needs one he goes and he spends six or eight months at a place building a church building. May the church make a contribution to him in some way to assist him, as he is involved in this? And again it doesn't make me any difference whether he is incorporated as a business or whether he's just strictly a private individual, that technicality doesn't seem to make any difference to me.

We agree that we can use institutions to carry out the command to save souls, to evangelize, to preach the gospel. The law is to go, preach and teach the gospel. The incidentals are to walk, or ride, or to use the travel company, a boat company, an airlines, or to use a travel agency, or if we're going to use tracts to do this, to use a Bible publishing company or all kinds of things and situations involved here.

We get bogged down in some details. I believe we all agree that twelve churches could agree to buy one month's time each for a TV program. But we get bogged down in who's going to sign the contract and how are you going to handle it from there on. The radio station, a TV station at least in most instances, would want ONE GROUP responsible for that contract. Well, if they would agree to receive twelve checks from twelve different places you know, we wouldn't have any problem. But if they have a problem with that, and they want one place responsible, we get all bogged down on whether the other eleven churches have to send their check directly to the TV station or whether they can send it to the church that signed the contract, and then that church pays the TV station. And I don't see any difference in that kind of thing. It's a matter of a person's word is his bond. And if churches agree together in principle to something, the little details of who writes

the check and to whom it's made out to and those kind of things, do not seem to me to be matters that should divide us, or create limitations in our accomplishing the work.

My preference certainly is for ELDERS TO BE OVER ALL THINGS having to do with Christian work and activity. I believe the church ... an elder should be involved in printing the Bible. But you see here's the Bible that we have, and Brother Parish says "the church is adequate to do..." well I believe the church is adequate. But I don't know of any churches that are printing ... well I know of a few churches that are printing Bibles, but they're doing it indirectly. Richland Hills here over in Fort Worth is translating but somebody else is printing the Bibles that they translate. They're working through an institution. But most of us are dependent upon an institution, such as the American Bible Society for the Bibles we have and use. And the church is adequate to print Bibles, but usually we don't. We work through an institution.

And then we talk about paying for product or service. Listen folks! When you pay the American Bible Society for a Bible, you're doing two things. You're paying, yes, part of that is for the cost of the English Bible you get. But part of that is a contribution for another Bible that they're putting out that they're going to distribute free of charge in Cambodia, or in some Indian tribe down in South America. YOU'RE NOT STRICTLY PAYING FOR THE PRODUCT YOU GET; YOU'RE PAYING MORE THAN THE COST OF THAT PRODUCT. YOU'RE PAYING... AND SOME OF IT THEN IS CONTRIBUTION FOR ANOTHER BIBLE THEY'RE GOING TO GIVE AWAY. And even when you buy something from the *Gospel Advocate*, you say you're paying for service when you buy a book from the *Gospel Advocate*, or you're paying some service when you buy Bible school literature from the *Gospel Advocate*. PART of it is paying for service, but PART of it is a contribution to subsidize the *Gospel Advocate* periodical.

WHY DO YOU THINK BROTHER LIPSCOMB BROUGHT BROTHER MCQUIDDY THERE IN 1885? ITS BECAUSE THE *GOSPEL ADVOCATE* PERIODICAL WAS NOT PAYING ITS WAY. And Brother McQuiddy came to start AUXILLARY ENTERPRISES, SUBSIDIARY ENTERPRISES in order to subsidize the *Gospel Advocate* subscription. And over a long period of time the *McQuiddy Printing Company* through its commercial printing, of course became a much bigger company. But through all of these years the *McQuiddy Printing Company* has subsidized the *Gospel Advocate Company* and during the five years I've been there, I know the *McQuiddy Printing Company* has subsidized the *Gospel Advocate Company* anywhere from 50 to 100,000 dollars a year.

So many other things we could say, but that's all. And I appreciate it, and I hope and pray that we can see through some of these things and come to greater unity.

Jamie Sloan - Moderator: We're thankful to and indebted to both these brethren for their efforts. And we look forward to the panel discussion and the question and answer session… (Tape ends here whs).

Congregations and Institutions
Day 3 Speech 1 Panelist: 1
Sidney Ellis

Introducton: *Ellis, Sydney. Known for 37 years of work in Boise City, Norman, and Owasso, OK, Lincoln, NE, Akron, Canon City, and Colorado Springs, CO. Presently with Owasso congregation and director of the School of Preaching.*

Brethren I want to say in the very beginning that it's certainly good to be here. I'm glad to be here, and I appreciate Brother Lanier and Brother Wolfgang and the fact that they have arranged this meeting. I appreciate the good spirit, the good attitude, that is being manifested on the part of all the speakers, all the participants. And I want you to know that I have relatives and friends on both sides of this issue. It's really not that big a problem between us. But one brother in the non-institutional side of the question recently told me, he said "We are all in agreement on the authority of God's word." He said, "We just differ in its application." And I think that's right. We believe in the authority of the scriptures, that we must have authority for all that we do in so far as the work of the church is concerned.

I appreciate and am in agreement wholeheartedly with most of everything that I've heard said this morning. Most everything that Brother Farish has stated and Brother Kearley has stated. I think they both gave great speeches. I believe, my friends, that just as we may differ on the war question and still have fellowship, I believe that we can differ on these issues and still have fellowship.

In the little town where I grew up there are two congregations, one of them is of the non-class persuasion, the other has Bible classes. And they attend each other's meetings, they announce each other's meeting, they disagree but yet they have fellowship together. And I think that's good. I think that's the way it ought to be.

For a number of years ago, when we lived in Colorado Springs, a man moved from Kentucky to Colorado Springs. His wife had divorced him, he had four children and evidently he was in trouble with the law back in Kentucky. Two of those children attended our services and two of them were members. They had come into contact with the church through an Aunt with which they had stayed for a particular period of time. But the law caught up with this brother, and he called me from jail and asked me, he said "Could the church there in Colorado Springs take care of his children, see that they were taken care of?" And so the elders agreed to do so, and so the result was that we took those children to Mountain State Children's Home. And brethren who had moved up from this area, two former elders and also a former preacher from Tennessee who were of the non-institutional persuasion, agreed with the way that we supported those children. We paid for their support in Mountain State Children's Home.

Now brethren, it seems to me that there is a way that we can do the Lord's work and be in agreement. And I believe that it is indeed a shame that we have been divided and that we have so little fellowship. We need to… we need…I'm glad that we have opened up the lines of communication, that we're talking, that we're visiting. We…you may never change your position, we may never change ours, but we can understand one another better, we can appreciate one another more.

I have a brother who is on your side of the aisle, and thank you. (Laughter. Time had expired and he stopped in mid sentence. whs)

H.A. Dobbs? - Panelist: Thank you for your presence. You said it; "I've got a brother on your side of the aisle." See there, I'm glad…I'm glad I got it. (Laughter, whs)

Sidney Ellis - Panelist: I heard that's on the tape. (Laughter, whs)

Congregations and Institutions
Day 3 Speech 1 Panelist: 2
Foy Vinson

Introduction: *Vinson, Foy. Has preached for 37 years in Sunray, Decatur, and Allen, TX, also Elgin, IL. Has been with Allen since 1968, also served as a pastor for the last 16 years. He is respected author for many brotherhood publications.*

Because of the constraints of time, I want to be very brief and first of all say that I'm happy to be here. I'm happy for this meeting. I have been inspired and encouraged by it in many respects. I have seen friends of yore that I've not seen in many years, and whom I have loved in the past and still love in the present. And I feel like that in many respects with regard at least to many of us, there's not as much difference as perhaps some of us have thought. Obviously I believe there are exceptions to that, and that will come out I think more in our discussions today.

But let me just briefly respond to some of the things that Brother Kearley said. And some of these things he said more in detail in his manuscript which time prevented for him… prevented him from covering further. But first of all, I certainly want to commend him for his expressed attitude toward those of us with whom he disagrees. He stated in his manuscript that he never made this a test of fellowship. And he said to us this morning that he believed a number of men that he alluded to, who differed with him on these matters and objected to many of his practices, were in his conviction, in Heaven above. I appreciate that and I'm sure that all of you appreciate that sort of attitude.

Brother Kearley, of course, is editor of the *Gospel Advocate*. And let me say for the benefit of historical accuracy and proper perspective, that such an attitude especially of one in a position such as he is has not always prevailed among us, as most of you know. In fact the very opposite disposition came clearly to the fore in the statement that's been referred to and there were some questions about just exactly how it was expressed. And I have it written down, which will briefly read to you at this time. It was found as

I said in December 1954 issue of *The Advocate* and it read thusly, "I trust that you will not consider me presumptuous if I suggest that perhaps the writers for the *Gospel Advocate* might wisely spearhead a movement to quarantine those preachers." And "those preachers" were many of us who are here today, "those preachers" who were opposed to a number of the projects, and the supportive institutions, that we've been discussing this week.

As it turns out, it was not thought presumptuous at all by at least most of the writers of the *Gospel Advocate*, from the editor on down, to spearhead such a quarantine. And this in fact became the clear policy of *The Advocate* and of other brethren and continued for years thereafter. It was as a result of this sort of hostile climate that caused my late father about the same time to pen these words in which he said, "To believe in the terms of pardon, the New Testament items of worship, and the church of Christ as the only and all sufficient organization through which and in which the will of God is to be executed by His children, appears to be inadequate with respect to ones faith today. We must believe in quote, 'our institutions', or else be marked and regarded as unworthy of the full fellowship and esteem of all the brethren."

I'm happy to see in this meeting this week an improvement over those attitudes. And I would say that had proper attitudes prevailed back then, and I don't mean to suggest just on the institutional side but on the non-institutional as well, had proper attitudes prevailed, I believe the course of 20th century church history would have been dramatically different.

A few years back, when I first saw a directory of churches of Christ that was published by my brethren with whom I differ on these issues, I was surprised to discover that in distinguishing themselves from us that they used the terms institutional and…time already. All right.

Robert Gabhart? - Panelist: That's a short four minutes.

Foy Vinson - Panelist: That's a short four minutes!

Congregations and Institutions
Day 3 Speech 1 Panelist: 3
H.A. Dobbs

Introduction: *Dobbs, H.A. Editor of the Firm Foundation, businessman and noted preacher for over 40 years, now lives in Houston area.*

Thank you Brother Steve Wolfgang and Brother Roy Lanier, for all the work you've done in order to make this meeting a reality. And I think the audience has been excellent, good attendance, good interest, good behavior, and so I think the audience needs a thank you as well.

Brother Farish, in the speech that you heard a few moments ago, told us very clearly that it's OK for the church to use institutions. He endorsed that, he approved that. In his speech, the written speech that I received, he wrote, "The nature of the authority for the employment by the church of service institutions is general." So the church has authority to use service institutions.

And then Brother Farish further illustrated that for us on his overhead.

Jamie Sloan – Moderator: It's the big bar.

H.A. Dobbs – Panelist: It's the big bar. There we are. (Farish's Chart #4) I'd like for you to look again at this overhead. I think it's excellent, excellent. And I'm sorry that I didn't bring any overheads, but I'm glad he brought this one. And this is a sermon that I could preach with as much energy and zeal as Brother Farish presented. I'd just like for you to look at the institutions that he tells us the church may use. He has the real-estate firm on there, a human institution. He has the utility company, the Power Company, the Gas Company, the Water Company, and all human institutions, some of them municipal in there. He has the contractor and his firm, his business; the church can use that institution. He talks about using the grocery store to purchase groceries for the widow. He even has the convalescent home on there. So the church can use the convalescent home to provide the need of widow women according to this chart, and I agree with that, I think that's right.

THE LOCAL CHURCH AND HUMAN INSTITUTIONS

B. Local church uses human institutions
  1. The activity must first be authorized (2 John 9)
  2. The institution used flows from the authorized work undertaken
     a. Hebrews 10:25, assemble – realtor, utility, contractor
     b. I Timothy 5:16; relieve widows – realtor, grocer, doctor, convalescent home
     c. Matthew 28:19, teach - Publishing company
C. (blocked, whs) Acts 20:28; 1 Peter 5:1-2 (rest blocked, whs)

But my dear brethren, may I respectfully suggest that you need now to stop calling yourselves non-institutional, because these are all institutions. And by your own consent, you commonly use them in order to allow the church to do its work. Now there's no difference, an expression that I sometimes use is not a dime's worth of difference, but there's not that much difference, and I sometimes say not two cents' worth of difference. But there is absolutely no difference, no difference that I can discern between what Brother Farish put on this chart concerning the church using institutions and what Brother Furman Kearley said in his excellent speech with reference to how the church may use institutions in order to do its work. And so I think we have here this morning a non-issue.

I think we are as agreed on this proposition as we are on the fact that the Bible is the inherit…inerrant and infallible word of the living God; and that we ought to accept its every declaration and commandment as an iron rule for our behavior. I just don't really see why we are talking about this issue if these are the positions, because there's just no difference here. And it may be that we need to turn to that ironclad word of God and pay some attention to His admonition that we are not to quibble about words to no profit.

I too, want to commend the attitude that I've seen in this meeting so far. And I want you to know, to reassure you, of my respect for you and of my earnest, sincere, Christian affection for you. May God bless you.

Congregations and Institutions
Day 3 Speech 1 Panelist: 4
Robert Gabhart

Introduction: *Gabhart, Robert. He is presently with the N. Beach St. congregation in Ft. Worth, TX, in his 8th year there. He formerly was with Haltom City for 12 years. Frequent author for several magazines and participant in joint book publications.*

I'm very thankful to be a part in this meeting with brethren I don't know very well. But we have been washed in the blood of the same Savior that I seek to serve. I share with Brother Kearley the attitude we should be able to talk and to study and to serve the Lord together more often than we have in the recent past. This next week I've been invited to speak to a congregation on Wednesday evening that ordinarily I wouldn't have been invited to. The events of this week have had something to do with that.

And though we be brethren in every sense of that word, children of the same Father, though we love each other dearly as we ought to, sometimes it's necessary to warn those we love.

We've seen presented this morning and throughout the week two pictures of the Lord's church in the 21st century. There's Brother Farish's picture and there's Brother Kearley's picture, and their vastly different brethren. They don't look alike. In the printed material that Brother Kearley sent us, he talked about this but didn't quote it. The quote says, "The Good Samaritan made use of an institution, now a hospital or a nursing home, to help a certain man. If the Samaritan could use an institution, I know individual Christians can, and I believe the church can, Luke 10:34-35." What we have there is a difference between what we can know from the scriptures and what we believe without scripture is approved of God. Brother Kearley's motives in saying that are absolutely pure. The ends which he seeks to obtain are notable ends. But the picture of the church he's drawn for us is unlike anything in the church's history and unlike anything described in the New Testament.

When Jesus was talking, in Matthew 16 and verses 21 and 22, about going to Jerusalem and dying there and be-

ing raised again, Peter heard that and it went right by him and he said, "That'll never happen" Lord, over my dead body. And in verse 23 the Lord said, "Peter you're a stumbling block to me. You're not setting your mind on God's interests but on man's."

The problem we've got to wrestle with brethren is whether we're willing for the local church to be the local church. Are we willing to set up no foundations and no institutions and no nothing that's going to supplant the church and the work God gave it to do? Are we going to seek to follow the local church into some kind of brotherhood wide functioning unit, or follow the simplicity of the New Testament church revealed by God? Are we going to seek to spread the gospel through the institutional concepts of men rather than through the divine arrangement of the kingdom of God? It's got to be God's work and it's got to be God's way, not man's way in religion. There's another way to establish and to accomplish the GOOD that Brother Kearley envisioned.

In Ephesians chapter 4 and verses 11 and 12, the apostle Paul says that when the Lord set it all up, "He gave some as apostles and some as prophets and teachers" and it was "for the equipping of the saints, for the work of service, to the building up of the body of Christ." When I teach my brethren, and I do, to care about the downtrodden and the forsaken of the world, to be active in relieving their hurts, I am equipping them for the work of service. Brother Kearley's picture has the church funding Parachurch organizations to accomplish that.

I call all of you brethren to join me in opposing the kind of institutionalism that removes the motivation of Christians to individually be involved in the lives of people the Lord brings into their lives. I plead with you to join me in opposing church support of the Para-church organizations which are unknown in God's New Testament revelation about the organization of the church.

Congregations and Institutions
Panel Discussion

Jamie Sloan – Moderator: All right now. For as long as time will permit, we're going to allow these 4 brethren to focus on different, problem areas, as they choose to do so. And we ask if one of the brethren from the other side we'll, over there we'll begin.

Panel Discussion

H.A. Dobbs - Panelist: All right, thank you very much. Foy and Bob, I'd like to raise this question of the 'how.' I know that the answer that we commonly get when we raise it is that "We're not talking about the how but the 'who.'" This morning however we ARE talking about the 'how,' we're talking about institutions. And the question is not 'who' but 'how.' And I want to know where we're going to get a detailed pattern telling us HOW the church in the 1st century, according to Acts 6, took care of widow women. I want to know if those widow women were kept in private homes. Were they kept in dormitories? Where were they fed? Were they given the food and allowed to cook it for themselves or was the food cooked and served on dining tables for them?

Now if your answer is that the 'how' is revealed in the fact that seven men were chosen, my response is no brethren, that's the 'who,' we need to talk about the 'how.' To understand that we have an obligation before God, and to understand who is to execute that obligation is not quite enough. We've got to go beyond that to know how we're going to do it. If the word of God stipulates the 'how,' if it tells us how those widow women were taken care of, then believe me I'll accept that absolutely. But if it doesn't stipulate it, then that puts it in the realm of the generic doesn't it?

And we can then use Brother Farish's convalescent home. Now that convalescent home is an institution separate and apart from the church, human in origin, unmentioned in the New Testament. But according to Brother Farish, it is perfectly legitimate for the church to use that human institution in order to discharge its responsibility and duty of taking care of these widow women. Now that's Brother Farish's way of telling us the 'how' of it. He didn't get that convalescent home out of the New Testament; he got that out of the generic command to care for the widows. So would you talk a little bit about the 'how' of that?

Jamie Sloan – Moderator: Let me just make one little comment about this particular session. This is not a criticism, you're asking a question. But you brethren are free to question one another, but I say to both sides that then, when you make a response it is not a part of the format that you are under obligation to specifically answer one of those questions. If you have something else in the way of the discussion that you want to say, you're free to do that. All right.

Foy Vinson – Panelist: Be fine, I'll be glad to respond to that. I would think after all these years of discussing these issues and even what's been said this week, but especially brother Dobbs as long as you have been around, I'm sure it's as long or longer than I have, that we would know that the issue is not, nor ever has been over methods, never has been over the 'how.' I've never heard of anybody creating any problem over the matter of how. The issue has to do with, again as you've anticipated, but it's still the answer. Who? Which organization is to do this?

Now let me go into something here that, four minutes wasn't long enough a while ago and two minutes won't be now and I don't know whether twenty will be. But the thing that I wanted to bring out and we need to talk about this morning, is the difference between SUBSIDIZING a human institution, and MAKING USE of a human institution, buying a product or a service from it. Now Brother Farish brought that out in his speech. And especially if you could see the manuscript of Brother Kearley and even some of what he said, I think came across to that effect. But his manuscript was ABUNDANTLY clear that he makes NO DISTINCTION WHATSOEVER between those two things, between purchasing a service from a human institution and simply putting that institution into the budget of the church. I've never seen anything that was more embracing of institutionalism than Brother Kearley's speech.

And there isn't anything akin to what Brother Farish was saying in the position that Brother Kearley occupies in that. And that's why I wasn't surprised when some brethren admitted that they are institutional, though at first I was shocked some years ago when I saw that admission in the directory of churches. But I can see now why many brethren at least admit that they are institutional. Some brother earlier in the week denied that but evidently Brother Kearley would not. I don't know how many here would.

Jamie Sloan – Moderator: Brother Ellis.

Sidney Ellis – Panelist: You brethren surely agree that 1 Timothy 5:16 indicates that the widow in deed should be taken care of by the church, in the absence of any relatives. And so since James 1 verse 27 mentions the fatherless and widows, why and if the church can rent a house and take care of these widows, get a couple to take care of them, isn't that an institution? Isn't that a home? And if the church can do that for the widows, since it mentions widows and the fatherless in James 1:27, why cannot the church also do the same for fatherless children? In other words, if a couple in your congregation had five kids and the parents were killed in a car accident, could the church take care of those children? That's all.

Robert Gabhart – Panelist: The question again as Brother Vinson has said, has never been whether the church could do that or not. It's never been. The question is does the church do it or does the church do it by supporting in the budget a Para-church organization? The thing that we are so concerned about, the thing that's alarmed me during the week is, after hearing on Thursday evening how we were so united on the hermeneutic, that we agree that Bible authority was necessary. And then speaker after speaker comes to the platform and says that the Good Samaritan Hospital ought to be used to help the sick, says that the Jesus Society helped the poor out of their bag.

The more I hear the kind of argument like that the more I am alarmed by what kind of that appeal to authority allows. If we're able to establish our authority for what the church does today by what the Son of God was involved in under the Law of Moses, our hermeneutical base is not what we thought it was and our agreement is not what we're hoping. We've gone back somewhere past Campbell's "Sermon On The Law," if that's the kind of argument. And I would wonder whether these two brethren, neither of you have said that and… but Brother Kearley's speech in the printed material clearly says that.

Another quote from that, "The churches have found it is more practical to have one large hospital doing nothing but caring for the sick rather than fragment this up each having its own hospital." I understand that to mean building and supporting a hospital out of the budget. That's what he was discussing there, the institutions. And I would envision that as being, one in Nashville, one in Houston, one in Dallas. And that's the thing that would disturb me. Is there anything in the hermeneutic that would prohibit that as you understand it? And as Brother Winkler seemed to say, other speeches aren't built upon that same basis, and that's very alarming.

Jamie Sloan – Moderator: Brother Dobbs.

H.A. Dobbs – Panelist: Brother Kearley is here and he is abundantly able to speak for himself as you all know. So I feel no need to defend anything that Brother Kearley may have written in his paper. However I have discussed this with Brother Kearley and Brother Kearley envisions a hospital where the only service performed is care for the indigent. And his concern was in foreign fields, not Houston, Dallas, New York City, but in foreign fields where the people are largely impoverished and unable to supply medical care. Now we would agree that we can supply that care. We can provide medical care for them, if it was right for the Good Samaritan to take the man to the inn and have him receive medical care. If the need is great enough, then the building of a clinic could very well be justified.

And I think that what we're called in question here about today is Brother Farish's convalescent home. He put the convalescent home on his chart, and said that's an institution that the church may use. And there's no difference between that and what Brother Kearley is saying when he talks about building a hospital exclusively for the care of the indigent. And we can provide the medical care just as we can provide their other needs, and including the need of preaching the gospel to them.

I want to get very quickly to this question of ability. Brother Farish says the church has no right to undertake something that is beyond its ability. Yet the church is charged with the responsibility of preaching the gospel to every creature in the whole world. And I wonder if you think the church really today, any local congregation would say that that's not beyond their ability? Now all of the churches together, all of the disciples together, as we multiply disciples, and that's what we really ought to be doing, would in time gain that ability, but we don't have it currently. So that's an obligation of the church that is beyond our ability. I think we need to pay some attention to that. Thank you.

Jamie Sloan – Moderator: Foy.

Foy Vinson - Panelist: I want to come back again to this distinction that I think is not being noted or observed between purchasing services and subsidizing institutions. Let's take the hospital for a moment. I again don't know of anybody that has a problem with, if there is someone who is regarded as a object of charity for a local church, and they are in need of a hospital or medical care, of taking them to a doctor or taking them to a hospital, and paying for the services rendered, in either case, to provide whatever is needed for that particular person. But it disturbs me to think that we can't see a difference between that and the church going out and creating an institution such as a medical clinic or a hospital and subsidizing that institution and thinking that there's no difference between that and simply using a human institution that exists to accomplish something that the work needs to accomplish.

Back in 1954 Brother Gayle Oler, whom I personally knew as a young man and my father was very close to him for a number of years, made the statement that "Boles Home is not an organization within the church nor of the church. There was never any organization under the elders of the New Testament church except the local congregation. We believe that the simple New Testament arrangement must be held inviolate. Private homes, hotels, radio stations, children's homes, or anything else that renders service to churches of Christ must retain their status as separate organizations, and there is where Boles Home stands." Brother Oler was very good and, I think, all together correct in his theory about Boles Home. We know he didn't practice what he preached on that. And thus he failed to make the distinction in practice between subsidizing, putting Boles Home in the budget of the church, and using it as a service institution. It's interesting to me he parallels it with hotels, and radio stations, and says they stand on the same footing. Now surely we can see a difference between paying a radio station for using its time to preach the gospel and simply putting that station into the budget of a local congregation.

Sidney Ellis – Panelist: Let me ask this question. If a disaster struck your congregation and it left a number of children without any parents. And those children grew up in your congregation but they needed a home. And suppose that your congregation could not fully support or pay for the expenses of those children. Could another congregation assist you in taking care of those children in that benevolent work? And if so, is that not an institution other than the church, or do you view it as a part of the church doing the work of the church under the oversight of the elders?

Jamie Sloan – Moderator: Robert do you want to…?

Robert Gabhart – Panelist: I want to look at the … I want everybody to be sure that they saw this chart that Brother Farish used, and that Brother Dobbs wants to preach from. Because 'C' is at the bottom, but just what Brother Vinson's been saying, "Oversight excludes donations and demands buying of services and products." That's the New Testament way. That prohibits the church then from going into the nursing home business, and the hospital business, and the clinic business. Brethren that would send us funds to take care of a disaster, the church is taking care of the disaster. We send funds to the Philippines, to the church there when a typhoon hits. That church there takes care of that need. That's vastly different, that isn't a second cousin, to an organization which builds hospitals or to subsidizing hospitals.

What is the authority for building a medical clinic in Zimbabwe? It's the same authority that would be used to build one in Nashville. It must stand on the same biblical basis. That kind of argument, that way of looking at the church, that kind of teaching, cannot help but cause hospitals and nursing homes, supported by the church, underwritten by the church, licensed by the state, unable to turn away those who are not members of the church, who are not the church's charge, who are not indigent, unable to turn those away. They're licensed by the state.

In the 21st century the picture will look exactly like the denominational churches. The seed was sown in the teaching about the church fifty years ago and the crop will be harvested fifty years from now. The basis of it, the authority of it, has got to be the same. It doesn't matter that it's 10,000 miles away. The difference will never be understood by anyone and certainly it won't be understood by the Lord.

H.A. Dobbs – Panelist: Bob I hope you're right. I hope that fifty years from now we have more facilities for providing the needs for sick people if they're not able to provide it for themselves. And I hope your prophecy comes true that the church is taking care of MORE orphan children, and taking care of MORE widow women than they are today. I think that's a little bit optimistic, but I'm glad to hear you make that prophecy. And I hope that you're the 7th son of a 7th son, because then it will all come true. But I could think of nothing that I would more delight in than to have the very thing that you fear come to pass, because I think we need to reach out in our benevolent concern. And with a hand as open as the hand of God who causes His sun to rise upon the good and evil and sends rain on the just and the unjust, to help people both inside and out of the church who are in need of it, and to alleviate human suffering wherever it's found. And that is the glory of the church. And to hope that that's retarded somehow, I think is unfortunate.

Now I want to get back to this question of the 'how.' And I must insist that we're talking now about how. And all of these things that you've brought up you've talked about the 'how' but you put it under the label of 'who.' Now can we talk about the 'how' and just call it the 'who'? When I talk about the 'who' now, I'm wanting to know precisely the details of how those widows were taken care of. I asked you for that information a little while ago, and you didn't have time. I know two minutes is short to get to that, but would you give me the details of how those widow women were taken care of by the church. Now the 'who' is the church. And the church designated these seven men, that was the church in action, how did they do it? There's just no details given. And since it's generic and the detail is not given, we're at liberty to do it in any way that does not violate a New Testament principle.

One other thing, if the only service that can be obtained is the care of orphan children in a specific institution, then a contribution to that specific institution is equivalent to purchasing the service of the care of orphan children. If, on our check instead of saying contribution, we wrote for the purchase of your services, would you then be satisfied?

Jamie Sloan – Moderator: All right, Foy.

Foy Vinson – Panelist: All right, back to your question as to the 'how,' and can I specify you've said that the New Testament doesn't specify, so obviously I can't specify. And again I would come back to the fact that I don't think there's where we have the problem at all. Now you've been asking me some questions, and Bob some questions, and that's fine.

I want to try to understand where you're coming from and what I want to understand is this. Are you saying that the church of the Lord Jesus Christ has authority to establish an institution other than the church, and to subsidize that institution, and to call upon brethren or churches throughout the brotherhood to make contributions to that institution? Now that's the question that I think needs to be dealt with, and it will help me to understand exactly what you're saying about institutionalism. I think there's confusion here as to what constitutes institutionalism. I've tried here to make the distinction here between simply using an institution as a service organization and making a contribution to an institution. And I…brethren back through the years have had no difficulty seeing the difference, at least theoretically, in that. Are we no longer making any distinction?

Jamie Sloan – Moderator: Our time … it is after 10:00 and we've not been consistent about where to cut this off. We can go one more round or just do it in the question and answer.

H.A. Dobbs – Panelist: Take one more round.

Jamie Sloan – Moderator: All right, let go again. All right. So this will be the last…

H.A. Dobbs – Panelist: Yea.

Jamie Sloan – Moderator: In this session.

Sidney Ellis - Panelist: OK, let me say this. If, you know… I think we need to be concerned about unity. And if you brethren want to do it that way, if you want to buy the services of an orphanage for example, to take care of some children, I have no objection to that. And also there are some Para-church organizations, for example a radio station that airs some religious programming, but also some other kind of programming. And I believe they would like to solicit church donations, but I believe we could buy time to preach the gospel on that radio station, but I do not believe that we ought to be subsidizing it or making a contribution.

So I think there's a lot of agreement here on a lot of these Para-church organizations. So we're not as far apart as you brethren think we are. And let me say this, some of the statements about abuses and references to them, and then laying those at our feet, I don't appreciate that, because we don't endorse that any more than you do. And so I think we need to have . . . know where we're all coming from and I believe we can have a lot more agreement.

Jamie Sloan – Moderator: All right Robert.

Robert Gabhart – Panelist: I appreciate Brother Dobbs concern for the needy of the world and certainly the unsaved of the world. And I share that. The answer though to the needs of a lost and dying world is, as Brother Earnhardt said so eloquently yesterday, to develop in the hearts of Christians a commitment to the things of God and to develop in the lives of the children of God a discipleship that puts nothing ahead of the things of the kingdom. And as we restore that kind of zeal and dedication, and… and equip the saints for the work of the service, they'll care for the downtrodden, they'll touch the lepers, they'll aid the abused children and the adults whom the Lord brings into their contact. And with that kind of an army of committed disciples we'll have the only thing that'll stem the Parachurch organizations that you say you oppose with us.

That ought to be our focus in the 21st century as we battle Satan on every front. To restore in the hearts of every individual a dedication to doing what the Lord did while He was here. But to make what He did here the authority for everything brethren want the church to get involved in is the kind of hermeneutic that you SAY that you oppose. And we pray that we'll hear it differently and hear it better and be able to work together to make the next fifty years what both of us want it to be. But in the way that God has authorized it to be.

Jamie Sloan – Moderator: All right. We're going to take just a brief break. We need to get back so that … we've got an 11:00 luncheon, please go see about those luncheon tickets (the tape ends. whs)

Congregations and Institutions
Question and Answer

Jamie Sloan – Moderator: (Beginning not caught on tape) be disappointed if they're get to answer all these questions. (Laughter, whs)

Robert Gabhart? - Panelist: Oh, sure! I'm already sick.

Jamie Sloan – Moderator: Our first questions will go to our speakers and then to brethren on the panel.

Question 1:

The first question is to Brother Kearley and it says, "When I buy a Bible from the Baptist bookstore, knowing the owner of the store is a heavy contributor to the Baptist Church, am I contributing to the Baptist Church?"

Furman Kearley – Rebuttal Speaker: To a certain extent, in two ways. Number 1. Of course you are contributing to a point in the fact that he is going to contribute. But number 2. And most importantly, in this situation, some of that money goes directly to the Baptist Association and they're going to use it to do what they're going to do. Now, you know, we're quibbling over percentages here you know, so to speak, Even when the Baptist Book Store sells a book at 50% discount to another store that's going to sell it, they're still making a certain amount even of that 50% that they're going to use for their own purposes. It's above the actual cost. It's profit, if you want to put it that way, and yet it's a non-profit institution. And so it's not profit in a technical sense or a taxing sense, but it's profit.

And so we have to make our decisions as to whether we buy a book from the Baptist bookstore or a hospital at a service from a Catholic hospital on other basis than the fact that some of that money is going to be used to further Catholicism. You know, the very fact that I walk into a Catholic hospital gives the Catholic Church a degree of influence and power. When I use services there, it is going to certainly advance the power of the Catholic Church, infidel hospital the same.

Jamie Sloan – Moderator: Thank you Brother Kearley.

Question 2:

Brother Farish, "Do you agree with Brother Furman's concept of purchasing from *Gospel Advocate* being a contribution? What about a church purchasing an ad in *Gospel Advocate* or *Guardian of Truth*, are not the prices too high to simply be a purchase?" (Laughter, whs)

Pat Farish – Main Speaker: Yes. (Laughter, whs)

Robert Gabhart? - Panelist: Go to the rest of your speech. (Laughter, whs)

Pat Farish – Main Speaker: I don't have any problem with any business making a profit, and what they do with it. And if it's an exorbitant profit, I ought to have sense enough not to trade with it. Making a reasonable profit, what they choose to do with it is their business. And that's the end of that.

Where's the switch? Where's the overhead? (Laughter over not finding the overhead snapping his fingers, whs) OK, while we're looking for that. Let me get one other thing over here and I can talk about…Thank you. (Farish's Main Chart #4) I appreciate this being brought up, because I had to kind of skim over this and didn't get to it the way it needed to be. But now you look at this. 1 Timothy chapter 5 and verse 16 Paul said, "If anyone of you that believeth hath widows, let her relieve them and let not the church be charged that it may relieve them that are widows indeed." Now here's a responsibility of the church. How is it going to alleviate this responsibility? Not by making a contribution to some society of some sort, to some home. But if it chooses to…whatever's necessary to accomplish the alleviation of this situation, whether this widow needs groceries, whether she needs medical attention, whether she needs to be put in a convalescent home, whether she needs to be put in a hospital.

Let me tell you something, there is all the difference in the world, considerably more than a dime's worth, between making a contribution to that institution and buying SERVICES from it. And we know that. I used the expression "seeing through a ladder" several years ago, and Brother Foy Vinson chided me about it so I won't use that now. But that's OBVIOUS. Buying a service is CONTROLLING the resource.

The statement of 1 Peter chapter 5, or of Acts chapter 20 and verse 28, the REQUIREMENT that the elders of the local church that they exercise… (time ran out).

Foy Vinson? – Panelist: The oversight.

Pat Farish – Main Speaker: The oversight. Thank you. (Laughter, whs)

Question 3:

Jamie Sloan – Moderator: Brother Ellis the question says, "As I understand your position, a local church may support parentheses (putting regularly into the budget) a human institution parentheses (that is college and benevolent home), would that also include a missionary society? And if local churches can support a Church of Christ Benevolent Society, or any human institution, can a local church support a denominational society or institution? Why or why not?"

Sidney Ellis – Panelist: I don't know where the individual got the idea that I would put a college in the church budget. That's ridiculous. And I resent such a question, because that's not my position. I agree with you on that, so that's my answer.

Unidentified Participant: The Missionary Society?

Sidney Ellis – Panelist: Well the missionary society would be the same.

Jamie Sloan – Moderator: All right.

Sidney Ellis – Panelist: I would not contribute to that.

Question 4:

Jamie Sloan – Moderator: Brother Vinson, "Would you please explain the terms used 'institutional' and 'non-institutional' as it relates to subsidizing versus using an institution."

Foy Vinson – Panelist: Well that has to do with a question that I wanted to ask these other brethren. Back in 1934, Brother W.E. Brightwell who was a regular contributor to *The Gospel Advocate* and the news editor at the time, made the prediction that the next religious war among brethren would be around the issue of institutionalism.

I'm curious as to what these brethren think institutionalism is. It sounds to me like they're saying that we can not only purchase the services of human institutions, we can create them, we can maintain them. And that's not institutionalism or, if it is, it's not bad. So there wouldn't be any religious war at all over that if all held to that particular view. The point is, that the church sustains a different relationship to an institution when it subsidizes it, as opposed to when it simply uses it to purchase a product or a service from it. One is authorized by the word of God and you're simply carrying out the work, and it is the 'how,' it's a part of the 'how' and the method. The other is simply unknown to the New Testament. And I just can't believe that brethren are not able to make that distinction. I won't refer to the ladder either, since I chided you for it. (Laughter) But that's OBVIOUS to ANYONE who stops and gives any thinking, or any thought to it at all.

Question 5:

Jamie Sloan – Moderator: Brother Dobbs the question, "Can you honestly see no difference between a church paying a widow's water bill on the one hand, and on the other hand have the church build and maintain a water system for her community?"

H.A. Dobbs – Panelist: Now let's talk about this business of honesty. I want you to understand that I am sincere. And I want all of you to understand that what I say to you I say to my heart. And when the question is phrased in that way, there is a tacit implication that maybe you're dishonest and so now for a little while we want you to be honest. And I think that whoever wrote that question ought to come around and see me after this session is over. (Laughing as he speaks, whs) Now I haven't gotten to the question yet, that's just the preliminary.

I understand that there would be certainly a difference between building a water company and building a hospital. I know that difference. Is that your question? Certainly I see that there is a difference with regard to those two things. A hospital's not a water company; a water company's not a hospital.

I understand, on the authority of Brother Farish, that the church however may use the Water Company, may purchase its services. And the church, according to HIS chart, may use a human institution. And so I think you institutional brethren need to deal with those kind of distinctions yourselves.

Jamie Sloan – Moderator: All right, where am I? Did I…I got all the panel, right? Part of it you did? You didn't get a question? (Pointing to Robert Gabhart, whs)

Robert Gabhart – Panelist: That's… that's OK.

Foy Vinson – Panelist: You got 90% of it.

Jamie Sloan – Moderator: 90% of it. (Laughter, whs). I'll catch up. I'll catch up, my bad.

Question 6:

Brother Kearley, "Why are you opposed to the missionary society that divided brethren, it's a human institution?"

Furman Kearley – Rebuttal Speaker: Generally with regard to this difference in contribution and pay for service…I do not want any church to ever use a DIME of its money, a PENNY of its money, where it does not believe it is not receiving a proper service or product, you see. And so if you're giving to Lubbock Children's Home…we give to Lubbock Children's Home because we are purchasing a service. We actually do it on that way at 3rd and Dwight. We pay for one day's service per year for the whole institution. They divide out their budget by 365 and we pay 1/365th of it. And in addition, we pay for one child for the whole year. We…we…but we write it as a contribution or whatever you… it doesn't make any difference. We feel we are getting product and service for what we do. If you're not getting product or service don't give it, or pay it or whatever.

With regard to the missionary society, and the differences involved in here. I don't have time. (Laughing as he talks, whs) I have here Brother Gus Nichols *Distinctions between Orphan Home and Missionary Society*. I do not believe that I get a commiserate product or service from the Missionary Society and, therefore, I don't give anything to it. I do not believe I get a product or service that I ought to get, so I do not give anything to it. That's the short of it. I could run into why I don't believe that by looking at this analysis from Brother Nichols in much more detail.

Question 7:

Jamie Sloan – Moderator: All right Brother Gabhart, try to restore your confidence in me, brother. "How are you taking care of orphan children and widows now without using any institutions?"

Robert Gabhart – Panelist: As we've been saying from the beginning in Brother Farish's speech outline, it's not a matter of taking care of the needy, it's a matter of whether the church is going to do it or whether an institution is going to do it, subsidized by church funds.

I would wonder if what I just heard Brother Kearley say, means that the missionary society is a matter of judgment. And that if I could get product and services commiserate with the money that I am spending from the local church treasury, that he would have no problem with the Missionary Society. I know that Brother Gus Nichols didn't believe that. But I'm wondering if that is the beginning and the ending of what he would say that the reason he's opposed to the Missionary Society.

As I read the manuscript that he presented us, the kind of authority that's given for building hospitals and nursing homes would certainly allow you, on a product gained from service rendered basis, to support from the church treasury the Missionary Society. If not, I just can not imagine why not. Those were the…that was the kind of authority that was given for that.

Question 8:

Jamie Sloan – Moderator: All right, now Pat. "Where is the specific pattern, book chapter and verse, for having several simultaneous Bible classes, some taught by women, using uninspired literature, on Sunday morning, just before the worship service? Please give specific authority with a specific pattern."

Pat Farish - Main Speaker: You didn't even say who this was to. It's for Pat Fisher. (Laughter, whs)

By definition, specific authority is explicit, in so many words. And I don't know, and I don't particularly care about it. I have the authority for the teaching, any number of passages, which instruct us to teach. And the various ways that we might carry it out, "simultaneous Bible classes, some taught by women, using uninspired literature, on Sunday morning, just before the worship service," that is the judgment of the people involved. Some folks even have it also on Sunday evening before the worship service; some folks have it Sunday evening period. It's authorized. We're instructed to teach. And the best way the folks can teach, the things that best accomplish, best discharge the matter of teaching are all that's important. The people involved make the decision. And we don't have, and I don't make any pretense of calling for specific authority for everything we do. There is another kind of authority.

I want to touch on something else that I thought Brother Dobbs said. I don't want to impute something to him here, but his comment about today the church being inadequate to go into all the world. To all the world. It did the job in the 1st century. The way it did the job in the 1st century was the folks working according to the instruction that God gave them. Now I have confidence in God's plan that it'll work today. I know a lot of folks, again I don't direct this to him (motioning to Brother Dobbs whs), but I know that there are a lot of folks in calling themselves members of the church, who don't think that the Bible is a sufficient pattern for us today. But I believe it... I believe that HE believes that it is. Let me have that (Reaching for notes left on podium whs)

Question 9:

Jamie Sloan – Moderator: Brother Ellis, "When the church purchases time from a radio station that has religious and non-religious programs, could it be that this is partly a donation which helps finance the non-religious programs? According to Brother Kearley's argument, when purchasing from publishing businesses, why can't you make general donations to the station from the church treasury?"

Sidney Ellis – Panelist: If I purchase, if the church purchases time to preach the gospel, that's what we're paying for, we're not paying for anything else. We're not subsidizing anything else.

And these brethren never did answer my question about a home with a number of destitute children, abandoned, with a couple taking care of them, is that home an institution other than the church? Is that the church or is that a home? And if the church is supporting it, then is not the church supporting, giving donations to another institution?

Question 10:

Jamie Sloan – Moderator: Alright sir! Foy, "Does the charter of Florida College allow it to support men to go out and preach the gospel?" Have you ever seen the charter of Florida College?

Foy Vinson – Panelist: I may have to observe the Passover. I would doubt it seriously. I've never heard of such an idea.

Jamie Sloan – Moderator: If you don't want to talk about that further. . . .

Foy Vinson – Panelist: I don't want to talk about that further.

Jamie Sloan – Moderator: ...Do you want to fill up two minutes?

Foy Vinson – Panelist: I know that's not the purpose of Florida College, and I know the men that are involved in it would not be engaged in that sort of thing.

I want to get back to the 'why' of this problem of institutionalism. And I believe that it grows out of a misconception of what the church is, and what it's all about. And also a feeling that somehow we cannot do what God wants us to do with the arrangements that God gave for us to do it.

The idea stated, for example, in the last issue of *Search*, the publication of The Search TV Ministry, to this effect. "That it isn't practical or even possible for every local church of Christ to use its effective television program. But we're learning that congregations can cooperate and do more than a whole bunch of us can by hacking it alone." And over on the last page of the same issue it says, "By working together in this ministry, Churches of Christ are telling the world we are sufficiently organized to preach the gospel to every creature." In other words, until we had things like this, institutions, sponsoring church arrangements, we were not sufficiently organized to do what God said we're to do, and which He provided for us to do through local churches. Now that's the mentality behind institutionalism and also the sponsoring church. That somehow we've got a greater responsibility than we can discharge as God left us. So we've got to make some other arrangement in order to do the will of God.

As Brother Turner pointed out in his lesson last night, in brother...at the dinner, and Brother Roberts last night, our concept to often is church-hood and not brotherhood. And we're trying in some way to bring about a collectivity of churches, an association of churches. That's what institutionalism is. That's what it is intended to accomplish. And if we didn't have that unscriptural concept of the church, we wouldn't be reaching out for institutions.

Question 11:

Jamie Sloan – Moderator: All right, Brother Dobbs you may have clarified yourself about this earlier, but the questioner wants to know. "Is it scriptural for churches to build a hospital for the care of the world's indigent sick and for churches to donate money to such a hospital?"

H.A. Dobbs – Panelist: Someone mentioned earlier that we need to use existing hospitals. You can go into some areas of the world and no hospitals exist. There are none. And the poor people in that part of the world have no medical care at all, virtually. And certainly what little medical care may be available to them is woefully inadequate. Now I'm not talking about a metropolitan center where these hospitals exist and where the very cost of trying to build and maintain them is prohibitive. I'm talking about areas of the world where there, hospitals do not exist, and where there are indigent people, who in large number, have need of medical care. And in that kind of a circumstance, yes sir, the church could build such a hospital. Now it might be not done under the oversight of elders, we haven't talked about the distinction between elders and the board and we need maybe to get into that. But I don't think we're going to have time in this two-minute speech to do it. But briefly put the answer to the question is yes, on the conditions that I've stipulated.

Question 12:

Jamie Sloan – Moderator: All right, Robbie this question may get into that.

Robert Gabhart – Panelist: Good.

Jamie Sloan – Moderator: "Would it be scriptural for a local church to incorporate an orphan's home to comply with state requirements and have the elders be the directors of the cooperation? Wouldn't they have oversight of that work? Or could the elders with exclusive rights under the terms of the articles of incorporation, appoint Christian men to be the directors of that orphan home and have oversight of that work?"

Robert Gabhart – Panelist: That's it? I need two minutes to read the question. Let me think about it.

Elders of the local church are certainly able to provide for all the needs that the Lord has given for that church to provide for. All the responsibilities that can be a part of the work of the church legitimately in the New Testament, the elders have the authority and the ability and the responsibility given by God to do that. We'd have to go back to all the outlines about what is the work of the church, and how it…to talk about how it might be accomplished.

The question is not whether or not, in my mind, the church is sufficient to do that which God has authorized. The question is whether or not that's what brethren have set up. Have they arranged the work of the church? Have they arranged the responsibilities of the church in a way that's consistent with New Testament authority? I would not ask for specific authority for those institutions. I'd ask for ANY KIND of authority, any kind of New Testament authority.

And the idea, referring to what we just heard, of building a hospital in areas of the world where there were none available really begs the question. Obviously that would be a need of that part of the world. The question is has the Holy Spirit through New Testament scriptures given the church that responsibility to care for the needy of the world? With that out of the way, then certainly we would find the ability and the responsibility of elders to do whatever it was that the church had been commissioned by God to do as a work of the church.

Jamie Sloan – Moderator: All right, am I back on track now?

Robert Gabhart – Panelist: Yes.

Question 13:

Jamie Sloan – Moderator: All right Brother Kearley, "Upon what evidence do you assert that Florida College sends teachers and preachers to proclaim the gospel? If I, as an employee of IBM, decide to go to China on my vacation to teach the gospel, has IBM sent me?" This may be getting the general area of the question intended for Foy earlier.

Furman Kearley – Rebuttal Speaker: Well of course I am speaking generically. I don't know that much about Florida College's business, but I have taught with other colleges. I have an opportunity to go as a teacher for Alabama Christian School of Religion to Russia and to teach some Bible classes. If I teach anything that is in the Bible from Genesis to Revelation, and especially if I teach the gospels, I am teaching the gospel and preaching the gospel. If there are people who come to those classes that are sitting there, and they are non-Christians, I'm going to try to convert them. I assume that if Florida College had an opportunity to teach a Bible class in Russia, they would send one of their professors to Russia. Is there somebody from Florida College here who would deny that you would send… Brother Owen, if you had an opportunity to preach the gospel…I mean to teach a class in Russia, wouldn't you send a teacher there? (Laughter…Brother Owen stands up and answers the question, but is not audible from the tape.)

Jamie Sloan – Moderator: Thank you Brother Owen.

Furman Kearley – Rebuttal Speaker: OK

Jamie Sloan – Moderator: Take 30 seconds.

Furman Kearley – Rebuttal Speaker: That would be…

you know I had no idea ... so I take it back with regard to Florida College. But certainly most all of us, if we have an opportunity to go and to teach a class to anybody, we go and teach a class to them. I have never thought in terms of, you know, charging with regard to that in relationship to any college...in other words auditors have always been free to come to my Bible classes. Surely those who are getting credit and doing all of that, we charge tuition, but I have never rejected an auditor from coming to my Bible class whenever, wherever I taught it, and I've taught it to them in South America, other places, as colleges and so on.

This deal what this says with...here. OK.

Jamie Sloan – Moderator: I sincerely regret that we're out of time. But we have promised that we would give, if they so desire, the two final speakers, two minutes. And out of fairness, I think, we've got another question for Brother Farish if he would like that, or wants that.

Question 14:

We will have this question for Brother Farish and then they'll have each a two minute summation. Brother Farish, "If Hebrews 10:25 authorizes the building of a building, where is the authority that limits the judgment of the kind of building that's built? Is this not the stewardship of each autonomous congregation?"

Pat Farish - Main Speaker: I'm not being facetious. Yes.

Now then, the question was raised about finding all the details for how they attended, in Acts 6, to tending to those needs of those widows. And someone, Foy or Bob, has already well answered that. That that's not a matter of specific revelation, but the instruction was there, the job was done. That's in the same class as the question as to how Noah went about building the ark, what tools he used, and what method of construction and so forth. I don't know how he did it. I just know he was told to do it, and I'm confident therefore, that he used whatever was necessary. He was authorized to use whatever was necessary to get the job done, the job that he was directed to do. With reference to the care of those for whom the church is responsible, for those widows in deed or whatever, they are authorized. The elders are authorized to use whatever is necessary to get the job done, while they maintain their oversight, while they continue to exert the...or to discharge the responsibility given them by God (Acts 20:28; 1 Peter 5:2). It's their responsibility to see to it that the

job is done, that the money is expended wisely and that's the thing that they do. And that's all that's involved in the matter of the 'how' it got done.

Congregations and Institutions
Day 3 Speech 1
Summation Speeches

Jamie Sloan – Moderator: All right, Brother Kearley.

Furman Kearley – Rebuttal Summation Speaker: No time is ever enough I don't suppose. But I would like to say I express appreciation to Brother Wolfgang and Brother Lanier and everybody else involved in putting this together. And I appreciate your presence in being here and I hope that we can work together to continue to communicate. And I see we need lots of communication.

I certainly do not know of anything that I said in my paper that would indicate the OK'ing of a United Christian Missionary Society. This is something, you see, that goes against the principles in Brother Farish's paper and in my concept either one. And I said I agreed with Brother Farish's paper. It talks about the autonomy of the local church. I do not agree that… you know, with the United Christian Missionary Society because it violates the authority of the church.

I agree with the Gospel Advocate Missionary Society. And so you know, if you want to give me $14.98 for a subscription for yourself or anyone you want to, I'll take and you can call it a payment. I'll call it a payment or I'll call it a contribution. But it's helping accomplish the mission that we have of trying to teach and preach the gospel.

Pat Farish – Main Summation Speaker: Brethren we've had two days and a little more of study together, and it's been good. It's been good to be together. It's been good to open the Bibles, to bring our convictions to the open, to be examined in the light of the word of God.

We're not through, there's another session after this. But today's going to see the end of it, and we're going to go our separate ways. And if we let that be the end of it, then we'll have just spun our wheels here in a grand old fashion. The thing that I want to do is appeal to you. That's why I put my glasses on, so I can see your eyes. (Laughter whs) I want to appeal to you just as sincerely as I know how, those of you who think I preach and practice the truth and those of you who don't think so, all of us. Let's not let this be the end of it in terms of our thinking about the things that have been brought up here, in terms of our examining that which we've been doing or which we intended to do, in terms of the direction that we see ourselves going, or see others going. Let's continue to come back to open the Bible and to think about these things. Don't leave here thinking, "Well it didn't change my mind so that's the end of that." Well, you know, I don't necessarily expect it to change our mind in the two days that we're here. But let the seed find lodgment in a good heart, from whichever side of the question we look at it. Jesus said, and here's the key to successful Bible study, and here's the way that we can know irrespective of methods. JESUS SAID "IF ANYONE WILLETH TO DO HIS WILL," that man's been raising his fist at me all day (Laughter, whs), "ANYONE WILLETH TO DO HIS WILL, WILLETH TO DO HIS WILL, HE SHALL KNOW OF THE TEACHING." And that's what we want. Thank you.

Jamie Sloan – Moderator: I guess I will not be up here again. But from a personal standpoint, I would like to express my appreciation particularly to every man that's been on the panels, the sessions that I have been associated with, to every man, every one of them to the man, for their expressions of patience with me in trying to do the little job that I've done up here. And the love and warmth that you've shown to me and the attitude of all, to be so honest in front of so many, so open to admit and to insist on what they do believe to be the truth. And it has been a most helpful experience for me. We're going to go to lunch now. There are eight tickets that need to be sold, and those can be bought at the luncheon. Let's please take care of that. We welcome these eight with open arms. Let's go. (The tape ends here, whs)

END OF SPEECH ONE, DAY THREE

Morning Meal

Day 3 Meal Speeches
Saturday, July 14, 1990

Participants

Non-Institutional Brethren
Bob F. Owen — Only Speaker

Day 3 Meal Speech 1
Bob F. Owen

Introduction: *Owen, Bob F. He presently serves as President of Florida College (sine 1982) and has been a speech, Bible and business teacher since 1952. He is a native of Memphis, TN and does extensive gospel meeting work across the nation and has worked with churches in Clearwater, Tampa, and Largo, FL. Has served in leadership in Rotary, chamber of commerce and city council positions in Temple Terrace and is presently chairman of the Commission on Independent Colleges in the American Association of Community and Junior Colleges.*

Maybe it's really not such a bad idea to eat in the church building. Because I've got an idea that if you're going to be eating while I am talking, that at least you'll stay awake, and that would solve one of the big problems that I frequently have when I'm trying to preach. The other part of the problem though is there's been a real question, and it was debated out there before we came in, to try to use this alternate approach, as to whether it was better for me to speak before you eat and therefore keep you from eating or to speak after you eat and maybe run the risk of you're losing what you'd already done. So I hope that it will all really work out well.

I've got a real good friend in Tampa named George Marcus. And as you might have guessed from the name, George is a Greek. Through him, I've become well acquainted with a man named Steve... named Mike Bilirakis who is a United States Congressman. When Mike was running for office the first time, George was a big supporter. And George said, "I want everybody to know that I'm not voting for Mike because he's a Greek." He said "I'm voting for Mike because I'm a Greek." (Laughter from audience whs) But I want to tell you, I voted for Mike also. And I've already forgotten most of the things I learned in Paul Southern's Greek Class in Abilene. I voted for him because philosophically we agree. He is a staunch conservative morally, politically, economically, socially, and he's been a good representative for the general area.

I sent him a donation just recently but it may not be to any avail because Mike is in serious trouble politically. Now, the area that we live in is strongly conservative. The area that he represents is very conservative, and he's had strong backing. But he's probably going to be defeated this year because he's opposed to abortion. And many of his long time supporters who philosophically and personally are committed to the same kinds of things that he is, have come to him and have said, "I'm not going to vote for you this time because of your stand on abortion." That single issue is causing people to line up with someone with whom they are diversely opposed philosophically.

I can't help but wonder if their might be a parallel among us. I know that there are differences among all of us. I don't know any person with whom I universally agree on doctrine. It's been pointed out to me that not all of us agree on all the things that's been said in these panel discussions. And that's obviously true with both sides of the issue. Yet all of us find birds with whom we can flock. And we all find birds with whom we will not flock.

For over four decades we've had a major point of separation over congregational cooperation and church support of human institutions. Some of us who are hear at this assembly see these things as non issues, and as matters of judgment or indifference. Some share MY feelings that these things violate scriptural authority because they involve group action and not just individual action. They put us in a position that cannot be treated as optional. This is different from the war question. It's different from the covering question. On those things brethren can differ and still not violate one another's conscience. But this is like the question of the instrument. If you bring it in, it commits the whole group. And when money is taken out of the treasury to support something where conscientious objection exists, you can't treat it as a matter of personal indifference.

I'm glad to say that after this week I could easily say that if wanting to please God were the only issue, or if wanting to follow Bible authority, or if loving brethren, or if wanting peace and unity, were the only issue we could solve the problem for several hundred Christians right here this week. But it's greater than that. But I join with so many who have said it already, "I am so pleased that at least we're talking."

And I want to complement Steve and Roy for the outstanding work they've done in putting this together. It's not easy and it hasn't come without flack and complaint to them. But they've done a super job and I think we're all indebted to them. And I'm grateful to all the people who have spoken and the excellent attitudes that have existed throughout. I think it's wonderful.

I can understand Roy not wanting to introduce me. When I went to Freed Hardeman, I had the fortune, he called it the misfortune I'm sure, that we room together for a semester there. Then a year or so later when we were at Florida College together, Florida Christian College it was known as then, we roomed together there. The next year we moved out to Abilene and we moved together… and we lived together there. So we've been roommates for a long time. After that episode though at Abilene, we married sisters and we both ended up with a great improvement in roommate situation. (Laughter from audience, whs) I've got a lot of respect for Roy. We don't agree on some things. But I've never stopped loving and appreciating the firm stand and the conviction and the basis from which he comes. I could say the same thing about so many others.

It's been a wonderful experience this week. We've sung together and we've prayed together. I heard somebody say the other day that he'd rather hear R. J. Stevens sing than to eat. I told him "I had too. I've heard him eat." (Laughter from audience, whs) But it's been a wonderful experience to… it's been a wonderful experience to worship together. As Brother Curtis Camp said so eloquently and ably the other day, and wasn't that a marvelous talk? And I could certainly have worshipped with that little group he described in New Mexico. That's not the issue, just like we can do this here. But if somehow we started doing things that would compromise the consciences of others, NOW we've got a problem that can't be swept under the rug or simply ignored.

I deplore the divisions that exist among us. And I fear that those with whom I associate are caught up, like OTHER people are, in a spirit of the world that sometimes maybe leaves the spirit of Christ. You know we

have to fight, not only our own personal feelings, but the influence of society. We live in a time when people are encouraged to not get along, to do their own thing, to make sure they get their own way. I've said sometimes "the theme song of our society today ought to be I Did It My Way." And the world pushes us to not get along, to not care about other people.

Did you hear about the guys that were on a shipwreck? The ship blown off course hundreds of miles finally broke up on a reef. Only six guys made it to an island. It's not a deserted island; nobody had ever been there before. And they knew they were there forever. There was no way out. Two of them were Catholics and they immediately went up on the north end of the island and found this beautiful little bay and built the Our Lady of the Lagoon Catholic Church. Two of them were Baptists. So two of the six went down on the south end of the island and built the Southside Baptist Church and set an attendance goal of eight. (Laughter from audience, whs) Two of them were members of the church and they immediately started the Eastside church of Christ and the Westside church of Christ. (Laughter from audience, whs) Now I laugh and you laugh and yet we all cry because tragically, like in most humor, there's enough truth in it. And I deplore it with you.

As in most church problems, most of us can recall events where an attitude was bad or an argument was misrepresented. I'm not talking about those kinds of abuses which all of us regret. I'm talking about honest differences among brethren who still share convictions on the authority of scripture.

Nashville was at least an eye opener, if not a SHOCK to many of us. Calls for a new hermeneutic and opposition to instrumental music in worship only because it had traditionally caused trouble in churches of Christ, made that experience sound more like an ecumenical council among liberal theologians than a discussion among our brethren. I'm glad to say "This week's different." I don't have a crystal ball, no sycamore trees, and claim no abilities of insight.

Forty years ago when we were first questioning the Broadway plan for Germany, where the *Herald of Truth* was trying to decide whether it was the work of all the churches of Christ or just the Fifth and Highland church in Abilene. I would have never dreamed of our brethren going into the extent in the social gospel that characterizes many today. And it can't be swept under the rug that it's just a few little old churches back in Nashville. Find a community where mainstream churches are not just INUNDATED with all kinds of socially oriented programs under the guise that we're going to reach the world through their stomachs.

I know many brethren hold a very conservative attitude toward scripture and demand Bible based preaching. And yet they live in separation from those of us who differ with them over sponsoring churches. And yet their practice seems to be, to maintain a fellowship with those who differ with them so much in attitude toward scripture. All of us know that it's far too simplistic to suggest that we could find unity if all of us would just give up any practice that's questioned by anyone else. On the other hand, is unity not worth our foregoing some things that we might claim as liberty?

Personally I have no objection to a church building being used for a wedding or a funeral. I know some highly respected brethren who do object. I think that if I were in a group where strong objections existed, I would be content to forego those practices FOREVER. On the other hand if I were in a group that opposed divided Bible classes, I possibly would have to do differently. My judgment might be that we were not reasonably doing our work in teaching without some kind of class arrangement and I could not permanently abandon the practice. I might or I might not, it depends on the condition there. What I'm talking about is more than a matter of freedom; it's a judgment call on whether our work for the Lord is jeopardized beyond reason. None of us is willing to forego those activities which we feel necessary to reasonably serve the Lord.

Almost two generations of Christians have known this division over institutionalism. We've developed separate flocks of birds. It would be naive to try to ignore the differences and I'm not suggesting we do that. I do wonder though how brethren who still demand strict biblical authority through commands and examples and inferences can continue to walk together with those who are POLLS apart from them philosophically.

I am told that Brother McGarvey never approved the use of instruments of music in worship. And he told people he didn't approve. Yet he worshipped regularly with those who used them. His practice and his association spoke more loudly than his filing verbal objections to the practice.

Is it different today? When brethren say they oppose the avert… overt denominational practices of many congregations, and yet that's expressed in a way that no one seems to really make an issue over. Obviously each person must make personal applications and decisions. I differ with some brethren that I respect very much. I see them as people who love the Lord and who respect His word as authority. For me to have unqualified participation with them, or to endorse their practices would demand a compromise of my conscience. This of course I cannot do. I truly wish the separations did not exist and I pray to God that both my actions and my attitude are proper. I don't want to be part of the problem. I'd like to be part of the solution. But there is no solution apart from a proper understanding of God's word and humble spirits that are content to serve the Lord and His people.

At Nashville last year, Brother Jimmy Jividen with whom I went to school in Abilene, mentioned his writing on *Worship In Song*. If you don't have this book you need it, everybody. It's great. He's made some of the best arguments and presents the arguments for the use of instruments and than answers those arguments beautifully. His last chapter, I wish I could just read it to you. His last chapter is entitled "Restoring Fellowship To A Broken Brotherhood." And it closes with what he calls a bold proposal. It's about two pages long; I'll not read it all. But the proposal, you might already have guessed, out of AGAPE LOVE he talks about, would be for people to care enough about unity that they would forego some things that are at their liberty.

I'm going to read you the last three sentences. There are three paragraphs. Three short paragraphs that close Brother Jividen's appeal to those of the conservative Christian Church who still believe in biblical authority but differ with us over the instrument.

> Would it not be a wonderful day if the conservative Christian Church in a thousand towns announced that they're going to give up the instrumental music in Christian worship because their brethren in the churches of Christ cannot accept it in good faith? Would it not be a wonderful day if members of churches of Christ in a thousand towns announced that they accept as brothers those in the conservative Christian Church who no longer use instrumental music? Would it not be a wonderful day if members of the churches of Christ and the conservative

Christian Church would sit down together in Bible study, not to prove their own tradition, but to seek to know the will of God? May God bless us with that kind of spirit.

Roy mentioned Brother Camp's lectures or talks at chapel about a preacher. I'd love to have heard those. Particularly I wish I could have heard that last one on the danger of pride.

And I close by saying, if a man's going to try to be a gospel preacher, and most here are trying to do that, #1 he's got to love the Lord. #2 He's got to love and respect God's word. I think Paul was perhaps as effective as a preacher as any could be, and I want to add the 3rd one from Paul's language. In 1 Thessalonians 2 he said, "But we were gentle in the midst of you, as when a nurse cherisheth her own children: even so, being affectionately desirous of you, we were well and pleased to impart unto you, not the gospel of God only, but our own selves, because you were become very dear to us."

When we love each other enough to use the real spirit of Christ, maybe we can reach across some chasms. Frequently on Sunday mornings we sing the song *I gave my life for thee, what hast thou given for me?* Maybe it's a shame that we sing that too close to the contribution time. And somebody thinks that giving to the Lord means an extra ten bucks. What he's talking about giving, is loving others above self and being willing even to be damaged for the cause of Christ, of putting the others first and self second, because we're more interested in one another, in going to heaven, than we are in our own personal pride. May God bless us to that end.

Thank you. (Applause, whs)

Fellowship Among Differences

Day 3 Cycle 2
Saturday, July 14, 1990

Participants

Non-Institutional Brethren
John Clark — Rebuttal
Ron Halbrook — Panelist 2
Charles Davis — Panelist 4

Institutional Brethren
Jimmy Jividen — Main
Maxie Boren — Panelist 1
Wyatt Sawyer — Panelist 3

Fellowship Among Differences
Day 3 Speech 2 Main
Jimmy Jividen

Introduction: Jividen, Jimmy. Native of Oklahoma, well-read author, known for his work in York College, and local churches in Wadena, MN, Montrose, CO, Van Nuys, CA, Norman, OK, Sheffield, Wichita Falls, and Abilene, Texas.

Thank you, Roy. If I were running, I wanted to get all the time I could. (Evidently responding to Roy Lanier's introduction not caught on tape, whs) To Steve and Roy I want to express appreciation, because they've gone through a whole lot, and to so many that have done so much. I want to say thank you for the powers that be that allowed John Clark to come back and to share with me on this very important subject. We were together last year and I'm thankful we can be together this year. I do have a little problem with Steve though. I hated for him to draw another line, and that young whippersnapper and cut us, all of those under 40 crowd off, I'm telling you. (Laughter, whs)

I am real humbled, and I feel heavy the responsibility of sharing 28 minutes with you. You have given me your ears to hear, your mind to understand, and I hope your spirit to change. Because we are always in a perpetual change as we endeavor to restore New Testament Christianity. You are here because you desire to strengthen your fellowship.

When I was a boy, my dad took me up into Harper County one time and there we saw two parallel fences running down through a pasture. I asked him what it was. He called it a Devil's fence. And that Devil's fence meant that there were two neighbors that were so selfish and so standoffish from one another that each of them built a fence on his property and would not even share a fence. We might not tear down that Devil's fence but I hope we can start talking over it. I hope and pray that what we have done here THIS WEEK will be able to cause SOME of us, in SOME of the places and SOME of the ways, to start talking to one another again.

There are some things that I fear. I fear the party spirit that has caused a lot of the division in the first place. In San Diego a few years ago, I was on a panel. It was an antagonistic audience, and they were trying to label me somewhere. And they finally…someone held up their hand and said, "Jimmy are you a liberal or a conservative?" I've never been asked that before. I had to think about it a moment. And then I said, "Well I try to be Biblical in doctrine conservative in practice and liberal in love."

I do not…I fear the fear of being labeled. "Many of the rulers believed on Jesus but would not confess Him lest they be put out of the Synagogue, for they loved the praise of men more than they loved the praise of God." I am what I am. I fear the misusing of terms and loaded words. Confucius said in his *Analex*, that what was needed was the rectification of terms. We need to call things as they really are instead of using terms that are loaded to alienate.

I am concerned about building straw men that do not really exist. I do not believe that some of you are orphan haters any more than I believe that some of us reject pattern authority, support Christian colleges out of the church, believe the work of the church is recreational, or accept the new hermeneutics. I am EMBARRASSED when I am charged with thus. Some of us, we have sought to fight and write rather than retreat and quit talking.

Why is it that we cannot enjoy fellowship because we disagree on cooperation, when there is fellowship extended to those who have head coverings, and different views of eating and drinking in the church building, and weddings and funerals, and the Holy Spirit? And yet there cannot be a stronger and deeper fellowship on those that disagree on cooperation.

There are certain presuppositions that I think we share, and I'm thankful for that. What is sometimes called, erroneously so but sometimes called, the new hermeneutic is rejected by us all I believe. I am thankful that you're listening, that we're not just two tape recorders on play blaring at one another but we have the recording button on. I am thankful to be accepted with all of my warts. I am more of a lover than I am a fighter.

My purpose is not to discuss the issues but to show the theological basis of restoring a greater degree of fellowship between us. And I hope and pray that some of us in some of the places will, like Jacob and Esau, come back and receive each other into arms and weep together. You know Jacob and Esau did some mighty unbrotherly things to each other before they separated. And it's time for some of us to shed some tears like they did and come together

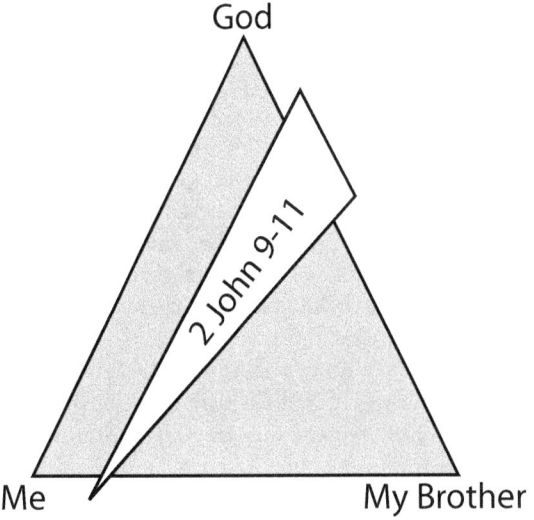

again, in Genesis 33:1-4.

(Chart #1) I want to share some charts with you. I apologize. I don't have any of these newfangled charts, all of these different colors and things. I just have some old ones that I've put together, and I want to use these charts, if I might, and…to show us some of the things about fellowship that I want to share with you. Number 1, I want to say that fellowship is defined in the New Testament; of course the word is KOINONIA. It is that that means a commonness, a sharing together, a communion, a partnership. It is used with reference to a partnership, a business partnership in Luke the 5th chapter, Peter, Andrew, James, and John. It's used in the ancient papyri of the domestic relationship.

But there was a new dimension given to it, particularly in the writings of Paul. He calls it an in Christ kind of fellowship. It is a caring, sharing, and bearing. It is estab-

lished by divine sanction. One is begotten by the word into the family of God. He has been washed by the blood of Jesus Christ, and he is indwelt by the Holy Spirit of promise. He becomes a child of God. It's not a decision of his brothers and sisters, whether he is going to be received. It is a decision of the Father that, if we're a child of God we're automatically, instantaneously, brothers and sisters in Jesus Christ. We did not choose our brothers; we only recognize them as our brothers.

There is a kind of relationship that exists and only can exist in a triune relationship; it is always God, me, and my brother. If we think that we can establish fellowship on some kind of a horizontal line because of different interests or party spirits, we are confused. We only have fellowship one with another if we are in fellowship with God.

Now, that fellowship can be broken. And according to 2 John 9 and following, "If any man goes onward and abides not in the doctrine of Christ, he hath not God." He has severed his relationship with God. Verse 10 and 11 says, "If anyone comes to you and brings not this doctrine, receive him not into your house, neither bid him Godspeed," because if you do "you become a partaker." That is a KOINONIA word, "a partaker with him in his evil doings." So if it's severed on one place, it is severed on another place.

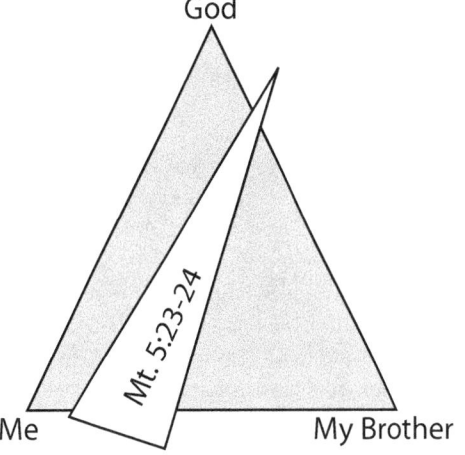

(Chart #1b) And if the relationship is severed between my brother and I, it affects my relationship to God, and that concerns me. (Quoting Matthew 5:23-24, whs) "If you come to the altar and there remember that thy brother has ought against thee, leave there thy gift at the altar, go and be reconciled unto thy brother and then come and offer thy gift." He says you straighten it out with your brother before you come to God and offer a sacrifice.

You remember in 1 Peter the 3rd chapter Peter told that those that were husbands to "dwell with their wives according to honor giving honor to the wife as unto the weaker vessel that your prayer be not hindered." Now that relationship that is estranged between the husband and wife affects your relationship with God. Now the relationship we have with one another is based upon our relationship with God and never let us forget that.

Scope Of Fellowship

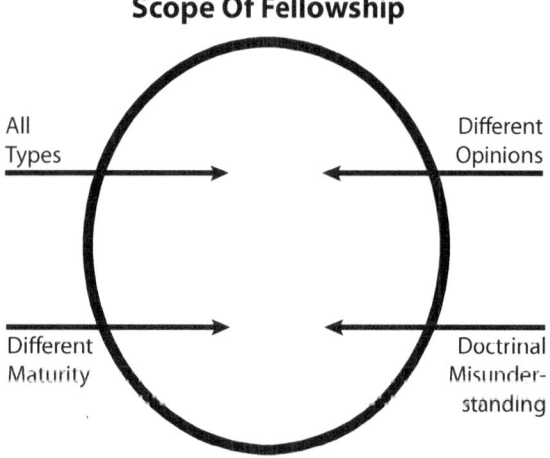

(Chart #2a) Briefly, I want to look at some of the scope of fellowship. There are different kinds of people that needs to be included in the fellowship. All types of individuals, difference of opinion, different stages of maturity, and even doctrinal misunderstanding. Now all types of people, Jew and Gentile, bond and free, male and female, as shown in 1 Corinthians 12:13 and Galatians 3:28. That includes all kinds of individuals. It means those with warts, and those whose feet stink, and those who have different interests, and different kinds of backgrounds than we have. We are brethren. "We be brethren." It means that we have all kinds of an opinion … you know the passages in… in first…the passages concerning this in Romans the 14th chapter, that we're to receive one another, even with the differences of opinion.

Now there are a lot of problems that come. You say, "Well, one man's opinion's another man's faith." I'll tell you, if you just go to the common sense way…the preacher told me one time when I was a boy. He held his hand out and said, "What's in my hand?" They guessed what was in his hand and he said "Well I'm going to tell you what's in my hand." He told him what was in his hand, and if you believed the man it was a matter of faith. And then he showed them what was in his hand and that's a matter of fact. We've heard the illustration. I want to tell you that that which God has revealed is not a matter of opinion. But that which God has not revealed, then that is in the realm of opinion.

We're to accept one another as in Romans 15:7 as Christ has accepted us, that is with all of our weaknesses and warts and with all of our inadequacies and all of the things that we do that are wrong. God has accepted us and we need to accept one another as brethren. There are different stages of maturity. 1 Corinthinas the 3rd chapter and Hebrews the 5th chapter speaks of the childhood, and the babyhood, and the maturity of the church. We have bawl babies in the church that are immature, we have adolescents that are always in a rebellion stage, and we have those that are matured and have gone to seed. We have them all in the church and they are to be included in the fellowship at their stage of maturity.

We'll…and then doctrinal misunderstanding; I want to stay there a moment. Open your Bibles if you will to 1 Timothy 1. There he is talking about some brethren in the church they're to not…they're to be cast unto Satan, technical terms for withdrawing of fellowship in verse 20. "Among those are Hymenaeus and Alexander whom I am deliver over to Satan so that they may be taught not to blaspheme." Now hold your finger there and go to 2 Timothy 2 and verse 16, "But avoid worldly and empty chatter for it will lead to further ungodliness and their talk will spread like gangrene, among them are Hymenaeus and Philetus, men who have gone astray from the truth saying that the resurrection has already taken place and thus have upset the faith of some."

Now here is the problem. Here at Ephesus, he's saying those who believe that the resurrection has passed already they are to be cast unto Satan. Over in 1 Corinthians 15 and verse 12, he speaks of how that those at Corinth that question the resurrection, he says, "How say some of you that there is no resurrection of the dead." And he calls them saints and he calls them the church of God in 1 Corinthians the 1st chapter. What's the difference? Those over here at Corinth, those were individual that questioned the resurrection and they needed to be taught. And the longest chapter in 1 Corinthians is the 15th chapter…individuals that needed to be taught about the resurrection. But over here at Ephesus individuals had gone astray. And they used vain speech and they were leading people astray, destroying the faith of some, and individuals that were forming a party, and individuals that were forcing a false doctrine to that party. Those individuals had to be cut off.

There is doctrinal misunderstanding that needs to be included in the fellowship, just as in 1 Corinthians 15. Now we'll look at those doctrinal differences that will cause a schism, and doctrinal differences that will cause individuals to teach and to practice that which is not a demand that you accept that which is unscriptural, then those are reasons for fellowship.

Limits Of Fellowship

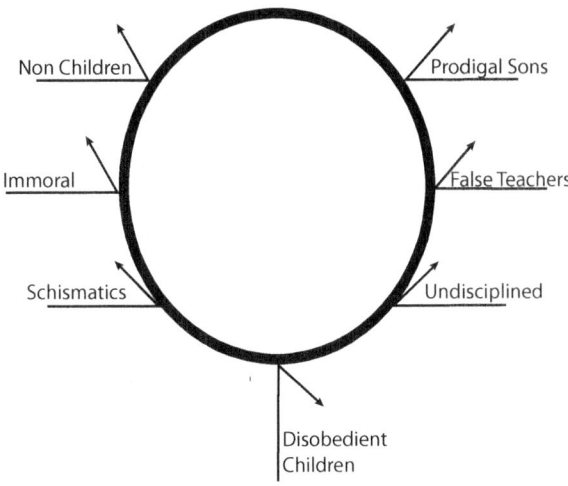

(Chart 2b) On down into the limits of fellowship, there are those that are non-children. Those that have not been born of God, that shouldn't really be in the chart, but some individuals think that you just open your arms of fellowship to everybody. Those that are not children of God cannot be included in the fellowship.

Those that are prodigal sons in 1 John 2 and verse 19, he says, "that they went out from among us that it might be manifest that they were not of us. Had they been of us they," no doubt, "would have continued with us." Individuals that have quit the church, by definition, they're not in the fellowship. You can't withdraw from them because there's no fellowship there to withdraw.

Those that are immoral, 1 Corinthians the 5th chapter, it speaks of the immoral brother, and he gives them about six different kinds of language. He says not to eat with such a one, deliver one… such a one to Satan, and casting out from among you, all that kind of terminology. Those that are immoral cannot be included in the fellowship.

Those that are false teachers in 2 John 9, those that are schismatics.…and open your Bibles if you will to Romans the 15th chapter. Those that cause division in the body of Christ, they…if there's a hotter place in Hell, it'll be for them, I do believe. In Romans 16:17 he says, "I urge you brethren, keep your eyes on those that are causing dissentions and hindrances contrary to the teachings that you have learned and turn away from them." There is… those individuals that cause division are not to be allowed to spread their party in the church. And a lot would be solved if we could just do that, those that are division makers that they could be marked, they could keep your eyes on them.

One of the powerful passages in 1Corinthians the 3rd chapter and verse 16 is talking about those that have parties in the church (referencing 1 Cor. 1:12, whs), "I am of Paul and I am of Cephas, and I am of Christ." In verse 16 he calls the church "the temple of the Holy Spirit." "Ye are the temple of the Holy Spirit. And the Spirit of God dwells within you. If any man destroy the temple of God, him shall God destroy. And the temple of God is holy, and such are you." He's saying the church is holy, and woe be unto that person that would seek to cause division in the body of Christ. Schismatics, we must not include in the fellowship those that cause division.

Those that are undisciplined, those that refuse to receive the admonition of the brethren when the church… "And take one or two with you and then at the mouth of two or three witnesses every word may be established," and so forth. "And tell it to the church and let him be unto thee as a heathen and as a publican" (Matt. 18).

Disobedient children, those who do not follow the tradition that had been delivered by the apostle. In 2 Thessalonians 3:6 the word that is translated "tradition" is PARADOSIS. It means that which has been handed down. "I have received," "I've delivered," are the technical words that are used for it in the New Testament by the apostle Paul. It doesn't have a bad or a good meaning at all. It's one of those neutral words. You can have the traditions of men, which are bad. You can have the traditions that come from the apostles that … he says, "I have received of the Lord that which also I have delivered unto you" in 1Corinthians 11 concerning the Lord's supper. In 1 Corinthians the 15th chapter he speaks of the gospel that he'd received, that he'd delivered. That kind of tradition cannot be altered. Those individuals that do not teach the traditions, these are the ones that are not to be included into the fellowship.

What's my time?

Roy Lanier - Moderator: You have 12 minutes.

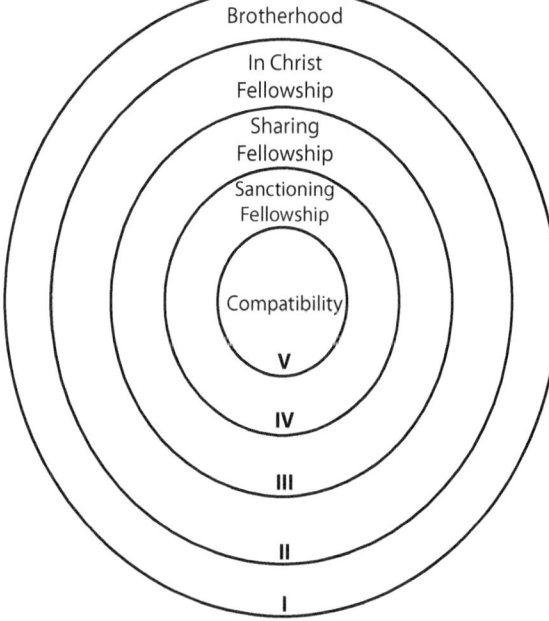

Jimmy Jividen - Main Speaker: OK. (Chart #3) I zipped through that to get to this (Laughter, whs), the basis. This is not in the book, this chart; there's a division in the book and I have chosen to deal with this right now because I believe that this is the forum to do it. I believe, and I have called this, levels of fellowship, degrees of fellowship. I want you to think with me and critique this, because I'm always learning. I hope I come to a better knowledge of the truth though by learning. And this is something that

I think may be a catalyst by which we can strengthen our fellowship. I do know that as any illustration, they break down when it's taken to the ultimate extreme, and I do not want this illustration to be taken out of its context. It is only to illustrate that there are different degrees, or levels, or dimensions, of fellowship in the body of Christ.

There is in this external circle, there is the "Brotherhood." Everyone that is born of God is a brother; that means an individual that has been baptized by an apostate preacher; that means an individual that is an old moral reprobate that was at one time baptized into Christ. That includes such individuals as "Diotrephes who loved to have preeminence among the brethren" in 3 John 9, and (referencing 2 Tim. 4:10, whs) "Demas who has forsaken me having forsaken this present world." It includes all of those individuals who are children of God but have apostatized. It includes those … all within this circle are brothers. We cannot unbrother anybody. All of God's children come with the bargain when we become a child of God.

Now that does not mean that all brothers and sisters will be saved. Nor does it mean that all brothers and sisters are in fellowship. It only means that when we talk about fellowship it is not to be totally equated with brotherhood. There are erring brothers. There are prodigal sons and daughters. They're individuals who have been cut off from the fellowship of the church. These are brothers and sisters in the Lord but they are not in fellowship. That is the external line. Anyone that has been begotten by God, has been washed in the blood of Jesus Christ, and has received the indwelling of the Holy Spirit of God, by definition he is a brother in Jesus Christ.

Line number two, there is another degree of fellowship called the "In Christ Fellowship." This term was first used, began to be used by Paul, and it speaks of a different dimension of fellowship other than just a business relationship, or a social relationship, or a domestic relationship. It speaks of that relationship which is in the sphere of grace. Where there is the blood of Christ constantly causing us to be cleansed. In 1 John 1 verse 7 and following, "If we walk in the light as He is in the light, then we have fellowship one with another and the blood of Jesus Christ, His son cleanses us from all sin." That "In Christ Fellowship" is precious. And it is so precious that we will do anything in order that we can reach out and help a brother because he is in Christ. In 1947, when the tornado destroyed Woodward, Oklahoma and left about 110 people dead in its wake, that I was just a boy. And it was just the next day that churches from all over began to send help, of economic help, and to come and help. Not because they knew us in the flesh but because we were brethren, because there was a tie that bound us closer than any other, any kind of physical tie in the world. Because the Spirit that dwells in me dwelt in them, and that the relationship was because we called the same Father, ABBA Father.

There is an "In Christ Fellowship" that is very precious. 1 Timothy the 6th chapter and verse 2 it says that slaves ought to be really obedient to their believing masters because they are brethren. And Abraham spoke to Lot "We be brethren." Galatians 6:10, "We ought to do good unto all men and especially unto those that are of the household of faith." There is an "In Christ Fellowship" that is known by everybody that has ever been born of God or in fellowship with Jesus Christ, whether or not we have seen them in the flesh. I have fellowship with brethren in Africa, and in Eastern Europe, and South America, and around the world that I'll never see their face in this world at all, but they are my brethren. I can tell you story after story of meeting a brother in some foreign land, or someone that we did not know who was a brother in Christ. And once we find out they're a brother or sister in Christ, our hearts open up, our spirits open up, because we are kin in the Lord.

Then there is another kind of…within this "In Christ Fellowship" there is another dimension, and that is a "Sharing Fellowship." In Philippians the 4th chapter and verse 15 that's been quoted several times here, Paul speaks of how that no church had fellowship with me in this matter of giving and receiving save you only, in Philippians the 4th chapter. Now tell me Paul, what about this kind of fellowship that you have with the church at Philippi? Don't you have fellowship with the church at Corinth, the church at Ephesus, and the church at Thessalonica? Oh yes, I'm in fellowship with them. Well what do you mean that no church had fellowship with me in this matter of giving and receiving only you, save you only? When we have a sharing together, it deepens and gives a different dimension of our fellowship.

When we share together…I'm hoping that we have yet deepened our fellowship, because we have shared together in our worship, that we have shared together in our study, we have shared together in exposing ourselves, who we really are in this fellowship that we have had together this week. I pray to God…there is a different dimension once we have shared with one another in the faith. This different dimension is because we do share. I'm sure that there are lots of missionaries that are scattered around the world, but those missionaries that you are most concerned about are those that you have a part in helping. You look…post on the bulletin board a letter from that missionary. And people are just thrilled to know what's going on out there with this brother because you have shared with him. He comes back and shares with you his heart and his experiences and that deepens the fellowship.

But there is another dimension of fellowship, and that is the "Sanctioning Fellowship." Open your Bibles if you will to Galatians the 2nd chapter and verse 9. And this…I have learned so much in researching on fellowship that I didn't know before. And I hope and pray that we can become a little more serious about the dimension and the nature of fellowship in the Lord, instead of letting party spirit, instead of letting suspicion and misrepresentations rule the day. Galatians 2:9 is talking, of course, about Paul and Barnabas coming there to Jerusalem. And he says and . . . those that were individuals in the church there and perceiving the grace of God that had been given to me, Paul . . . or "James, Cephas, and John, who're reputed to be pillars gave to me and Barnabas the right hand of fellowship that we might go to the gentiles and they unto the circumcision."

You know the context of that don't you? You know that there was the right hand of fellowship. Now Paul tell me, "Did you not have fellowship with the church at Jerusalem?" Surely you did. In Acts the 9th chapter, he says that he went in and out among them. He was preaching there in the church at Jerusalem. But still there was given unto them and Barnabas the right hand of fellowship. "Barnabas didn't you have fellowship with the church at Jerusalem?" "Sure I did. It was the church at Jerusalem that sent me up to Antioch." "Well tell me what did they give you that you didn't have?" "It was the right hand of fellowship."

I don't know the difference between the right hand and the left hand, the right foot and the left foot of fellowship. You can get a lot of theories about that. It could be like shaking hands. You use your right hand to shake hands because that's your sword hand, and if your shaking hands with someone they can't stab you in the back because they don't have the hand to do it with, you know. That might be it, I don't know. It could probably relate to the laying on of the hands, you know. In Acts the 13th chapter it spoke of how Paul and Barnabas received the laying on of the hands. And when they were sent out he gave them sanction. Timothy received the laying on of the hands of the presbytery and was warned in the 5th chapter to lay hands suddenly upon no man. He's saying you be careful in giving individuals sanction. There is a "Sanctioning Fellowship" that is involved.

Now individuals… you might have this kind of fellowship, an "In Christ Fellowship," a sharing, but you can't give him a "Sanctioning Fellowship." Often times I get letters of individuals that are wanting to know about a preacher or a congregation. And they'll ask me to give me as a reference. I tell exactly what I know about them right there. "Hey, I know his character, he has a good character. I know his family; he's got a good family. I don't know too much about his preaching, I've never heard him preach, you'll have to judge that for yourself." You tell him exactly. I can sanction what I know. He said, "Be careful what you sanction." But you are to give sanction and credibility.

So this…and then this last one, I'm not going to even say much about because that is a "Compatibility Fellowship." That really shouldn't be in here because it doesn't have a spiritual dimension; it just means that you're compatible. Now there are a lot of people that I have an "In Christ Fellowship," a "Sharing Fellowship," and a "Sanctioning Fellowship," that I don't have a very good "Compatibility Fellowship" with. But we get together and we fuss and fight like cats and dogs. And if we… it just gives us all a little tension because we have different personalities. I'm sure it's because he's so hard to get along with, not me (Laughter). But you know there is a compatibility. Paul had that with Timothy, and Paul lost that with Barnabas in Acts the 15th chapter. And there is that "Compatibility Fellowship."

In closing I just want to say, "We be brethren," because of a common divine relationship. I want to say we are in Christ. Some of us have a "Sharing Fellowship" in some things and cannot have a "Sharing Fellowship" in other things because of conscience. No problem with a person being included in the fellowship that has a doctrinal misunderstanding, until that doctrinal misunderstanding is taught to form a party, or is forced to include some kind of a practice or is some kind of a faith destroying doctrine. I can open my arms and receive many as long as it is just a doctrinal misunderstanding to be taught.

Some of us cannot give a "Sanctioning Fellowship" to a person, though we can have a "Sharing Fellowship." We must recognize that those of us that are here today cannot establish fellowship by some kind of an ecclesiastical decision, or an arbitrary act. But WE CAN CEASE TO BE A PARTY and accept one another as Christ has accepted us, on an individual and a congregational plane. But we cannot give some kind of an ecclesiastical decision, but we can accept one another on certain levels of fellowship. WE CAN GROW in fellowship and hold up the ideal of a divine church and an inspired authoritative scripture. There'll always be some who bind and loose more than God, like Peter at Antioch, or like those at Corinth. But we MUST NOT, we CANNOT surrender the ideal. I STILL DREAM THE IMPOSSIBLE DREAM, AND REACH FOR THE UNREACHABLE STAR, AND WILL CONTINE SO THAT FELLOWSHIP IN ALL OF ITS GLORY MAY ONE DAY BE REALIZED IN JESUS CHRIST IN GLORY.

Fellowship Among Differences
Day 3 Speech 2 Rebuttal
John Clark

Introduction: *Clark, John. He was reared in Orlando, FL but born in Malden, Massachusetts. He has preached for 36 years in Missouri, Michigan, Ohio, Alabama, Kentucky, Florida and Texas. He has specialized in studies on evolution and the family and is a frequent speaker on both subjects. He taught at Florida College (1976-1980), and recently moved to Kansas City.*

I'm delighted to be here this afternoon. That's not the total truth about it, but I'm deeply stirred as I look over this audience. Consider what I've heard during the time that we've been together. And as they talked about having a meeting of young preachers, I thought about the young preacher that I used to be, when I first began preaching. Full of dreams and ideals and hopes, thinking it was real simple that people wanted to hear the word of God and I want to preach it. That's going to be real easy. And I found out it wasn't easy.

But I came on the scene in preaching when these issues that we've been talking about during this period of time were heating up. And sometime in my revelry, I wonder what the young preacher that I was would think of the older preacher that I have become. Am I a bitter or better man? What have the years done to me? Have I lost my idealism, my hopes, my dreams? The idea that I thought then that through my efforts and with my wonderful companion Ruth, that we could help people go to Heaven.

And one thing I've had to tell my children since then, and I've been through the fire. I've seen a lot of things, and all of us have a lot of stories to tell. But between each line of pain and glory, has been this aspiration. I've tried to say it to my children. I don't care what other people do, but this family is committed as Joshua was. "As for me and my house, we want to serve the Lord." I don't want to be like the movie I saw one time of a preacher, a Methodist preacher I think it was, and his little 8 year old boy said, "Daddy, suppose I don't want to go to Heaven." He said,

"Son you're going whether you want to or not, so get used to the idea." (Laughter whs)

But I can tell my story and all of us can, of the pain that's taken place. But I don't know about all this with this week, where it's going. And I don't think it's the end of the beginning or the beginning of the end, but maybe it's the beginning of the beginning. And I can hope and pray, and make some effort. And I'm delighted to be here with Jimmy Jividen. One of the great benefits of this is to know this man, to meet this man. I've read after this man. He is a man committed to a study of the word of God. He loves the scriptures. He makes a real effort to go to the word of God. And I love and admire that. And God forbid that I should misrepresent him or anybody else here. That's not what I'm here for. But I'm here to firmly speak my heart and my conviction about things, and to show you why I think the fellowship has been broken, and what might be done by us in order to restore it someway.

1. <u>Authority</u> - Mt. 28:18-20; Eph. 1:18-23
2. <u>Reality</u> - Luke 12:54-57
3. <u>Study</u> - 2 Tim. 2:15; 2 Pet. 3:15-16
4. <u>Humility</u> - Mt. 5:3; Phil. 2:1-4

(Chart #1) I want to quickly look at some things here with you. And I just want to get these lightly. The need for authority in the study of fellowship is that we serve a king the world did not crown, and we're a part of the kingdom that'll never be destroyed. And I believe like I did at the beginning, that He's been raised up to sit in heavenly places and He is with God the Father. He's far above all principality and power and might and dominion. And if I'm not committed to His will, to do His will, then it's just fun and games. It's a serious business and so the whole question of "What did He speak to us?" is mighty important. I want a word from Christ. I want to submit to His authority.

And the reality, Jesus chided His own generation for saying they could look at the weather, look at the sky and they could determine if a storm was coming. And then he said, "Why don't you discern the sign of the times?" Reality means we have got to see how bad it is. We've got to recognize what's going on. And then with reality in our mind, then we make an effort to try to do something about this, the best that we possibly can.

And study, commit ourselves to study. Folks, I used to, as a young preacher, stay up all night and study. I can't any more. And the older I get, I realize that when I really know what I ought to study, I don't have quite the energy I used to have when I was going in all kinds of different directions.

And humility, the door that enters the kingdom is marked with humility. "Blessed are the poor in spirit for theirs is the kingdom of God." And it must continue there as Paul says in Philippians 2 for "every man to think of his brother above himself. Not looking only on our own things, but the things of others."

    5. <u>Energy</u> - John 3:17; Jas. 1:22-25
    6. <u>Vulnerability</u> - Acts 20:19; Eph. 4:32
    7. <u>Agony</u> - 2 Tim. 1:12; Col. 2:1; Eph. 4:30-31

"Spend And Be Spent"
2 Cor. 12:15

(Chart #2) And energy and I don't have as much as I had. But I'll tell you this, as the days dwindle down to a precious few, I want my efforts to be made in behalf of something that's going to outlive me and has eternal implications. So I'm not interested in party spirits. I'm not interested in pushing someone back. I'll tell you this, this knotty problem of fellowship, and it is a knotty problem, I don't want to be on one end pulling and another bother on the other end pulling, and pulling it tighter. I want to do something to loosen it and make it possible for us to communicate and to deal with one another as we really ought to. There's a story of a faithful Phrygian king who tied the Gordian Knot, and it was presented to Alexander the Great. What he was going to do, could he untie it? So he looked at, he pulled out his sword and cut it. And a lot of solutions that people are pretending to give us to the problem of fellowship, they're not untying anything. They're not unraveling this knotty problem, they're just simply cutting it, and they're not solutions at all.

Vulnerability, people have got to see in my eyes, not in some pretense, but they've got to see in my eyes, tears as they saw in the eyes of Paul, when he begged those brethren to do what was right. People have got, hopefully, to feel in their heart my pain, and I have to feel yours in mine and understand that I am vulnerable. And I learned one thing in living, that if you love people you run the risk they could hurt you. And if you think that I'm unwilling to go any distance or to work any length of time, if you think I'm unwilling to do that to resolve this, you're mistaking me, you're misreading me.

Vulnerability, we've got to feel the pain and the agony. Paul says, "For this cause I suffer many things, nevertheless I am not ashamed for I know whom I have believed and am persuaded that He is able to keep that which I have commit unto Him against that day." I know whom I believe. And I'm convinced brethren, that there are people… I've heard it in this room, there are people who are hurting because we cannot be together, as perhaps people think we used to be. But we cannot sacrifice our commitment to Jesus Christ for any kind of a relationship with human beings. Now spend and be spent, that's my goal.

(Chart #3) So is this a Humpty Dumpty situation we're in? Is this what this whole problem among our brethren is? "Humpty Dumpty sat on a wall. Humpty Dumpty had a great fall. And all the king's horses and all the king's men couldn't put Humpty Dumpty together again." Is that

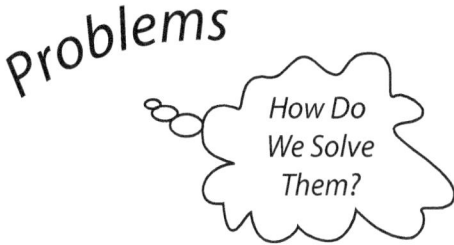

1. Understand How Bad It Is
2. Be Fair -- Even Handed
3. Optimism -- Believe That A
Solution Is Possible

what it is? Is that our situation, it's impossible, this impossible dream? Well I'll go on dreaming and daring, but I do it through the eyes of realism. But realism has helped me, or my experience has helped me, to understand this. You learn something when you're older that you didn't have when you were younger. And that is as Paul said it in Romans chapter 5, that he "gloried in tribulation for tribulation worketh patience, and patience works proven character, and character hope, and hope makes not ashamed."

I know that you cannot accomplish in a few days, what it may take many many years to accomplish. But I have hope; I think hope born of experience. As Kipling said, "If you can meet with triumph and disaster and treat these two imposters just the same, our triumphs are never as great as we think they are, and when we have these triumphs sometime we lose our head. And our defeats are never as bad as we think they are, and then we lose our heart." Keeping our heads and our hearts, I'm trying to commit myself to talking today about these problems, and then what we can do about them.

(Chart #4) And I just have to speak bluntly to you and plainly. That this is the kind of thing that, these three points I want to make is what I make when I'm talking… counseling a couple who are having marriage problems. And I have wept over this, and I have agonized over that, and three things I tell them right up front. I've got to know how bad it is. I have to know what really is going on, how bad it is. Secondly, I have to be fair; I have to be

evenhanded. And thirdly, I need optimism born of reality, not just pie in the sky by and by. But knowing how bad it is to have an optimism that says, "I believe that a solution is possible."

And I want to tell you how bad I think it is. (Chart #5)

> Thus, it is not what the church buys with the money, or what the church does, so much as why is the church doing this work or spending this money. If the church is doing the work or spending the money with the clear goal of saving souls, then it is justified.
> Whenever the motive comes to be to satisfy pride, to have the biggest and best church building in town, or to have the finest Christian Country Club anywhere ....
> And the congregation has lost sight of saving souls ... then what is taking place is not the work of the Lord.

The End Justifies The Means

This is not to make a personal attack. God forbid that I should be seen in that light. But this article that appeared in November of 1988 is one of the things that, I tell you my brethren, that troubles me deeply. By all means save some. When I read a statement like this "Thus it's not what the church buys with the money or what work the church does, so much as why is the church is doing this work or spending this money. If the church is doing the work or spending the money with the clear goal of saving souls, then it is justified." Now if that's not "the end justifies the means," please help me. I'm willing to be persuaded. I'm willing to be changed. But what that sounds like to me is that principle of that "the ends justifies the means."

And that gets to the focus, the issue here of what we're going to talk about when we talk about recreation. We're talking about the dreams of reaching the whole world with the gospel. What's it all about? The truth of the matter is that experience will teach you that the means form and shape the end. And you may start off with this idea, but when you get to that point, the means that you have used to accomplish it have shaped the end and made it into something entirely different.

When I left the Baptist Church, I did so because believing the Bible and believing in Christ and loving the scriptures. I found by serious study of the scripture that I could no longer, after a period of time, go on convincing myself that I loved Christ, that I wanted to do His will, for I had not done His will. And despite the fact that it was painful and difficult within the family and other things, I had to be true to a heart that says I want to do what's right. And having found out what's right, I will do what's right. That's why these things are so serious.

Now I've got a set of charts, and I got laughed at the last time because I went through these charts so fast. (Flashing Chart #6, #7, momentarily whs) And I'm just going to tell you, I got charts, and I got charts (Laughter), and I got charts, and oh boy this is kind of silly because

KOINONIA
- Acts 2:42 - Rom. 15:26 - "Contribution"
- 1 Cor. 1:9; 1 Cor. 10:16 (2) - "Communion"
- 2 Cor. 6:14; 2 Cor. 8:4; 9:13 - "Distribute"
- Gal. 2:9; Eph. 3:9; 2 Cor. 13:14; Phil. 1:5;
  2:10; 3:10; Phile. 6; Heb. 13:16 - "Communicate"
                                 1 Jn. 3:1-3, 6-7

KOINONOS
- Mt. 23:30; Lk. 5:10; 1 Cor. 10:17, 20; 2 Cor. 1:7; 8:23; Phile. 17; Heb. 10:33; 1 Pet. 5:1; "Partner," "Sharer," "Partaker"

KOINONIKOS
- 1 Tim. 6:18 - "Communicate"

SUNKOINONIKOS
- Eph. 5:11; Phil. 4:14 "Fellowship with," "Communicate with"

SUNKOINONOS
- Rom. 11:17; 1 Cor.

METOCHE
- 2 Cor. 6:14 - "Communicate"

METOCHOS
- Lk. 5:7; Heb. 1:9; 3:1, 14; 6:4; 12:8 "Partners," "Fellow," "Partakers"

METECHO
- 1 Cor. 9:10, 12; 10:12, 21, 30; Heb. 2:14; 5:13; 7:13 "Partake," "Take Part," "Pertaineth To"

what I wanted to get to was this one. (Chart #8) But what that illustrates is, all of us could take time and go to a concordance and we could run down all of the references and study this word fellowship. It's a rich and wonderful word. And I do not want it diluted, robbed of its glory, and turned into something that is vastly different from what inheres in the word.

If I read my Bible right, this word that as Brother Jividen has helped…he's done a wonderful study on the subject of fellowship. And I've appreciated it. And a brother that I differ with, and he has on the cover this, "KOINONIA a place of tough and tender love." I like that, Jimmy. Because love has got to be tough enough to say and do the thing that must be said and done. We don't love people unless we love them enough to correct them. And when you become, you know, too kind to correct on the one hand, or you become too convinced to be compassionate on the other hand, there's no hope for us being able to resolve problems. The church is a place; the fellowship is a place of tough and tender love. And there are times, as it says in Ecclesiastes, "A time to embrace and a time to refrain from embracing." There's a time when I must reach out to my brother and hold him and say, "I'm here for you and you can count on me." But there are some times when I have to push you back from me and say, at arm's length, "I cannot agree with what you're doing. I do not believe it is right, and as my… as your friend I want to start standing in harm's way." It has to be both tough and tender.

And Brother Jividen has done wonderfully in this book, discussing the matter of discipline. Discipline is that very thing of being tough enough to insist that if a person will not do right by the direction of their own conscience instructed by the word of God, then the people of God must act. As 1 Corinthians 11 says, "Lest we be judged with the world." If I will not correct myself, then I force the people of God to act upon it. And then there is some kind of hope that I won't be judged with the world. That's why these issues are so strong and so volatile.

KIONONEO   Verb Form

- Rom. 12:13; 15:27
- Gal. 6:6; Phil. 4:15
- 1 Tim. 5:22; Heb. 2:14; 1 Pet. 4:13; 2 Jn. 11

> "Share, Have A Share; Give
> Or
> Contribute a Share"
> Arndt & Gingrich

In Each Case The Thing Shared Is Specified And Has Spiritual Implications

(Chart #9) And what I want to point out here is the word "fellowship" is a rich term. To share, to have a share, to give or contribute a share. In each case, the thing shared is specified and has spiritual implications. I hear too much talk, in my judgment, correct me if I'm wrong, instruct me so that I may know better, but the term "fellowship" has been given such application to things that are not of a spiritual nature. And it's the camel's nose in the tent. We start off by talking about, "well now people could share a room… share a meal and that could be fellowship." And then the next thing you've got is, people being then involved in the church having on its calendar, directing these certain things. And then next we have this proliferation of gymnasiums and all that. I'm not charging people with believing in the end result of that.

But I am making the charge that if we cannot see that

when we allow the camel's nose in the tent, and then later on during the night the camel climbs into the tent, and we wake up in the morning and say, "There's not much room here." And he says, "If you don't like it you can get out." (Laughter, whs) Who's at fault? Is there not a problem here? We're talking about how this thing can develop to the point that the term "fellowship" loses the connotation in the Bible of being IN CHRIST, because of the BLOOD OF CHRIST, because of the LOVE OF GOD for us, because of something that is deep and of such dimension that it cannot be diluted by trivializing it in the way in which I see it being done.

Uses — Study Reveals

> The Word Is Not Used To Describe Social or Secular Activity

In Every Instance The Word Has Spiritual Connotation

Fellowship of Jesus

1. *Basis*
   is Being in Fellowship
   with God - 1 Jn 1:7

2. *Means* - The Message
   Declared By Apostles - 1 Jn. 1:1-4; 4:6

3. *Test* - "Hearing us" - The Apostles
   Christ's Witnesses - 1 Jn. 4:6

(Chart #10) The uses of the word do not describe social or secular activity. In every instance, the word has spiritual connotations. (Chart #11) I quickly make this argument that the basis of this fellowship in Jesus is being in fellowship with God, as our brother has said. Excellent material arguing with that Jimmy, and I appreciate it. And that's what more of us may . . . must do. In fact, I've seen during this week and the other one that, "John, you just assume well the practical help to many people is not going to be there in talking about these things." We've got to go back, study them, and talk about them, and teach them. And we got ourselves…look at ourselves and see if we're really on the beam. Being in fellowship with God is the basis of fellowship.

The means of this is the message declared by the apostles. What John says is, "That which we've seen, which we've heard, we've handled the word of life." And then he says "We declared unto you that your fellowship may be with us." And then he says in 1 John chapter 4 and verse 6, "We are of God, he that heareth God, heareth us, he that heareth not God, heareth not us. Hereby know we the spirit of truth and the spirit of error." The only way that I can have this fellowship is to be able to receive the message and test my life, my behavior by the message, hearing the apostles.

(Chart #12) And this is this, which we've seen. God sent Christ into the world for which we are thankful. And He instructed the apostles. And then promised them the Holy Spirit, and He said, "I have yet many things to say unto you that you cannot bear now. But howbeit when He the Spirit of truth is come He will guide you into all

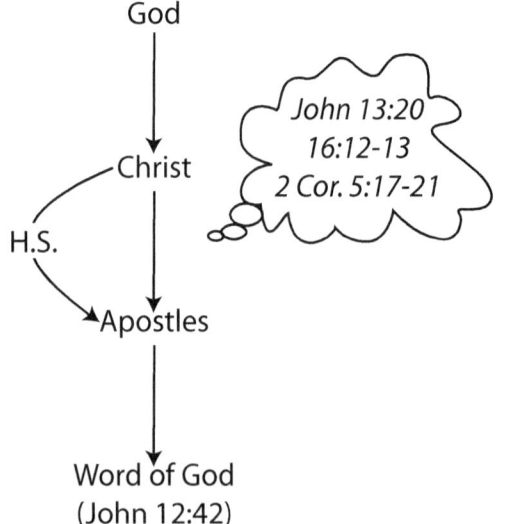

truth." And we believe, as a result of that, that the word of God came. And we have that, and we're thankful to God for that. And Jesus says, "He that rejecteth me and receiveth not my words hath one that judgeth him." He told us that the only way you could receive His word, was to be willing to receive those that He sent, John 13:20. "That you receive whomsoever ye send, you receive me. He that receiveth Me, receiveth Him that sent Me."

What we're talking about here, is this fellowship can only be maintained by continuing to listen to the message that has been given, IF YOU PLEASE, to the apostles by Jesus Christ and the Holy Spirit. (Chart #13) And that's why I absolutely, completely agree with the charts that Jimmy has put in his book. And this is the point about

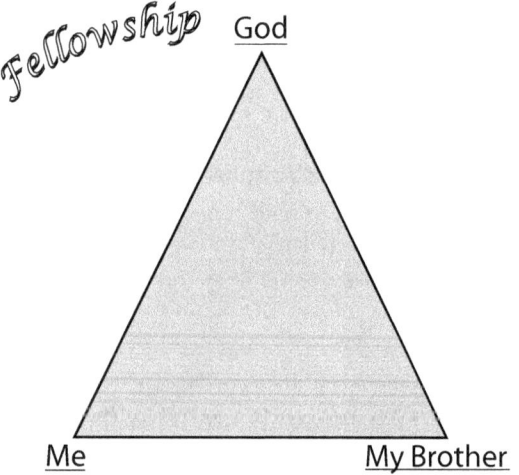

"the fellowship that I have with my brother is based upon my fellowship with God." And I agree with him that no matter what the warts are, all the difficulties are, this is my brother. And I must understand that, and we're in the same family.

(Chart #14) Now, I'll also agree that it can be broken. It can be broken by my brother. "Whosoever goeth onward and abideth not in the doctrine of Christ hath not God." And so the point that we must understand is, I may love a person and I just…it breaks my heart. But I cannot afford to set aside the fellowship that I want to maintain with God because I want to have a relationship with this my brother. And we're in agreement upon that.

(Chart #15) And then with regard to my behavior, and

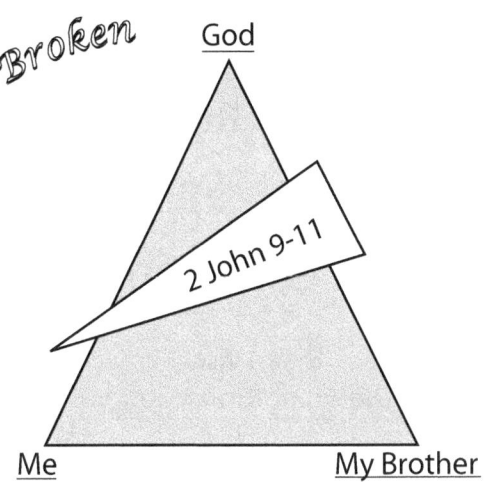

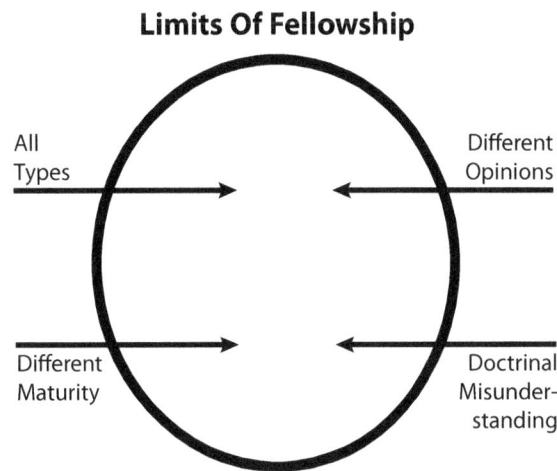

Jimmy talked about that and I don't want to repeat that. I just want to go through this very rapidly. (Chart #16)

verted and they're a problem (Laughter). You see, someone said, "If you find a perfect church don't become a member of it. Why? Because you'll ruin it" (Laughter). So the scope of the fellowship is we understand that there are doctrinal misunderstandings, there are different opinions.

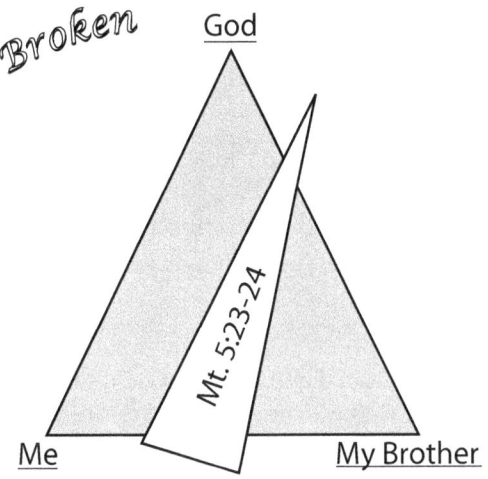

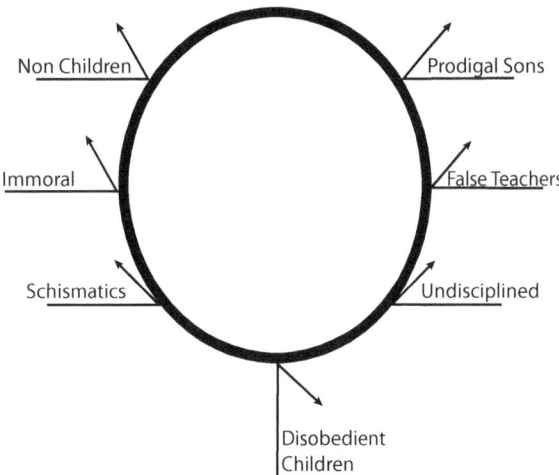

I want to agree with him absolutely that with regard to the scope, all types are in the church. Different opinions are in the church, different maturity, doctrinal misunderstanding. How many preachers have gone off someplace, they've been tired of wrangling and fussing and things. They go off to some place out here and they say, "I'm going to start this church, and this church is going to be exactly…I'm going to make that…I'm not going to have any problems in that congregation. I want to just teach a little bit and never have these problems" (Laughter). And then what happens is, what happens someone else is con-

(Chart #17) We also agree, and this is what I appreciate about Brother Jividen. He just comes right up to the lick log and points out you can't have people that never have obeyed the gospel. You can't tolerate the immoral, the schismatic. And that doesn't mean you don't do everything you can to correct the situation. The prodigal sons, the false teachers, the undisciplined, and the disobedient children, there are limitations to fellowship. And he insists, in the end of this book, that we must work harder as a local congregation on this matter of discipline. Now the truth of the matter is brethren, have you ever seen one of your children, I have 5 of them, I've had 5 of them. Well my wife has had 5 children but (Laughter), she reminds me of that (Laughter), but one of them isn't around the house for 2 or 3 or 4 weeks. And one of them, one of the parents says to the other, "You know I haven't seen Jason around the house for 2 or 3…" "You know I've noticed that. One of these days I'm going to have to go out and look that boy up." You don't hear that (Laughter). But in God's family does that not happen? And you can't be your brother's keeper until you're a brother's brother. I've learned that. Now we're all in agreement on that.

But I want to say this and when I read this, I can hear this man's voice, his son's voice, here tremendously impressive person to me and his daddy was too. (Chart #18) And I listen to Brother Foy Vinson, and I hear what he said,

Fellowship

"A Broken Fellowship With Brethren Is More Grievous Than, Perhaps, Any Of Us Can Appreciate ..."

not Foy but this is Brother Bryan Vinson. "A broken fellowship with brethren is more grievous than perhaps any of us can appreciate." Now isn't that what we're talking about, the sadness of what's going on?

(Chart #19) But then I listen to this too. "But a broken fellowship with Christ, the Father, and the Holy Spirit is eternally catastrophic." And that's why these issues have come up, because we really believe that the nature of this

"... But A Broken Fellowship With Christ, The Father, And The Holy Spirit Is Eternally Catastrophic."

Bryan Vison
The Arlington Meeting,
Pg. 332

whole thing involves a revelation of the mind of Christ. As Paul said, "We have the mind of Christ." And we believe that that's the result of what Paul wrote in verse 13. "Not in words which man's wisdom teacheth, but in words which the Holy Spirit teacheth. Comparing spiritual things with spiritual words." We believe we have a revelation of the mind of God. And what we believe about that is, that what people are teaching and practicing with a disrespect for that, is catastrophic. And that's why this issue is so important.

(Chart #20) And I agree with Brother Jividen. Now I may sound like an echo Jimmy, but you said it so well.

"It makes little difference what happened 3 generations ago. The emotional desire to want more men and women to join in the fellowship is irrelevant. The judgment and statement of recognized leaders is not what is important. What is fundamental is what sayeth the scriptures? It is the scriptures not man which determine the limitation of fellowship."

"It makes little difference what happened 3 generations ago. The emotional desire to want more men and women to join in the fellowship is irrelevant. The judgment and statement of recognized leaders is not what is important. What is fundamental is what sayeth the scriptures? It is the scriptures not man which determine the limitation of fellowship."

Barriers To Fellowship

Jimmy Jividen

"The attitudes that are barriers to fellowship must be overcome for the church to be heathly. Fear, ignorance, selfishness, and indifference must not rob Christians of their, if you please, family rights and responsibilities in fellowship. Their present happiness and their enternal security are involved."

"If an individual really wants to resolve some of the schisms in the Restoration Movement, then let him do so by doing some good scriptural exegesis and refute the errors that threaten the movement."

(Chart #21) "If an individual really wants to resolve some of the schisms in the Restoration Movement, then let him do so by doing some good scriptural exegesis and refute the errors that threaten the movement." And that's exactly what I would say to you. And I see our getting back and studying some of these questions that it has allowed us to see efforts being made. I think some very bad argument have been made in defense of positions. But one thing that I want to… I try to put things in a good light. The positive thing about that is that people feel somehow compelled to try to get scriptural authority for what they're doing. They may make bad arguments, but when you start doing that, you're admitting we've got to have authority.

(Chart #22) Now, "The attitudes that are barriers to fellowship must be overcome for the church to be healthy. Fear, ignorance, selfishness, and indifference must not rob Christians of their," if you please, "family rights and responsibilities in fellowship. Their present happiness and their eternal security are involved." Now what I want to do having said all of that, is to say that we're very much in agreement.

I want to focus in the last part of this, some questions which I think we need to really get in and study. I'm telling you this. When we look in the past sometimes we're

afraid when we look backward. Somebody says "those that forget the past are going to have to repeat it." And there's truth in this. That when you or I look back in the history of the Restoration Movement, we got some great lessons we can learn there. And I'll just guarantee you this, that if our past history has been painful, and for me personally it has, it's not nearly as painful as it's going to get. It's going to get worse. And if we do not make some effort to change the future, WE WILL HAVE TO ENDURE THE FUTURE. And that's why these things are important.

Question

I Want To Ask

Are We Dealing With This Matter Of Recreation?
- Work Of The Church?
  - John 18:36
- Sacred & Secular?
  - Ezek. 22:26

(Chart #23) That's why I'm saying the question in this last 5 minutes that I want to pose here, then we can ventilate this. And I appreciate Ron Halbrook, Charles Davis, and those who are working here and the men who are going to be working there, and they're going to be doing the lion's share of this matter. Are we dealing with this matter of recreation? I want to ask that brother. I don't believe that we can deal with it if we just say "Well now we can"…and some will suggest that well "we've taken that word recreation and we said it smells like coffee" and so on. And they look like that they're saying "Well there's a real problem about that and I don't agree with that." What we need, what we need among all of us, is a willingness to come up and see and say what is a real problem. If the word "fellowship" has been diluted in the way in which I believe it has, let us be willing to see that, as painful as it is to see that. And then to see what we're going to be able to do about it.

I'll tell you this. Our Lord said, "My kingdom is not of this world, if it were then My servants would fight that I should not be delivered hence." He was teaching us that the nature of the church determines the function of the church. If I believe the church is holy, and I listen to the language of Old Testament prophets about the failure of the priests to make a distinction between the sacred and the profane. I see today that people that are flirting around with recreational activities and all that idea, with the idea that it'll make the church grow. Let's tell you this; growth for the sake of growth is the philosophy of the cancer cell. Now when we're talking about the matter of growth, and the matter here of let's get involved in all these kind of things. I believe that a church engaging in recreation makes no more sense than having the Lord's Supper in a Boy Scout meeting. I'm not trying to be flippant. I'm not trying to recognize distinctions that are there. But I want to tell you, that's a major problem to me.

(Chart #24) And I want to ask you this, and this is on my heart brethren. When I accepted the truth and looked at the church and talked about the local congregation, and talked about getting back, restoring the primitive

Are We Saying We Believe In The Local Church Concept While Seeking To Activate The Church Universal?

church, and understanding the distinction to denominationalism, the concept of the independence and autonomy and equality of local churches. And then I began to read history, I saw that Alexander Campbell would say and a church could pass it along, they moved and you see a movement flourishing. And then lo and behold he begins to write and says, "How can we harness the energies of the tens of thousands of Israel without a greater cooperation? And how can we have a greater cooperation without a more thorough going church organization?" And moving that out from the autonomy and equality of the local churches they dreamed of greater days. And I'll tell you, the means to which they moved have destroyed the church in the process, in my judgment. I'm convinced of that. And what I'm asking "Are we saying that we believe in the local church concept while seeking to activate the church universal?"

I have not the time now, but I recommend that you read William Banowsky's discussion of *The Mirror of the Movement* in which he talked about how congregational cooperation developed among us as a people. And the brethren kept complaining that we just do not have… we've got a bunch of little churches, little churches they can't do anything. And the truth brethren, is that 89% of all of the churches of Christ no matter what they are, have less than 200 members. So someone today would say "Little groups of people." And what he began to talk about was that they looked around with obvious envy at the efficiency of denominational machinery and they started dreaming of better things. And what they attempted to do was to claim that they could still cling to the commitment of the local congregation, congregationalism, yet at the same time put all the churches together and have the results of denominational activities. And I call that, what they call today, cognitive dissidence. And that is trying to hold two contradictory ideas at the same time. And you cannot maintain your commitment to the concept of local bodies of Christians and that being the limit of this fellowship and activity, and at the same time dream and dare to build things that can put it all together. It is not compatible. We are deceiving ourselves into thinking that we believe a thing when what we're doing is moving in another direction.

Time has taken its toll. Conclusion. (First part of the sentence inaudible from tape whs) We are the children of God when we love God and keep His commandments. One of the ways that you can know I'm a child of God is that I love His children. And when we love God we're going to keep His commandments.

I thank you. May God bless US ALL in the CONTINUAL QUEST on this earth to serve God and to go to Heaven.

Fellowship Among Differences
Day 3 Speech 2 Panelist 1
Maxie Boren

Introduction: *Boren, Maxie. Fulltime meeting and lecture speaker, director of the Brown Trail School of Preaching, rioted (sic) for evangelistic efforts and presently lives out of his "pickup and fifth-wheel trailer." Has been preaching for 36 years at works including Hasting, NE, Marietta, OK, Nocona, Dallas, Snyder, Austin and Corsicana, TX.*

I'm going to dispense with all the niceties of bragging on Steve and Roy because four minutes doesn't allow much time. But perhaps I express the sentiments of a number of you when I feel like I've been somewhat on a roller coaster. One minute I'm just so hopeful and thrilled and encouraged and I think, "Well boy, there's no differences among us, I agree with what I've been hearing." And then maybe the next moment something is said or something I infer perhaps that causes me some concern. And I'm thrilled about this meeting. I am excited about the possibilities of good that can come from it. And certainly my fervent and ardent prayer is that there can be some sort unity and fellowship among us. I think that's the way it should be.

At the latest count there are some 5 billion people on planet earth. That's rather mind boggling within and of itself. And those who study population trends tell us that by the year 2040 there's going to be somewhere in the neighborhood of 10 billion people on the face of this earth. And at very best all the churches of Christ represent, as far as I've been able to determine, somewhere around 2 and a half million people. That's all the different persuasions among us from the extreme left to the extreme right and all those in between. And if you'll put your pen to that and do a little figuring, you'll find out that that's representative of somewhat less than 1/100th of 1% of the world's population.

It seems to me like that we have such a momentous task ahead of us, that we could put aside some of these petty grievances that separate us and find the basis of fellowship. We don't have to agree on every single thing. In fact, I am persuaded that there's no two of us, if we sat down

and discussed EVERY matter that relates to the cause of Christ, somewhere along the line we're going to disagree. And brethren if we allow these disagreements to cause us to splinterize, it's going to be a hopeless situation.

Somehow we've got to be big enough to understand that the Lord's will is that we be united. His prayer was for that in the 17th chapter of the book of John. And the apostle Paul in the 4th chapter of Ephesians verse 3 urged Christians "endeavor to keep the unity of the spirit in the bond of peace." And yet we have fragmented and we've divided into warring camps. Jesus said, "Blessed are the peacemakers for they shall be called the sons of God" (Matt. 5:9). I for one urge you, let us all unite together to have more love and more compassion and more harmony and more unity among us and lay aside some of the grievances in some of the areas wherein we differ.

I realize the importance of these issues. But you see it comes across to brethren of my persuasion that you fellows perhaps think that we're the ones that are responsible, and we see it a little bit different from that. You see a definite pattern for EVERY ASPECT of what we've been talking about. I definitely see a pattern for the Lord's church. I've preached as hard as any of you on Hebrews chapter 8 and verse 5; there's no doubt a pattern. But I don't see all of the pattern that you see evidently, in the how that we're to do every little thing that comes along. There's got to be a realm in there for your judgment and my judgment. And yet all of us get along together as brethren in one united front to take the gospel to a world that's steeped in ignorance and darkness and dying in sin, and DESPERATELY and urgently needs the gospel of Jesus Christ.

Thank you so much.

Fellowship Among Differences
Day 3 Speech 2 Panelist 2
Ron Halbrook

Introduction: *Halbrook, Ron. Resides and works in West Columbia, TX and has done local work in Belle Glade, Trenton, and Clearwater, FL, Kenosha, WI, Pine Bluff, AR, Athens and Birmingham, AL, Nashville, TN and Dayton, OH. He is a staff writer for Guardian of Truth, debater, and author of several books and tracts.*

Thank you for your love in making this opportunity possible.

---

2 John

9 Whosoever transgresseth, and abideth not in the doctrine of Christ, hath not God. He that abideth in the doctrine of Christ, he hath both the Father and the Son.
10 If there come any unto you, and bring not this doctrine, receive him not into your house, neither bid him God speed:
11 For he that biddeth him God speed is partaker of his evil deeds.

Hebrews 9

16 For where a testament is, there must also of necessity be the death of the testator. 17 For a testament is of force after men are dead: otherwise it is of no strength at all while the testator liveth. 18 Whereupon neither the first testament was dedicated without blood. 19 For when Moses had spoken every precept to all the people according to the law, he took the blood of calves and of goats, with water, and scarlet wool, and hyssop, and sprinkled both the book, and all the people, 20 Saying, This is the blood of the testament which God hath enjoined unto you. 21 Moreover he sprinkled with blood both the tabernacle, and all the vessels of the ministry. 22 And almost all things are by the law purged with blood; and without shedding of blood is no remission.

Hebrews 10

9 Then said he, Lo, I come to do thy will, O God. He taketh away the first, that he may establish the second. 10 By the which will we are sanctified through the offering of the body of Jesus Christ once for all.

(Chart #1) My reflection on both of these speakers is that they've done a wonderful job in focusing on a principle of truth in 2 John, where we learn that in order to abide in the love and grace of our Lord that we must abide within His doctrine. And so I see our meeting as an effort to study that, and to come to that common ground.

(Chart #2) I also think, in reflecting on this, of Jesus in Hebrews chapters 9 and 10, as being the focal point, the one who shed His blood, in order that the death of the testator, the new covenant might come into effect. And so in the sprinkling, the shedding of His blood, the new covenant is sanctified, "By the which will we are sanctified through the offering of the body of Jesus Christ once for

all." The world needs to hear about that savior.

(Chart #3) And these blessings that He gives must be according to the pattern, the covenant. The new covenant is sealed, of course, in the blood of our Lord. When we talk about baptism, immersion is in the blood sprinkled way. Other actions have no blood, not in the new covenant. The Lord's Supper, we have a Bible pattern. When we have other elements and other days beyond the pattern, there's no blood sprinkled there. And we're not taking the crucified Lord to a lost world when we introduce something that's not in the new covenant, sealed and sanctified with His blood.

When we sing we walk in the blood sprinkled way. When we play the instrument, there's no blood sprinkled there. And we need to be serious, and I think we're all trying to be, about understanding what is the work of the church revealed in the blood sprinkled way, that we

New Cov. Sealed By Blood (Heb. 9:16-22; 10:9-10) **Blood Sprinkled:**	Not In New Covenant **No Blood:**
1. Immersion (Acts 8:38)	1. Other Actions
2. Lord's Supper (Matt. 26:26-28; Acts 20:7)	2. Other Elements, Days
3. Sing (Eph. 5:19)	3. Other Music
4. Work of Church (1 Tim. 3:15; 5:16)	4. Other Works
5. Organization of Church (Acts 20:25; 1 Pet. 5:2)	5. Other Organizations

might walk in that way. Evangelism and limited roll of benevolence, we can read about. But when we have other works, entering into these recreational matters, we have to cry out against it. Not because we despise brethren, but because we love souls and we care about walking in the blood sprinkled way.

The same principle is involved in these questions of organization. In Acts 20 and 1 Peter 5, we agree there is a limitation, as God designed the organization, as to the oversight of the elders. If we add levels beyond that, then we're getting beyond the blood sprinkled way. This is above all our deepest concern.

Furman Kearley, Editor of *Gospel Advocate* on the Mission of the Church

"The church may assist with child Day Care Centers, Christian Schools, Christian Camps, & Other expedient means that provide an opp. to save Souls" (G.A. Nov. 1988, pg 5). Kearley Includes "A kitchen or Fellowship hall as well as the Gymnasium (Letter, Furman Kearley [5 July 1989], G.A. 1990, 77)

(Chart #4) Yet there was a time when we could read in the *Gospel Advocate* on the mission of the church. In 1948, "That it is not the mission of the church to furnish amusement. That such perverts the mission and degrades the mission of the church." But in an editorial that's already been replied... referred to, we see that day care centers, Christian schools, camps, and to include kitchens and gymnasiums, can be included.

One of the heart wrenching things for me, is to learn that men that I have read after and respected and benefited from and that I feel have very conservative feelings, like Brother Dobbs, Brother Connley, Brother Warren, now say that the church gym is "just a judgment call."

GYM Battle Over? H.A. Dobbs, Andrew Connally, & Thomas B. Warren Say Church Gym "A Judgment Call"
(Quotes On Question & Answer Tape 5-25-88)

Q: "If a church was large enough & they felt that a gym for them was just like a little church supper for somebody else, & it didn't tie up their whole church program, you couldn't say they are sinning."

DOBBS: "That's what you're hearing me say (illegible).

(Chart #5) Dear brethren if the gym battle is over, we're not approaching one another, we drifting much further apart than EITHER of us ever IMAGINED.

(Chart #6 had the title: Brief Survey of Medical Works of Churches of Christ, but the rest was illegible) And when we talk about the new hermeneutic, then I think about this latest issue of *Pulse*, "The right hand protests the new hermeneutic, but the left hand promotes it." The magazine is full of articles about Medical Missions and church supported Hospitals.

(Chart #7 illegible) And if you think there are one or two little things like that, here's one of the article's listing over twenty such, over twenty. If that be the case, we're drifting further and much further apart. There's a GAPING difference there. Not because somebody hates somebody else, but we're not following the same pattern of teaching on this.

(Chart #8) And so I would remind you that Brother J.W. McGarvey made the observation to Brother Sewell a long time ago that you cannot successfully combat error

> **2 Cor. 6:14-18; 2 John 9-11**
> **A Voice From The Past**
> **J.W. McGarvey**
>
> "You are on the right road, and whatever you do, don't let anyone persuade you that you can successfully combat error by fellowshipping it and going along with it.
>
> "I have tried. I believed at the start that was the only way to do it. I've never held membership in a congregation that uses instrumental music. I have, however, accepted invitations to preach without distinction between churches that used it and churches that didn't.
>
> "I've gone along with their papers and magazines and things of that sort. During all these years I have taught the truth as the New Testament teaches it to every young preacher who has passed through the college of the Bible. Yet I do not know of more than six of them who are preaching the truth today. It won't work."

by fellowshipping it. He said he tried that, he preached in the churches that had the instruments and those that didn't, went along with their papers, tried to teach the truth. Finally he said, "I don't know of more than six men who are preaching the truth today. It won't work."

Thank you.

Fellowship Among Differences
Day 3 Speech 2 Panelist 3
Wyatt Sawyer

Introduction: *Sawyer, Wyatt. Presently works with the Midtown congregation in Ft. Worth, Texas, noted publisher and author, respected for many works for 49 years in Houston, Dallas, Port Arthur, and Ft. Worth, TX churches.*

My utmost desire brethren, is to see every one of you in Heaven some day. And I personally am willing to do whatever it takes to see us ALL there together. If that scares you, be scared. But open up your heart, open up your mind. And everything I'm going to say from here on will come down to one concluding thought that could solve this thing.

First of all I am impressed. I'm impressed with you. I'm impressed with the spirit, of what I've seen in here, the things that have been said on all sides. This is good. You didn't solve family difficulties until you sit down in a family conference and got to it. Right? We are a young church. The Lord's church is still young and we're just kind of bantering about here, there, and yonder.

Truth is one. It is united with reality, and God establishes reality. Truth emanates from one source, God, Father, Son, the Holy Spirit, to us the Bible. Truth does not change to accommodate generations. From beginning to end it is truth. Truth is capital "T" as the Greeks even thought about it. God's mind revealed. And then there's small "t", truth about agriculture, truth about mechanics, and this sort of thing. The capital "T" is religious, it is absolute, it is unchanging. Why are we not getting together on it? Religious truth has been given to man, and God expects man to get together. Why did He give it? If we're not going to use the Bible, why do we have it? Isn't that a simple question?

Our goal, I believe, in agreement with everybody seemingly, is to study, to pray, to meditate on God's will until we can move the church along to its goals and purposes as one body. Now I have a wishful plan. I've thought this for months, and it would work. I'm not saying it's going to

happen this way, but it would work. If God said "close the doors and lock 'em. Now you sweet, wonderful, beautiful, people have the word of God, and I expected you to operate together on it. Now you stay in that room and you'll never go home until you get it worked out." We might go to glory straight from here (Laughter) but I don't think so.

So what I'm saying is, we need to study and get together and we need to hash this thing out and get mature and adult about the job of reaching 6 billion souls.

Fellowship Among Differences
Day 3 Speech 2 Panelist 4
Charles Davis

Introduction: *Davis, Charles. He is a native of Somerville, NJ and presently works with a congregation in Pine Bluff, AR. He began preaching in 1974 and has served churches in Alabama, Tennessee, Florida, and Minnesota. Works extensively in meetings and debates.*

The Psalmist said that "Righteousness exalteth a nation, and sin is a reproach to any people." My beloved brethren, there's sin in the camp. And as long as there is sin in our camp, we will be divided. Platitudes, smiling, making gestures, making jokes, is not going to solve the division that has divided the body of Christ. We must recognize that this is reality.

It's going to take more to get to Heaven than desiring so. It's going to take more than singing a beautiful song to get to Heaven. It's going to take men and women, boys and girls, of every race, color, and creed, to lift up the blood stained banner of Jesus, and speak where the Bible speaks, be silent where it is silent, do things in Bible ways, call things by Bible names. We have left that divine pattern. As long as we remain in the pattern that we are going in now, in diversity, we will never get to that great celestial kingdom.

The problem is that fellowship has become a word of recreation. It has become a word that we have lost Biblical fervor for. It has become an attitude that reflects our socialization and not our scriptural determination. We need to get serious about Heaven because God is. If we think that, because we wear the name Christian, God is going to overlook the sin that is in our camp, we have got a problem.

The Bible says in Isaiah 34 and verse 16, "Seek ye out of the book of God and read, none of these shall fail or want for her name. I have commanded it, the Spirit of the Lord shall gather them in." If we desire to go to Heaven and do what is right, we're going to have to "seek ye out of the book of the Lord and read." We're going to spend more time in the word of God, determining what God wants of us, than we are right now.

Looking back over the two speeches just briefly for a moment, I realize Brother Jividen's speech was an excellent speech, I have no problems basically with what he said, but really he didn't deal with the issue. The issue should be "What are we going to do with the word fellowship?" Are we going to continue to let it be given a recreational name? Are we going to continue to let fellowship, be that which divides us? Because we're not walking on the same principles and the same patterns that our forefathers walked on. Because some of us are not militantly and aggressively contending for the faith. Brethren it's not a joke. This is a sad commentary of affairs.

And we must sit down together to iron out our differences. When yes there are billions of men and women, not only in Africa, not only in Asia, not only in Germany, but right here in this country, who are groping in darkness and we are fighting over hermeneutics. We'd better get our act together. We'd better realize that God is not playing, and that the word fellowship has divided us. It's not a matter of opinion; it's a matter of doctrine. If it's a matter of opinion, let us bury that hatchet right now. Let's leave this building, and let's go out and preach the word of God to those that are dying and lost. If it's a matter of doctrine, somebody had better repent, because that's what it's going to take in order for this schism to be brought back, and the body to be made one.

May the Lord bless us all as we labor diligently to get to that Promised Land.

Fellowship Among Differences
Panel Discussion

Roy Lanier – Moderator: Now we're ready for our discussion between…our quite discussion, between these panelists (Laughter, whs). And Brother Halbrook do you want to start it off.

Panel Discussion
Ron Halbrook - Panelist: Thank you brother…

Roy Lanier – Moderator: Remember you're talking to each other, not to that bunch out yonder (Laughter).

Ron Halbrook - Panelist: Thank you Brother Lanier. Something that has been mentioned a number of times is that, as in the editorial that I just showed a minute ago from the *Advocate*, that if we use these recreational things as a part of our evangelistic effort, that it's just a matter of a method.

(Chart #1) And I can remain seated and just let you glance at this. I understand methods to be things like, under "PREACHING" you'd have tents, and black boards, and Bibles, and charts. Under "RECREATION," what would the method be? The method would be balls, gloves, bats. Now, here though what I'm hearing is that under "PREACH" we have methods. We, all agree, could use a chart, use a tent, that those are methods. But then somebody is bringing in the ball fields and the gymnasiums and the bats and calling that a method for preaching. I believe that's a method for recreation.

And I'm saying those kinds of things will continue to separate us. We're using the word "method." Where what we've got is an entirely different activity it seems to me, and what Brother Jividen called a faith destroying activity or doctrine, in the sense that it leads to more and more and more of those activities. And introduces a spiritual nature, or I meant to say a secular nature, to the work that God gave us to do in saving souls. If all these billions of people are lost in the world, what in the world are we doing building gymnasiums and having a fuss over that, when the world needs to hear about the savior that died and his precious blood? And why can't we say those other things are sinful, if we can't produce book, chapter and verse for them, and then try to slide them in as a method? It seems to me, we need to address that.

Thank you.

Roy Lanier – Moderator: Who were you looking at while you were having a quiet discussion? (Laughter, whs)

Ron Halbrook - Panelist: (Possibly Ron utters something indiscernible from the tape whs)

Maxie Boren – Panelist: Well, first of all, my response would be, I don't think he's talking to any of the brethren here. I know all the brethren that share my convictions quite well, and I don't know of any of us that are advocating what you're suggesting. I think we've got to look way out to the left field for brethren that are in that persuasion. I'm basically in agreement with you.

Ron Halbrook - Panelist: That those things are sinful or bad judgment?

Maxie Boren – Panelist: Well, I may not go as far as you in denouncing them as totally sinful. I think there are some areas of judgment pertaining to some of that. I'm certainly not for gymnasiums or anything like that. But you're implying that we're the ones that are involved in this. So I'm basically on your side.

Charles Davis - Panelist: But dear brother if you don't make a definitive statement as to whether or not it is sinful or not, then basically you are taking a side. The side is that you're not committed either that it's an opinion or that it's a matter of division, and that it's a matter of sin.

Maxie Boren – Panelist: So in other words, we've got to concur with your judgment…

Charles Davis - Panelist: I didn't say that.

Maxie Boren – Panelist: …before we're acceptable, is that…?

Charles Davis - Panelist: No. No.

Maxie Boren – Panelist: See I think that's the point that really causes the dissension. I really do. Because I get the distinct impression that sometimes you fellows are saying "unless you agree with us and call it like we think it should be then you fellows aren't desiring to obey the Lord and all."

Charles Davis - Panelist: No, I think we should agree with the apostle Paul. I think we need to speak where the Bible speaks and be silent where it is silent. I'm not asking for you to agree with Charles Davis, he has no position, he has no church, certainly he hasn't shed his blood for anyone, can barely save himself. But what I'm asking for ALL of us to do, is to go back and to contend for the faith. There was a time when we would stand up, and would have no problems admitting what our stands were, as versus denominationalism or whatever the case may be. And now it seems like we're not willing to put our two feet to the fire. And that's what we've been hearing all week, and I think even the audience would concur, we need to hear a definitive statement that if these things are wrong you need to say so, and if they're not you need to say that as well.

Ron Halbrook – Panelist: (After a long pause, Ron asks Brother Sawyer if he wants to speak next. whs) Brother Sawyer did you…?

Roy Lanier – Moderator: Wyatt.

Wyatt Sawyer – Panelist: Fellows we're in a day of many needs. For people, Christian people, are people trying to be like Christ. Do we recognize a responsibility of the church on one hand in taking care of many of these needs, and the responsibility of the Christian family taking care of some of the other needs, social needs?

Ron Halbrook - Panelist: Are you saying that some of these recreational things, for instance, should be taken care of by the family and therefore it would be a sin if the church did it? If so we're agreed. And I appreciate that you're trying to say that you have even a strong judgment that the church ought not to be involved in those things. I've discussed with a number of the brethren who hold that.

But the thing that seems to me we fail to see, if you leave them in judgment, no matter how strong your judgment is against it, then you have no absolute Bible pattern there. And therefore you're going to have to do with them what you're asking us to do with you. "You're going to have to go along to get along."

Now Isaac Errett insisted the instrument ought not to be used, it'll bring choirs, it'll discourage participation, but he said that's my judgment. And you know what happened in time with the *Christian Standard*. Because he predicated that on judgment it didn't hold. And your position won't hold. As much as I love you and want us to be together, the position that these gyms are only judgment matters, brethren it won't hold. And they're going to surround you and then they're going to take you. I mean you're going to go, the brethren as a large, are going to go that direction. You've got to put up a Bible barrier or else quit making a lot of protests against it.

Wyatt Sawyer – Panelist: I didn't know I had taken a position yet.

Ron Halbrook - Panelist: Well I was going on Brother Boren's statements. Excuse me.

Maxie Boren – Panelist: Well I've already told you, I am not for that. So I don't know what you are talking about.

Wyatt Sawyer – Panelist: But you need to reply to Brother Boren when you're talking to him. But now I asked you a question and you bypassed me.

Ron Halbrook - Panelist: All right, I didn't realize I did, I'm sorry.

Wyatt Sawyer – Panelist: I forgive you.

Ron Halbrook - Panelist: He said all of us.

Maxie Boren – Panelist: I think I did.

Wyatt Sawyer – Panelist: I forgive you.

Ron Halbrook - Panelist: I thought that includes you.

Wyatt Sawyer – Panelist: Yeah. I ask the same question are people being human beings, are there some of these things church's responsibility and some of them family responsibility? Let me give you one I've wrestled with. In Port Arthur, Texas I was working with families, which I had predominately always done, Christian families to provide Christian recreation to Christian young people. Are you with me? I want you to stay with me and not Maxie, or Jimmy, or anybody, stay with me.

Ron Halbrook - Panelist: All right! And no church involvement as you're explaining it now, right?

Wyatt Sawyer – Panelist: No.

Ron Halbrook - Panelist: OK.

Wyatt Sawyer – Panelist: You haven't heard me yet.

Ron Halbrook - Panelist: I'm trying to follow you.

Wyatt Sawyer – Panelist: Yeah. We were working with families to take care of the needs of our young people socially to keep them out of the Devil's dens and all that sort of thing. Talking to one of the local brethren, we got into a dilemma that bothered me a long time. He took this hard line that there is complete separation of church and family. Church could have nothing whatsoever to do with the recreational functioning in the family or the children. So I asked him, "Are you telling me that here's a kid goes over here to Bridge City and goes to a Honky Tonk and dances with these lewd women and drinks beer and gets drunk and gets thrown in jail and you're going to withdraw fellowship … disfellowship … I mean to withdraw from him. You're going to withdraw fellowship from an immoral Christian, right." That's church action. Now I want you to come over here and sit down with me in my office and for about six weeks and I want you to help me help families provide wholesome Christian activities for their children. Now as the church, you'll damn them. But as the church, you run when we say what do we do to keep Christian families Christian.

Charles Davis - Panelist: First of all, it's not the responsibility of the local church to provide recreation for the members of the body. Second of all, if recreational activities will keep us from ungodliness, then we need to all run right now to the park (Laughter). Dear brother I love you. I wish that were so. But unfortunately, recreational activities is just a straw man. It is an excuse that we use to propagate our beliefs and to further our doctrines. I've never found, and I've done some counseling, I've never found that providing a place to go, a park, barbecue facilities or whatever, I've never known those things, those amenities, to keep a young man or woman from fornicating or from drinking or from being in the wrong company.

What it takes is for the mother and father to put the V.I.P. treatment on that child, and that means some <u>V</u>ery <u>I</u>ntense <u>P</u>ain (added underscores to show speaker's emphasis, whs) when he's young (uproarious laughter and applause, whs). And what that also means is that bring him up in the nurture and the admonition of the Lord. It's not the Lord's nurture and admonition for me to discharge my responsibility by allowing the local church to go out and to build a recreational facility that my son and daughter might grow up to be model Christians. That's daddy and mommy's responsibility. That's why we've got so many children now, we've got babies having babies, because mommas and daddies are to busy doing other things than raising them children.

Wyatt Sawyer – Panelist: Question!

Ron Halbrook - Panelist: I'd like to comment on that, but I don't want to get out of turn.

Wyatt Sawyer – Panelist: Well you can't follow your own speaker though (Laughter).

Ron Halbrook - Panelist: OK.

Wyatt Sawyer – Panelist: You have to be in order (Laughter). Yeah.

Ron Halbrook - Panelist: That's fair. OK.

Wyatt Sawyer – Panelist: Elders, as shepherds of the whole Christian person, will discipline problem situations but are totally unresponsive to guidance to avoid the need of discipline situations.

Charles Davis - Panelist: I'll respond again. Again, the elders are the spiritual overseers of the flock. And you're right. You're absolutely right. I think the elders should be taking a greater roll in disciplinary actions that go on with the local body. But by the same token when the elders overstep those boundaries, and become mother and father, then now you're creating an entity that God had never intended. In the beginning, it was Adam and Eve, mother and father. It will always be mother and father. There's a discharge of responsibility the church has.

And I think the problem is, going back to the first series of lectures we had on "The Individual And The Church," we still have not understood there is a DEFINITIVE difference between what mother and father MUST do, and what the church has an obligation to do. And I've seen it go too far.

In Memphis there is a series of studies being conducted now, and churches in Memphis are gathering together to implement this program which they have broke ground for, it's called FWS. And it's called <u>F</u>ellowship <u>W</u>ithout <u>S</u>in, or <u>F</u>un <u>W</u>ithout <u>S</u>in (added underscores to show speaker's emphasis, whs). Several local churches get together, bought a tract of land, they're going to build this great amusement theme park, only Christian boys and girls can go in there, and there'll be no fellow… there'll be no sin, only fellowship while they're in this parks. And it's such a ludicrous idea for us to believe, first of all that fellowship is a physical thing, and number two that we can have fun in a place where there's no sin, and that we're totally insulated in this place. That's ludicrous, and again, that's the responsibility of the parents, not for the churches of Memphis to cooperate, putting their money together, and purchasing this land, and then LABELING it a place where we can have Fellowship Without Sin (added underscores to show speaker's emphasis, whs). I don't know of such a place as that on the face of the earth, that's Heaven.

Maxie Boren – Panelist: Well I don't see…

Roy Lanier – Moderator: We're…

Maxie Boren – Panelist: I personally feel…

Roy Lanier – Moderator: We're going to have to cut this out in just a moment to get our questions. So Maxie make your comment

Maxie Boren – Panelist: Well I was just going to personally say, to me this is a much ado about nothing, because I'm not involved in that. We don't advocate that. I thought we were going to be discussing things that pertain to this group here. I'm not responsible for what some brethren way out in left field are doing. I thought we were trying to work on unity among the ones that are represented here. If we're going to talk about some of these things, then we need to go way out there and get a bunch of the brethren way out in left field here.

Ron Halbrook - Panelist: (Ron begins to answer Maxie… whs)

Roy Lanier – Moderator: Point of order! Point of order! Hold it, hold it. We're going to have to take a break, so you can turn your questions in. Do we have any questions? (Laughter).

Wyatt Sawyer – Panelist: I'm surprised.

Roy Lanier – Moderator: They haven't settled all these questions?

Wyatt Sawyer – Panelist: No.

Roy Lanier – Moderator: Then we will take a two and a half minute break and then we'll get to our question session.

Fellowship Among Differences
Question and Answer

Roy Lanier – Moderator: Beginning not caught on tape whs) It's time for us to begin this session. And if any of you would come up, you could write a book if you'll answer all those questions.

Question 1:

Here is a question for Jimmy Jividen. "Can you fellowship Christian Churches? Why should we fellowship you? Is this not a parallel?"

Jimmy Jividen – Main Speaker: I think the question should better be asked, "Can you fellowship individuals in Christian Churches?" Fellowship is not on congregational level; it is on a personal level. And then individuals within the Christian Church that teach and practice that which there is no authority for, we cannot extend fellowship to them because of the things that I suggested in the charts. If a person does that which is without authority, Biblical authority, such as instrumental music and demands that as a practice of their fellowship, then you cannot have fellowship with that which is erroneous. If indeed, they have formulated a party that is distinct from the body of Christ into a human denomination, then that would be definitely that which you could not have fellowship with.

Now an individual who might have a doctrinal misunderstanding concerning instrumental music, or with a doctrinal misunderstanding concerning the nature of the church, I can extend fellowship to him in that doctrinal misunderstanding as I try to teach him the way of the Lord more perfectly. Now if they did not form a party, and they did not force that which is a practice that is unbiblical, then I could receive them into my fellowship as Paul did those that disbelieved or questioned the resurrection in 1 Corinthians 15. That isn't to sanction that, but to recognize that there is doctrinal misunderstanding. But to practice or to form a party is the thing that causes the break in the fellowship, it is not just a doctrinal misunderstanding.

Roy Lanier – Moderator: You are keeping our two minutes. OK. That was a long two minutes (Laughter, whs).

Brother Davis… Oh wait a minute. I should give this to Brother Clark. I don't know whether I have one for him or not.

Charles Davis – Panelist: That's OK, give him mine.

Roy Lanier – Moderator: Do you want yours, Brother Davis?

Charles Davis – Panelist: I give way to the senior.

Question 2:

Roy Lanier – Moderator: Brother Davis, "Is the sin in the camp the problem of institutions and sponsorships, or is it the making of laws about opinions?"

Charles Davis – Panelist: That's a good question. If it was based upon opinion, and if it is based upon opinion, then I think really we should be able to sit down right now and come to a harmonious understanding. But as it is, we have clear-cut Bible principle that's being violated. And therefore institutionalism cannot stand based upon a fact that it's an opinion, especially when we just went through an extensive study of 2 John.

2 John 9 and 10 tells us, "Whosoever transgresseth and abideth not in the doctrine of Christ hath not God." We must realize that there's transgression here brethren. As long as we keep looking at our problems, especially the problem of fellowship, the uses of fellowship, as being an opinion, it's our opinion that it's wrong to have a fellowship hall, it's wrong to have fellowship meetings, it's wrong to have fun and frolic and recreation attached to the word (fellowship it doesn't mean of the word), as long as we start thinking that and continuing to think that way, and think it's opinion, we'll never bridge the gap that divides us.

We must sit down and do some serious study, and desire to love the Lord more than men. And to love the Lord more than we do any human practice that we have previously held to. Thank you.

Question 3:

Roy Lanier – Moderator: This is addressed to either, well it addressed actually to both sections of the situation today. I believe I'll give Brother Clark, if he wishes to, a first comment on this. "Would you say the greatest threat to our unity in Christ is, #1 some brethren going beyond specific patterns in the scriptures, #2 some brethren making and demanding patterns where God has not made them, #3 both." Would you like to comment? Do you understand the question?

John Clark – Rebuttal Speaker: Yes. Let's read that again. "Would you say that the greatest threat to our unity in Christ is some brethren going beyond specific patterns in the scriptures, or some brethren making and demanding patterns where God has not made them, both 1 or 2." You're talking about greatest, I mean it'd be difficult for me to answer what's the greatest problem. The greatest… if I were going to answer that I'd have to do like the Lord, "What's the greatest commandment?" And he said, "Thou shalt love the Lord thy God with all thy heart, with all thy soul, with all thy mind."

My answer would be that our greatest problem is our failure to fully and completely and absolutely respect the authority of the scriptures. That's a general answer. But I think both of these are problems. If we are committed to a pattern, where God has revealed what He wants, and I'm telling you this, when God speaks that means it's important. And I may not think it's important, but when God speaks it's important. And this matter of, if God has told us something, the principle "see that you make all things according to the pattern." We may not think… what's the big deal about putting all that stuff in the tabernacle the way it was? Because God said to do it, and it was important to God. And if something that's important to God is important to us, if our love of God is right.

But the second one, "Some are making and demanding patterns where God has not made them." This is where we need serious study to determine whether or not, you know here's what we're insisting upon something. You see when someone insists upon specific information for which . . . what we're arguing and defending is that you have generic authority for it, and you demand the specific, you see. That's a clear problem. But it can be addressed by us doing further study on the nature of authority, about how God authorizes and discussing distinctions that are there, but both of them are serious problems.

Did I go over?

Roy Lanier – Moderator: Was that a 1-minute signal or a time signal? Ok. I… he's still giving us time signals so… incidentally you were late. (Further discussion takes place out of microphone range, whs).

Let's see, Maxie Boren.

Maxie Boren – Panelist: You want me to respond to the same question?

Roy Lanier – Moderator: No!

Maxie Boren – Panelist: Well, I thought you said that…

Roy Lanier – Moderator: Oh, I'm sorry.

Maxie Boren – Panelist: That you wanted…

Roy Lanier – Moderator: Have you got the question? Here it is. I believe it was to both of you. I'm sorry.

Maxie Boren – Panelist: I believe that's what you said.

Roy Lanier – Moderator: Yes, you're right. I'm sorry.

Maxie Boren – Panelist: My response would be both of them are very definitely destructive to the cause of Christ. To go beyond with that which is written is very bad, and we want you brethren to know, and I think I speak for all the brethren that feel as I do, that we're just as concerned with the liberal trends in the church as you all are. You know, sometimes maybe y'all think y'all have a monopoly on a love for the truth, but we love it, too. And we're very muchly concerned with these trends to the left, but I'm also equally concerned with this attitude, and that's the way I would call it, that binds where I don't believe God has bound.

One thing that really troubles me that has been brought up in this meeting, for instance, here's a man that's injured by the wayside and an individual Christian can help him but a church couldn't help him. To me, that is picking at straws, nitpicking if ever there was any. I gave an illustration to some. A busload of Christians, say 45 members of a congregation, going down the road and here's a man injured by the side of the road. The whole church is there in the bus, two or three elders, the preacher, and everybody else, here he is hurt and we get out there and the fellow's unconscious and all, and we see he's in need of a hospital. Could the brethren there, the church, take action and write a check to the hospital for his care? The answer of the one or two fellows I asked was, "No, we'd all have to write individual checks." See, to me that's binding where

God has not bound, and to me that's what's dividing us, that nitpicking.

And so I think the answer to your question is both of those are very hurtful to the cause of Christ, either to the far left or to the extreme right of that judgmental attitude.

Question 4:

Roy Lanier – Moderator: Ron Halbrook, "Can't," that's a contraction, "Can't two churches be in fellowship and love and accept each other when one supports an institution and the other doesn't?" I guess you could answer it can they do it or can they not do it, either way, just whatever you want to answer.

Ron Halbrook – Panelist: Thank you, Brother Lanier. There would be of necessity deciding is this a matter where the Lord bound something or is this a matter of where He did not. If it's the question of cups and classes, we all agree that the Lord did not bind in that area, and that it's an expediency. But if it's this question of having a church supper and a kitchen and then when the baby grows up it's a gymnasium, and we want to say but that's just a method of encouraging young people, keeping them out of trouble, having fellowship with the brethren and all of that. Well, the problem is that violates a pattern. And when you talk to those that use the instrumental music, they will say, "Well, you people are binding where God didn't bind." And, "Why can't two churches differ?" And all of that. You know how to answer that question. When you answer that, you'd have the same answer I have to give when it comes to the issues that WE'VE been discussing here.

Now let me take a moment to add to this point, "Well what are we going to do about the young people?" It's an unintentional insult to young people to suggest that we can't keep them faithful to the Lord, and their heart won't be deeply touched by the gospel unless we can have parties, entertainment, and feed them. We can't save lost souls even of young people by getting in a war over recreation with the denominations. We give them a hot dog and the church down the street gives them a foot long hot dog and we've lost them.

The only thing we can give them is the TRUTH. And that has power. And you can touch their SOULS. And that's what we are doing about it where I live. We're teaching the young people that a savior DIED and SHED HIS BLOOD and that means more than all the world, and to make a commitment on that basis.

And then when we go to our homes, yes we also teach parents that young people need occasions for clean recreation. But we do not mix that as being the work of the church, and young people need to learn to get out and earn an honest living, and we teach on that. But the church doesn't set up a business so they can be employed and stay out of some DISHONEST business. What to do is, dear brethren, teach the TRUTH, the PLAN OF GOD. And it will reach their souls.

Charles Davis – Panelist: Amen.

Question 5:

Roy Lanier – Moderator: This is a question for Jimmy Jividen. "According to 1 John 1:6, are there levels of walking in darkness, and if so when does it become light?" Now I'm assuming that the question is because you're saying there are levels of walking in the light, then this question is are there levels of walking in the darkness, and when is the change?

Jimmy Jividen – Main Speaker: 1 John 1:6 and following about "walking in the light as He is in the light, then we have fellowship one with another and the blood of Jesus Christ cleanses us from all sin." If there was not some kind of darkness in there then the effectiveness of Jesus' blood and the sphere of grace could not be effective. There are... you can't have absolute white or light and still be cleansed from sin.

Question 6:

Roy Lanier – Moderator: Brother Davis I have one here for you. "Are social activities present or absent in Acts 2 verse 41 through 47?" And then in parenthesis "(Luke 2:52)." "Are social activities present or absent in Acts 2:41 through 47 and Luke 2:52?"

Charles Davis – Panelist: Thank you very much. Let's open our Bibles and read. Let's see what the Bible says. Acts 2:41, "And they gladly received the word were baptized. The same day there were added unto them about 3000 souls. They continued steadfastly in the apostle's doctrine, fellowship, breaking of bread and prayers. Fear came upon every soul and many wonders and signs were done by the apostles. They all that believed were together and had all things in common. They sold their possessions and goods, parted them to all men as every man had need. They continued with one accord in the temple breaking of bread from house to house, did eat their meat with gladness and singleness of heart, praising God and having favor with all the people. And the Lord added to the church daily such as should be saved."

Now the question, if I remember correctly, is asking "Is there any social intercourse with this gathering?" Is that correct brother?

Roy Lanier – Moderator: Social activities.

Charles Davis – Panelist: Social activities. Now you can't put me to a minute, this is too long. Just kidding. No! No, I'm just… (Laughter, whs). OK, the answer is obviously no. And when you to look at the scriptures here, we determine that what happened is simply men and women obeying the gospel of Jesus Christ. And everything that transpired from that point forward was of a spiritual nature. Obviously physical people have to gather together, physically sell their possessions, physically do some things together. But being together physically, selling your possessions and being together as this one crowd is together, doesn't mean that there's a social involvement, as it is the spiritual involvement is what is being emphasized here. And the same thing would be appropriate in Luke.

Ron Halbrook – Panelist: I don't know if he has time, but I think what they're wanting you to comment on is verse 46. How do you think that fits in?

Charles Davis – Panelist: Do I still have time to do that? I have 20 seconds.

Roy Lanier – Moderator: Yes or no.

Charles Davis – Panelist: No (Laughter, whs).

Roy Lanier – Moderator: OK.

Question 7:

Maxie Boren, smile you're on candid camera (laughing as he speaks, whs). "Have you ever preached in local work or meetings at a congregation that had a gymnasium? If so did you preach against such and try to get them to cease their practice?"

Maxie Boren - Panelist: I never have preached in one that has a gymnasium, that I can think of. Never have.

Ron Halbrook – Panelist: Would you feel compelled to if you did?

Roy Lanier – Panelist: Wait a minute, I'm asking the questions (Laughter).

Ron Halbrook – Panelist: I thought he had more time.

Roy Lanier – Moderator: No he has 2 minutes, but now he can use it as he wants to.

Ron Halbrook – Panelist: Oh, OK.

Maxie Boren - Panelist: Would I feel compelled to, Ron asked that question. I'm not so sure that I would. There's many very, very important issues. Usually in our meetings in this day and time, at least most of mine, are Sunday through Wednesday night. I get to teach a combined class Sunday morning, the Sunday morning sermon, the Sunday night, Monday night, Tuesday night, Wednesday night, generally 6 sermons. I personally feel I can spend my time much better than dwelling on one issue.

See to me Ron, you fellows are making a mountain out of a mole hill. Not that it's unimportant, don't misunderstand me, but there are other issues, other items that are so very, very important. And so I doubt that I would feel compelled to preach on it. First of all I don't think any of those that have gymnasiums are going to ask me, so I'm not really worried about it that much.

Question 8:

Roy Lanier – Moderator: Brother Clark, "To be in fellowship, which verses of the 8000 in the New Testament, must we agree on in faith and practice? All of them? Is there any verse in the New Testament that we could disagree on and still be in fellowship?" And I'm glad I don't have that one (Laughter, whs).

John Clark – Rebuttal Speaker: Is it possible for me to address anything that's been said before, or must I talk about that?

Roy Lanier – Panelist: Well, you have to answer the question first.

John Clark – Rebuttal Speaker: OK. Where's the question again. Is there 8…was there about… how many passages of scripture and… (Laughter, whs).

Roy Lanier – Moderator: "Of the 8000 in the New Testament, which must we agree on in faith and practice? All of them? Is there any verse in the New Testament that we could disagree on and still be in fellowship?"

John Clark – Rebuttal Speaker: This type of a question is interesting from the standpoint of what fellowship is based upon. As I tried to say in my lesson, was that our fellowship is based upon our relationship with Christ. And that we come into this relationship with Christ as a result of listening to the testimony of the apostles. I would develop that case from the first epistle of John. And that the whole point of our fellowship is that it is a result of us listening and doing the very things that the New Testament says are essential for us to do to be in that fellowship. And it seems to me that when John says "if we walk in darkness" and claim we have fellowship, we're just deceiving ourselves, "if we walk in that light as He is in the light we have fellowship one with another." So the commitment of a person who obeys the gospel, it seems to me, is to a lifetime effort to find out what Jesus taught and correcting myself all along the way.

When you talk with people, and sincere people, and they look up at you and say, "Do you think the Lord could forgive me?" you know. One minute! And then they'll go on and they'll say, "But I don't know everything," and they are worrying about, do they really know and then do they really have an understanding? And what I try to say to them is this that if you come and obey the gospel and I try to say this to kind of make them cautious . . . about rushing into it. I said, "You may know a lot of things but you don't know everything you'll ever know. But what you have to know above everything else is this one thing and if you don't know that, you really don't know anything, and that is that whatever you find Christ desiring, teaching you that He wants you to do and to be, that's exactly what you will do."

And brethren, our problem it seems like here, is, in talking about what will be done and what won't be done.

I'm going to turn over and answer this question over here. I'm not trying to press anybody. I'm not trying to accuse a brother of believing something. But I tell you this. A locomotive of logic doesn't stop because somebody screams. And going down the road here brethren, as we start with…I talked about the nose of the camel…we start with a thing and another thing goes to another thing. And when they build these gymnasiums, somebody's going to say why didn't you say stop? (Laughter as time ran out, whs)

Roy Lanier – Moderator: I did say stop (Laughter, whs).

Question 9:

Brother Sawyer, "If you could justify gyms and ball teams as aids to preach the gospel, would you reject as sinful a Jim and Tammy type theme park like Heritage USA, and where would you draw the line?"

Wyatt Sawyer – Panelist: So many issues in this discussion, to me and I'm pretty simple and pretty dumb, but have been stretched way out of proportion, way out of proportion. Part of our problem is we don't even try to see what the other fellow's thinking. We judge him by our view and then we start working him over on our view and so forth.

Let me say this to that. Every good thing that has ever come into this world can be abused and misused, every good thing. I've known people who hesitate to start a congregation of the Lord's church because of all the problems churches can have. I don't believe in that. I believe in going forward and doing right.

I want to ask this question, if I can, in response to that. Can Christian families build wholesome youth centers, period? Yes or no?

Roy Lanier – Panelist: You're not really supposed to be in the question asking business Wyatt. You've got part of two minutes left if you want it.

Wyatt Sawyer – Panelist: Yea. My answer is a question. Can Christian families build wholesome youth centers? I'd like both the brethren here to respond to that please. Do you agree? Do you agree?

Charles Davis – Panelist: Only if we can respond back to your question. But no I'm not going to…

Wyatt Sawyer – Panelist: When I…You…I want to…I just want to…

Ron Halbrook – Panelist: We both believe that.

Charles Davis – Panelist: Yes, I want the chance to ask the question.

Wyatt Sawyer – Panelist: Well…

Roy Lanier – Moderator: Go ahead Wyatt. Go ahead.

Wyatt Sawyer – Panelist: All right take each issue. Yes or no on my question. And then if you've got a question, that's fine I'll take all you've got. OK, then we're in agreement on that. Now what have you got? That's all I advocate brethren, as far as I know.

I was the first youth minister in the Churches of Christ beginning in 1946. And we have worked toward Christian families providing the social outlets and the elders helping us in our work to provide our young people. Life is work, play, love and worship. And you leave play out and you've blown the whole thing. That's just as important as any other part for a balanced life. I'm for the Lord's pattern. And I believe the family's responsible…

Roy Lanier – Moderator: Time.

Wyatt Sawyer – Panelist: For providing this responsible…

Roy Lanier – Moderator: Tiiiiiiiiiiiiiiiimmmmme.

Wyatt Sawyer – Panelist: Pattern here. OK, you have a question?

Roy Lanier – Moderator: Now, no, no, I'm… that's time. I've got another question.

Wyatt Sawyer – Panelist: All right.

Roy Lanier – Moderator: But now I know how my daughter and her children feel. Can you ever believe that he was a youth minister? (Scattered laughter). Oh, that's ugly, shouldn't have said that.

Question 10:

This is for Ron Halbrook. "Canadian Christians say that movies are sinful." Whether that's right or wrong. It says "right or wrong?" "If sinful, will one be lost in Hell over such sin?"

(Roy Lanier answering Ron Halbrook's head nodding asking if that was it, whs) Yep.

Ron Halbrook – Panelist: Well, my answer would be that if something is sinful, in terms of the absolute standard of truth, in other words it's equivalent to drunkenness or immorality, if attending a movie is like that, and we can prove that from the Bible, then yes a person that practices that and won't repent of it and hardens himself and just goes on like that would be lost. Now the Lord didn't give us a catalogue and look under M and go to movie. We have to deal in principles of truth, and you have to take the issues one by one. And my best discernment of scripture is that the movie is no more wrong than the TV set.

And so the difference though with that and these other things is, that you're violating a principle of truth. Brother Boren says he can spend his time better preaching on other things rather than against a gym. Well can he spend his time better on other things rather than preaching against instrumental music too? Is the instrument a mountain or molehill, which is it? These things are sinful and 2 Timothy 4:2 teaches we've got to contrast truth and error. We've

got to reprove and rebuke. Have we got something better to do than that?

Now it says also exhort. And yes we have to be positive in our preaching too. But I don't say either is better than the other. And we are letting souls down when they are in sin and when they depart from the pattern of New Testament teaching and we don't address it. We can address that with all the love of our Lord. But Jesus didn't go in where there was sin and say "well I don't want to make a mountain out of a molehill" and all of that, He addressed it. And we've got to do that because we love people, not because we have failed to love them, but because we do love them. That's the whole point of it. Love requires toughness and tenderness as was mentioned earlier. And part of the toughness is that we've got to address apostasy and departure. And I would hope you deal with instrumental music. And if you do, the gym is wrong for the same reason that the instrument is wrong.

Roy Lanier – Moderator: Time! OK, it just so happens that's the next question.

Question 11:

Brother Boren, "Do you believe that it is sinful to use instrumental music?" Now I assume that means in worship.

Maxie Boren - Panelist: Absolutely.

Roy Lanier – Moderator: Well wait a minute, I'm not through (Laughter). This is about a 10-part question.

Maxie Boren - Panelist: Ohhh (Laughter).

Roy Lanier – Moderator: There I assume they're talking about in worship, since that's the context. "Do you believe it's sinful to use instrumental music, or is it just bad judgment? How would you respond to those who use it who are members of the church?"

Maxie Boren - Panelist: Well I definitely believe that it's sinful. I've preached against it all my preaching life, of going on 37 years. I think it's an innovation into the worship of God that has no authoritative basis whatsoever. So the answer is definitely I'm against it.

But may I respond to Ron here?

Roy Lanier – Moderator: You have the rest of your two minutes.

Maxie Boren - Panelist: OK, I've got a couple of minutes here. Ron asked me a question while ago, "If I would feel impelled to preach on gymnasiums." I've got six lessons say in a gospel meeting, most of them. I do have many meetings with day services but not all of them. Would you not agree with me Ron that it's in the realm of judgment as to sermon selection? I've got to try and surmise the needs of a given congregation and then choose lessons that I feel are relevant and needful at that particular place. And, you know, with six lessons to choose, would I have to preach on a particular subject in order to be a faithful preacher of the gospel, in your estimation?

Roy Lanier – Moderator: One more minute.

Maxie Boren - Panelist: OK. Let me make a quotation here that I think hits at the issue. And the man that I'm about to quote, I loved him as a person. I disagreed with him often times and I refer to Reuel Lemons. But he did make a quotation some time ago that I think is very good. He said, and I quote, "Through the centuries, sects have sprung from the sinful practice of making matters of opinion, matters of faith." No man has the right to bind where God has not bound. Some have staggered not at carving the body of our Blessed Lord into sectarian ribbons. The fellowship of saints is precious. The unity of the body is precious. In the shadow of the cross, Jesus earnestly prayed for it. The tenderest terms of apostolic language are used to plead for it. And the sharpest terms of condemnation are used to rebuke those who would destroy it." I think that he had a valid point. And to me that's the main issue.

Fellowship Among Differences
Night 3 Speech 2
Summation Speeches

Roy Lanier – Moderator: Now we have two minute wrap ups by our two major speakers. We try to reserve time at the end of each of our sessions to give them a two-minute wrap up. Brother John Clark.

John Clark – Rebuttal Summation Speaker: I want to give my thanks, and that's expected but it's deserved, to all the effort made by all those that participated in this coming together, and willingness to do this. I know that Chester one time said that even a bad shot is honored if he agrees to a duel. I wonder if us fellows coming here have in some way some honor because we agreed to participate and put ourselves up here and take the shots? I think people did that because they thought it was worthwhile and they care, people care, I care. And it's been a joy to be with Jimmy Jividen. I hope that we'll . . . we were talking about I wish we were closer together, where we could study more and that together, and good can come of that.

And what of the future? I suggest let's try to do that. Communicate with one another. Perhaps the time will come when, maybe in the papers, be willing to share time and space and that sort of thing in the papers for those things. I urge you to do that. But of all else, I wish you, I wish all of you, Jimmy, you good brethren and everybody here, the joy in the Lord. Sometime in our pain and in our problem we feel we're lacking it. And so if you're searching for joy, the secret of joy, it seems to me, is shown by Paul in the Philippians letter. He could see the worst in the best and the best in the worst. And if you have your choice of choosing the better of two bests and there's no better thing. He could look at even when brethren don't preach the gospel with the right motives and all that, he was in prison and adding affliction to his bonds, he said, "But none the less I rejoice that Christ is preached." Meaning that he could see even in the worst situations good things. The bad, stress and strain, I can have joy if people, honest people are striving to do right.

And secondly we need to see the worst in the best, be- cause sometimes we think these are great things we get involved in. But if anything, anything in this life keeps me from the single-minded loyalty to Jesus, that's the worst. And that's why he says that he counted everything he ever achieved as dung and nothing. And then he could say, and I would like to be able to say, he says, "To live is Christ, to die is gain." There's nothing better than living a life so that you're going to have to ultimately choose the better of two bests. I wish you joy brethren.

Jimmy Jividen – Main Summation Speaker: Thank you for this opportunity to speak to you. And to those of you that have worked so hard to put this together, I give a special thanks, because this is not an easy thing to do.

I want you to know that I'll probably be ostracized because I've been eating in the same room that we have been preaching in, and I have heard clapping during teaching, and I have put my arms around unapproved brothers, and all of this. I will just not fit the party line. And I really believe we're talking about parties.

There is more than just a few issues, there's a whole lot of issues that face us in the church. And as we go about to do the Lord's will, it's not my side and your side but the Lord's side. We're to love the unlovable. I can…Brother John is such a dear brother. I want to know him a whole lot better. I can feel the pain that comes from many of our hearts because of the disruption of our fellowship. And I can remember that Paul and Barnabas had hard times, and they separated one from another. But yet Paul can speak of Barnabas three times later in such endearing terms and over John Mark say that he was profitable unto him in the ministry.

I hope and pray that even if there is not a merging of fellowship within the congregation that there will be a common interest. We must get rid of our party lines, and line up with people and paper and schools and to look to the Lord Jesus. And we need to learn to listen. The blind man said, "I told you already and you did not listen. Why do you not hear it again? Do you want to become His disciples too? I want people to know that I don't support institutions out of the church. I want people to know that the recreation's not the work of the church. I want to know that the gospel is not a social gospel. And let's quit accusing people of things that they are not guilty of.

Maxie Boren – Panelist: Amen.

Jimmy Jividen – Main Summation Speaker: I want to draw together in fellowship in Jesus Christ under His authority as revealed in the word and study the word and not some party line.

Roy Lanier – Moderator: For the good behavior of all of these that have been here today on this panel and on these speeches, I want to give my personal thanks. And for of course this session, your being here and your interest in it. On behalf of Steve Wolfgang, who has been the single prime impetus, I believe, in this meeting as well as the former meeting in Nashville that was of a similar nature, I give my thanks. It's been very good to work with him. Will you please stand as we have a closing prayer?

 END OF SPEECH 2

 END OF DAY 3

 END OF 1990 DALLAS MEETING

www.ingramcontent.com/pod-product-compliance
Lightning Source LLC
Chambersburg PA
CBHW060231240426
43671CB00016B/2909